40.00

Festive Drama

FESTIVE DRAMA

PAPERS FROM THE SIXTH TRIENNIAL COLLOQUIUM
OF THE
INTERNATIONAL SOCIETY FOR THE STUDY OF MEDIEVAL THEATRE
LANCASTER, 13–19 JULY, 1989

Edited by
MEG TWYCROSS

D. S. BREWER

© Contributors 1996

All Rights Reserved. Except as permitted under current legislation
no part of this work may be photocopied, stored in a retrieval system,
published, performed in public, adapted, broadcast,
transmitted, recorded or reproduced in any form or by any means,
without the prior permission of the copyright owner

First published 1996
D. S. Brewer, Cambridge

ISBN 0 85991 496 8

D. S. Brewer is an imprint of Boydell & Brewer Ltd
PO Box 9, Woodbridge, Suffolk IP12 3DF, UK
and of Boydell & Brewer Inc.
PO Box 41026, Rochester, NY 14604–4126, USA

British Library Cataloguing-in-Publication Data
Festive Drama:Papers from the Sixth Triennial
Colloquium of the International Society for the
Study of Medieval Theatre, Lancaster,
13–19 July, 1989
I. Twycross, Meg
809.202
ISBN 0–85991–496–8

Library of Congress Cataloging-in-Publication Data
Société internationale pour l'étude du théâtre médiéval. Colloque
(6th : 1989 : Lancaster, England)
   Festive drama : papers from the Sixth Triennial Colloquium of the
International Society for the Study of Medieval Theatre, Lancaster,
13–19 July, 1989 / edited by Meg Twycross.
   p.   cm.
Includes bibliographical references.
ISBN 0–85991–496–8 (hc : acid-free)
   1. Drama, Medieval – History and criticism – Congresses.
I. Twycross, Meg. II. Title.
PN1751.S6   1989
809.2'02 – dc20   95–49180

This publication is printed on acid-free paper

Printed in Great Britain by
St Edmundsbury Press Ltd, Bury St Edmunds, Suffolk

CONTENTS

Contents	v
Abbreviations and Acknowledgements	vii
MEG TWYCROSS (Lancaster University): Some Approaches to Dramatic Festivity, especially Processions	1
Households and Fraternities	
PETER H. GREENFIELD (University of Puget Sound): Festive Drama at Christmas in Aristocratic Households	34
OLGA HORNER (Lancaster University): Christmas at the Inns of Court	41
SHEILA LINDENBAUM (University of Indiana): Rituals of Exclusion: Feasts and Plays of the English Religious Fraternities	54
CLAIRE SPONSLER (University of Iowa): Festive Profit and Ideological Production: *Le Jeu de Saint Nicolas*	66
Religious Processions and Plays	
RONALD E. SURTZ (Princeton University): Masks in the Medieval Peninsular Theatre	80
RAFAEL PORTILLO & MANUEL J. GOMEZ LARA (Universidad de Sevilla): Holy Week Performances of the Passion in Spain: Connections with Medieval European Drama	88
PAMELA M. KING (QMW University of London): The *Festa D'Elx*: Civic Devotion, Display and Identity	95
ROBERT POTTER (University of California at Santa Barbara): The *Auto Da Fé* as Medieval Drama	110
Secular Processions and Shows	
JOHN CARTWRIGHT (University of Cape Town): Forms and their Uses: The Antwerp *Ommegangen*, 1550–1700	119
DAVID MILLS (University of Liverpool): Chester's Midsummer Show: Creation and Adaptation	132
JAMES STOKES (University of Wisconsin, Stevens Point): The Wells Shows of 1607	145

Shrovetide and Carnival: Farce and Fastnachtspiel

ALAN E. KNIGHT (Pennsylvania State University):
The Bishop of Fools and his Feasts in Lille — 157

MARJOKE DE ROOS (Koninklijke Vereniging van Archivarissen in Nederland):
Battles and Bottles: Shrovetide Performances
in the Low Countries (c.1350–c.1550) — 167

FEMKE KRAMER (Rijksuniversiteit Groningen):
Why a Peasant is Taught How to 'Shoot': Rhetoricians,
Militiamen and a Late Medieval Dutch Farce — 180

TOM PETTITT (Odense Universitet):
Mankind: An English *Fastnachtspiel?* — 190

LEIF SØNDERGAARD (Odense Universitet):
Two Carnival Plays from Late-Medieval Denmark — 203

WIM HÜSKEN (University of Melbourne):
Analysing French Farce and Dutch Pre-Renaissance Comic Drama — 212

JEAN-MARC PASTRÉ (Paris):
Fastnachtspiel et recit bref: L'Interférence de deux genres littéraires
en Allemagne aux 15e et 16e siècles — 223

Folk Customs and Characters

SALLY-BETH MACLEAN (Records of Early English Drama, Toronto):
Hocktide: A Reassessment of a Popular Pre-Reformation Festival — 233

MALCOLM JONES (University of Sheffield):
'Slawpase fro the Myln-Whele': Seeing between the Lines — 242

CHRISTINE RICHARDSON (Florence):
The Medieval English and French Shepherds Plays — 259

JARMILA F. VELTRUSKY (Paris):
The Old Czech Apothecary as Clown and Symbol — 270

Epilogue

JOHN COLDEWEY (University of Washington, Seattle):
Carnival's End: Puritan Ideology and the Decline of English Provincial Theatre — 279

ABBREVIATIONS

Since these essays come from so many different contexts, abbreviations have been kept to the minimum.

EETS OS	Early English Text Society, Original Series.
EETS ES	Early English Text Society, Extra Series.
EETS SS	Early English Text Society, Special Series.
OED	*The Oxford English Dictionary (A New English Dictionary on Historical Principles).*
PL	*Patrologiae Cursus Completus Series Latina* edited J.-P. Migne.
REED	Records of Early English Drama (in titles and as an institution).
STC	*A Short-Title Catalogue of Books Printed in England, Scotland, and Ireland and of English Books Printed Abroad 1475-1640* compiled A.W. Pollard and G.R. Redgrave; revised and enlarged by W.A. Jackson and F.S. Ferguson, completed by Katharine F. Pantzer, 3 vols (Oxford University Press for Bibliographical Society, London, 1986).

We use the standard British palaeographical and codicological abbreviations:

MS	manuscript.
fol.	folio.
mb.	membrane.
sig.	signature.

ACKNOWLEDGEMENTS

I would like to thank all those who have helped to complete this last and, as it transpired, most difficult volume of the 1989 SITM Colloquium papers. My most particular thanks go, as usual, to Olga Horner, for support both practical and psychological. In Toronto, Sally-Beth MacLean and Miriam Skey found me addresses and references which were not available on this side of the Atlantic, while in the British Library, Joanne Lomax tracked down pictures and references: where would today's editor be without E-mail and generous colleagues? Steve Jenkins of Lancaster University Information Systems Services magicked text – though often in strange shapes – out of the most arcanely encoded disks, and Lyn Hitch patiently typed from hard copy where even he found them completely impossible to unravel. Sandy and Alison Grant gave me the benefit of their DTP experience. And finally, the contributors have shown exemplary patience: though several wish to point out that these are their thoughts of 1989, not of 1995, and were they to write them again, they would probably look quite different.

ILLUSTRATIONS

Fig. 1	Bristol misericord of 1520	245
Fig. 2	King's Lynn brass c.1349: Tournai manufacture	245
Fig. 3	Flemish lead badge from the collection of of J.B. van Beuningen	246
Fig. 4	Roast Pig, Roast Goose, and Perambulating Boiled Egg from Pieter	246
Fig. 5	Brueghel *Luilekkerland*, engraved by van der Heyden (1567) Woodcut by Erhard Schoen for Hans Sachs *Das Schlauraffenlandt*.	249

Figure 1 is reproduced from a photograph by Malcolm Jones, by his permission; Figure 2 is adapted from a drawing, after John G. and Lionel A.B. Waller *A Series of Monumental Brasses* (London, 1842–1864) by H.K. Cameron in illustration to his article 'The Fourteenth-century Flemish Brasses at King's Lynn' in *Archaeological Journal* 136 (1979) 151–72, and is reproduced by his permission; Figure 3 is reproduced by permission of J.B. van Beuningen; Figure 4 consists of details from FIG. 32 of H. Arthur Klein *Graphic Worlds of Pieter Bruegel the Elder* (London, Dover, 1963) and is reproduced by permission of Dover Books; Figure 5 is reproduced by kind permission of the Graphische Sammlung Albertina, Vienna.

SOME APPROACHES TO DRAMATIC FESTIVITY,
Especially Processions
Meg Twycross

The papers in this book were all originally given at the Sixth Triennial Colloquium of the International Society for the Study of Medieval Theatre (SITM) held at Lancaster on 13–19 July 1989, under the heading of 'Festive Drama'. It is important in the era of computer catalogues that the title of a book should contain at least two keywords which accurately describe its contents. This collection of papers, though widely varied, feels coherent. *Festive Drama* is a good upbeat title: but to modern ears it could be misleading. What might our catalogue browsers imagine they were getting?

Festive, therefore something connected with a festival; therefore something cheerful and celebratory? But the cheerfulness requirement would disqualify the papers on Good Friday ceremonies; and the *auto da fé* of which Robert Potter writes was hardly a bundle of laughs: yet they clearly belong here. We adapt *festive*, then, to imply 'celebratory', but sometimes in a more solemn sense. It also implies something traditional and (except for individual *rites de passage*, weddings and funerals) recurrent, usually annually. *Drama*, therefore to do with plays? But a lot of these papers are about processions or folk customs which fall a long way short of being full-blown plays. Are we talking about festive mimesis? Perhaps: but it is a clumsy title for a book, and it too misses things out.

In fact, this problem of nomenclature is purely modern. A fifteenth-century English reader would understand perfectly if we were to call the book *Festive Plays*, or even *Festive Games*, or *De ludis festivis*.[1] It is a pity that, following the rise of professional theatre, semantic change has mirrored the segregation of drama from other kinds of play, so that these words no longer have the wider meaning which reflected the wider concept, where a *ludus* could be a theatrical drama or a game of football, and when the Banns of a mystery cycle could entice its potential audience with

> Of Holy Wrytte þis *game* xal bene,
> And of no fablys be no way.[2]

Incidentally, the fact that for us the noun *play* means 'theatrical entertainment' has probably caused us to read the fifteenth-century word *play* in what C.S. Lewis called 'the dangerous sense'.[3] 'At vj of þe belle we gynne oure play' may have referred on this particular occasion to the entertainment we now call 'The N.Town Play', but it did not necessarily convey a purely theatrical meaning to its original audience. 'The fun starts at six bells'? The same problem has led many earlier historians of theatre

1

into quicksands over *ludus*. (I have a theory that we would save ourselves a lot of problems if we translated medieval Latin written by Englishmen into medieval English.) In the same way, the semantic range covered by this collection is medieval rather than modern, and we should think of it in medieval terms.

The subject-matter of these papers seems to fall into two main categories, though there is inevitably some overlap. First, there are plays and entertainments performed on a festive occasion, often plays written specially for performance on a festive occasion (Pettitt, Søndergaard, Kramer, Sponsler, Pastré, Hüsken). A sub-group (Greenfield, Lindenbaum) looks not so much at the material as at the social dynamics of the performance: this is a matter of approach rather than content, and I shall return to it later. Secondly, there are the festive ceremonies and customs that are inherently or overtly 'dramatic' (Horner, King, Portillo and Gomez, Potter, Surtz, MacLean, Stokes, Cartwright). A branch of this looks primarily at the organisation and content of festive occasions (Knight, de Roos, Mills, Horner, and King again). Besides this there is a third category: folk characters and customs or folk-entertainers' routines and turns included in other plays which may or may not be specifically festive (Jones, Richardson, Veltrusky, and Pettitt again).

The material comes from Spain, the Netherlands (modern Holland and Belgium), France, Germany, Britain, Denmark, and ancient Bohemia (now the Czech Republic). Interestingly, though Spain, probably inevitably, is heavily represented in the second category, national differences are less visible than international links. Tom Pettitt's explication of *Mankind* depends on a knowledge of North European *fastnachtspiele* and Shrovetide customs for which there is little remaining evidence in Britain. From their knowledge of Spanish Holy Week ceremonial, Portillo and Gomez suggest a structural source for English Passion Plays. Besides this, two of the papers describe living ceremonies and organisations, which necessarily seem more complex than those historical ones for which we only have limited evidence, and raise questions about their ancient but defunct forebears, as well as about modern revivals of ancient festivities.

The authors display a range of critical stances. This begs the question: how does one approach festive drama? Not 'what is the correct approach?' as if there were only one, but what are the most useful lines to follow? I have allowed myself here to suggest a few possibilities. If I ask more questions than I answer, that is all to the good. Constructive criticism and further suggestions are welcome.

Before the setting-up of the professional theatres and touring companies, almost all drama was by definition festive. This book could quite as legitimately have covered the Corpus Christi Play of York or the *Quem Quaeritis* as it does *Mankind*, though the conventions this collection appears to have set up suggest that an article on York, for example, should demonstrate the particular thematic or sociological relevance of the play to the occasion. Of course, the appropriateness of a play for a particular occasion can be purely contingent, often as slight as 'festivities call for entertainment; this play is entertaining'. There does not seem to be any particularly striking thematic reason why the play of *The Dirty Bride* should be featured in Brueghel's painting of 'Carnival and Lent', though I am sure that reasons could be invented if one thought long and hard enough.[4] A festive play must not, of course, be inappropriate to the occasion: one would hardly commission a performance of *Othello* for a wedding unless, like Hamlet with *The Murder of Gonzago*, one had an ulterior motive. But most of the *Fastnachtspiele* described by Pastré, Kramer, and Søndergaard, though specifically written for Shrovetide, seem designed merely to suit the mood and tone of the occasion and taste of the audience without any of the more subtle awareness of the wider ambivalences which Pettitt finds so convincingly in *Mankind*. This in itself seems to suggest that *Mankind* had not only a more sophisticated audience but a more serious approach to religion. It is not only a play for Shrovetide, but a play about Shrovetide. But it partly expresses these ambivalences by calling up the patterns, and in some cases reproducing the actual details of folk customs dramatising the strife between Carnival and Lent, Feast and Fast. Why?

Plays on apparently serious subjects can make a very subtle, sometimes a startling use of traditional folk characters and motifs. Jarmila Veltrusky's description of the rôle played by the Old Czech Apothecary, a scurrilous and scatological figure, in a Resurrection play, at first seems bewildering. What has all this shit and anti-Semitism to do with the solemn celebration of Easter? She suggests a kind of typological chiaroscuro, throwing the figure of Christ into more radiant relief, a technique perhaps distantly connected to the Wakefield Master's use of Mak and Gill and the sheep. But it seems a very strange contrast in tastes. Perhaps, since the Apothecary is a quacksalver, and would therefore suggest popular entertainment of a gross kind, the author's intentions are partly technical, a short-cut to getting the audience on his side? If he can pull the right strings to make people laugh, it provides a platform of familiarity which he can then subvert? Or perhaps he just made the equation *Salvator*/(*quack*)*salver*, and allowed his imagination to range? But the disjunction is so violent that it must have set the serious audience thinking

One would expect plays written for a traditional event to supply the reassuring pleasures of the familiar, and festive plays tend to be very strongly generic. Wim Hüsken finds the plots of *fastnachtspiele* so much so that they can be expressed by a well-honed collection of structuralist symbols. One would be interested to see how this technique would work with the traditional British pace-egging and mumming plays, where the plot is linear and cumulative. How would it cope with non-verbal elements like running gags?

We have fewer techniques for approaching the quasi-dramatic festivities, i.e. ceremonies or customs that are not plays in the sense of being fully mimetic with characters, dialogue, costumes, and a developed plot, but which are somehow essentially akin to plays. As William Prynne said in 1633, even after the rise of the public theatre,

> if you consider them as they are here applied, you shall finde them all materially pertinent to the theame in question; they being either the concomitants of Stage playes, or having such neare affinity with them, that the vnlawfulnesse of the one are necessary *mediums* to evince the sinfulnesse of the other. Besides, though they differ in *Specie*, yet they are homogeniall in their genericall nature, one of them serving to illustrate the quality, the condition of the other ...[5]

Prynne is of course not concerned to assess what makes the 'New-yeares-gifts, May-games, amorous Pastoralls ... luxurious disorderly Christmas-keeping [and] Mummeries' *dramatically* akin to 'Stage-playes': for him the important likeness lies in their immorality and disorderliness, which is due to their pagan and papistical origins. We, who feel them as less of a threat either to morals, religion, or public order (we have other bugbears), can look at them more dispassionately, though not without our own prejudices. Some of us rather like the idea of immorality and disorderliness, provided it can be safely labelled 'carnivalesque' and does not actually threaten our personal property or composure. But we shall return to this.

Presumably because these 'Festiuities, Customes, [and] Ceremonies'[6] have something of the same 'genericall' quality as 'Stage-playes', they seem to have a strong potential either to become plays themselves, or to adopt features we connect with plays (for example, costumed characters), or to associate themselves with plays. They have an odd fluidity this way, particularly when we consider that they are traditional and thus, one would imagine, fixed. Mumming plays, for example, seem to give an almost endless scope for improvisation and 'improvement', both verbal and sartorial. Conversely, as we have seen, plays very easily absorb such customs and ceremonies, as incidents and routines, or even as structural devices.[7]

To take the most familiar example, medieval Christian ritual gave the impetus and the initial setting[8] for liturgical drama: though the ritual is not in itself drama, it shares a lot of the theatrical techniques and features of drama. As we know – and as Prynne[9] later points out – one theory of the Mass saw it as a sacred tragedy, the main differences between it and other forms of mimesis being first (and less important) its allegorical mode, and second (and distinctive) its power to effect a mystery in the here and now. But the problem of sacred anamnesis is a complex and highly technical one, and I do not want to tangle with it here. Leaving this aside, many religious processions and ceremonials were and still are read as mimetic by their participants:

> Many ȝerys on Palme Sonday, as þis creatur was at þe processyon wyth oþer good pepyl in þe chirch-ȝerd & beheld how þe preystys dedyn her obseruawnce, how þei knelyd to þe Sacrament & þe pepil also, it semyd to hir gostly sygth as þei sche had ben þat tyme in Ierusalem & seen owr Lord in hys manhod receyuyd of þe pepil as he was whil he went her in erth.[10]

Margery Kempe's churches left this mimesis to her 'ghostly sight', but others actualised it with costumed characters and/or brief scenarios. So the procession of the Guild of St Mary at Beverley for the Feast of the Purification in 1389 provided lights, and guildsmen dressed to represent the Virgin Mary, Joseph, and Simeon, and two Angels to bear the lights. When they arrived at the church, *offeret ibi dicta virgo filium suum Simeoni ad summum altare instar Purificacionis gloriose virginis Marie* ('the said Virgin shall offer her son to Simeon at the high altar, in the likeness of the Purification of the glorious Virgin Mary').[11]

To their contemporaries, these features were seen not as a movement towards drama, but as embellishments to the body of the ceremony. Philippe de Mézières' 1372 ritual for the Feast of the Presentation of the Blessed Virgin Mary, which we would call a full-scale liturgical play, was described by its author as *aliquam ... solempnitatem cum representationibus quibusdam deuotissimis verbis, nouisque actibus, et signis ornatis ...* ('a certain solemn celebration with various representations adorned with most devout speeches, new actions, and signs ...').[12] In her Colloquium paper,[13] Mary Erler told us how London Palm Sunday processions were 'adorned' (despite the Sarum rubrics forbidding this) with new costumed characters, Prophets, who did not actually belong to the biblical narrative: they were significant mouthpieces for the liturgical prophecies in the service. Conversely, in the mystery cycles the Prophets Plays, which we do not see as being particularly 'dramatic' (no conflict, no plot-development), obey the dynamics of the procession: we need to extend our perceptions to recognise this as an acceptable scenario.

It is of course easier to read Christian ceremonial as narrative because Christianity is based on history. Pedagogically, too, it was easier to teach the laity to perceive the human story behind the ceremony – or for the laity to perceive it for themselves – than it was to explain its theology. The spiritual dimension could be conveyed non-verbally by symbols and 'theatrical' effects – light, colour, movement, significant gesture. Also Christian ceremonial has words, so can more easily accommodate scripted drama. But the same tendencies can be perceived in secular ceremonies and customs.

As historians and critics of theatre, we tend not to be familiar with the tools used by folklorists to describe these ceremonies and customs. At the 1989 SITM Colloquium we atttempted to rectify this by holding a half-day workshop run by folklife specialists. They were, as I recall, mainly interested in modern survivals, and their approach seemed to the theatre historians to be largely sociological. Since then, Tom Pettitt and Leif Søndergaard, in their introduction to the Proceedings of the 1992 Odense Symposium on *Custom, Culture and Community in the Later Middle Ages*,[14] have provided a very useful set of criteria for an analysis of these customs. They suggest we should look at their incidence – are they seasonal or occasional? – their social auspices, their motivation, their varying dramaturgy, and their content. I would like to follow through some of these looking at some of the material covered by these essays, and add some of my own.

Pettitt and Søndergaard suggest that 'While cultural historians might be more interested in the mentality motivating [these] customs, for the theatre historian a more significant feature is their varying dramaturgy'.[15] Several of the papers in the present volume are biased towards cultural rather than to theatre history, and I shall return to them: but for the time being I would like to stay with the second concept. How can customs and ceremonies be said to have a dramaturgy? What features might we look at? Have they a plot, and if so of what kind? Is there mimesis? Is there a script? What theatrical 'concomitants' have they? How do they relate to their audience?

Can customs and ceremonies have plots? (I talked about plays adopting them as structural features, which implies that they can.) Though at their most stripped-down they do not tell a story, nonetheless we sense that many of them have a scenario. This may be more or less developed: either explicit, implicit, or potential. Why do we get this sense? (Nb. that I am talking about *scenario*, not *message*.) One current popular handbook of critical terms[16] says that 'Drama is usually expected to show situations of conflict between characters'. Pettitt and Søndergaard suggest plausibly that one of the main structural feature of customs and ceremonies is the 'encounter', 'a deliberate and traditionally structured interaction between two distinct groups', of which one is usually active and one passive, though some customs (including football matches, and presumably tournaments, and combat-dances) involve 'a collision between two opposite (but equally mobile) groups'. This, and particularly the distinction between active and passive groups, is a very useful starting point.

The encounter of two active groups is, on the face of it, most like drama. If one tones down the violence implicit in the word 'collision', this could also apply to singing and/or dancing games between two equally balanced groups, as in the Holly and Ivy carols[17] and the 'Welcome mine own' song in the penultimate scene of *Wit and Science*.[18] (Dance is potentially highly mimetic – see Arbeau[19] for sixteenth-century evidence.) It also, of course, applies to all games between two persons or teams, which is why chess so easily becomes a metaphor for the game of love, or death, or (with the chessmen as team) politics. None of these, it is worth pointing out, necessarily need an audience, though they may have one.

Most 'encounter customs', according to Pettitt and Søndergaard, take place between an active and passive group. Hocking, as described in this volume by Sally-Beth MacLean, they define as the less-frequent 'interception' variety of encounter, in which the active group lies in wait for the passive. 'At the opposite extreme of magnificence' though similar in structure, are Royal Entries, where the active group receives (welcoming rather than ambushing) the higher-ranking passive though mobile one. In the reverse pattern the active group is on the move: in parades and processions it passes through the larger passive community; while mumming belongs to the widespread 'house-visit' genre, where the active group penetrates the living space of the passive group.

The active/passive divide is a useful concept provided we look very carefully at the nature of the 'passive' rôle. At first, and particularly in respect of processions and parades, there is an obvious and tempting correlation with actors and audience. But Pettitt and Søndergaard make it clear that both active and passive groups are involved in the action, even though the passive group is responsive rather than initiatory. We seem to have two possible distinctions here. Either the passive group is a particularly responsive audience (which suits what we know of medieval and folk audiences),[20] or there are potentially three groups involved, active (initiatory) players, passive (responsive) players, and spectators. Is the presence of the latter a factor of the size of the community involved in the festivity, or is it a reflection of the nature of the performance? Once a custom becomes a Show, there has to be an audience. Or vice versa: once there is an audience, a custom will become a Show.

The basic drama lies in the encounter, but it can be developed according to context and intention. In hocking, the plot is ambush-capture-(?torture-)ransom-release. It does not seem to have developed any further, as there was presumably sufficient excitement and entertainment in the event itself.[21] The mumming house-visit is an invasion by unknown strangers into a household which then (in some cases) tries to guess who they are. After propitiatory hospitality, and (in some cases), reciprocal entertainment offered, the mysterious guests disappear. For various reasons, this has great potential for development (notice that I have already started to motivate the action), and I will come back to it. The Royal Entry shows the ruler coming to the boundaries of his city whose citizens may reject him (i.e. prove disloyal): however, they welcome him and he passes into it to take possession, though often, especially in the *Blijde Inkomsten* of the Low Countries, on their terms. All of these have the potential for suspense:[22] will the hockee escape? will the mummers prove destructive? will the citizens refuse entry? though the traditional scenario (and in the case of hocking, brute force) in most cases dictates that the suspense will be satisfactorily resolved.

The mimetic element in all these at its most basic is the very act of performance – in other words, sustaining a particular kind of behaviour in public for effect. This of course applies to all social events where we are on show, and it could be argued that all formalised public social interaction is in some way mimetic, emphasising a particular facet of our social relationships. A ceremony merely formalises this further: the king, queen, or duke in a Royal Entry enact themself in their rôle as ruler, the welcoming party enact themselves as subjects. Should we make a distinction here between mimesis and performance?[23] The difference between a Royal Entry and hocking, for example, is that in the latter the behaviour is not normal: one is acting against one's everyday public character (though it can be perceived as paradigmatic of a more complex social situation, of which more later). Women do not usually lie in wait for men and tie them up; nor, for that matter, do men women. Both are thus rôle-playing, one stage down the road towards drama.

The mumming house-visits are very interesting in this respect. Here, for the active group, the immediate *intention* is not to be recognised as oneself: not to assume a character, but to abolish one's own. To achieve disguise, the visitors wear garments other than their own or their own garments turned inside-out, conceal or alter their faces with masks or soot or bootblack, and their voices either by silence or the mummers' peculiar characteristic 'ingressive' or 'reverse' speech.[24] But there is also a scenario: the visit, in which hospitality is demanded and extended. In some versions, guest-gifts are given.[25] The narrative imagination gets to work: what kind of guests are these who are unknown to their hosts, are not even recognisable beings from our world, and apparently cannot communicate by normal speech? The question is often put in the form 'What do they represent?' (even when the intention seems to be not to represent anyone), and was often linked to the question 'Where does this (obviously pagan) custom come from?' The answer is not infrequently 'Ghosts', and its origin seen as a pre-Christian propitiation of the dead. In England an attenuated but popular (in both senses) version of the custom is still played on Hallowe'en. However, in the later Middle Ages and Tudor period, when it was part of Christmas, it could be worked up not as a visitation from the other world of the spirits, but as a full-blown Epiphany scenario as seen in some of Lydgate's mummings,[26] or Henry VIII's visit to Wolsey:[27] ambassadors from an exotic land, bearing gifts, but unable to speak the language, so requiring 'an interpreter or *truchman*'.[28] This begins to look more like a Show than purely a custom. This scenario can then be translated to the holiday 'otherworld' Christmas scenario of the kingdom of the Lord of Misrule. George Ferrers, Edward VI's Lord of Misrule in 1551/2, came 'out of the mone'.[29]

By this time costumes and props have appeared to grace the event. In the Inns of Court Christmas festivities described by Olga Horner, this even involves mobile scenery – the 'Tower' to which pretend malefactors are condemned. At the Royal Household, George Ferrers had his 'pyllary gybbatt heddinge axe & blocke, stockes, and lyttellease',[30] as well as lavish costumes from the Revels wardrobe for his entourage.

What degree of genuine mimesis can we detect? Were there mini-plots, or even dialogue? In these lavish and complex entertainments, everyone had his separate rôle, and presumably acted in character. It would seem likely that the props were used as part of a scenario. It would also seem likely, especially within the Inns of Court, that the actors improvised dialogue, though there was no script in our sense.

When we come down the social scale to, say, Robin Hood Games, we suffer from a lack of information. The person called Robin Hood had a traditional character, was apparently dressed to match, and had his traditional entourage, also dressed to match. But what did he actually do and/or say? His rôle seems variously and in various places to have involved morris-dancing, mock-combat, and acting as host and master of ceremonies to an outdoor ale.[31] Was this all improvised? Were there traditional formulae of greeting or challenge? The question is complicated by the

SOME APPROACHES TO DRAMATIC FESTIVITY

existence of various fragments of Robin Hood plays, but no evidence to tell us how integral these were to the festivities themselves. It seems more probable that, like the Coventry Hock-Tuesday Play, they were adjuncts rather than central.

Since the scenarios of these festive customs were traditional, we can assume that the audience as well as the actors knew their parts. The generally interactive style of medieval drama suggests that they were less diffident about being tackled than we are, possibly because they were already trained in their rôle. This may have been confined to the medieval equivalent of 'Oh no he didn't'; but it is noticeable nowadays that audiences of mummers' plays are much more ready than your usual theatre audience to offer unsolicited suggestions or even play an ancillary part ('Hold that axe!') – though the boy on roller-skates who in the 1995 Lancaster Pace Eggers' Play interpreted this piece of audience involvement as carte blanche to beat up St George with his own weapons was probably becoming too involved even by medieval standards.

I find the procession the most difficult to fit into the 'encounter custom' format, and since I am particularly interested in processions, both in themselves and as potential engenderers of the mystery-play cycles, I would like to look at them in some detail. This may make this article rather top-heavy, but since processions are not usually thought of as dramatic, and yet display a lot of the features and processes with which these essays deal, they repay study in this context.

Classifying them as 'an encounter custom' depends upon the spectators being cast in the 'passive' role, the participants as 'active'. But some processions do not need spectators. Others are pointless without them. So have all processions the same basic scenario? Well, what actually happens? A body of persons proceeds in an orderly and formal fashion along a predetermined route. If we see it from the participants' point of view, it is a journey. If we see it from the spectators' point of view, it is a succession of persons, or of modules of information, passing a fixed point. It is going to matter whether the procession is designed primarily for the participants or for the spectators.

Even in the former there are various types of scenario depending on the intention of the event. In the 'pilgrimage' type, which is usually though not always of a penitential nature, the scenario is 'I walk the prescribed route at some cost to myself'. In the Elche Roá, as described by Pamela King, some people do this barefoot. The participant makes an affirmation primarily for him- or herself. Spectators, if there are any, may draw their own lessons from this, and some of the more flamboyant Good Friday processions in Spain or Italy may appear to the outsider to have turned private penance into a dramatic and extravagant symbol of mass penitence, just as Bob Potter's *autos da fé* turned the justice of the Inquisition into a figure of the Last Judgement: but the endurance is nonetheless real. The fact that it is a group exercise and the knowledge that it is traditional helps to strengthen one's own sense of affirmation. The route in itself is not particularly important, except in so far as it is familiar and provides the testing ground.

The difference between this sort of procession and the audience-centred one is usually quite clear. In Elche, I felt it necessary to join in the Roá to be part of the occasion (even though I was a foreigner and a non-Catholic), whereas on the following day it was equally obvious that I was required to act only as spectator to the funeral of the Virgin. The grey area of course comes where the organisation of such a procession becomes so complex, and needs so much preparation, that it has to be delegated to executive sub-groups such as individual parish fraternities, as with the Semana Santa in Seville: the more complex the organisation the more exclusive – and competitive – it is bound to become.

In another kind of all-active procession, the Rogationtide Beating the Bounds, the route is all-important. Here the processional group lays claim to its territory by perambulating it, stopping at the boundary stones to beat them and renew the traditional chalk-marks. The procession also has a mnemonic function, which in earlier times was reinforced by beating the choirboys (the next generation) as well. Nowadays threats are deemed to suffice. George Herbert claimed that it fostered 'justice in the Preservation of bounds ... Charitie in loving walking and neighbourly accompanying one another'.[32] The name of the Flemish *ommegang* ('going round about') suggests a sort of Beating the Bounds, except that by the time we meet it, it has had for practical reasons to go through the main thoroughfares, but the message is the same – this is our territory. Because of the presence of the patron saint or relic, it also becomes a lustration: as Prims says, 'Deze heilige, dit relikwie, is het palladium van de paraecia'.[33]

In such a procession the participants are all 'active'. Often, however, an all-active procession will have some sort of primary focus: a Good Friday procession may be led (in the social sense – physically the focus may be situated at the front, the back, or in the body of the people) by a Cross; a saint's day procession will centre on the statue of the saint. In that case the participants are partly 'responsive' (though not passive), not only in playing follow-my-leader, but also doing honour to the focus by escorting it. (It does not of course have to be religious: a Trades' Union banner or a regiment's colours come under the same heading.) Once the welcoming group in a Royal Entry have done their turn, they too become an escorting group leading the ruler to the various set pageants which take over their rôle of welcome. There are thus different degrees of activity within the action.

Context obviously affects how the scenario is perceived, and how mimetic it can become: a Palm Sunday procession, as we have seen, consciously imitates the Entry into Jerusalem. It will also be affected by the shape and nature of the route. A Good Friday pilgrimage which proceeds to the top of a hill, particularly if that hill bears a Calvary, either permanent or temporary, implicitly or explicitly commemorates the Way of the Cross. (Such a procession inside a Catholic church will be marked out physically by its Stations: here the details of the route do matter, because it is also mnemonic. It recalls incidents in the original event.) If, as in Portillo and Gómez's Spanish ceremonies, the procession also escorts a statue of Christ, it is only a step to creating the meeting-and-greeting scenarios they describe, in which the statue itself is made to interact mimetically with other statues or with costumed characters. These may echo the incidents of the Way of the Cross, and so apparently arise from the original story, but they can also in practical terms be encounters of the main procession with subsidiary processions from other churches. The perceived nature of the mimesis may be complicated here by the situation described by Pamela King, in which the statue itself is seen as being a person with power, not merely a figure of a character in an historical event. (We are back to anamnesis and the Catholic/Protestant divide again.)

In these 'active' processions, everyone is an actor, though with different degrees of autonomy. But the more theatrical ones can very easily become Shows as well. This type of procession exists mainly for the spectators. The participants actually get the worse of the deal, because they never see the entire show.

Shows are thus like plays, but with several marked differences. Since they are mobile, they provide a series of snapshots. Any action is very limited in duration. Characters do not recur – cannot recur unless they are represented by different people each time – does this sound familiar? In Van Alsloot's 1615 painting of 'The Triumph of Isabella',[34] there are two Isabellas (not counting the Archduchess herself, who was in the audience), and three Virgin Maries. And the communication is largely through spectacle, not words, though sound – explosions, music – is possible, provided it is loud enough to carry, and written labels, banners, and mottoes can give essential information. (Since I first wrote this, I have seen the Bruges revival of the Procession of the Holy Blood, in which some groups manage very effectively to present short – roughly ten-line – playlets as they go along. These are short enough to be taken in by that section of the audience which they are passing at the time, and are replayed on a continuous loop. This was a revelation of the practicality of the projected missing link between the Corpus Christi procession and the Cycle.)

Complex plots are out. Nonetheless there can be an overall scenario. Some ordering is essential from the practical point of view, and which kind is chosen will depend on the nature of the occasion, the content of the procession, and the amount of cerebral activity that has gone into its organisation. For example, where different segments of the procession are provided by different groups, they can be arranged according to the status or seniority of the participants. This is particularly likely when the Show consists largely of groups of marching men, with banners, standards, or figures of patron saints. This pattern emphasises social hierarchy and the power of tradition. Then there is the competition pattern, in which each of the pageants seeks to outdo each other in ingenuity and theatricality for a prize, as with the entries in the sixteenth-century Netherlandish Landjuweel (which were themed), or our homegrown Lancaster Carnival (which is not). Here the organisers, not having seen the displays in advance, can only guess at a suitably theatrical and varied order. Most usually, however, they will attempt to impose some coherent pattern on the event, on a literal or symbolic level.

Since a procession is by nature linear and sequential, there is a strong tendency for the spectators to experience it as a narrative. There can be different kinds of narrative, perceived on different levels. One way is to present it as history, as time passing. The Elche *Pobladores* march in a chronological sequence.[35] The present-day Valencia Corpus Christi procession, a revival, displays, with interpolations, the history of the Bible from the Fall[36] to the Apocalypse.[37] In the Leuven, Antwerp, and Brussels *ommegangen* of the sixteenth and seventeenth centuries, the waggons showing incidents from the life of the Virgin were arranged chronologically. This seems an obvious kind of ordering: an historical sequence feels more natural than a random one, and is easier to remember. There are signs, however, that during our period a considerable amount of tidying up in this direction went on. The histories of the Leuven and Antwerp *ommegangen*, at least,[38] seem to show that in the fifteenth century the religious waggons were much more varied in topic, and only settled down, or were deliberately 'themed', into their later order around the beginning of the sixteenth century.[39] In the absence of any documentary information, we do not know whether the pageants in the earlier English Corpus Christi processions were once ordered on another principle (perhaps according to the status of the guilds which provided them?) and then rearranged chronologically, or whether some guilds were told to bring forth pageants to fill gaps in the sequence:[40] but the parallels are clear. A procession like this is not a play in our sense, but each snapshot segment might acquire a script (as they do in Bruges) and become a play in its own right, while still being subordinate to the overall design of the grand Play. If this was the process, the English processional Corpus Christi Cycle is the ultimate example of the change from festive ritual to drama while still keeping its processional matrix.[41]

There is also the feeling that this progression denotes progress. John Cartwright points out how in Antwerp, when the image of the turning of the Wheel of mercantile Fortune was straightened out into a sequence of pageants, these started at a point which ensured that the cycle would end on an optimistic up-turn. This also fits in with the theatrical dynamic of processions. There is a tendency to leave the most important feature until last, so that the onlookers get a sense of build-up and suspense, though the Host or the statue of the Virgin or the Lord Mayor or the Queen must be properly enfolded in a protective cordon of their escort, so they will not be exactly the last item in the sequence.[42] Thematically (which we shall come to in a moment), it postpones the key to the central meaning until the very end.

It is however not entirely true that these sequences are always up-beat. One would hardly expect on a celebratory civic occasion to present a sequence of events showing the road to ruin: but the chapbook description of the new devices in the Antwerp *ommegang* of the Circumcision on Trinity Sunday 1562[43] shows that the three new waggons represented the Golden Age, Morning or Youth, accompanied by Happiness, Security, Peace, and Innocence; the Silver Age, Midday or Maturity, with Art, Ambition, Temerity, Cupid, Virtue, and Pleasure; and the Age of Iron, Evening or Old Age, with Care, Misery, Fraud, Avarice, Discord, and Infirmity. Though it is not made explicit, those who know their Ovid will remember that the Age of Iron engendered both Commerce and War.[44] The chapbook for 1561, despite the optimistic sequence of allegories, and the sentiment 'God makes everything good in His time', ends with the line *VVel hem die in alle gauen volstandich waeckt* ('Well is he who in all prosperity [lit. gifts] is thoroughly on his guard'), after which comes the ominous ending *Hier naer volcht dordeel Godes, het welcke dat al besluyt* ('Hereupon follows the Judgement of God, which concludes everything').[45] Like the Corpus Christi Cycles, here the overall mood may be celebratory, but the ending displays a qualified optimism, especially when followed by the *schroomlijck backhuys* ('terrifying oven') of Hell.

There can be other systems of ordering than simple narrative history or a simple narrative allegory. Another is to emphasise an underlying pattern of conceptual relationships. Thus many of the Old Testament characters marching in the Valencia *Corpus* are selected as types of the Eucharist: Abraham preparing to sacrifice Isaac, Melchizedek, the Spies of Canaan. There are thus two organising principles running at the same time, historical and typological. This in turn reflects on the venerated focus of the procession. When it finally appears, the Host takes on multiple meanings: guarded by the clergy and preceded by the laity in ceremonial costume, but playing themselves, it is the Sacrament made available to us today; as the Body of Christ it has been foreshadowed typologically in biblical history; seeing it following on the four-and-twenty Elders and the Eagle of the Revelation of St John, it is easy to read it as the Christ of the Second Coming enshrined in the tabernacle of the New Jerusalem. It thus manages to focus past, present, and future in itself. But this third is my personal perception, not made explicit in the programme,[46] which on the whole presents the material of the procession in a eucharistic light, even to the extent of interpreting folk figures like the Giants as the four continents profiting from the Eucharist, and the curious mummers' dance, reminiscent of the engravings by van Meckenem,[47] as Virtue overcoming the Seven Deadly Sins.

Some processions do not use sequence to present a history, but to pile up information around their focus. This can be a person (like the Archduchess Isabella)[48] or a city (like Antwerp). Complimentary processions like this take their meaning from the person or institution being complimented: without them, the essential key is missing. For example, what could the following possibly have in common: a fishing boat; a crowned dolphin; a leopard ridden by a Moorish king scattering largesse; a lemon-tree with a pelican in its piety and five maidens sitting round its base; an arbour with the effigy of William Walworth, Lord Mayor of London during the Peasants' Revolt; a Merman and a Mermaid; King Richard the Second in state? All becomes plain if you know that these are the pageants devised for the Lord Mayor's Show of 1616; that the Lord Mayor in question was a fishmonger; and that he was called John Leman. The fishing boat is obvious: the dolphin is on the Fishmongers' coat of arms and the merpeople are its supporters.[49]

The five maidens seated by the onomastic tree are the Five Senses, because the lemon tree is 'an admirable preserver of the sences in man, restoring, comforting, and relieving any the least decay in them'.[50] William Walworth, Lord Mayor for the second time in 1381/2, was also a fishmonger, who, to quote Stow,

> did by his arrest of *Wat Tyler* (a presumptuous Rebell, vppon whom no man durst lay hands) deliuer the king [Richard II] and kingdome from the daunger of most wicked Traytors, and was for his seruice knighted in the field.[51]

Only the leopard and the King of the Moors do not allude directly to the Lord Mayor, his name, or Company: they represent the Goldsmiths, the Fishmongers' 'combined brethren', reciprocating a similar compliment made in 1611, when the Lord Mayor was a Goldsmith.[52]

There seems no particular reason why the pageants should have appeared in this order, save that the Richard II pageant, which comes last, is the most elaborate and theatrical, and the fishing pageant, which comes first, possibly the most semantically transparent. Here the effect is cumulative rather than linear: rather like an AngloSaxon riddle it displays different aspects of its subject, challenging the spectator to construct an answer in which and only in which all these seemingly unconnected things can be made to connect. It thus also celebrates its subject's uniqueness.

Puns, rebuses 'forto accorden with the Meirys name',[53] heraldic and historical allusions, allegories, all turn the Lord Mayor's Show into a mobile conundrum pleasantly decipherable by those in the know. It is assumed that these are all the citizens of London watching the event. This is, of course, from the point of view of the spectator; the devisor starts with the answer and brainstorms around that. This, together with the Valencia programme mentioned above, opens up the whole question of intention and audience perception, and the possible gap between them. Interpretation very much depends on what the spectator brings to the show. The Valencia procession demonstrates biblical history, with which we are still assumed to be familiar, through a sequence of exemplary figures. You have to be able to recognise them by their attributes: Jonah with his whale, Moses with his horns and the Tables of the Law. Whether the audience recognises the more abstruse typological ones (Melchizedek, Joshua and Caleb) without the aid of the programme I do not know. To unriddle the Lord Mayor's Show you need to be familiar with his name, the Fishmongers' arms,[54] the history of the Company and of London, even their special relationship with the Goldsmiths. You also need to be good at reading emblems.

Since a Show demonstrates rather than saying, there is ample opportunity for the audience to get it wrong – or as we would now say, to construct their own meanings.[55] It is interesting, considering our assumptions about the visual literacy of the Middle Ages and early modern period, how often this subtext had to be put into words, either because it was non-traditional – John Cartwright's 1561–64 descriptions are of the *nieuw puncten*, the 'new displays' – or because the artefact has been pressed into a different service from that which was originally intended, or possibly because the spectators are expected to be tourists, or even just ignorant of their own traditions. Royal Entries, with their more complex and sophisticated allegories, regularly had explanatory speeches,[56] and the habit also grew up of issuing commemorative booklets, at first purely as presentation copies but, with the spread of printing, as souvenirs for a wider market. There then arises a whole industry in chapbook programmes for popular as well as one-off events. This seems to reflect or even to be the cause of an increasing desire to be educated in one's own heritage. A particularly pleasant example from Antwerp (1648)[57] purports to cast *een kinderactighe ooghe* ('a childlike eye') on the figures of the ommegang, thus targeting one possible market, but it is addressed to *Ghy Curieusen 't sy vremdeling, 't sy inwoonder* ('You enquiring people, whether you be foreigners or residents'). Like most of the other chapbooks, it adds a measure of moral and patriotic interpretation to the bare description of the pageants. It is interesting, in comparison, how the accounts of spectators (often, naturally, foreigners) seem to tend to disregard interpretation altogether, confining themselves to the literal and theatrical content of the shows.[58] An useful project here would be to do a detailed analysis (and where possible comparison) of the emphasis and content of each type of reportage.

Processions like the seventeenth-century Lord Mayor's Shows were very carefully 'themed', and therefore coherent. The same can be said of those late medieval and early modern Royal Entries where the 'devisors' kept a firm grip on content and quality, even though the individual contributors had a right over their own pageants. Here we can speak with some confidence about the intended meaning of the Show. However, many popular processions were far more eclectic, firstly, as I have said elsewhere,[59] because they had a magpie tendency to acquire successful items from other events, and secondly because they were composed of different organisational groups which transmitted different messages.

The 1615 Brussels *ommegang* is a case in point. Denis van Alsloot's surviving paintings[60] appear to divide it very neatly into its component parts (though there may have been more, lost, paintings):

1. the *ambachten* (the Trade Guilds) with their standards;
2. the *serments* (the militia guilds of various types of 'shooters' – see Femke Kramer's paper) with their patron saints;
3. the pageant waggons, in this year enhanced in compliment to the Archduchess Isabella;
4. the city officials; and the clergy, with the statue of Our Lady of the Sablon.

Each of these groups is organised visually in a different way, because of its different history, and because of its differing ethos. (In practical terms, too, some groups – the clergy from the Cathedral, the civic officials – actually joined the procession at different points on its route.)[61] The trade guilds with their standards (Adam and Eve in Eden for the Greengrocers – compare Norwich; wind- and watermills for the

Millers) emphasise their crafts and products, and their group solidarity and consequence. The militia guilds, like the English armed watches, but much more highly structured socially, process carrying their characteristic weapons (longbow, crossbow, handgun, sword and buckler) and all firing their muskets (a very immediate expression of readiness for war as well as being theatrically exciting), led by their banners, and costumed persons representing the patrons of their guilds (e.g. the giant St Christopher and his hermit, St Michael and the devil and St Gudula and her devil). They march in reverse order of foundation, with the most senior last.[62] They make a clear statement about military strength and preparation (which also depends upon group solidarity and training), reinforced by divine protection.

The parade of pageant waggons incorporates an historical sequence of great antiquity showing incidents from the life of the Blessed Virgin, and a selection of secular ones, some of which are traditional, and some of which were specially devised to compliment the Archduchess. Like the fish-, lemon-, and London-pageants of the Lord Mayor's Show which took place the following year, these latter only make sense as a sequence if you know about the event and person they commemorate. What has a giant cage of parrots to do with the double trump of Fame and the goddess Diana and her huntress maidens? The pattern only slides into place when you are told that the Archduchess had won for herself the title of King of the Old Crossbow Guild in their annual competition to shoot the popinjay fastened to the top of the spire of the Church of Our Lady of the Sablon. The message of the first three waggons is thus 'vanquished parrots speak her fame as a chaste huntress'. We then notice that the parrot-cage is escorted by Amazons (conspicuously male) carrying crossbows.[63] Labels on the second and third waggons make it clear that Fame is celebrating this *grande victoire*, and that the Archduchess has surpassed even Diana, who has come to pay her homage. Next in line, Apollo, Diana's brother and also an archer – the inscription on the front of the waggon urges him to relinquish his bow, presumably to Isabella – and the Muses sing her victory in a Parnassus pageant probably originally designed (on analogy with Antwerp) to celebrate the arts of the city.[64] At the end of this section the funeral nef of the Emperor Charles V, also a regular feature of the *ommegang* since its creation in 1558, not only provides a truly theatrical culmination but in this occasion compliments Isabella by showing her as a worthy successor to her grandfather as Ruler of the Netherlands. The parrot cage also picks up the theme of the second section of the nef complex, the Pillars of Hercules with Charles' motto *Plus oultre* ('Go further'), for the cage is accompanied by persons dressed like living parrots who are in fact copied from costume books showing the garb of the inhabitants of the newly-colonised Americas. This waggon is dressed overall with the monogram of the Society of Jesus, and must have suggested its mission to the Indies.

Isabella was an immensely popular ruler who associated herself enthusiastically with local customs and causes. It is interesting that it seems to have been felt perfectly appropriate that these waggons should coexist with those celebrating the explicit focus of the *ommegang*, which comes in the last section, escorted by magistrature and clergy: the statue of Our Lady of Sablon. It would be tempting to see this as a secular takeover, but it would be wrong. There was no direct competition: Isabella was not herself riding in the procession – the triumphal waggons represent her by actors. Our Lady of Sablon is still the undisputed mistress of the procession, but her role as protectress of the city is shared on a lower level by (delegated to?) Isabella. In the ordering of the procession, the waggons celebrating Isabella's triumph enwrap those celebrating the Virgin, as if they were escorting them, though this may be an accident of arrangement. The contiguity of the two may suggest that Isabella shares in some of the qualities of the Virgin – female power, exalted ancestry, piety, a maternal love of her people – but there is no usurpation. The very fact that Isabella's waggons are new and neo-classical, while the Virgin's are traditional and biblical marks the difference between them. As some verses composed in honour of her feat declare, she was *Bataillant soubz lestandart du Vierge Mari*.[65]

So far I have been looking at what might be called the rhetoric of processions: how they dispose and present their material. Earlier writers, such as Withington, concentrate largely on their stock vocabulary: the individual theatrical ingredients like giants, mountains, trees, fountains, ships.[66] There remains what is currently the most popular critical approach to early-modern drama and folk festivity, the socio-historical one. Over the last decades, appraisal of surviving folk drama and festivities has moved from the not very helpful traces-of-ancient-mystery scenario first popularised by Chambers (after Frazer) to the sociology of the event itself; while, as Pettitt and Søndergaard point out, earlier records provide 'an unusually clear window on the vernacular cultures of the late-medieval and early-modern periods'[67] which has been much used by social historians for their accounts of popular attitudes and movements. Current writing shows the obvious influence of the theories and techniques of New Historicism. The titles and subtitles of some of the papers in this book reflect this: 'Forms and their Uses'; 'Civic Devotion, Display and Identity'; 'Rituals of Exclusion'.

This approach attempts to see how these festivities worked in and for their social setting. As David Mills asks of the Chester Show, 'What are its functions?'. There appear to be two main schools of thought. The first, which we might call the collective point of view, starts axiomatically from the concept of community, and emphasises the contribution of such festivities to its sense of its own wholeness and identity. When looking at processions, for example, it sees participants and spectators as sharing and celebrating essentially the same values and aspirations. The participants have been delegated by the community as a whole to express these shared values.

The urban procession confirms the sense of community in various ways. It may be made up of a series of discrete groups, but merely the fact that they have all consented to take part, if for different reasons, communicates a sense of solidarity.

The subliminal message to both participants and spectators is 'In unity is strength'.[68] This may be presented as commercial or military strength or as strength of faith or conscience, but the effect is the same: we all support each other – and God, through the mediation of His saints, supports us. If there are differences of opinion or dissensions, we forget them for the duration of the show, for the promotion of the greater good.

It is also an expression of identity, in both senses of the word. Individual sections can express a group identity by uniforms or concerted actions; but the Show as a whole also expresses an corporate identity – 'We belong together'. It also usually attempts to express the other kind of identity: 'What are we like?' martial? maritime? commercial? cultured? Catholic? A civic Show will often demonstrate this allusively by allegorical pageants, and symbolic floats like the Antwerp Ship and Mount Parnassus. Identity itself is often displayed by a personification of the city, like the Maid of Antwerp,[69] or the Genius of London.[70]

The sense of tradition, what David Mills calls 'past-consciousness', that this Show has been going out in the same form for time out of mind, confers dignity and worth: we have a history, a place in the world. To call it *heritage* is a kind of shorthand for a right of access to a shared past,[71] a communal resource to draw on. Even apparently random floats and figures like the Antwerp Giant, Elephant, and Whale, or the Brussels funeral nef, which were made specifically for other events, belong here, even before they are written into the official allegorical script, because they are part of this communal history. This is *our* Giant, he tells of our heroic origins, he was created when we welcomed Philip II;[72] we were once privileged to entertain this Elephant, this Whale was cast up on *our* beach.[73] It also creates a sense of continuity and familiarity which must have provided reassurance in an unnervingly unstable world. Particularly in the Low Countries and at that time, the image of the Wheel of Fortune discussed by John Cartwright must have had a powerful resonance, and the citizens were both brave and thoughtful to confront its implications.

And finally, display. The dressing-up, the spectacle, the strange devices, the lavish pleasures of the eye, all transform the everyday streets and people. We (at least, the English) tend when talking seriously about these things to forget that sheer excitement and enjoyment, and doing something like this really well, may be proper ends in themselves, as well as good for morale: and this despite our current preoccupation with the feel-good factor.

These are all valid assumptions. They work if the event is truly communal, if the spectators are at one with the actors and with each other. Cracks begin to appear in this reassuring edifice if they are not. The second version of the deep structure of these events sees them as political, part of a power play rather than agents of social cohesion.

One approach emphasises subversion and dissent, and sees popular festive activity as a powerful agent of these, largely because, being popular, it is assumed to be giving the masses an otherwise inaccessible voice. A Show necessarily makes a statement of some kind. It can be used by one group to make a statement against another group: the charivari is a case in point, as are James Stokes' Wells Shows of 1607. It is perhaps unfortunate that much of our information about such shows necessarily comes from the records of courts of law: we could be forgiven for the impression that they are always an instrument of dissent and subversion. Current scholarly sympathy here seems to be on the side of civil unrest, with the paraders rather than those paraded against, no matter what the subject, with somewhat inconsistent ideological results: when is someone going to speak up for the victims, the unfortunate mismatched or adulterous couples who have offended against society's norms (the charivari is surely an instrument of repression, not liberation?), the Puritan who was only acting in accordance with his conscience in trying to stop 'disordred unrulie & contemptious persons' from disturbing the Sabbath? Carnival and its associated riots are equally popular for the same ideological reasons. It is assumed (post Ladurie and Bakhtin) that they express the class struggle, in which the underdog has his day but is in most cases brought to heel again smartly. Drunkenness and hooliganism are just part of the package.

As for official processions and shows, these are seen as the instruments of the opposite side in the power play. The (passive) community does not delegate the (active) procession to make a statement for it: the (active) oligarchy impose their ideology on the disempowered (passive) audience. Much could be made here of William Walworth and the irony of his rôle in the Peasants' Revolt. Any sense of community is specious, if not a downright confidence trick. We should not be lulled into forgetting the creative dissensions which will lead to social justice. Our present preoccupations with the clash of cultures in our communities and awareness of the disempowerment of a large part of the globe have led to the current interest in the marginal and in liminality: we are very much aware of and seek out evidence for the possibility that such ideologies were not communal, that some of the spectators must have felt excluded. Hence any social event can be read as a ritual of exclusion.

This view emphasises historical change rather than, like the previous, 'collective' one, taking a snapshot of history at any one time. It specifically looks for contradictions and dissensions. Its weakness is that it has to operate by hindsight, and is therefore apt to distort the picture as seen by the actual participants – and can also tend to patronise them for not realising what was 'really' happening. Its strength for us is that it does, at its most flexible, allow for the multiplicity of influences on any popular event. Its emphasis on change is particularly interesting when it is applied to *traditional* popular festivities. We are currently very much aware of the perception that tradition can become unthinking conservatism, and that heritage can be marketed in neat, spurious packages. Several papers in this collection tackle the question of the nature and implications of tradition, and, then as now, its involvement with tourism.

Both these views are of course viable. Equally we would be wrong to espouse either view to the exclusion of the other, though it does make for simpler critical approaches. One appeals to our idealism, the other to our cynicism: I suspect it depends on personal temperament which one we incline to most. Myself, I know that my usual feeling when watching a procession is one of association, not alienation, even if the ethos it expresses is very foreign to my own upbringing – perhaps especially when it is, because it expands my imaginative capability. But I also felt a chill in Valencia when to the engulfing beat of drums the army went by *in fatigues* and at the double to join the clergy in escorting the Host. It was a dramatic statement of the collaboration – I almost said, complicity – of Church and State, but it jarred my own pacifist conditioning and I remembered too clearly what I as an Englishwoman had been told of the history of twentieth-century Spain. It was both too alien for me to sympathise with and too close for comfort.

This in a nutshell is our problem when we attempt to study the festivities of the past. We can try to observe and understand their intentions and traditions, but we do not belong to their community. Equally we are trapped in our own traditions and presuppositions, and unconsciously judge them accordingly. We need to empathise with their enthusiasms (or why study them at all?), but we may not believe in their religion or their politics or accept their world view. Unnervingly, some of the things which attract us most as imaginative constructs may be based in or associated with ethics which we deeply distrust.

What then can we usefully do?

Clearly, we need to recognise where we ourselves are coming from, and that our preoccupations were not necessarily theirs. Much criticism starts with the laudable admission that 'we cannot transcend our historical situation'[74] and then proceeds regardless to impose our values on their events. A little humility and many caveats are in order.

We cannot totally reconstruct the past, but we should at least make sure that we have all the *available* details before deciding what they might reveal. There is too much of a temptation to lay every festive event on the Procrustean bed of fashionable theory. In a paper given at the Colloquium but destined for another journal,[75] Alan Somerset gave a cautionary tale of how further information made him change his mind over what at first had seemed 'a textbook example of surveillance and control' in 1590s Shrewsbury. Again, not all Christmas mock-kingdoms were subversive in intent: Olga Horner stresses how at the Inns of Court 'underlying the licensed foolery were serious ambitions, and opportunities for attracting royal favour'. Any account of Carnival has to accommodate the facts that in Ferrara the Duke, in Rome the cardinals, and in France the King and his minions behaved in just as riotous a way as the temporarily liberated underclasses.[76]

Similarly, any account of hocking, which seems so promising from the feminist point of view, must allow for the fact that, as Sally-Beth MacLean emphasises, it was a double-sided event: women hocked men but men also hocked women. If we disregard the latter fact for the moment, the custom makes a very nice status-reversal ritual. According to the theory, an underclass (women) are given licence for a day to behave in the way in which they would like to behave all the time (exercising power over men, the overclass) but at the end of the day are returned to the status quo. Moreover, through their behaviour during this period of licence, they prove that they are more effective than the overclass (they make more money).

This immediately raises questions. Why were the women more efficient as fundraisers? Were they more shameless, more devious, more terrifying (the picture of 'jolly matrons' lying in wait behind their foaming tankards somehow suggests considerable muscle, besides psychological terrorism), or, as hockees, more agile or more tightfisted than the men? Were the men more easily caught, or more chivalrous, or more lascivious? Or did they just have more cash? Was there a flat rate? Dr MacLean tells us that the present-day Hungerford Tutti-Men demand a penny from the men and a kiss from the women. How was one supposed to measure hocking success, economically or in minor sexual satisfactions? There are more ways than one to cut the cake.

Then, how does one accommodate the men's hocking-day into the scenario? A free-for-all for natural predators? Licensed sexual assault? Revenge for the previous day, and a reassertion of customary power? (That one would depend upon the order of events, and as Dr MacLean points out, this was different in different places.) Social behaviour and relationships are more complex than that. We looked at the surface dramaturgy of hocking earlier. The sub-plot, it would appear, especially from the Bishop of Worcester's scandalised edict, is that a lot of the victims (male *and* female?) found the torture enjoyable, and even went on to prolong it with 'scandals, adulteries and other misdemeanours'. Both scenarios could be seen as an extreme expression, extended into the public domain, of the alternative possibilities in customary private relations between men and women, even though the first was not socially sanctioned. 'Women on top' would not be so funny if it were not felt to be at least partly true.

Structure may be important, but the actual content of these customs is important too. A procession of flagellants does not communicate the same message as a military parade. When it comes to writing about the possible social structure of a performance-event, it seems to me important that we should know what the actual performances were. Peter Greenfield's thesis partly depends on assuming that local landlords 'rewarded local commoners for performing plays that presumably involved elements of carnival inversion and travesty of social order and authority'. But as he says, we have no actual evidence of the kind of shows they performed. The players from Whalley might have done a contemporary version of the Antrobus Soul-Cakers' play (not in itself particularly subversive, though certainly anarchic): but they might equally have done a Nativity Play. They might have done *Pyramus and Thisbe*. They might have done *Youth*.[77] Presumably they were not sophisticated enough for the likes of *Respublica*, or *Gorboduc*, or Edward VI's *Comedy of the Whore of Babylon*,[78] or fortunate enough to have John Bale as their parish priest, and the opportunity to play

Three Laws.[79] But if these were all equally possible Christmas plays, where does it leave the theory of containment?

Pushing this a little, if the *material* of the plays is not potentially subversive, then it is the actors and the performance which have to be contained. But if actors and acting are subversive, then they have to be repressive as well, because they take over your space (this is especially true of plays before the custom-built theatre) and force you to accept their ideology – for the time being. All acting is a power-play. Unless an actor can command your attention and make you believe what he wants, he has failed. At this level, it is unrealistic to talk about 'containment', because by taking them under your patronage you have given them their platform, even if they end by humbly thanking you for the opportunity: and it is long odds that their performance, *if it is good*, will last longer in the audience's memory than your patronage. The only way of 'containing' them is to pay them to go away, or attempt to abolish them altogether, which is of course what Puritans like Prynne wanted, and finally succeeded in doing.

It is fatally easy with this approach to treat the players as a paid cipher. We have to allow for the possibility that most of these events happened largely because the actors wanted to act. Forget political significance, or the exploration of the human condition, or even economic necessity (there are other ways of earning an honest penny): actors are basically show-offs, and they need an audience. I used to laugh at E.K. Chambers and his 'mimetic impulse of the folk', but the older I get the truer it seems.

But performers cannot perform in a vacuum. If we want to get as accurate a picture as feasible of a festive Show, we need to look closely at the practicalities of putting it on. Who planned it? Who organised it? Who paid for it? Who gave permission for it to go forward? How much control had any of these over the finished product? If there were formal controls, what were they, and how effective do they seem to have been?[80] It helps here to hold it up against modern equivalents, both in order to compare and contrast, and to revive our sense of just how complex an event like this can be. Anyone who has ever had to arrange a public event will know how many legitimate vested interests are involved and have to be appeased. Some are external, like the police and the fire service and local traders. Other, internal, interests may be at daggers drawn over aesthetic questions which are possibly mutually insoluble (Pamela King in her account of the Elche *Festa* describes the various tensions between the parties of tradition and of scholarly reform); others over matters of funding or casting ('for thomas poolles child bycose he plednot our god' was apparently only the tip of an iceberg of resentment and jockeying in the Chester Painters' Guild).[81] All of these will alter, however slightly, the shape of the final product and the dynamics of the event.

A performance of any kind is a complex biological structure. Its own particular DNA is what makes it distinctive. We need some kind of classification system to get a grip on it, but there is a danger that the convenient abstractions of socio-historical theory, like 'shared values' or 'the dominant ideology', or 'the community' or 'the ruling classes', will oversimplify the real thing to the point of uselessness. Even 'tradition' needs human agents to keep it running.

Take for example a procession, probably the most obvious 'showcase' event, and therefore the most susceptible to such classifications. If it is to be organised to express 'shared values', who determines what these values are and how they shall be expressed? Individual participants (thus leaving the coherence of the values and their expression to the Zeitgeist)? A democratically-elected committee? (Elected from and by whom?) The City Council? An artistic director? If an artistic director is appointed, who appoints him/her, and how much autonomy has s/he?[82]

In fact, the sheer practicalities of the event usually determine this, and incidentally explain a lot of our socio-political perceptions. The more ambitious an event is, the more people it involves, the more difficult it is to organise without massive delegation. This is easiest to arrange through existing structures (especially if they volunteer to pay) – or, conversely, existing structures will insist on playing a part. 'The community' here is the sum of its effective organisations. This will inevitably mean that those who are not involved in these will be sidelined.

It often also means that those who cannot raise the money to put on a Show (play, processional float, or whatever) will not have a voice. This does not necessarily mean, however, that these shows are always mounted by socio-economic groups A and B. Above the poverty line, your disposable income is the income of which you think you can dispose, or there would be no Rio or Notting Hill Carnivals. But there are also many different kinds of funding structure. Does the one who pays the piper always get to call the tune? How?[83] Can we prove it?

If a popular event is 'traditional' (i.e. recurrent), that will ease certain organisational and funding problems. There will be precedents:[84] organisers and participants will know their rôles; costumes, floats, and giants can be recycled, and there will not have to be the same massive capital outlay as at the beginning. But this increased efficiency will also inevitably lead to conservatism. This may give the sense of pleasant familiarity and reassurance I spoke of above, but it also has its dangers: not political dangers, but theatrical ones. A Show of any kind is a theatrical event. (Thomas Hardy did traditional drama a great disservice by implying that a mummers' play is only truly authentic if it is completely undramatic.)[85] It needs energy, and suspense, *and surprise*, or it will suffer from the law of diminishing returns. This implies a modicum of change.

Exactly how much change and of what kind is arguable. Tradition in itself is not necessarily stultifying: a traditional event provides a safe framework within which players and devisors can experiment. There is bound in any case to be some change, because of wear and tear and fashion. Costumes and actors have to be replaced, and will be unconsciously updated.[86] But really enthusiastic actors and designers will always be trying to improve theatrically on a traditional event. New features will be added. The Elche *Festa* has been played continuously (more or less) for centuries, but has obvious musical strata dating from the thirteenth to the seventeenth centuries, and the seventeenth-century angels' bodices, on show in the museum, are delightfully masque-like and totally unlike the current twentieth-century Botticelli drapes. We are continually presenting a revised view of the past.[87]

Every now and then, it would seem that a major facelift is necessary if the event is to survive at all. Here the past might have lessons for the present day: take, for example, the recent history of the York Mystery Plays in the context of the (now apparently defunct) York Festival.[88] Sometimes a new festival arises from the corpse of the old. Its demise can be brought about by events which are beyond the participants' control: war, government suppression, bankruptcy of the funding body. Or the event may become so out of step with the times that it starts to die for lack of popular support. David Mills' account of the life and death of the Chester Show demonstrates what kills popular events as well as what sustains them,[89] and seems to include a warning that 'the marketing of heritage' is not the answer: a revival mounted purely for touristic purposes will die when the tourists move on.[90] (The Elche *Pobladores* looks set to succeed because it cannily draws on the theme of joint racial origins, with which the ordinary Ilicitano can identify.) Do all such events have a natural life span, and die when the culture which created them fades? There is no room here to discuss the relationship between popular festivals and religion, and the delicate balance between Christianity as belief and Christianity as a shared culture; or the complexities of accommodating modern sensibilities with an ancient form.

Finally, because this was the real world, there ought to be a place in it for Small Catastrophe Theory. So many imaginary reconstructions assume a perfect fit between plan and execution. Th'experience woot well it is noght so. Some of the more spectacular as well as the more humdrum disasters of the past have come down to us. The *Bal des Ardents*.[91] The repeat fireworks performance at the Joyous Entry into Bruges which nearly terminated the career of the Emperor Charles V before it had begun.[92] The rainstorm which obliterated the welcome of Margaret of York into Bruges when she came to marry Charles the Bold.[93] The Show at Micklegate Bar which was not finished in time for the Royal Entry of Henry VIII and Katherine Howard into York in 1541.[94] The devil who was accidentally ignited in hell, but played on spartanly, though he was badly burned.[95] The Antwerp Giant who was decapitated going round the street corner of the Oude Beurs and the Wolstraat and remained suspended against the first-floor windows peering gravely down into the houses, to the hysteria of his audience.[96] There must have been many others left unrecorded (possibly because the audience never noticed that something had gone wrong): the angels who did not fly, the worlds which obstinately refused to be set on fire. Or of the hasty improvisations which became a traditional part of the event, and may be the simple explanation behind many an iconographical puzzle. To all those whose well-laid plans have collapsed in humiliating disaster through no fault of their own, let me recommend Étienne Jodelle's account of his *triomphe à l'antique* for the Victors of Calais, for which he was given three days to design and paint the scenery and cartouches, and write, cast, and rehearse two musical masquerades, while playing the leading rôle himself, and having to memorise 100 lines of verse which he had only written that morning; with costumiers who failed to deliver the wings and body-stockings for the Cupids or the complimentary wreaths for the Royal Family which were the whole point of the second masquerade; successfully manoeuvring two rocks – even if the lament *qu'on m'avoit fait au lieu de rochers des clochers* ('that instead of *rochers* – rocks – they had made me *clochers* – bell-towers') is not, his editor says, to be taken literally – and a large ship (with mast) through a very narrow doorway into the hall only to discover that the half the tables had not been cleared, and that the audience would not stop talking so that no-one could hear the actors ... His anguished voice rings recognisably across the centuries:

> ... comment se pourroit il faire qu'un homme s'estant tourmenté par quatre jours, ayant quasi perdu le repos de toutes les nuits, s'estant mille fois extremement faché de ne voir son entreprise aller selon son desir, ayant la memoire embrouillée d'une meslange et confusion de choses qui toutes se tiroient d'une mesme tonneau, appellé à l'execution de son affaire avant quasi que d'estre à demi prest ... renversé et voyant renverser ses gents l'un sus l'autre à l'entrée du lieu où il falloit entrer, ayant esté fort malade environ une heure devant et se trouvant fort mal dedans le lieu mesme ... voyant tous ses appareils rompus avant que d'en rien faire, voyant demeurer des choses necessaires par le desordre, ne trouvant presque point de place pour le reste, voyant des le commencement par la faute d'une musique se naistre une rizée, voyant mesme qui est le pire du jeu les premiers interlocuteurs qu'il avoit soulagés et asseurés faillir outre son esperance, eust peu tellement se commander à soymesme, que de donter le courrous, l'apprehension, et la honte, et au lieu de crever et desirer d'estre cent piés sous terre, montrer un visage impudent et une vois de meurdrier entre tant de fautes, qui n'eussent pas laissé pour tout cela de lui estre imputées?[97]

> '... how could a man [who], having been tormented for four days, having lost almost all his sleep each night, been infuriated a thousand times over at not seeing his undertaking going as he wanted, his mind fogged with a mixture and confusion of things which were all different facets of the same problem [lit. which had all come out of the same barrel], summoned to perform the whole thing before he was halfway ready ... having been tripped up (?) and seeing his people being upended one on top of the other in the doorway to the place where they were supposed to make an entrance, having been very ill about an hour before, and still feeling very ill even on stage ... seeing all his stage-machinery broken before he could do anything with it, seeing things he needed left behind because of the chaos, and hardly able to find any room to put down the rest, seeing a giggle start up at the very outset because there was something wrong with the music, even seeing – which is the worst of the

whole farce – the opening speakers, whom he had jollied along and propped up, collapse beyond his wildest expectations: [how could such a man] have been able to get a sufficient grip on himself as to suppress the rage, the sick panic, and the shame, and instead of crumpling up and wanting to be a hundred feet under the ground, present a brazen face and the voice of a hardened criminal in the midst of so many blunders, which were inevitably going, in spite of everything, to be seen as his responsibility?'

So recognisable it makes your blood run cold, this is truly Festive Drama from Hell. But Jodelle was determined to have the last word: to allow us to appreciate the Platonic beauty of his original design, he published it as it had appeared on the drawing board. We are lucky that his hurt pride also spurred him to describe, in all its cringing detail, its less-than-perfect execution. Who knows how many other disasters are masked behind the fixed smile of an official sixteenth-century press release?

Lancaster University

NOTES

I owe a great deal to discussions on this topic with Olga Horner, Pamela King, Rosemary Phizackerley, and Robert and Alison Samuels.

At the time of writing, the book of essays entitled *Moving Subjects: The Semiotics of Processional Performance* and edited by Kathleen Ashley has not yet appeared.

1. Though they did not actually, to my knowledge, use that adjective with those nouns.
2. *The N. Town Play 1: Introduction and Text* edited Stephen Spector EETS SS 11 (1991) 21: *Proclamation* lines 520–1.
3. C.S. Lewis *Studies in Words* (Cambridge University Press, 2nd edition 1967) 12–14.
4. The play of *Valentine and Orson* is presumably there for calendrical reasons: its hero is for part of the play a Wild Man of the kind which appears in the end of Winter masquerades, nowadays especially in Switzerland and Austria.
5. William Prynne *Histriomastrix* with preface by Arthur Freeman (Garland, New York and London, 1974; facsimile of 1633 London edition by Michael Sparke) Introduction (no pagination) fifth page. I have reversed the italicisation of the original here. Prynne's 'concomitants' include 'effeminate mixt Dancing, Dicing ... Face-painting, Health-drinking, Long haire, Love-lockes, [and] Periwigs', some of which we would see as part of the social context, some as theatrical accoutrements.
6. Prynne 20.
7. We could classify the degrees of this theatricalisation as a continuum from simple custom to developed drama: but I want to avoid anything which might suggest an evolutionary approach, as if ceremonies became more 'advanced', and therefore better, or more successful, the more complex and the nearer to 'Stage-playes' they became. Equally I want to avoid implying a primitive purity in the simpler forms. So if I start with the simpler and end with the most complex, this is merely because it is convenient to describe it as if it were a process of accumulation.

8. I am thinking partly of Elche, described in this volume by Pamela King, where the play of the Death, Assumption, and Coronation of the Virgin is both a detachable entity and part of the celebration of the Vespers and Feast of the Assumption, as its names suggest.
9. Prynne *Histriomastrix* 112–113. O.B. Hardison deals with this topic at length in his *Christian Rite and Christian Drama in the early Middle Ages* (John Hopkins Press, Baltimore, 1965) 35–79.
10. *The Book of Margery Kempe* edited S.B. Meech and Hope Emily Allen *EETS OS 212* (1940) 184. See also:

    On þe Purificacyon Day er ellys Candilmesse Day whan þe sayd creatur be-held þe pepil wyth her candelys in cherch, hir mende was raueschyd in-to beholdyng of owr Lady offeryng hyr blisful Sone owr Sauyour to þe preyst Simeon in þe Tempyl, as verily to hir gostly vndirstondyng as ȝyf sche had be þer in hir bodily presens for to an offeryd wyth owr Ladys owyn persone. 198

    For other examples see my article 'Books for the unlearned' in *Drama and Religion* edited James Redmond (Themes in Drama 3: Cambridge University Press, 1983) 65–110, especially 106.
11. From Diana Wyatt's transcription of the Beverley records for REED: quoted with her permission in my article on '"Transvestism" in the Mystery Plays' *Medieval English Theatre* 5:2 (1983) 123–180, on pages 129–130.
12. *Philippe de Mézières' Campaign for the Feast of Mary's Presentation* edited William Coleman (Toronto Medieval Latin Texts: Pontifical Institute of Mediaeval Studies for the Centre for Medieval Studies, Toronto, 1981) 84: *aliquam ... solempnitatem cum representationibus quibusdam deuotissimis verbis, nouisque actibus, et signis ornatis* ... Its setting was the Office for the Feast of the Presentation: *Officium Presentacionis Beate Marie Virginis in Templo* 55.
13. Published as 'Palm Sunday Prophets and Processions and Eucharistic Controversy' *Renaissance Quarterly* 48 (1995) 58-81.
14. *Custom, Culture and Community in the Later Middle Ages* edited Tom Pettitt and Leif Søndergaard (Odense University Press, 1994). They also point out that 'The distinctions between custom, drama, and pageantry are modern rather than medieval' and suggest that it is a strength rather than a weakness to ignore them (10).
15. *Custom, Culture and Community* 13–14.
16. Chris Baldick *The Concise Oxford Dictionary of Literary Terms* (Oxford University Press, 1991) s.v. *drama*.
17. *The Early English Carols* edited R.L. Greene (Clarendon Press, Oxford, 1977) cxxiii–cxxvi.
18. *Tudor Interludes* edited Peter Happé (Penguin, Harmondsworth, 1972) 215–217, lines 988 sd –1020.
19. Thoinot Arbeau (pseudonym and anagram of Jehan Tabourot) *Orchesography* translated Mary Stewart Evans, introduction and notes by Julia Sutton (Dover, New York, 1967, second augmented edition of 1948 edition by Kamin Dance Publishers). See especially Arbeau on the 'mute rhetoric' of courtship in dancing (16), and on mimetic branles (153–67).
20. E.g. Theseus' court in *A Midsummer Night's Dream*, or the courtly (but extremely discourteous) audience in *Love's Labours Lost*. Both of these are representations of private occasions.
21. The St Brice's Day Play, as it is recorded, does not appear to have arisen structurally out of the custom, but as an adjunct, an explanation of how (one half of) the custom arose.

22. The suspense lies in the possibility of going against the expected scenario.
23. There must have been considerable tension when Elizabeth I attended a celebratory play and was, as at King's College, Cambridge, in 1563, set on the stage: by performing her role as monarch and the cynosure of all eyes, she cannot but have distracted attention from the student actors who were performing a play: *REED: Cambridge* edited Alan H. Nelson, 2 vols (Toronto University Press, 1989) *1* 234
24. See e.g. *Christmas Mumming in Newfoundland* edited Herbert Halpert and G.M. Storey (Toronto University Press, 1969). For more on the subject of mumming, see my paper '"My visor is Philemon's Roof"' *Fifteenth Century Studies 13* (1988) 335–46.
25. Usually disguised as prizes won by the host at mumchance: see e.g. the famous mumming on 26 January 1377, when the Commons of London gave gifts to the young Prince Richard, soon to be Richard II. The account is in British Library MS Harley 247, fol. 172^v, and is quoted by among others, Paul Reyher in *Les masques anglais* (Hachette, Paris, 1909) 16.
26. John Lydgate *The Minor Poems Part 2: Secular Poems* edited H.N. MacCracken EETS OS 192 (1934 for 1933) nos 45 and 46.
27. George Cavendish *The Life and Death of Cardinal Wolsey* edited R.S. Sylvester EETS ES 243 (1959) 25–28.
28. *Documents Relating to the Revels at Court in the Time of Edward VI and Queen Mary* edited Albert Feuillerat (Uystpruyst, Louvain, 1914) 89, of the Lord of Misrule's interpreter: *truchman = dragoman*. In Lydgate, the interpreter is a *poursuyant* (695), or *heraude* (698); in Cavendish the Lord Chamberlain interprets for them: 'Syr for as myche as they be strayngers And can speke no Englysshe they haue desired me to declare vnto your grace thus ...'
29. Feuillerat *Revels* 89.
30. Feuillerat *Revels* 81.
31. See Sally-Beth MacLean 'King Games and Robin Hood: Play and Profit at Kingston upon Thames' *Fifteenth Century Studies 13* (1988) 309–320; Alexandra F. Johnston 'Summer Games in the Thames Valley Counties' in *Custom, Culture and Community* edited Pettitt and Søndergaard (see note 13) 37–56.
32. George Herbert *A Priest to the Temple, or, The Countrey Parson, his Character and Rule of Holy Life* (1652), in *The Works of George Herbert* edited F.E. Hutchinson (Clarendon Press, Oxford, 1941) 284. I acquired this quotation from Richard Mabey's 'Country Life' column in *The Independent on Sunday Review* for 4 June 1995, page 81.
33. Floris Prims *De Antwerpsche Ommeganck op den Vooravond van de Beeldstormerij* (Mededelingen van de Koninklijke Vlaamsche Academie voor Wetenschappen, Letteren en Schoone Kunsten van België, Klasse der Letteren 8, no 5: Brussels, 1946) 5.
34. See below note 59.
35. See Pamela King in this volume.
36. Though oddly enough, the Fall is not represented by Adam and Eve (who appear later in the casts of the mystery plays associated with the procession), but allegorically by St Michael leading one White Soul and one Black (actually dark blue). St Michael is the patron saint of the town.

　　Pamela King and I were at the procession on Corpus Christi Day 1994 in order to shoot material for a video. Together with Asuncion Salvador-Rabaza, our host, we shall be writing more about it in the future.

37. So does the Bruges Holy Blood procession, though it finishes, like some French cycles, with the Resurrection. Both are demonstrating the function of Christ's body and blood as the culmination of biblical history.
38. Edward van Even *L'Omgang de Louvain* (Louvain/Brussels, 1863); Leo de Burbure (de Wesenbeeck) 'De Antwerpsche Ommegangen in de XIVe en XVe Eeuw' *Maatschappij der Antwerpsche Bibliophilen 2* (1878).
39. This may have something to do with the popular devotion to the Rosary. One organising principle is that of the Joys and Sorrows of the Virgin. Rather than the secular waggons being detached from the religious ones because of an increasing secularisation, it would appear that at first the religious ones were grouped together in order to make a more coherent statement about the focus of the procession. Non-religious processions, such as the London Midsummer Watch (see Ian Lancashire *Dramatic Texts and Records of Britain* (University of Toronto Press/Cambridge University Press, 1984) no. 969, pages 188–190) were more random.
40. The Corpus Christi processions at Dublin (see E.K. Chambers *The Mediaeval Stage* 2 vols (Oxford University Press, London, 1903) 2 363–5), and Whitsun Plays at Norwich (Chambers 2 387: *Non-Cycle Plays and Fragments* edited Norman Davis EETS SS 1 (1970) xxvi–xxxi) seem to have had this mixed pattern, with some attempt to arrange the religious pageants in chronological order. For a 'random' Corpus Christi procession, see the records of Ipswich in *Records of Plays and Players in Norfolk and Suffolk, 1330–1642* edited David Galloway and John Wasson (Malone Society Collections 11: Malone Society, Oxford, 1980/1) 169–84.
41. I have written about the processional qualities of the York Cycle as experienced in action in *The Cambridge Companion to Medieval English Theatre* edited Richard Beadle (Cambridge University Press, 1994) 47.
42. According to the numerologists, the centre of a triumph is the place of honour: see Alastair Fowler *Spenser and the Numbers of Time* (Routledge and Kegan Paul, London, 1964) 149. In longer and more heterogeneous processions, the honoured person or object usually occupies the central position in the final segment.
43. *Ordinancie, Inhoudende de Poincten vanden Heylighen Besnijdenis Ommeganck der Stadt van Antwerpen, geschiet inden Iare M.D.LXII* (Hans de Laet, Antwerp, 1562).
44. *Metamorphoses* Book 1, lines 127–150.
45. *Ordinancie, Inhoudende de Poincten vanden Heylighen Besnijdenis Ommeganck der Stadt van Antwerpen, geschiet inden Iare M.D.LXI* (Hans de Laet, Antwerp, 1561).
46. Jose Maria Rey de Arteaga *Corpus de Valencia* (Ajuntament de Valencia, 1994): leaflet.
47. For a good range of illustrations of the *Moriskendans*, and a brief discussion, see Thea Vignau Wilberg-Schuurman *Hoofse minne en burgerlijke liefde in de prentkunst rond 1500* (Nijhoff, Leiden, 1983) 31–7 and plates 24–31. The Lady in the Valencia dance is played by a man.
48. Or the Virgin Mary: though religious processions are more likely to be narrative.
49. W.C. Hazlitt *The Livery Companies of the City of London* (Swan Sonnenschein, London, 1892) 215.
50. Frederick W. Fairholt *Lord Mayor's Pageants: Part 1* (Percy Society, London, 1843) 41, quoting Antony Munday *Chrysanaleia, or the Golden Fishing* (1616): see edition by J. G. Nichols (Worshipful Company of Fishmongers, London, 1844).

51. John Stow *A Survey of London* edited Charles Lethbridge Kingsford 2 vols (Clarendon Press, Oxford, 1908) *1* 107, retold at more length 219–20. Stow repudiates the story that he also 'slue Iacke Straw' (215). He also seems to have owned property in the stews of Southwark (2 55).
52. Fairholt *Pageants: Part 2*, 256 (the Goldsmiths' leopards bearing the Indian king and queen 251). See Hazlitt *Livery Companies* 223.
53. See e.g. John Lydgate 'Henry VI's Triumphal Entry into London' line 345 in *The Minor Poems of John Lydgate Part Two* edited H.N. MacCracken *EETS OS 192* (1934) 642: quoted by Fairholt *Pageants: Part 1* 7, from an earlier edition. The mayor on this occasion was called Wells. The Lord Mayor's Show of 1591 for Sir William Webb showed a child representing Nature spinning a web (Fairholt, 28); in 1609 the Show for Sir Thomas Campbell, Mayor was entitled 'Camp-bell; or the Iron-mongers' Faire Field' (Robert Withington *English Pageantry, An Historical Outline* 2 vols (Harvard University Press, Cambridge Mass., 1926: reprinted Arno Press, New York, 1980) 2 29–30.
54. Also in fact the arms of all the preceding Lord Mayors of London who had been Fishmongers.
55. See e.g. the cautious comments of the English herald reporting on the marriage festivities of Margaret of York with Charles the Bold:
    the pageauntes wer so obscure that y fere me to wryte or speke of them because all was countenaunce and noo wordes
    (British Library MS Cotton Nero C 9, fol. 173^v).
56. The Walworth pageant was part of a static spoken scene.
57. *Den triumphanten Omganck van Antwerpen* (Ian van Hilten, Amsterdam, 1648).
58. Like Juan Christoval Calvete de Estrella *El Felicissime Viaie d'el Muy Alto y Muy Poderoso Principe Don Phelippe* ... (Nucio, Antwerp, 1552); Jan de Pottre *Dagboek (1549–1620)* (Maatschappij der Vlaamsche Bibliophilen 3:5, Ghent, 1861), the various accounts of the Royal Entry of Mary Queen of Scots into Edinburgh in 1561 cited by Anna J. Mill *Mediæval Plays in Scotland* (Blackwood, Edinburgh and London, 1927) 189–91, etcetera. What exactly do they notice, and how far do they suggest interpretations?
59. 'The Flemish *Ommegang* and its Pageant Cars' *Medieval English Theatre* 2 (1980) 17.
60. See Geoffrey Ashton *Catalogue of Paintings at the Theatre Museum, London* (Victoria and Albert Museum with the Society for Theatre Research, London, 1992) 1–4; Edgard Goedleven *De Grote Markt van Brussel* (Lannoo, Tielt, 1993) 68–91; Fr. V. Baesten S.J. 'L'Ommeganck de Bruxelles en 1615 d'après les tableaux de Denis van Alsloot' *Précis historiques* 38 and 39 (1889–1890) 5–19, 193–28, 337–361, 437–56, 533–53. The question of how many paintings there were originally, and therefore how much of the procession the surviving ones show, is complex. Van Alsloot was paid for six, and then another two, making eight in all. Four survive (two in the Prado, two in London, one of which, belonging to the Victoria and Albert Museum, was sliced in half by its Victorian owner), together with two copies (one of the mutilated London painting showing the Shooters' Guilds, one of one of the Madrid paintings showing the Trade Guilds), which are in Brussels. The famous painting in the London Theatre Museum is labelled 'LA CINCQVIESME' at the bottom. Without this it would be tempting to assume that the eight comprised two sets of four: but the Archduchess appeared to have six on show at Tervuren in 1619: Leo van Puyvelde 'De Ommegang te Brussel in 1615 naar de

schilderijen van Denijs van Alsloot' *De Koninklijke Vlaamse Academie voor Taal- en Letterkunde 1–2* (Ghent, 1958).L 118–121.
61. Alphonse Wauters *L'Ancien Ommeganck de Bruxelles* (Briard, Brussels, 1848) 9–10.
62. The Fencers Guild 1480 (St Michael and St Gudula); the Hackbut guild 1477 (St Christopher and St Barbara, patroness of guns and gunpowder); the Longbow guild 1477 (St Sebastian and St Antony); the Little Crossbow Guild 1381 (St George). The Old Crossbow Guild 1213 (Our Lady of Sablon) is not featured as it was escorting Isabella in the Broodhuis.
63. One is Semiramis, Queen of Babylon, descendant of Nimrod, the great hunter: Baesten 117.
64. Baesten points out that the waggon is a simple flat-bed construction (125). He does not seem to recognise it as a simplified Parnassus – or indeed Diana on the previous waggon. The costumes may have been adapted from a static display in honour of the entry of the Archduke Ernest of Austria into Brussels in 1594 (Jacques Stroobant *Brusselsche Eertriumphen* (Peeter de Dobbeleer, Brussels, 1670) 33).
65. Contemporary engraving entitled *Trophee aux Dammes*, reproduced in L. Hymans *Bruxelles à travers les âges* (Brussels, 1882–1889) fig. 24. Isabella is shown seated on a throne, Apollo, Diana, and three huntresses surrendering their bows to her: on the canopy of the throne is a representation of the statue of Notre Dame de Sablon being brought by ship from Antwerp by Béatris Soetkens, with the label *Supreme Gloire*. This very nicely suggests the hierarchy.
66. Withington *English Pageantry* (see note 52) 1 3–84: chapter 1: 'Elements of the Pageant'; see also Glynne Wickham *Early English Stages 1300–1660: Volume One, 1300–1576* (Routledge and Kegan Paul, London and Henley, 2nd edition 1980) 41–45 (tourneys), 90–92 (street pageants), plates 12, 13, 16.
67. *Custom, Culture and Community in the Later Middle Ages* edited Tom Pettitt and Leif Søndergaard (Odense University Press, 1994) 9.
68. Demos in support of the disempowered usually make their point by the sheer weight of numbers.
69. She was originally not an allegorical figure but a Beauty Queen. Jervis Wegg *Antwerp 1477–1559* (Methuen, London, 1916) 21
70. Withington *English Pageantry* 2 24
71. I owe this phrase to Rosemary Phizackerley.
72. Cornelius Grapheus (de Schryver) *Spectaculorum in susceptione Philippi ... An. M.D.XLIX Antverpiæ Æditorum, Mirificus Apparatus* (Antwerp, 1549) sigs L3^v–M1^v; also Calvete de Estrella *El Felicissimo Viaie* (see note 57) 245^v–246^r. Gaspar Bouttats *Verbeeldinghe vanden triumphanten Ommeganck van Antwerpen ...* (Hieronymus Verdussen, Antwerp, 1685) attributes it to Pieter Coeck van Aalst. Voet *Antwerp: The Golden Age* (Mercatorfonds, Antwerp, 1973) says that the Giant first appeared in 1534 (452).
73. Bouttats: 'Vele houden dat desen Vis gemaeckt is tot memorie , naer eenen die over die hondert jaren hier inde Schelde ghevanghen was, andere seggen, datmen de *Walvisschen* die in groenlant gevangen wierden, al-hier aen-gebrocht wierden, en dat die *Traenbranders* die doen hier woonden, desen soude gemaeckt hebben ... Men seght desen *Oliphant* ghemaeckt is naer eenen die over hondert jaeren her tot Antwerpen gheweest is.' Voet *Antwerp* 34 publishes a print of an elephant in the streets of Antwerp in 1554. It was a present from the King of Portugal to the Emperor Charles V (Voet *Antwerp* 46).

74. Raman Selden *A Reader's Guide to Contemporary Literary Theory* (Harvester Wheatsheaf, Hemel Hempstead, 2nd edition, 1989) 104.
75. Alan Somerset 'New Historicism: Old History Writ Large? Carnival, Festivity, and Popular Culture in the West Midlands' *Medieval and Renaissance Drama in England 5* (1991) 245–55.
76. Bernardino Zambotti *Diario Ferrarese dall' anno 1476 sino al 1504* edited Guiseppe Pardi (Rerum Italicarum Scriptores vol. 24 part 7: Zanichelli, Bologna, 1937) *passim*, especially 60 for a classic egg-fight; Fabrizio Cruciani *Teatro nel Rinascimento Roma 1450–1550* (Bulzoni, Roma, 1983) 301, 330; Pierre de l'Estoile *The Paris of Henry of Navarre* translated Nancy Lyman Roelker (Harvard University Press, Cambridge, Mass., 1958) 99.
77. A quick trawl through Ian Lancashire *Dramatic Texts and Records of Britain* (University of Toronto Press/Cambridge University Press, 1984) comes up with the following Christmas plays in similar circumstances: 'le Mary & Gabriel' at King's Lynn in 1445/6 (162), taken to seat of Lord de Scales at Middleton, Norfolk (227); the Nativity in the Guildhall at Exeter 1430/1 (134: see also *REED: Devon* edited John Wasson (Toronto University Press, 1992); masquerade of masked men at Mount Edgecombe, Cornwall, c.1556 (229); many other visits by local troupes, but content unspecified; many maskings and disguisings, but usually put on by the household itself.
78. *Respublica* for Queen Mary, Christmas 1553 (Lancashire 212); *Gorboduc* Inner Temple 1551/2 (see Horner); *Comediam de meretrice Babylonica* by Edward VI, Hampton Court, 1547/8 (Lancashire 149)
79. John Bale's *Three Laws* (aborted) at Bishopstoke, Hampshire, Christmas 1551 (Lancashire 85). Perhaps literacy and sophistication had both increased dramatically by 1632, when a group of men in Warrington were brought before the Justice of the Peace charged with performing *Henry VIII* on a Sunday (*REED: Lancashire* edited David George (Toronto University Press, 1991) 95–7).
80. Some agents of control, such as fines, can only operate *post hoc*, though they may affect the next time's performance. The threat of them is presumably meant to deter, but there is enough evidence even in this book to show that they did not, if people were really determined.
81. *REED: Chester* edited Lawence M. Clopper (Toronto University Press, 1979) 100. I owe this information to my ex-student Alan Hamilton: unfortunately he was unable to complete his MPhil thesis on the Chester Painters' Guild and their play.
82. In the medieval and early modern period, it was unlikely to be a 'she'. In the Flemish *ommegang*, he was usually the official town painter: see my 'The Flemish *Ommegang* and its Pageant Cars' *Medieval English Theatre 2* (1980) 95 note 68. See e.g. *REED: York* 137–143 (1486) for the mechanics of arranging a Royal Entry.
83. To give an obvious example, if costumes are being paid for *and made* by the mothers of participants, they have the ultimate control over the product; but the design may well have been provided and the material specified by someone else. On the other hand, how much artistic freedom did the painters (e.g. Thomas Poole) in the Chester Show have?
84. See *REED: York* 271: the joiners and painters charged with making a scaffold for a show at Micklegate Bar for the Royal Entry of Henry VIII and Katherine Howard in 1541 'hadde delyuered vn to them a Copy of an olde precydent of the furst commyng of kyng henry the vijth to this City' in 1487.

85. *The Return of the Native* Book 2 chapter 4 (e.g. in the Wessex Novels edition (Macmillan, London, 1912) 147–8).
86. The generation gap determines that our parents' taste always looks old-fashioned and 'wrong': respect for tradition begins with our grandparents.
87. See Pamela King and Asunciòn Salvador-Rabaza 'The *Festa* or *Misteri* of Elx' *Medieval English Theatre 14* (1992) 4–21 for more on the latest revisions to the production.
88. The annual Festival of Early Music, which is currently on a sounder financial basis, provided a showcase for waggon plays in 1994. There is local enthusiasm to keep the plays as an annual event, though it seems to be directed to replacing them in their 'traditional' (since 1951) setting in St Mary's Abbey. This is popularly assumed to be the original medieval method of performance.
89. John Coldewey's account of the end of drama in Maldon is a simpler scenario.
90. Even in the sixteenth century, substitute festivities did not always catch on: at York Grafton's Interlude, which was attached to the Midsummer Show of armour, in 1584, and possibly intended to replace the banned Corpus Christi Play, did not last more than two years (*REED: York* 405–406, 409–412, 414–23).
91. John Bourchier, Lord Berners *Froissart's Chronicles* (London, 1523–1525) fol. ccxliii[r–v].
92. In 1515. See Remy Du Puys *La tryumphante Entree de Charles Prince des Espagnes en Bruges 1515* edited Sidney Anglo (Theatrum Orbis Terrarum: Johnson Reprint Co., New York, 1971) 13. As one might expect, there are a fair number of firework disasters, too many to annotate.
93. British Library MS Cotton Nero C 9: *The mariage of the Ryght highe and myghty Prince the Duc of Burgoigne with the Right high and excellent Princesse Margarett suster vnto ... Kyng Edward the iiij*[th] ... fol. 173[v]: 'And than the storme of the rayne come soo fast I myghte nott wryght the certayn of the presentancion ...'. Rain is a not infrequent disaster – see Withington *English Pageantry 2* 28 (Lord Mayor's Show, 1605); Grafton's Interlude *REED: York* 423, the various incidents in Meredith and Tailby (see below note 94).
94. *REED: York* 276.
95. *The Staging of Religious Drama in Europe* edited Peter Meredith and John Tailby (Early Drama, Art, and Music Monograph Series 4: Medieval Institute Publications, Kalamazoo, 1983) 261. Philip Butterworth 'Hellfire: Flame as a Special Effect' in *The Iconography of Hell* edited Clifford Davidson and Thomas H. Seiler (Early Drama, Art, and Music Monograph Series 17: Medieval Institute Publications, Kalamazoo, 1992) 67–10, has a lot of information about this hazardous form of stage effect.
96. In 1647: Daniel Papebrochius S.J. *Annales Antverpienses* 5 vols (J. Buschmann, Antwerp, 1847) 4 495.
97. Étienne Jodelle *Œuvres complètes 2: Le Poète dramatique, Le Poète satirique* edited Enea Balmas (Gallimard, Paris, 1968) 219–56: *Le Recueil des inscriptions, figures, devises, et masquarades ordonnées en l'Hostel de ville à Paris le jeudi 17 de Febvrier 1558*: quotation from page 251. For *rochers/clochers* see 249. Notes to the work, see 462–7. The first masquerade was on the subject of Jason and the Argonauts. The rocks were meant to follow Orpheus (who was also on Argo), drawn by his singing. I would like to thank Dr Zara Zaddy for helping me with this translation.

FESTIVE DRAMA AT CHRISTMAS
In Aristocratic Households

Peter H. Greenfield

'There is no slander in an allow'd fool ...'[1] So Olivia, in *Twelfth Night*, excuses Feste's humorous inversion of their roles, the fool proving his mistress more foolish than he. Yet such inversions must remain in the realm of the playful. When Sir Toby's transgressions of the rules of the household turn from the inversion of early and late with quaffing and caterwauling at ill hours, to the violent disorder of the duel between Cesario and Sir Andrew, Sir Toby learns at the cost of a bloody coxcomb that he 'must confine [him]self within the modest limits of order'.[2] Aristocrats of Shakespeare's time and earlier must have held an attitude like Olivia's toward festive misrule in their households at Christmas. Not only did they often appoint a Lord of Misrule from among the members of the household to reign over the Twelfth Night festivities, but many also rewarded local commoners for performing plays that presumably involved elements of carnival inversion and travesty of social order and authority. Ultimately, however, this allowed misrule served to set the 'limits of order' and reaffirm the authority of the lord over his household and the surrounding countryside.

Evidence of dramatic performance at Christmas in aristocratic households by local amateurs is as yet relatively rare. Many household records remain in private hands, and the difficulty of gaining access to private collections led the Records of Early English Drama project initially to declare such records beyond its ken. Individual editors, especially of county volumes, have nevertheless pursued household records, finding them a valuable part of the total picture of dramatic activity in a county, and REED has since relented and even begun sponsoring editions of family records. Still, little of this recent scholarship has as yet seen print, forcing this paper to range from the early fifteenth century to the early seventeenth – well beyond what even medieval theatre scholars are willing to call 'medieval' – in search of a rather meagre sample.

We have long known that much of the dramatic activity at court was concentrated in the period between Christmas Eve and Epiphany, and the same holds true for private households. The famous book of regulations for the household of Henry Percy, fifth Earl of Northumberland, provides for a Master of the Revels responsible 'for the overseinge and orderinge of his Lordships Playes Interludes and Dresinge that is plaid befor his Lordships in his Hous in the xijth Dayes of Cristenmas', and details the duties of the Earl's performers at that time of year.[3] Most masques, disguisings and other entertainments performed by members of the household tended to occur during those twelve days. The household account book of Elizabeth Berkeley, Countess of Warwick, records '*diuersis* disgisingez *factis hoc festo*' at Christmas 1420.[4] The Children of Northumberland's Chapel received 20s. 'if they doo play the Play of Nativitie uppon Cristynmas-Day' while their Resurrection play for Easter and their Shrove Tuesday play are the only entertainments at other times of the year the regulations mention.[5] A 1515 wardrobe account of Edward Stafford, third Duke of Buckingham and Northumberland's brother-in-law, lists *vj vlne* Canvas *pro ffactura vnius lez pagent & ostensione ... coram prefato domino duce in ffesto Natali domini ...*[6]

Professional players often visited the households at this time of year as well. The Northumberland book specifies the amounts to be paid to players 'that comyth to his Lordschipe betwixt Cristynmas and Candilmas', but makes no reference to companies that arrived at other times.[7] Accounts of Henry Lord Berkeley show that he paid acting troupes for performing at Caludon Castle (near Coventry) only at Christmas, between 1600 and 1605, although he rewarded travelling musicians throughout the year. This pattern does not, however, hold true for the majority of households. In fact, none of the several visits of professional players to Lord Berkeley found in an earlier account book came at Christmas.[8] The more common pattern occurs in the accounts of the Walmesleys of Dunkenhalgh, Lancashire, in which only three or four of the 83 visits by itinerant professional companies between 1612 and 1639 are recorded as happening during the Christmas season. Instead, the Walmesleys got their Christmas entertainment principally from groups of players from nearby towns who were almost certainly amateurs. They came to Dunkenhalgh Manor House from Downham (twelve miles away), Ribchester (nine miles), Clitheroe (nine miles), and most often from Whalley, only five miles away.[9] Similar evidence that local amateurs performed in the households almost exclusively at Christmas appears in most of the available household records. Elizabeth Berkeley welcomed minstrels of Lords Stafford and Clarence and Lady Abergavenny to Berkeley Castle in 1420/1421, but at Christmas it was villagers from Slimbridge and Wotton who played before the Countess.[10] Many professional entertainers came to the powerful Duke of Buckingham's household at Thornbury Castle in Gloucestershire, including at Christmas 1520 a French company with two female members, yet in 1508 it was players from the Duke's own manor of Writtle, Essex, who travelled across the country to entertain him at Christmas.[11] Professional troupes visited Smithills, Lancashire, at various times during the year, but at Christmas 1588 it was players from Preston and Nantwich, in 1590 from Downham, and in 1591 from Rochdale, Garstang, and Blackburn.[12]

What lords stood to gain from welcoming to their households these real-life cousins of Bottom, Quince, and company went beyond the solace Olivia derived from Feste's fooling. Many aristocrats returned to their country seats at Christmas, and there engaged in entertaining intended to reaffirm patron-client relations with local gentry and officials, as well as relations with members of their extended families. Dramatic entertainment, like feasting, contributed to this reassertion of power by acting as a gift from lord to guests. The giving and receiving of this gift symbolised a reciprocal promise of continued beneficent paternalism on the part of the lord in exchange for continued loyal service on the part of the guest. Both disguisings and plays given by professional companies could function as gifts in this way, but plays performed by local amateurs offered an even greater potential for serving the lord's political needs. They emphasised the reciprocity of the relationship between the lord and those under him, for at the same time as the performance acted as gift from lord to invited guests, it acted as a gift from the players and the local people they represented to the lord, and that gift was reciprocated when the lord rewarded the players.

Such gift-giving is of course appropriate to the feast of Epiphany, and when the records date performances precisely, they occur most frequently on Epiphany itself.[13] The Magi presented gifts to the Christ Child as a gesture of obeisance and humility before a greater lord, and this humility is a central liturgical theme of the feast, as R. Chris Hassel Jr shows in his *Renaissance Drama and the English Church Year*.[14] Hassel does not explore, however, the possibility that, in addition to offering thematic inspiration for the content of masques and plays performed on the feast, the liturgical significance of Epiphany could be appropriated for political purposes. He notes that the audience at a court masque 'had just attended the Epiphany Evensong en masse and observed its sovereign reenact the Magi's homage to Christ'.[15] When the masque concluded with a similar gesture of homage to the sovereign, the two events together had powerfully enacted a reaffirmation of the hierarchy of God, monarch, and subject. Local amateurs presenting a play before the lord in his household provided a similar opportunity to appropriate the liturgical message of Epiphany to reinforce the hierarchical relationships between the lord and his client-gentry, tenants, retainers, and others in some way dependent on him.

Furthermore, this celebration of harmonious social community appropriated the other Epiphany theme discussed by Hassel: the achievement of concord out of discord, of unity out of plurality and conflict.[16] The entertainments most likely to have been imported into aristocratic households by local players were the Christmas games or plays they performed in their own towns and villages.[17] What we know of these folk entertainments – Robin Hood plays, King Games, Lords of Misrule, and the like – suggests that they would have offered images of resistance to authority before culminating in gestures of concord and obeisance. As C.L. Barber has said, 'The village saturnalia of the Lord of Misrule's men was in its way a sort of rising; setting up a mock lord and demanding homage for him are playfully rebellious gestures, into which Dionysian feeling can flow'.[18] Yet the amateurs' plays never intended genuine subversion; in fact, Michael J. Bristol finds festive misrule fundamentally conservative: it 'seeks to restrain and limit all radicalisation from below in the form of individual deviation from socially accepted norms, and all radicalisation from above in the form of departures from traditional and customarily tolerated patterns of governance'.[19]

This social conservatism of misrule is of course enhanced when the ruling authority – the local lord – authorises the very misrule ostensibly subversive of his authority. As Leonard Tennenhouse says of A Midsummer Night's Dream, 'If Theseus authorises certain inversions of power relations by permitting them to exist within the frameworks of festival and art, it is also true that the introduction of disorder into the play ultimately authorises political authority'.[20] Plays performed by local amateurs thus function within the larger event of the lord's Christmas entertaining much as the antimasque does within the masque proper. The antimasque images forces subversive of the dominant social order, legitimising the exercise of power by the monarch to ensure the maintenance of order.[21] Similarly, authorised festive misrule within the household reaffirmed the authority of the lord, by providing aristocrats and commoners alike with a reassuring representation of the lord's power to contain the forces of disorder.

Even if the entertainment did not specifically image discord and misrule, its occasion can be seen as an invasion of aristocratic space by commoners who do not belong. Yet the reciprocal gift-giving transforms this apparently discordant intrusion into a representation of social harmony.[22] The lord, his guests, and the intruding performers act out their social relationships to one another, and as David Harris Sacks has said of the court masque, 'This acting out is as important as – perhaps more important than – the poetic message offered by the text'.[23]

While we can only guess at the extent to which lords were conscious of the political value of Christmas performances in their households by local players, we do have evidence that aristocrats actively encouraged such performances. In 1606 Francis Clifford, Earl of Cumberland, paid 4s. 'to the yonge men of the toun [Skipton] being his lordships tenants & servants, to fit them for acting plays this Christmas', presumably at his seat, Skipton Castle.[24] That some lords would have been especially interested in encouraging performances by amateur groups like these 'Players of Skipton' can be seen in the cases of Elizabeth Berkeley, the Duke of Buckingham, and Thomas Walmesley.

As the only child of Thomas, Lord Berkeley, Elizabeth Berkeley claimed title to all the Berkeley property on the death of her father in 1417. Her right to those estates was challenged, however, by James Berkeley, the nephew and closest male relative to Lord Thomas, and the legal battle which ensued ran for nearly two centuries. In the absence of legal resolution of the claim, Elizabeth's husband, Richard Beauchamp, Earl of Warwick, took possession of Berkeley Castle by force in 1420. He then left his countess and her household to hold the castle and surrounding estates while he accompanied Henry V to France, and hold it she did, despite James's threats of attack against the castle and eventual occupation of the Berkeley manor house at Wotton-under-Edge.[25] It was in the midst of this dispute that players from Wotton and Slimbridge came to her household at Christmas, came at a time when she desperately needed to enlist the support of local officials, tenants, and others in her struggle with her cousin.

PETER H. GREENFIELD

A century later but only a few miles to the south, Edward Stafford, Duke of Buckingham, launched a programme of repair and new construction designed to make Thornbury Castle rival the royal residences as a symbol of power, the personal power he expanded until it threatened that of the king, and brought Buckingham to the block in 1521. At Christmas 1507, though, the Duke was still regaining the influence his family had lost when Richard III attainted and executed his father. He needed to build a local power-base in Gloucestershire, since the previous dukes had kept their principal residence at Writtle, in Essex.[26] The hundreds of guests he entertained on Christmas and Epiphany included several who possessed considerable Gloucestershire estates of their own: Maurice, Richard, and James Berkeley; Sir Robert and Anthony Poyntz; and William Kingston. Also present were the Abbot of Keynsham, bailiffs and receivers of the Duke's estates, twenty-two people from the town of Thornbury, and thirty-two from the surrounding country.[27] The amateur players from Writtle filled a small but important role in this entertainment on the grand scale. Their performance demonstrated the loyalty and affection of the tenants of the manor where the Staffords formerly kept their principal residence; through welcoming and rewarding the players, the Duke could show his benevolence to those dependent on him. The performance thus provided the members of the Gloucestershire audience with an example of the relationship Buckingham wished to establish with them.

Even minor gentry could exploit Christmas performances by amateurs to increase their standing in the local community. When Thomas Walmesley welcomed many groups of local players to Dunkenhalgh Manor House in the early seventeenth century, the estate had belonged to his family a relatively short time. His grandfather, also Thomas Walmesley, made his fortune in London at the Bar, eventually becoming Judge of Common Pleas and receiving a knighthood. In 1571 he purchased Dunkenhalgh Manor from one Ralph Rishton, and in 1612 it passed to his heir.[28] The many payments to travelling professional companies mentioned above indicates that Dunkenhalgh was a frequent stop on their northern itineraries, but the Christmas visits of players from places like Whalley may have been more important for solidifying the Walmesleys' influence in that part of Lancashire.

Whether or not they had the special motives of Elizabeth Berkeley, Edward Stafford, or Thomas Walmesley, the English aristocracy of the fifteenth, sixteenth, and early seventeenth centuries seem to have enjoyed the plays of local amateurs at Christmas time, perhaps not just because there was no slander in these allowed fools, but also perhaps because in the very act of allowing, and in the performing of what is allowed, authority is exercised and reaffirmed. Just as the aristocracy followed the royal example in becoming patrons of itinerant professional players, so they followed the royal example of the masque in employing amateur acting in their households at Christmas as a means of appropriating the power of theatricality to protect and enhance their own local power.

University of Puget Sound

FESTIVE DRAMA AT CHRISTMAS IN ARISTOCRATIC HOUSEHOLDS

NOTES

1. *Twelfth Night* 1.5.94; from *The Riverside Shakespeare* edited G. Blakemore Evans (Houghton Mifflin, Boston, 1974).
2. Twelfth Night 1.3. 8–9.
3. *The Regulations and Establishment of the Household of Henry Algernon Percy, the fifth Earl of Northumberland* edited Thomas Percy (1827) 339–44; quoted in Paul van Brunt Jones *The Household of a Tudor Nobleman* (University of Illinois Studies in the Social Sciences 6:4: Urbana, 1917; reprinted Torch Press, Cedar Rapids, Iowa, 1918) 321–2.
4. Longleat House MS Misc. 9, fol. 57. Although the manuscript is catalogued as a household account book of Richard Beauchamp, Earl of Warwick, the accounts actually reflect the expenses of the household of his wife, the former Elizabeth Berkeley, as the Earl spent most of the period covered by the accounts in France with Henry V. The records of the Berkeleys and of Edward Stafford, third Duke of Buckingham, used in this paper have been printed in *REED Cumberland/Westmorland/Gloucestershire* edited Audrey Douglas and Peter H. Greenfield (University of Toronto Press, 1986).
5. Jones *Household* 231.
6. Public Record Office: E 101 631/20, mb 20.
7. Jones *Household* 231.
8. Berkeley Castle Muniments: General Series Bound Book 109, fols 2, 47, 103, and General Series Bound Book 107. See Peter H. Greenfield 'Entertainments of Henry, Lord Berkeley, 1593–4 and 1600–05' *REED Newsletter* 8: 1 (1983) 12–24.
9. *REED: Lancashire* edited David George (University of Toronto Press, 1991) 184–212.
10. Longleat MS. Misc. 9, fols 43, 57, 68.
11. Public Record Office: E. 36/220. page 12 and Staffordshire Record Office: D (W) 1721/1/5, pages 46–58.
12. *REED: Lancashire* 167–9
13. Even where precise dates of performance are not given, the records suggest that Epiphany was the day of greatest entertaining. Buckingham's accounts for 1507/1508 indicate only that the *'lusores de* Writell' were present from 25 December to 7 January, but the lists of those present at dinner indicate that 519 persons of various ranks were entertained on Epiphany, as opposed to 389 on Christmas Day, and far fewer on the intervening days (Staffordshire Record Office: D (W) 1721/1/5, pages 46–60).
14. R. Chris Hassel Jr *Renaissance Drama and the English Church Year* (University of Nebraska Press, Lincoln, 1979) 54–8.
15. Hassel *Renaissance Drama* 54
16. Hassel *Renaissance Drama* 58.
17. Extant household records unfortunately provide no clues as to the nature of what the local players actually performed in the households at Christmas. The French troupe that played before the Duke of Buckingham at Thornbury Castle on 1 January 1521 performed 'the passion of oure lorde', but that was a professional company (Public Record Office: E. 36/220, page 12). The amateurs probably would not have offered even something as sophisticated as the unintentional travesty of aristocratic entertainment of 'Pyramus and Thisbe'.
18. C.L. Barber *Shakespeare's Festive Comedy* (Princeton University Press, 1959) 29.

19. Michael D. Bristol *Carnival and Theatre: Plebeian Culture and the Structure of Authority in Renaissance England* (Methuen, London, 1985) 52.
20. Leonard Tennenhouse *Power on Display: The Politics of Shakespeare's Genres* (Methuen, New York, 1986) 74.
21. Stephen Orgel *The Illusion of Power: Political Theater in the English Renaissance* (University of California Press, Berkeley, 1975) 40.
22. A well-known example of such an 'invasion' is the 1377 visit of disguised 'Comons of London' to Richard II, with whom they played at dice, intentionally losing to him gifts of gold, the occasion ending in a general dance: British Library MS Harley 247, fol. 172^v; quoted by E.K. Chambers *The Mediaeval Stage* 2 vols (Oxford University Press, London, 1903) *1* 394–5.
23. David Harris Sacks 'Searching for "Culture" in the English Renaissance' *Shakespeare Quarterly* 39: 4 (1988) 471.
24. John Tucker Murray *English Dramatic Companies 1558–1642* (Constable, London, 1910) 2 255.
25. C.D. Ross 'The Household Accounts of Elizabeth Berkeley, Countess of Warwick, 1420–1' *Transactions of the Bristol and Gloucestershire Archaeological Society* 70 (1951) 82–3.
26. Carole Rawcliffe *The Staffords, Earls of Stafford, and Dukes of Buckingham 1394–1521* (Cambridge University Press, 1978) 87; and A.D.K. Hawkyard 'Thornbury Castle' *Transactions of the Bristol and Gloucestershire Archaeological Society* 95 (1978) 51–2.
27. Staffordshire Record Office: D (W) 1721/1/5, page 46.
28. *REED: Lancashire* xxxvii–xxxviii.

CHRISTMAS AT THE INNS OF COURT
Olga Horner

Sir John Fortescue, a former governor of Lincoln's Inn, writing c.1470 in praise of the English legal system, fostered the impression that the Inns of Court were essentially finishing schools for the landed gentry, where the study of legal science, of Holy Scripture, and of chronicles 'was secondary to the real purpose of acquiring the manners and accomplishments of a courtier. Although entered as law students, the sons of knights, barons, and nobles were taught 'to sing and to exercise themselves in every kind of harmonics ... to practise dancing and all games proper for nobles, as those brought up in the king's household ...'[1]

The few surviving early records of the Inns of Court and Chancery[2] seem to confirm Fortescue's view that the curriculum was heavily weighted towards the social graces. Inn members held regular Saturday-night dances and apparently celebrated the various festivals of the canonical year with indiscriminate enthusiasm. In common with the community at large, they kept the major religious feast days of Christmas, All Hallows and Candlemas. In addition, Ascension Day, Shrove Tuesday, and All Saints, plus other feasts which fell in Christmastide, might also be kept by individual Inns. For example Furnival's, one of the Chancery Inns, began the Christmas festivities of 1471–1472 at All Hallowstide and continued for three months until Candlemas, with minstrelsy and revels every Saturday and, in accordance with the custom of the Inn, extra revelling on the days dedicated to St Hugh (17 November), St Edmund (20 November) and St Katherine (25 November).[3]

Outside the Inns, the judges, Serjeants, Benchers, and students of every grade were actively involved in official Court and City life: as hosts to royalty and to foreign and civic dignitaries at the splendid Serjeants' Feasts, and as participants in national ceremonies and Royal Entries.[4]

Within the Inns, Grand Christmasses and the March and August Readers' Feasts were occasions of solemn ceremony, lavish banquets, and dramatic entertainments, when 'the better sort of the Gentlemen of the Society' performed 'Galliards, Corrantoes, and other Dances; or else ... Stage-Playes' for the amusement of their distinguished guests.[5]

It appears that Fortescue's claim for the Inns as 'a kind of academy of all the manners' was to some extent quite justified. Members were expected to be at least competent, and preferably proficient, singers and dancers, in order to take part in and contribute to the cultural life of the Inns. By developing the accomplishments with which a courtier entertained his monarch, and by the example and training at formal feasts in carrying out the duties of officers of the royal Household, an education in the Inns seemed to prepare a student more for life at Court than to equip him with the necessary expertise to practise at the English Bar. Certainly many young men entered the Inns without any intention of completing their legal studies for a career in the law. Some were there to acquire the necessary grounding in land law needed to manage family estates: some concentrated on their literary talents in the intellectual and social freedom found within the club-like fraternity of an Inn: others hoped to use the Inns' historical, professional, and geographical closeness to the royal Court as a stepping stone to preferment and political advancement.

At the same time Inn directives and regulations testify to a rigorous educational scheme. Every barrister and judge of the Common Law was required to qualify in one of the Inns of Court: trained, supervised, examined, and finally called to the Bar by his fellow Benchers. Deliberately and for historical reasons,[6] revels were limited to those feast days kept by everyone, and also the three-week midsummer holiday, and the long Christmas break. As this usually ran from the end of November to 12 January, it allowed time for Inn members to plan and prepare the sometimes lengthy and ostentatious Christmas revels, with the least interference to law court terms and the educational exercises of Reading and Learning Vacations. All the revels of 1461–1472 at Furnival's Inn (see above), although extensive, nevertheless fell within the sanctioned Christmas period.

The generic term 'revels' applied equally to an evening of music or dancing, by and for the students only, to the full-scale festive programme of a 'grand' Christmas, lasting several days, or to the 'private' Christmasses, limited to Inn members, for whom less extravagant food and simpler pastimes were provided. The extent and cost of the Christmas celebrations varied from year to year, and was governed by income, numbers in commons, or outside circumstances. In times of plague, Christmas might not be kept at all (for example at the Inner Temple in 1505, 1506, 1513, 1517, 1521, etc.);[7] in other years there were extraordinary entertainments, as in 1561–1562 at the Inner Temple. Held to honour Lord Robert Dudley and to show the Inn's gratitude to him,[8] the revels were lavish, elaborate, and expensive, every member having to contribute 20s. equally, irrespective of age or seniority; an unprecedented method of financing the celebrations.

D.S. Bland has reconstructed the order of events of these revels from Gerard Legh's imaginative literary dialogue:[9]

i   The masque of Desire and Beauty.
ii The feast of the Prince Pallaphilos.
iii The feast ended, the High Constable does honour to 'the ambassadors of foreign nations' (guests from the other Inns?).
iv Presentation of twenty-four knights to the Prince.
v   Presentation of the Prince's coat of arms.

vii   A procession to 'the Temple' (presumably the Temple Church) for some form of 'sacrifice'.

viii   Return to the Hall of the Inn where the proceedings are brought to a conclusion with dancing.[10]

Presumably the programme lasted more than one day but it still cannot be a complete summary of the festivities. Apart from the first performance of *Gorboduc*, known to have taken place on Twelfth Night, references to payments for unspecified 'masks, plays, disguisings, or other like' during this Grand Christmas, and particularly to 'a special admission, without payment' to Arthur Broke (who was not an Inn member) 'in consideration of certain plays and shows at Christmas last set forth by him'[11] suggest a more varied dramatic content to the proceedings than the events listed above.

Three more accounts support the overall picture of the variety and scope of Christmas entertainment at the Inns. The eulogistic description of 'sumptuously performed' Grand Christmasses at Clifford's Inn singles out that of 1482–1483 as an example. It lasted from 21 December to 10 January and was enlivened with 'selected songs, choice music, majestical masks, stately stageplays, bountiful banqueting, dicing, dancing and many other card invented courtly pastimes, with like rarity of oratory speeches ...' On some occasions, entertainment conducted 'with like magnificence and no less reputation' included 'martial stratagems, heroical inventions in matters of honour and arms and other witty devices ... acted and contrived' by the members. These items may have been either masques or the courtly pastimes of tourneys and combat at the barriers, but where the author is fulsome about the quality of the amusements, he is annoyingly lacking in hard facts.[12]

A later official report commissioned by Henry VIII (c.1540) on the organisation and system of legal training at the Inns of Court is a succinct, prosaic, and probably more reliable document. It relates how the members at Christmas time 'have all manner of pastimes, as singing and dancing; and in some of the Houses ordinarily they have some interlude or tragedy played by the gentlemen of the same house, the ground and matter thereof is devised by some of the gentlemen of the House'.[13]

The third account, William Dugdale's compilation of how the Inner Temple organised its revels in the sixteenth and seventeenth centuries, is an amalgam of events which took place on some, but not all Christmasses, 'extracted out of the accounts of the House'.[14] Dugdale provides valuable information on planning and procedure and some factual background for Gerard Legh's version of the 1561–1562 revels. He identifies the elected officers and the titles they assumed for that Christmas period, the most important of whom were, besides Lord Robert Dudley as Prince Pallaphilos and 'Constable and Marshal':

Mr Onslow	'Lord Chancellor'.
Anthony Stapleton	'Lord Treasurer'.
Robert Kelway	'Lord Privy Seal'.

OLGA HORNER

John Fuller	'Chief Justice of the King's Bench'.
William Pole	'Chief Justice of the Common Pleas'.
Roger Manwood	'Chief Baron of the Exchequer'.
Mr Bashe	'Steward of the Household'.
Mr Copley	'Marshall of the Household'.
Mr Paten	'Chief Butler'.
Christopher Hatton	'Master of the Game'.

There were also four 'Masters of the Revels', a 'Lieutenant of the Tower', a 'Carver', 'Ranger of the Forests', 'Sewer', and 'fourscore of the Guard; besides divers other not here named'.[15]

According to Dugdale the most important officers were chosen from among the senior Inn members as early as Trinity Term (June), allowing time for others to be selected at All Hallowtide if those originally named could not, or would not, serve, and fines were levied for refusals. (Meg Twycross suggests that appointing members unlikely to be available might be an accepted way of financing the festivities.)[16]

Lesser officers were appointed as required nearer Christmas, probably at the Parliament held on the Eve of St Thomas. If it had been decided to proceed with the Grand Christmas, a formal announcement was made then and the officers named. But for the more lavish revels, initial preparations would have to be started before this Parliament on 21 December, and the Masters of the Revels who were to organise the food and entertainment already known. The St Thomas' Eve proclamation perhaps marked the formal and official commencement of that year's festivities for the 'whole Society of gentlemen', when at the close of business 'in token of joy and good liking, the Bench and Company pass beneath the hearth, and sing a carol, and so to boyer' (an issue of drink).

The Christmas celebrations proper began on Christmas Eve, when revels and dancing before and after supper set a pattern for the following twelve days. After dinner and supper the 'ancientest' (most senior) Master of Revels sang a carol or song, commanding all those present to sing with him, 'and so it is very decently performed'. Dugdale deals at great length with prescribed ceremonial and the Marshal's responsibilities at dinner. He seated the guests and members by age, rank, and status, supervised the very precise order of service of the meal, the duties and conduct of the other elected officers, and where and when the musicians played and sang.

On Christmas Day the gentlemen attended church, after which they breakfasted on brawn, mustard, and malmsey. At dinner the first course was a boar's head, its entry accompanied by minstrelsy. Strangers 'of worth' were admitted to take this meal in the Hall at a cost of 12d. Musicians and trumpeters supplied music during the first course at supper, and at service time 'the two youngest butlers are to bear torches in the Genealogia'.[17]

After the comparative solemnity of the feast of the Nativity, the festivities on St Stephen's Day were an elaborately constructed mockery of royal court pageantry. At dinner, after the first course, the Constable Marshal entered the hall in 'a fair, rich, complete harness, whit and bright gilt' with a nest of feathers on his helm, carrying a gilt pole-axe, and accompanied by the Lieutenant of the Tower similarly accoutred. With them were sixteen trumpeters, four fifes and drums, and four men in white half-harnesses carrying the Tower on their shoulders. After the Constable-Marshal and the Lieutenant had curtseyed and knelt to the Lord Chancellor, the Constable-Marshal delivered an oration begging to be taken into the Lord Chancellor's service. Next came the Master of the Game, dressed in green velvet, with the Ranger of the Forest in green satin carrying a green bow and arrows. Both blew three blasts of venery on the hunting horns round their necks and paced round the fire three times. The Master of the Game made three curtseys and also asked to be admitted to the Lord Chancellor's service.

What followed was a curious and problematic diversion. A huntsman came into the hall 'with a fox with a purse-net; with a cat, both bound at the end of a staff; and with them nine or ten couple of hounds, with the blowing of hunting horns'. The fox and the cat were set upon by the hounds and killed beneath the fire. (In a hall with a central hearth this would be the side nearest the screens and furthest from the High Table). 'This sport finished ...' the second course of the meal was served.

Modern views of this activity are divided between those which reluctantly and distastefully accept that real animals were used in a ritual rooted in folklore[18] and those in favour of a mimic hunt, either an allegorical 'device' or a burlesque of the outdoor sport, staged by students costumed as animals, with all the attendant possibilities for comic horseplay in keeping with the season of misrule.[19] On practical grounds, as Bland points out, an entirely human mock hunt would be a more sensible project inside a hall measuring approximately 21 metres by 9 metres, with a central fire, numerous large tables, and full of members, guests, and servants.[20] However, student parties have never been renowned for sensible activities. In such a cluttered space, a performance requiring a Master of the Game, a Ranger of the Forest, and a huntsman with twenty wildly excited dogs and a frenziedly terrified fox and cat, might well be a recipe for disaster, involving a fair amount of personal injury and damage to property, but enthusiastically staged as a time-honoured tradition.

After this excitement, Dugdale reports that there were speeches or a debate (probably satirical) by the Common Serjeant and the King's Serjeant, followed by the senior Master of the Revels singing a song with the assistance of the company. At supper the hall was 'served in all solemnity, as upon Christmas Day' and when the meal was finished, the Constable-Marshal, mounted on a scaffold carried by four men, circled the fire three times, descended, and took part in the dancing. He then called his court by their assumed names, such as 'Sir Randle Rackabite of Rascal Hall, in the County of Rakehell' and 'Sir Bartholomew Baldbreech of Buttocksbury, in the County of Breakneck'.[21] This done, Dugdale writes, 'the Lord of Misrule addresseth himself to the banquet, which ended with some minstrelsy, mirth, and dancing, every man departeth to rest'.

Clearly the 'Constable-Marshal' was the Inner Temple's Lord of Misrule and the 'Lord Chancellor' was at the centre of the ceremonial; he heads the list of officers elected for the 1561–1562 revels and was normally the presiding officer of the Christmas festivities. Dugdale nowhere mentions a Christmas King or Prince; the 1561–1562 revels were exceptional and unique with Lord Robert Dudley as the Constable-Marshal and also Prince Pallaphilos, to mark his role as ruler of the imaginary kingdom invented for this special Christmastide.

On St John's Day (27 December), the Lord of Misrule held power, gathering his followers for breakfast after church and ruling over the evening programme. After supper some kind of mock trial took place, in which the King's Serjeant accused the Constable-Marshal and the Common Serjeant of disorder. The latter defended himself, the King's Serjeant replied, the parties rejoined, and the guilty officer was committed to the Tower (the edifice which was brought into the hall on St Stephen's Day).

On New Year's Day, breakfast was 'as formerly' and 'At dinner, like solemnity as on Christmas Eve'. For Twelfth Day Dugdale notes only that the food at breakfast and the service at dinner were the same as on St John's Day. An entry for 'The Banquetting Night' comes between those of New Year's Day and Twelfth Day but it is unclear whether it was allotted to a particular night or not. It was an occasion when all the Inns of Court and Chancery were invited by the Butler to the banquet and to see a play and a masque. Scaffolds were provided 'for ladies to behold the sports' – barriers perhaps? – before the banquet, which was served by the gentlemen of the House. The ladies dined separately in the library while the Lord Chancellor presided at a table in the hall, where he called to him 'the Ancients of other Houses, as many as may be on the one side of the table'. The banquet over, the Constable-Marshal, 'fairly mounted on his mule', came into the hall and devised some sport to pass the rest of the night.

It is impossible to say how far Dugdale's account also reflects the Christmas customs of the other Inns; the St Stephen's Day Hunt seems to have been exclusive to the Inner Temple, as does the choice of Constable-Marshal as Lord of Misrule. The other Inns followed the example of the Universities in having Christmas Kings; at Gray's Inn c.1500 he was chosen by 'the clerks of the third table' to rule on the festival days and he was paid homage by the members in solemn and ceremonial fashion,[22] apparently with true respect, not with the mocking deference accorded to the Lord of Misrule.

Ironically, Lincoln's Inn chose the name of Jack Straw for their King. His Christmas reign must have been as anarchic as his namesake's activities, since the Benchers were impelled to curtail the King's authority in 1519, prohibiting future excesses at Christmas and utterly banishing Jack Straw and his adherents. To improve behaviour, the same order appointed the Marshal to sit on New Year's Day 'for lerning of young Gentilmen to do service' and forbidding the King of Cockneys, who ruled on Holy Innocents' Day (27 December), to 'medyll neyther in the buttry' nor in the office of Steward.²³

From time to time, Gray's Inn, Lincoln's Inn and the Middle Temple elected a Prince comparable to the Inner Temple's Prince Pallaphilos; respectively the Prince of Purpoole, the Prince de la Grange, and the Prince d'Amour. Like their royal cousin, Prince Pallaphilos, each of them was a monarch of a fantasy kingdom and only reigned at long intervals to mark special events: the expense probably prohibited more frequent appearances.

Common to all the Inns were the excessively popular pastimes of dicing, card play, and other gambling games referred to in the 1482 Clifford's Inn Revels. They were notorious as the cause of disorder and violence and periodically Inn governors banned gambling altogether, even during the normally permitted Christmas period. In 1521, Inner Temple players of 'Shoffeborde' and 'slypgrote' were under a penalty of 6s.8d., and in 1532, 'Shodebord', dice, and cards were forbidden, with players fined 3s.4d., but the prohibitions were never permanently nor rigidly enforced. Outsiders were freely admitted to the games and the Inns tacitly condoned a practice which yielded a substantial daily profit – almost enough to pay for the entire Christmas celebrations – literally legalised gambling.²⁴

On a somewhat higher cultural level, Dugdale confirms the importance of songs, dances, and the peculiar legal ritual of circling the hearth common to all the Inns. A Gray's Inn Member, Sir John Spelman, predates Dugdale's information with some notes in his legal commonplace book of the order of events at Christmas c.1500 in his Inn, and lists the titles of the accompanying songs. After Vespers on Christmas Day, the Marshal returned to the Inn leading his company with 'a song called "There shall none rain down rain" etc., [followed by] "Round about the fire" more quickly than before with a shout at the end'. On Twelfth Night, after supper and Revels:

> the marshal and steward shall come solemnly to the fire with torchlight, singing 'Farewill and have good day'.²⁵ After singing which twice they shall go out of the hall, continuing to sing until they have finished their song. And in the mean time, the marshal and steward shall break their staves and rods of office and burn them.²⁶

And Christmas was over for another year.

Instructions for the steps of a dance have survived, written down in an early sixteenth-century moot book of Lincoln's Inn. Entitled 'The howe of the howse', a seventeenth-century hand has glossed this 'or the old measure':

> Fyrst half turn and undo yt agayn, flower iij forth, the fyrst man and the second folowe, flower and roll into other placys, hole turn, flower, and then roll into other placys.

J.H. Baker suggests that this is the courtly hove-dance referred to in Gower's *Confessio Amantis* (Book 6, line 144): 'Wher as I moste daunce and singe / The hove dance and carolinge'.[27] As to the likelihood of a dance known to Gower still being performed at the Inns in the sixteenth and seventeenth centuries, Baker comments:

> Lawyers being conservative spirits, the oldest forms of entertainment were kept up long after ordinary folk had moved on to newer fashions ... the solemn revels, with the old measures and songs performed on such occasions ... [28]

The remaining diversions of Christmastide, ranging in dramatic content from tourneys and barriers to what can be recognised as conventional drama, appear indeterminately in the records and chronicles as 'interludes', 'plays', 'disguisings', 'shows', 'inventions', 'devices', or 'masques', rarely well-enough documented to be unquestionably classified into separate genres. But more non-professional entertainments must have gone completely unrecorded; unless the interlude, play, etc. cost money, caused a fracas, or was in some way sensational, it was unlikely to be entered in the Inns' accounts and orders or referred to in contemporary chronicles.

As early as 1412 there was a paid performance of some kind at Furnival's Inn: *Thomas Thwaits solvit pro Interludio vjs viijd* followed by entries in 1416: *pro Lusoribus et Ludo suo* and 1417: *Pro Coena Ludensium* which show no payment although they appear in the general accounts for Christmas.[29] Lincoln's Inn paid for plays in 1494 and 1498;[30] the Middle Temple paid 6s.8d. to *ludatoribus* in 1509;[31] and the Inner Temple allocated money for Christmas players in 1522 and 1523.[32]

No Gray's Inn records earlier than 1550 have survived, but an order of 1551, that there should be no interludes out of term time except when Christmas was solemnly observed, implies an earlier and continuing dramatic tradition.[33] The 1526 Christmas production had the dubious distinction of a mention in Halle's *Chronicle* for its effect on Cardinal Wolsey and the subsequent imprisonment of Serjeant Roos, the eminent lawyer-author. But if Halle is correct, and he was a Gray's Inn member himself, the 1526 performance was actually a revival of a production originally staged soon after 1500.[34]

Gray's Inn became renowned in the later sixteenth century for its legal literary men. The translator of *The Supposes*, George Gascoigne, and his follow collaborators on *Jocasta*, Francis Kinwelmarshe and Christopher Yelverton, were all Gray's Inn members. They reputedly presented these plays in 1566, exactly where and when is not known, but even if the plays were intended for Court, it is likely that they were first previewed for their fellow members in their own hall at Gray's Inn, during the favoured period of Christmastide.

The same reasoning might apply to William Baldwin of the Inner Temple and his lost play of 'love and lyve'. When he offered it to Sir Thomas Cawarden, Queen Mary's Master of Revels, he explained that 'there be of the Innes of court that desyer to have the setting forth thereof' and on Christmas Eve his cast of 62 was already in rehearsal and would be ready in ten days time.[35] It is not recorded if Queen Mary saw the play or not, but with so many of the Inns' members involved, it would surely have been seen by the societies, either as a dress-rehearsal or in lieu of its presentation at Court.

Assigning John Heywood's *Play of Love* to the 1528 Christmastide at Lincoln's Inn naturally raises the issue of where his other interludes were performed. Given his close legal connections through marriage, and the form and content of his plays, he could arguably have written some of his dramatised debates especially for an audience of lawyers trained to appreciate verbal point-scoring and rhetorical agility.[36]

With *Gorboduc*, the play written by the distinguished Inner Templars Thomas Norton and Thomas Sackville for the 1561–1562 Christmas celebrations at the Inner Temple, we are finally on solid ground. There is a verifiable date and occasion of performance, known authors and even a published text, as well as recognition of the play's significance in English dramatic history: the first English tragedy, the first play in blank verse, and the forerunner of later 'succession' plays.[37]

Some unsolved mysteries remain. For example, what role did 'the keeper of the lions' (or for that matter the lions themselves) play in Furnival's Inn Revels? In 1473 the Inn paid 4d *In regardo Ductori Leonum*; in 1494 'They had lyons, the waites the harpur and other perticulers etc' and in 1497 the intriguingly named 'Pescod, the keeper of the Lyons' earned 8d. There are also Christmas payments recorded *In Regardo Ductori de le Marmosett et Jennet* in 1480 (compare the Constable-Marshal entering on his mule at the Inner Temple, above) and to 'the keper of the Babone' in 1485.[38] Were they bit-players in a masque, victims of an exotic version of the Inner Temple's St Stephen's Day Hunt, or participants in those 'Toyes' so despised by Francis Bacon?

> For *Iusts*, and *Tourneys*, and *Barriers*; The Glories of them, are chiefly in the Chariots, wherein the Challengers make their entry. Especially if they be drawne with Strange Beasts; As lions, Beares; Cammels, and the like; Or in the Deuices of their Entrance; Or in the Brauery of their Lueries; Or in the Godly Furniture of their horses, and Armour. But enough of these Toyes.[39]

As autonomous self-governing bodies, the Inns, types of fraternities of professional guilds, declared their position in society and the state with lavish and costly ceremonial and entertainment. They had independence and influence, the necessary wealth, the facilities to stage elaborate Revels, and a continuous supply of clever, literate, and creative young men to 'set forth' their devices. In range, style, and scale, then, Christmas at the Inns of Court could compete, and was often interchangeable with, the festivities at the royal Court. The Inns' Lord of Misrule seems to have existed as long as his court counterpart and Lincoln's Inn's Master of Revels is known to pre-date, by some 70 years, the officer appointed to that post in Henry VII's household, while a sixteenth-century Lincoln's Inn member, George Ferrers, took charge of Edward VI's Christmas Revels in 1551–1551/2 and 1552–1553, inventing two splendid imaginary kingdoms with all the exotic panoply of their foreign rulers, in the best traditions of the Inns.[40]

Apart from the magnificence of the celebrations, what distinguished the Inns' Christmasses from those of other communities or households is their identification with the royal Court. Where other Lords of Misrule, such as University Christmas Kings or Boy Bishops, parodied the forms and offices of their own institutions, the Inns' Lords mockingly usurped the Crown itself and the full apparatus of State. Jack Straw, a real-life pretender to the throne or anti-king, was the Inner Temple's 'Constable-Marshal' (an official seen by Henry VIII as a rival to himself),[41] and ruled over alternative 'governments' with the necessary complement of officers of the royal household.

But underlying the licensed foolery were serious ambitions, and opportunities for attracting royal favour. Among those named in Dugdale's 1561–1562 list, the Revels 'Lord Chancellor', Mr. Onslow, was Speaker of the House of Commons; Roger Manwood ('Chief Baron of the Exchequer') became the Lord Chief Justice; Robert Keilwey ('Lord Privy Seal') a Serjeant-at-law; and Christopher Hatton ('Master of the Game') eventually rose to the office of Lord Chancellor of England. With the evidence of the subsequent careers of many Inn members and the official Bacon Report's acknowledgement that the election of Christmas officers was 'done onely to the intent that they should in time to come know how to use themselves',[42] Fortescue was not entirely wrong to claim in 1470 that the great advantage, then as later, of a legal education was the social competence acquired and exhibited during the Christmas celebrations at the Inns of Court.

Lancaster University

NOTES

Abbreviations

Black Books	*The Records of the Honourable Society of Lincoln's Inn: The Black Books* edited J.D. Walker, W. P. Baildon and Sir Ronald Roxburgh, 5 vols (Lincoln's Inn, London, 1897–1968).
Furnival's Inn	*Early Records of Furnival's Inn* edited D.S. Bland (Department of Extramural Studies, King's College, Newcastle-upon-Tyne, 1957).
Pension Book	*The Pension Book of Gray's Inn: Records of the Honourable Society, 1569–1800* edited R. J. Fletcher, 2 vols (Chiswick Press, London, 1901–1910).
Inner Temple Records	*A Calendar of the Inner Temple Records* edited F.A. Inderwick and R.A. Roberts, 5 vols (H. Sotheran and Co., London, 1896–1936).
Middle Temple Records	*Minutes of Parliament of the Middle Temple (1501–1703)* edited Charles Trice Martin, 3 vols & Index (Butterworth, London, 1904–1905).
Dugdale	William Dugdale *Origins Juridicales or Historical Memorials* 3rd edition (1680, first published London, 1666).
Three Revels	*Three Revels from the Inns of Court* edited D.S. Bland (Avebury Publishing, Amersham, 1984).

CHRISTMAS AT THE INNS OF COURT

1. Sir John Fortescue *De Laudibus Legum Anglie* edited and translated S.B. Chrimes (Cambridge University Press, 1942) 119. In Fortescue's time there were four Inns of Court and ten Inns of Chancery, with, he claimed, 200 students at each Inn of Court and 100 at each Inn of Chancery. Writing in exile, and as tutor to the future King Edward IV, Fortescue was perhaps presenting an idealised recollection of life at the Inns, as well as promoting the abilities of his own profession to advise and take office under the king.
2. Although legend associates the arrival of lawyers in the Temple with the dates 1320 and 1328, and Lincoln's Inn may have been in existence in 1310, only one record, dated 1422, has survived earlier than 1501. Material from Furnival's, a Chancery Inn, is in a seventeenth-century compilation of records dated 1407–1422, 1447–1506 and 1528–1553.
3. *Furnival's Inn* 30–31, 33, 40.
4. For example the Serjeant's Feast of 1523, held in Ely House, lasted five days. King Henry and Queen Catherine, foreign ambassadors, the Mayor and Aldermen of London, judges and senior legal officers, nobles, merchants, and important London citizens: all dined on various days (*Dugdale* 127–8). Numerous entries record the Inns' contributions to events such as the visit of the Bastard of Burgundy, the accession of Henry VIII, and Edward VI's coronation (*Black Books 1* 45, 236, 281–2, *Inner Temple Records 1* 14, 21, *Middle Temple Records 1* 2, 36, etc.)
5. *Dugdale* 205.
6. For the complicated question of the origin and development of law terms, as governed by the religious feasts of the medieval Church, see Sir William Holdsworth *History of English Law* 16 vols and Index (Methuen, London, 1903–1972) 3, App.VIII, 275–8.
7. *Inner Temple Records 1* 3, 7, 29, 66, 67.
8. In a dispute between the Middle Temple and the Inner Temple over control of Chancery Inns, Inner Temple Benchers approached Dudley who took up the matter with the Queen, resulting in a favourable decision for the Inner Temple (*Inner Temple Records 1* 215–19, and *Three Revels* 12, 13).
9. Gerard Legh *The Accedence of Armorie* (H. Ballard, London, 1597) 118.
10. *Three Revels* 20.
11. *Inner Temple Records 1* 219–20.
12. W.C. Richardson *A History of the Inns of Court* (Claitor, Baton Rouge, Louisiana, 1975) 217, quoting the *Brerewood Manuscript* 109, 110.
13. *The Bacon Report*, temp. Henry VIII, published by Edward Waterhouse in *Fortescutus Illustratus* (London, 1663) 543–6.
14. *Dugdale* 153–7. Some of the records apparently still available in the seventeenth century to Dugdale have not survived.
15. *Dugdale* 150.
16. According to the Lincoln's Inn records for 1510/1511, Sir Thomas More 'was ij tymes appoynted to be Marshall and lettid by divers casualtes the seid Thos shall paie to the seid Companie v li': *Black Books 1* 163. His duties as Under-Sheriff of the City of London may have prevented him from serving. Fines were frequently imposed, as for example in 1516/1517, when three Christmas Butlers refused office and were each fined 26s. 8d., and two Masters of the Revels refused and were also fined 26s. 6d: *Black Books 1* 180.

17. Bland believes that this unexplained reference may be to 'an imaginary family tree of the kind produced by the King of Arms in the 1561 revels to prove the descent of Prince Pallaphilos (Robert Dudley) from Jupiter': *Three Revels* 123, note 6.
18. For a discussion of the tradition of solemn slaughter which hangs around Martinmas and Christmas, compare the Inner Temple St Stephen's Day hunt with hunting by boys on foot of normally protected squirrels, owls, and especially wrens, on the same day: see E.K. Chambers *The Mediaeval Stage* 2 vols (Oxford University Press, London, 1903) *1* 256, 257; and Enid Welsford *The Court Masque* (Cambridge University Press, 1927) 3, 23, who also associates the Lord of Misrule with the chasing and killing of an animal.
19. A case can be made for a mock hunt parodying the outdoor sport. Hunting was a popular Inns of Court activity; Lincoln's Inn maintained a large warren; the open country was close at hand where Inns' members regularly hunted together as well as joining the London nobles who hunted in Gray's Inn Fields and elsewhere (Richardson 478). Christopher Hatton, Master of the Game for the 1561–1562 Inner Temple Revels, was granted a special admission to the Inn 'without payment, in respect of his charges' while in office (*Inner Temple Records* 1 220): was this because he also arranged real hunting parties with dinner and amusements?
20. *Three Revels* 124.
21. These nonsense names for the Christmas King's courtiers, typical of student humour, are a regular feature of revels. For other examples see the 1617–1618 *Gesta Grayorum* (*Three Revels* 78–87).
22. Sir John Spelman 'Christmas in Gray's Inn' *Reports of Sir John Spelman 1* (Selden Society 93: London, 1977) 233.
23. *Black Books 1* 189–190. Jack Straw, leader of the Peasants' Rebellion of 1381, was especially vindictive towards lawyers; he and his followers burnt some of the law buildings and legal records and killed several judges and lawyers: see Sir John Froissart *Chronicles of England, France, and Spain* translated Thomas Johnes, 2 vols (William Smith, London, 1848) *1* 658.
24 *Inner Temple Records 1* 63, 100; Richardson 478–9.
25 J.H. Baker 'The Old Moot Book of Lincoln's Inn' *Law Quarterly Review* 95 (October 1979) 507–12, believes this to be the Epiphany carol:
>Now fare ye well, all in fere
>Now fare ye well, for all this yere
>Yet for my sake make ye gud cher
>Now have gud day.

(In *The Early English Carols* edited R.L. Greene (Clarendon Press, Oxford, 2nd edition 1977), carol 141, page 85.) See John M. Ward 'Apropos "The olde Measures"' *Records of Early English Drama Newsletter* 18:1 (1993) 1–21 on the 'measures' danced at the Inns.
26. *Reports of Sir John Spelman 1* 233–4.
27. J.H. Baker 512. John Gower himself was reputedly a member of an Inn.
28. J.H. Baker 510. The last solemn revels at the Inner Temple were held on Candlemas Day 1734.
29. *Furnival's Inn* 24, 25.
30. *Black Books 1* 119, 121.
31. *Middle Temple Records 1* 30.
32. *Inner Temple Records* 1 75.

33. *Dugdale* 285–6.
34. Edward Halle *Chronicle, containing the History of England (Henry IV to Henry VII)* edited Henry Ellis (London, 1809) 719. Halle also reports on the rich and costly apparel and the 'Masques and Morrishes' which were part of the 1526 revels.
35. *Documents Relating to the Revels at Court in the Time of Edward VI and Queen Mary* edited Albert Feuillerat (Uystpruyst, Louvain, 1914) 215.
36. John Heywood married the niece of Sir Thomas More (Lincoln's Inn). She was the daughter of Elizabeth More and John Rastell, Lincoln's Inn member and legal printer. Their son William Rastell, Heywood's brother-in-law, was also a member of Lincoln's Inn and a Common Law judge.
37 For an examination of the political significance of *Gorboduc* and the later 'succession' plays, see Marie Axton *The Queen's Two Bodies* (Royal Historical Society, London, 1977).
38. *Furnival's Inn* 31, 32, 33, 34, 35, 36.
39. Francis Bacon 'Of Masques and Triumphes' in *Essays* (Oxford University Press, London, 1962) 159.
40. Feuillerat 56–61, 89–90.
41. The last Constable-Marshal of England was the Duke of Buckingham, attainted by Henry VIII and his office subsequently left vacant (see Axton *Queen's Two Bodies* 42).
42. *Bacon Report* 545: see note 13.

RITUALS OF EXCLUSION:
Feasts and Plays of the English Religious Fraternities
Sheila Lindenbaum

I

The religious fraternities of later medieval England sponsored plays and ceremonial drama of all kinds, ranging from the humble Robin Hood gatherings at the Somerset village of Croscombe to the more ambitious *naviculum Noie* ('Noah's ship') carried through the streets of Boston, to the magnificently costumed procession of St George at Norwich and the great Paternoster Play of York. If the London parish clerks are considered a lay religious fraternity, as they were by Henry VIII's Privy Council in 1547, we can even include a cycle play in this list, since the clerks were responsible for the sumptuous four-day Biblical drama at Skinners' Well 'in which scenes from both the Old Testament and the New were presented in dramatic form'.[1] Moreover, guilds were a major employer of musicians for their religious observances and all kinds of entertainers for their annual feasts.

It is therefore puzzling that medieval English drama is so rarely considered in the rich context provided by the religious fraternities (also called 'guilds', 'brotherhoods', and more rarely 'confraternities'). It has been fifteen years since Stanley Kahrl wrote that 'the *usual* organisations producing the plays in Lincolnshire were religious guilds, both in town and village', and almost as long since Richard Beadle, followed by David Galloway and John Wasson in their Malone Society edition, confirmed the significance of religious fraternities in the dramatic and ceremonial life of East Anglia.[2]

Meanwhile historians of medieval popular culture have produced a virtual avalanche of studies on the religious fraternities, many of which are very helpful in interpreting the dramatic records. We have, for example, the pioneering works of Brian Pullan, Richard Trexler, and Natalie Zemon Davis on European fraternities.[3] Studies of English fraternities have been less ambitious, perhaps because the relevant letters were lost or scattered when these guilds were dissolved by the Chantries Act of 1547. Still, historians have discovered much useful material in the 1389 returns to a royal writ demanding information from the guilds about their history and governance, meetings (including feasts), and property; and more guild ordinances and accounts survive than is generally acknowledged. Susan Brigden, J.J. Scarisbrick, and Caroline Barron have recently made important contributions to our knowledge of English religious guilds.[4]

The works on English fraternities divide into two camps. While the ones I have just cited tend to emphasise the role of the fraternities in sustaining communal bonds and traditional religious cultures, some of the more recent studies have followed the European ones in stressing the fraternities' exclusiveness and dedication to special class interests.⁵ It is the latter line of thought I would like to pursue here, since it encourages us to question some well-established notions about the drama, specifically the idea that except for entertainment at court and in the noble households, medieval drama and ceremonial was largely a collective enterprise – a communal ritual in which all took part and which gave diverse groups within the community a sense of unity and shared identity.⁶ What we discover in the activities of the fraternities, I will suggest, are rather rituals of exclusion. Whether an event is a religious ceremony or a form of dramatic activity, sponsorship by a religious fraternity implies almost by definition that it will be enacted in the interests of an exclusive group, often an élite group of citizens or the ruling body of a town.

II

Recent studies of the fraternities emphasise that they were the 'characteristic institution of late medieval popular religion'.⁷ From the late fourteenth century, when fraternities sprang up in great numbers all over England, the majority of people, perhaps most people, belonged to a religious fraternity of some kind. Because of the spiritual benefits offered by these groups, many people associated salvation more closely with their parish fraternity than with the parish church itself. In fact, religious fraternities employed more ordained priests than any other kind of organisation.⁸ Given the scope of the fraternities' influence and membership, it seems only natural to stress the collective nature of their activities and to see them as promoting mutual interests and communal solidarity: after all, were they not, as one recent study describes them, 'voluntary associations of men and women linked together to provide mutual charitable help and communal prayers for living and dead members'?⁹

Indeed, the religious guilds did function as a kind of communal chantry, providing funeral services and prayers for the souls of dead members, and soliciting the intercession of saints by burning lights at their altars. That such activities were meant to express in some degree a solidarity with the larger Christian community appears in the stipulation by many guilds that prayers were to be said not only for the members but for the larger community of 'alle Christen souls'.¹⁰ Guild ordinances also suggest a communal spirit in their attention to resolving disputes. Like many other fraternities, the London Guild of St Peter at Cornhill stipulates 'that if there falle ony debate distaunce or discensioun by twene ony persones of this same fraternite ... wele consciencyd bretherne of the fraternite shulle do her trewe and tentif diligence to make unite, and accorde by twene the parties so beyng in distaunce'.¹¹

The annual feast, which provided the context for most of a fraternity's dramatic and ceremonial activities, was also conceived as a communal event. A feature of most guilds, whether rural or urban, it was called 'the common feast', and it was to be held 'in such a manner that brotherly love shall be cherished among (the bretheren and sisteren), and evil speaking be driven out; that peace shall always dwell among them, and true love be upheld'.[12] To demonstrate their sense of community the guild members often wore a common livery. And to demonstrate their desire that 'brotherly love' be extended to the larger Christian community, they shared food with the poor: as this is described in the ordinances of the Lincoln Guild of the Blessed Virgin Mary, for example, the guild invited as many paupers as there were members to partake of bread, ale, meat, and fish.[13]

It would be a mistake, however, to identify the guilds' professions of brotherly love, as expressed in their ordinances and the 1389 returns, with their actual practice. While the professions were no doubt sincere, the ordinances themselves include much evidence of unfriendliness to outsiders, and it has been shown that some of the charities mentioned in the returns are significantly exaggerated.[14] The preponderance of evidence indicates that, especially in towns, religious guilds did not extend their fraternal feeling in significant ways to the larger community. As Natalie Zemon Davis has pointed out, the fraternities 'could not engage and unite all city people', because they were 'local and particularistic in character, devotion, and imagery'.[15]

The guild's membership practices are perhaps the most important indication of their exclusive nature. Although almost everyone may have belonged to a fraternity, they did not all belong to the *same* fraternity, or to equally important ones. Thus while many guilds drew their membership from the artisan class within a particular parish or district in a town, élite fraternities like the Jesus Guild at St Paul's in London enrolled mainly wealthy men who had risen to high office in the city companies and corporation, together with their important associates from outside the city; and other guilds, like the Conception Guild in St Sepulchre at Newgate, were founded primarily 'for the poor people of the parish'.[16] Significantly the guilds which enrolled the less fortunate had as exclusive a mentality as those who charged high entrance fees and so limited themselves to the rich. The Lincoln Guild of St Michael, for example, specified 'that no one of the rank of mayor or bailiff' should be admitted unless by common assent, and that if admitted, he must not 'meddle in any matter' nor 'take on himself any office in the gild'.[17] Similarly, some fraternities – like the Cambridge Guild of the Annunciation, which would not enrol a chaplain or baker – excluded certain occupations;[18] and of course many trade guilds maintained religious fraternities exclusively for their members. These practices suggest that for many fraternities 'brotherhood' had been redefined to mean 'class affiliation', and that the closed-shop principles of the trade guilds were taken by many to apply in the religious sphere as well.[19]

Even the guilds' religious activities look more exclusive than communal when viewed in the light of these membership practices. Though the fraternity priests were supposed to pray for 'all Christian souls', it is evident that most of the fraternities' prayers were devoted to delivering the souls of the members inscribed in their own bede rolls. It was for these persons that the fraternity made clear, 'whoso ever ... wyll have the Parden, Prevylege and Profet thereto graunted and ordeny'd must pay to the seyd fraternityte the Some of x.s. iiij.d. sterlynge'.[20] Thus it was that the Lollard reformers could object to the guilds' religious activities on the grounds of their exclusiveness: 'special preyeris for dede men soulis mad in oure chirche preferryng on ... name more than anothir, this is the false ground of almesse dede ... for ... peerfythe charite accepte no persones'.[21] And thus it was that Calvin and the later Reformers could criticise private masses, the kind said by fraternity priests, as divisive, 'drawing the people hither and thither, when they ought to have formed one meeting'. Such private masses were 'a kind of excommunication' rather than the 'communion' ordered by the Lord.[22]

The fraternities' charitable activities follow a similar pattern. Miri Rubin has shown that the fraternities contributed to a 'shift from communal and co-operative forms of charitable organisation towards a more personal and individual search for religious and social benefits'. Thus most of the fraternities' charity took the form of doles to honour deceased members, with the result that the poor 'were no longer lodged, fed, and cared for but rather ... appended to funerary and commemorative occasions'.[23] Those otherwise deemed worthy of help were most often the fraternity's own members who had fallen on hard times, or persons who like themselves had once been productive members of the community. Those who had never been self-sufficient were stigmatised as the 'undeserving' poor. These attitudes are encoded in the ordinances – in those of the Chesterfield Guild of the Blessed Mary, for example, where there is a firm distinction between the deserving brother who suffers losses 'by fire, by murrain, by robbers, or by any other mishap' and the undeserving one whose losses come 'through his own lust, or gluttony, or dice-play, or other folly'.[24] While the distinction is ostensibly between deserving and undeserving members of the fraternity, the ordinance is actually a rationale for denying aid to outsiders and the hard-core poor, who were thought to be idle and immoral. Despite their ostensibly communal ethic, the fraternities had become an instrument for perpetuating a social order based on individual productivity.

Such impulses can also be discerned in the fraternal feasts, which increasingly became an occasion for conspicuous consumption rather than the expression of brotherly love and charity. The way in which the language of corporate feasting could sanction a display of the guild's wealth and status can be seen in the cases of several guilds which sponsored plays or dramatic ceremonies, particularly the larger more powerful organisations in major towns. In the late fourteenth century, the Beverley Guild of St Elene was apparently satisfied with going home to dinner after their procession and returning later to 'eat bread and cheese and drink as much ale as is good for them'.[25] But, even at that time, a moderately prosperous guild like that of Saint Giles and Julian at Bishop's Lynn was producing a substantial banquet requiring two cooks and two helpers to prepare. Their feast pales by comparison, however, with some recorded by larger fraternities, especially in the later period. In 1534, an inventory of St Mary's Guild of Boston mentions 15 tables in the guild hall and an array of cooking equipment weighing 1053 pounds. The Corpus Christi feast held by this large and powerful guild in 1514/1515 cost over £21, but even this was exceeded by the Assumption Guild at Westminster which spent nearly £40, a vast amount, on its feast in 1489.[26] Needless to say, the last sums far exceeded the amount spent by these organisations on poor relief. The four cottages for the poor maintained by the Assumption Guild must have used up a very small fraction of that fraternity's resources, and the Boston guild's fifteenth-century accounts show no trace at all of the 1000 loaves of wheaten bread and 1000 herrings mentioned in their 1389 return as being designated for the poor at the annual feast.[27]

III

Only in rural areas do we glimpse a collective spirit governing the production of the religious fraternities' plays and dramatic ceremonies. The Robin Hood plays at Croscombe in Somerset provide an example. Here the entire parish, or close to it, seems to have enjoyed guild membership and thus to have benefited from the altar lights maintained by the guilds. The membership was determined primarily by age and occupation (the Young Men, the Webbers, the Hogglers), but the 'incres' or profit from the activities of all the guilds, including the play of Robin Hood and his Archers, was returned to the parish churchwardens apparently to benefit the whole congregation.[28] Other plays sponsored by religious guilds as a way of earning money for a parish may have been similarly collective in nature.[29]

But rural guilds like the ones at Croscombe are barely recognisable as such. They burned lights at the parish altars, like all of the religious guilds, but they apparently were groups to which one automatically belonged by virtue of living in the parish, as opposed to the selective groups of laymen we have been discussing under the rubric of religious fraternities. The latter frequently had an altar in the parish church and sometimes contributed to the church expenses, but they were otherwise independent of the parish, governed by their own ordinances and frequently hiring their own priests. They flourished in towns, serving the needs of tradesmen and artisans, or in large villages, rather than rural areas. Some of these guilds in effect functioned as the ruling body of the town (the Guild of St Mary in Boston) or were in some way an instrument of civic government (St Anne in Lincoln, several guilds in Louth, the Corpus Christi Guilds in York, Ipswich, Plymouth, and other towns). Others were closely identified with the group of citizens from which the town's officers were chosen (the Guild of St George in Norwich, the Corpus Christi Guild of Northampton, the Jesus Guild of St Paul's in London). These were the religious fraternities that became responsible for a significant amount of English civic pageantry in the century prior to the Reformation.[30]

Almost all religious fraternities seem to have participated in some kind of procession, most frequently prior to the mass for their patron saint and the subsequent feast on the guild's 'general day'. The well-known Beverley procession, in which the Guild of St Elene enacted the story of the True Cross, took place prior to a mass and feast.³¹ Similarly, even though the Jesus Guild of St Paul's did not process to the mass, they ordered a procession to announce it, consisting of:

> vj Weights, with banners, paynted conysances, embrowdered with Jhesus goyng all the stretes and suburbs of London playing with their Instruments, to gyue warnyng and knowledg to the people of the said ffraternitie for the said ffeastes of Transfiguracion and Name of Jhesu.³²

For many guilds, however, and especially for the more substantial ones, civic pageantry was a larger enterprise. Frequently, a Corpus Christi Guild's annual procession doubled as the Corpus Christi procession of the town, and the annual procession of several St George Guilds (Norwich, Nottingham, Morebath) also became a civic event. In several places (Hull, Boston, Grimsby), pageant ships sponsored by religious guilds were drawn through the streets at annual festivals, likewise extending the guilds' activities out into the town. When these guilds put on their shows, they made a variety of arrangements with the civic government, sometimes retaining their own independence, sometimes serving as the agent of civic government in the production of a pageant, and sometimes serving to organise the trade guilds and other civic organisations in a co-operative production.

Still, we should not conclude from these arrangements with civic authorities that the religious fraternities undertook their pageantry in a communal spirit. This is the view expressed by Mervyn James when he concludes that the procession of the Corpus Christi Guild of York – combined with the trade guilds' cycle play – worked as a 'symbolic system' expressing 'wholeness'.³³ Once again, the symbolic system arising from the cult of Corpus Christi and the 'concept of the body' needs to be interpreted in the light of actual practice. In interpreting the symbolism of the body, it is helpful to recall that when the burgesses of Berwick-upon-Tweed determined that there should be only one guild in their borough, so that 'all shall be as members having one head, one in counsel, one body, strong and friendly', they also restricted membership to those ('saving the sons and daughters of guildmen') who could pay an entrance fee of at least 40 shillings.³⁴ In this case, as with the civic pageantry we have been discussing, it is clear that the cultural symbol – the idea of the body unifying many members in a smoothly functioning whole – should not be taken as a description of actual power relationships but as an instrument for disguising social inequalities and for gaining assent to the structure of power that existed in the town.

Nor should we follow James in concluding that, when a procession 'gathered in unity and concord', it was necessarily 'joined in this by the massed crowds through which it moved'. As James himself makes clear, a procession, with its necessary order of precedence, expresses 'a vertical structure of status and authority', and so works against a spectator's identification of himself with a common body.³⁵ Similarly, the guilds' special symbols and livery (like the Jesus Guild's 'painted conysaunces') differentiated the participants from the spectators, pointing to the guilds' wealth, and implying their authority over the physical space traversed by the procession. Insofar as it displayed and expended their resources, the pageantry also gave the guilds a chance to illustrate the virtue of productivity which they habitually invoked to differentiate their members from the less privileged townspeople and the urban poor, many of whom were onlookers of the pageantry. The guilds were also differentiated from the 'massed crowds' by their seemly behaviour in procession, where they were instructed to walk *bini et bini ... lento passu* ('two by two ... at a slow pace').[36] Such spectacles may well have been popular with urban audiences, but those who welcomed them were in effect assenting to the guild's power and exclusive ethic rather than joining in a celebration of true wholeness. Furthermore, the frequent disputes over precedence in civic processions give us good reason to believe that, in towns where there was any sort of challenge to the urban élite, there would be groups of spectators who withheld their assent to the procession's image of authority.

IV

The fraternities' exclusive character and productive ethic are also important in interpreting the private entertainment at their annual feasts. While none of the named plays associated with religious fraternities was certainly performed at a feast,[37] it is clear that even the middling sort of fraternity in a market town did hire entertainers to help celebrate important occasions. At Wymondham in Suffolk, between 1500–1544, the fraternity of St John the Baptist and other guilds regularly paid modest sums to entertainers, mostly single persons termed *Mimus*, *Mynstrell*, or *wayte*. Some of these payments, like the one to 'Thomas Bylowe [a 'mynstrell'] for Goyng To Chyrche with ye gyld' were evidently for music during a procession, but references to 'ij Mynstrelle(s) for gyff of songys To ye brethern' and a 'Berward pleynge with the ape' indicate that others were for the annual feast.[38]

The major guilds of Bishop's Lynn, where records survive from the late fourteenth century, could afford to pay more and to hire whole troupes of players, including a group belonging to one of their own members (William Wylde) and the travelling troupes of great noblemen. Travelling troupes were also hired by affluent guilds at Boston, Coventry, Norwich, and Westminster, and doubtless by many other guilds whose accounts do not survive.[39] In the latter part of the period, these entertainers included some known to have performed actual plays – for example, John English and the King's Men, who performed for the Holy Trinity Guild of Coventry in 1519 and the Guild of St Mary in Boston in 1525/1526.[40]

While it is unlikely that any one kind of dramatic play dominated the guild feasts, there is one kind that repeatedly suggests itself for discussion in the fraternity context, and that is the morality play. In fact, one of the earliest references linking the religious fraternities to drama concerns the Pater Noster play of York, which the Pater Noster Guild's 1389 return describes as a kind of morality, a play 'in which ... many vices and sins are reproved and virtues commended'.[41] And Ian Lancashire has argued that *The Castle of Perseverance* and other early moralities were the work of clerks, some of whom must have been the local chaplains of religious guilds.[42] Of course, the Pater Noster play and *The Castle* were designed for outdoor performance; but other moral plays linked to fraternities may have been for indoor feasts. The morality-like prologue and epilogue known as the *Reynes Fragments* were found in a commonplace book that also contained poems to be read at the feast of a Guild of St Anne;[43] and the '*ludo de* Mankynd' to which William Brokshaw of East Retford (Notts.) made a bequest in 1499 also belonged to a guild.[44] Most pertinently, a *moralite* is said by a court observer to have been in the repertory of John English and his troupe during the years when they performed for religious guilds.[45]

It is not surprising, then, that although moralities were far from being the exclusive property of religious guilds, they nevertheless embodied, more than any other kind of drama, the mentality represented in the fraternities' ordinances and ritual activities. Partly, this is the result of a common basis in the cultic observances that grew up around the sacrament of penance. Fraternity ordinances and morality plays share a preoccupation with the individual sinner and with helping him achieve a 'good ending' by all the means the Church makes available. In both are inscribed the desire of lay people to control the practice of their religion and the arithmetical approach they took toward organising their devotions.

More deeply rooted than these common preoccupations, however, are the assumptions about language which the guild ordinances and morality plays share. In the ordinances, language is the major index to virtuous or corrupt behaviour. Virtuous conduct is defined as keeping one's verbal oath of loyalty to the guild and engaging in harmonious communication at the guild's 'spekyng-to-gedyr' or business meeting. Conversely, the kind of conduct most frequently prohibited is the misuse of language, whether in quarrels or slander. One repeatedly finds the command that 'no brother nor sister of the saide Fraternite from hensforth fray nor missay ne pyke bate (debate) or quarrell one agaynst a nother', and that none 'be rebele of his tongue again þe aldirman' of the guild.[46] The moralities' equivalent measure of behaviour is the notion of 'active' versus 'idle' language that Paula Neuss has shown to be at the heart of *Mankind*, and that is characteristic of the morality play generally.[47]

The guilds' more elaborate strategies for regulating conduct also find a counterpart in the morality plays. The texts of guild ordinances were often read aloud at the annual feasts, so that they became potent instruments of social control, employing strategies similar to those used in the morality play to prohibit certain kinds of behaviour. One common technique was to hold up for scorn and rejection the life history of a sinner – a creature born capable of saving himself by profitable activity, but deserving to be shunned for the sins of idleness. As one London guild puts it:

> ... if any man be of good state, and use hym to lye in bed; and at rising of his bed will not work but [ne] wyn his sustenance and keep his house, and go to the tavern, to the wyne, to the ale, to wrastling, to schetyng, and in this matter falleth poor, and left his cattel in his defaut for succour; and trust to be

holpen by the fraternity: that man shal never have good, ne help of companie, neither in his lyfe, ne at his dethe.[48]

Fraternity ordinances often incorporate life histories that, like this one, suggest the skeleton plot of a morality play, even to envisioning the sinner as being determined, despite repeated admonition, to 'perseuer and continew' in his fault. The ordinances do not describe the sinner's last-moment rescue, as the early moralities do, but they similarly threaten the sinner and his counterparts in the audience with permanent exclusion from society and a terrifying loss of identity. In the ordinances this is explicit: 'Let the name of such an yll lyuer be stryken owt of boke of elect person[es] and not cownted amongest the good men'.[49] In the moralities the threat is expressed on the level of dramatic form, where it appears in the protagonist's desertion by his worldly companions, his final isolation, and such devices as characters called 'I wot nevere whoo'.

Finally, the guild context offers a new way of understanding the festivity in morality plays. As we have noted, guild festivity was described in ordinances as exemplifying fraternal love, as distinguished from the prohibited kind of revelry represented as 'noyse' and 'debate'. What is most interesting about these descriptions is that, in rejecting unseemly forms of revelry, the fraternities were rejecting a pejorative interpretation of their own activities; for reformers often argued that guild festivity was nothing more than 'gluttony and drunkenness' in the guise of good works.[50] The unseemly revelry that characterises the morality protagonist's Life in Sin may well have been a similar defence against criticism. In the context of a guild feast, the effect would have been to dissociate the sponsors of plays from immoral entertainment and to link them instead with profitable festivity – the kind that, like the guilds' devotions and selective 'charity', would accumulate spiritual capital for the audience.

University of Indiana

NOTES

1. *The Westminster Chronicle: 1381–1394* edited L.C. Hector and Barbara F. Harvey (Clarendon Press, Oxford, 1982) 477.
2. *Records of Plays and Players in Lincolnshire* edited Stanley J. Kahrl (Malone Society Collections 8: Oxford University Press, 1974 for 1969) xxx; Richard Beadle *The Medieval Drama of East Anglia* 2 vols (University of York PhD dissertation, 1977); *Records of Plays and Players in Norfolk and Suffolk, 1330–1642* edited David Galloway and John Wasson (Malone Society Collections 11: Oxford University Press, 1980/1).
3. Brian Pullan *Rich and Poor in Renaissance Venice* (Blackwell, Oxford, 1971); Richard C. Trexler 'Charity and Defense of the Urban Élite in the Italian Communes' in *The Rich, the Well Born, and the Powerful: Élites and Upper Classes in History* edited Frederic Cople Jahr (University of Illinois Press, Urbana and London, 1973) 64–109; and Natalie Zemon Davis 'Some Tasks and Themes in the Study of Popular Religion' in *The Pursuit of Holiness* edited Charles Trinkaus (Brill, Leiden, 1974) 307–36.

4. Susan Brigden 'Religion and Social Obligation in Early Sixteenth-Century London' *Past and Present* 103 (May 1984) 67–112; J.J. Scarisbrick *The Reformation and the English People* (Blackwell, Oxford, 1984), chapter on 'The Importance of the Lay Fraternities', pages 19–38; Caroline M. Barron 'The Parish Fraternities of Medieval London' in *The Church in Pre-Reformation Society* edited Caroline M. Barron and Christopher Harper-Bill (Boydell Press, Woodbridge, 1985) 13–37. See also Benjamin R. McRee *Bonds of Community: Religious Guilds and Urban Society in Late Medieval England* (Indiana University dissertation, 1987).
5. The guilds' exclusiveness was emphasised in a 1942 essay by Sylvia Thrupp, 'Medieval Gilds Reconsidered', primarily on the trade guilds: reprinted in Sylvia Thrupp *Society and History* edited Raymond Grew and Nicholas H. Steneck (Michigan University Press, Ann Arbor, 1977) 226–36. A recent study that takes the same line is Miri Rubin *Charity and Community in Medieval Cambridge* (Cambridge Studies in Medieval Life and Thought: Cambridge University Press, 1987).
6. This viewpoint is best represented by Charles Phythian-Adams 'Ceremony and the Citizen' in *Crisis and Order in English Towns* edited Peter Clark and Paul Slack (Routledge and Kegan Paul, London, 1982), and Mervyn James 'Ritual, Drama and the Social Body in the Late Medieval English Town' *Past and Present* 98 (1983) 3–29.
7. Brigden 'Religion and Social Obligation' 94.
8. George Unwin *The Gilds and Companies of London* (The Antiquary's Books: Methuen, London, 1908) 111.
9. Barron 'Parish Fraternities' 13.
10. For an elaborate version of this prayer, see *English Gilds* edited Joshua Toulmin Smith EETS OS 40 (1870) 22–23.
11. *Reports of the Royal Commission on Historical Manuscripts* (HMSO, London, 1888-): Sixth Report, Appendix 414.
12. Toulmin Smith *English Gilds* 217.
13. McRee *Bonds of Community* 83.
14. McRee *Bonds of Community* 223; Barron 'Parish Fraternities' 27.
15. Davis 'Tasks and Themes' 317: see note 3.
16. McRee *Bonds of Community* 57, and Unwin *Gilds and Companies of London* 122 point out the wide range of entry fees. See Brigden 'Religion and Social Obligation' 99–101, on guild membership; Barron 'Parish Fraternities' 35; and Toulmin Smith *English Gilds* 40, for poor people's guilds.
17. Toulmin Smith *English Gilds* 179.
18. Toulmin Smith *English Gilds* 271.
19. On these points, see Trexler 'Charity and Defense' 105, and Lionel Rothkrug 'Popular Religion and Holy Shrines' in *Religion and the People* edited James Obelkevich (University of Carolina Press, Chapel Hill, 1979) 39.
20. Statutes of the Guild of Jesus, the Virgin, and Saint Barbara in St Katherine's by the Tower: see John Stow *Survey of London* edited as *A Survey of the Cities of London and Westminster ... brought down to the year 1637 to the present time by J.S.* (John Strype, London, 1720) 1 Book 2, page 6.
21. Quoted in Rubin *Charity and Community* 96.
22. Quoted in Rothkrug 'Popular Religion and Holy Shrines' 84.
23. Rubin *Charity and Community* 295, 299.

24. Toulmin Smith *English Gilds* 166.
25. Toulmin Smith *English Gilds* 148.
26. McRee *Bonds of Community* 79; Pishey Thompson *The History and Antiquities of Boston* (n.p., Boston, 1856) 145, 138: Assumption Guild, Wardens' Accounts, Westminster Abbey Muniments.
27. Thompson *Boston* 134, 138.
28. *Church-Wardens' Accounts of Croscombe ... 1349 to 1560* edited Bishop Edmund Hobhouse (Somerset Record Society Publications 4: London, 1890) 1–44.
29. The sums range from £7 at Mildenhall in 1505 (Galloway-Wasson *Norfolk and Suffolk* 191) to 12d in Morebath in 1533/34 (*REED: Devon* edited John Wasson (University of Toronto Press, 1986) 209). The Croscombe Robin Hood play brought in over £4 in 1526/27 (Hobhouse 38).
30. Published records are easily available for at least thirty communities in which religious guilds sponsored civic pageantry, and many more references could doubtless be uncovered through a careful search of local histories.
31. Toulmin Smith *English Gilds* 148.
32. *Registrum Statutorum et Consuetudinum Ecclesiae Cathedralis Sancti Pauli Londiniensis* edited W. Sparrow Simpson (London, n.p., 1873) 457. For an announcement to the Nottingham Guild of St George and St Mary, see *Account Books of the Gilds of St. George and St. Mary in the Church of St. Peter, Nottingham* translated R.F.B. Hodgkinson (Thoroton Society Record Series 7: Nottingham, 1939) 1.
33. Mervyn James 'Ritual, Drama and the Social Body in the Late Medieval English Town' *Past and Present* 98 (1983) 15.
34. Toulmin Smith *English Gilds* 339–40.
35. James 'Ritual, Drama and the Social Body' 11.
36. *Cambridge Gild Records* edited Mary Bateson (Cambridge Antiquarian Society Publications 8° series 39: Cambridge, 1903) 101.
37. For example, the St James play *in sex paginis compilatum* ('compiled in six pages/?pageants') left by William Revetour to the St Christopher Guild in York in 1446: *REED: York* edited Alexandra F. Johnston and Margaret Rogerson, 2 vols (University of Toronto Press, 1979) *1* 68, or the 'plays for the ascencion' at Sleaford, Lincoln in 1480 (Kahrl *Lincolnshire* 86), or the 'play off Sent Thomas' played for his guild at Mildenhall in 1505 (Galloway-Wasson *Norfolk and Suffolk* 190).
38. Galloway-Wasson *Norfolk and Suffolk* 121–30. A similar pattern, though on a scale befitting a modest village, emerges from the records of the Corpus Christi Guild of Creeting St Mary in the same county (Galloway-Wasson *Norfolk and Suffolk* 149–54).
39. Kahrl *Lincolnshire* 4; McRee *Bonds of Community* 81 (see note 4).
40. *REED: Coventry* edited R.W. Ingram (University of Toronto Press, 1981) 115; Kahrl *Lincolnshire* 4.
41. *REED: York 2* 863.
42. *Dramatic Texts and Records of Britain* edited Ian Lancashire (University of Toronto Press, 1984) 15.
43. Ruth Wilson Tryon 'Miracles of Our Lady in Middle English Verse' *Publications of the Modern Language Association of America* 38 (1923) 374–8.
44. Lancashire *Dramatic Texts and Records* 128.
45. Lancashire *Dramatic Texts and Records* 315.

46. Toulmin Smith *English Gilds* 95.
47. Paula Neuss 'Active and Idle Language: Dramatic Images in *Mankind*' in *Medieval Drama* edited Neville Denny (Stratford-upon-Avon Studies 16: Edward Arnold, London, 1973) 41–67.
48. Toulmin Smith *English Gilds* xl.
49. *The Gild of St Mary, Lichfield* edited F.J. Furnivall *EETS ES 114* (1920) 6–7.
50. Rothkrug 'Popular Religion and Holy Shrines' 84: see note 19.

FESTIVE PROFIT AND IDEOLOGICAL PRODUCTION:
Le Jeu De Saint Nicolas
Claire Sponsler

One of the vexing problems of investigating cultural representations is that of determining how texts relate to the cultures they are part of. Most theorists of culture, especially those who are committed to tying cultural productions in some way to material forces, see the relationship as moving in two directions simultaneously: from the text to material reality and from material reality to the text. In this way the text is seen as both product and producer of particular social and economic conditions. The mediating factor – that which makes it possible for texts to shape material conditions and, less problematically, for material conditions to produce texts – is usually identified as ideology, the set of symbolic configurations that can be used to refigure material forces as cultural productions and vice versa. Because ideology occupies this powerful mediating position, tracking its elusive movements has naturally been of interest to cultural critics. But ideological investigations are never easy. How far, for example, can we go in inferring what a text says about the material conditions that produced it? And to what extent can a text be said to have created those material conditions by formulating an ideology that valorises them? These are difficult yet crucial questions for understanding the cultural functions of any text. In the case of medieval texts, separated from us by linguistic and historical distance that has obliterated most evidence of their production and consumption, these questions prove particularly challenging.

Jean Bodel's Le Jeu de Saint Nicolas has enjoyed continued attention from critics for a number of reasons, chief among them a textual richness that makes interpreting the play a complex undertaking. My object in this paper is not, however, to offer a new reading of the play, but rather to ask instead what cultural functions it might have served for its original audience. Although urban drama has generally been interpreted as the public enactment of communal harmony, it is well worth remembering that from the point of view of consumption urban drama might also have led to the exclusion of certain groups or individuals – that is, the message of collective solidarity that the performances sought to impose might not have been swallowed by all observers.[1] Nevertheless, and especially in the case of Bodel's play, it seems clear that urban drama at the very least strongly encouraged a sense of communal feeling, even if that encouragement was rejected by some. If we cannot confidently say that urban dramatic performances inevitably resulted in social cohesiveness, we can at least suggest that they often made available an ideology of communal accord for any who wished to view them that way.

Le Jeu de Saint Nicolas, whatever its actual effect on its viewers, seems in fact to have gone even further, not only offering the possibility of affirming social bonds but making resistance to its ideological thrust well-nigh impossible. Although we do not now know the precise details of the play's performance or the response of its audience, we do have the text of the play, whose narrative, structure, and themes seem manifestly designed to express the idea of social unity. Potential divisions based on real economic and social inequities are inscribed in the play but then displaced into a safer imaginative realm of battle between pagans and Christians. Even there, in that harmless fictional space, the rivalry is not played out to a violent conclusion but is instead harmoniously resolved. Crucial to this resolution of oppositions is the fact that the play is a festive drama dealing with a miracle of St Nicholas. It is here, in the focus on St Nicholas as an agent of profit that, I would argue, the play's ideological possibilities are most visible. The play need not have, and probably could not have, held one meaning for all its spectators; it does offer, however, a point of departure for ideological production, a place where material and spiritual gain could be shown to mesh in a way that might have contributed significantly to the social and economic life of a twelfth-century Arrageois audience. In the remainder of this paper I would like to discuss the ideological possibilities offered by Bodel's play, looking first at clues suggested by the text when it is examined with recent cultural theory in mind, and then considering why the ideological potential of the text might have been useful for twelfth-century Arras.

Le Jeu de Saint Nicolas was written in Arras somewhere between 1191 and 1202,[2] and is generally credited with being the first vernacular French drama. This alone would be enough to win it critical fame, but its complexity has also contributed to its continued popularity. The play seems at first glance, however, not so much complex as chaotic. It is constructed out of a *mélange* of genres, locales, verse forms, characters, tones, and themes, whirled together in a way that resists interpretation. The play's title suggests that it is a saint's play and indeed a miracle of St Nicholas, who saves the Preudom's life and restores the Saracen king's treasure, forms part of the action. But the play also includes elements drawn from the *chanson de geste* and from the *fabliau*. The difficulty for most critics has been how to derive a coherent meaning out of these disparate parts. Which element is to be foregrounded as the controlling aspect of the play – the epic scenes, the religious events, or the tavern's comedy? Or if no element dominates, how do they all fit together?

Although the action of the play takes place in five separate locales – the Saracen king's palace, the tavern, the prison where the Preudom is held, the distant lands of the emirs, and the crusaders' battlefield – these five locales are generally treated as if they comprised two distinct and opposing frames, the Court (which includes the palace, the prison, the emirs' lands, and the battlefield) and the Tavern (which is usually equated with contemporary Arras). In a recent analysis of the cultural function of the play, David Raybin addresses the problem of the apparent incongruity between the two frames. He argues persuasively that there is, in fact, no incongruity, but that the two different settings are played out as 'two distinct political, religious, and social environments, existing in separate but parallel frames of dramatic reality'.[3] According to Raybin, the Court is presented as African, pagan, aristocratic, exotic, and distant both temporally and spatially, while the Tavern is presented as French, Christian, bourgeois, ordinary, and grounded in what would be for its original audience an immediately present time and place – Arras.

This interpretation of the play's two frames as forming separate but parallel environments is convincing, yet it does not steer us safely away from some logical errors. For from this view of the play as split into two distinct frames comes the temptation to see it consequently as a representation of two separate ideologies corresponding to those frames, the Court encoding the values of a feudal aristocracy or urban élite and the Tavern the values of an urban bourgeoisie. A number of critics have followed this line of reasoning, arguing that the two parts of the play respond in some way to specific class interests or conflicts, usually involving pitting the aristocracy or urban patriciate against the bourgeoisie.[4] The audience of the play is then assumed to identify with one of those two sides, either the Court or the Tavern, depending upon whatever the audience's actual social composition is taken to be.[5] What all of these interpretations share is the attempt to see a certain social representation within the play as reflecting the ideology and class consciousness of an actual audience.

Recent cultural theory would, however, caution against assuming a direct correspondence between a literary representation and a real social group. It is understandably tempting to take the 'realism' of the tavern scenes as reflecting bourgeois life, as giving the audience 'the enjoyment of seeing themselves as in a mirror', as one critic has put it.[6] Unfortunately, at its most literal this supposed equivalence of tavern characters and audience assumes that the viewers were all thieves and gamblers.[7] Advocates of this form of reflection theory ignore that fact that realism was to some extent a convention, even in Bodel's time. As Alfred Adler has stressed, the tavern scenes present life *non pas telle qu'elle est, mais telle que la présente un poète* ('not as it is, but as a poet presents it').[8] In other words, the tavern is an imaginative representation not a literal re-creation of reality. Similarly, there is no reason to assume that the court scenes would have had meaning only to a patrician audience. Once again, these scenes are conventional forms of representation, derived from the motifs and actions of the *chanson de geste*. Even though the original audience for the *chanson de geste* was almost certainly aristocratic, reworkings of this genre such as Bodel's do not necessarily imply an aristocratic audience. In any case, there is no compelling reason to believe that the actual viewers of the play are mirrored in either the Court or the Tavern.

Even if we could accept theoretically such a neat homology between the representation of social groups and an audience's real social composition, *Le Jeu de Saint Nicolas* does not so much polarise ideologies and social groups as these critics argue, by forcing identification with one side or the other, as it draws them together by encouraging the audience to assimilate the two sides. The point is not that the play makes the rich identify with the rich and the poor with the poor, but instead that it invites each individual member of the audience, whatever his or her status, to identify with all of the social groups represented in the play. What the audience is given is not a reflection of themselves but rather a chance to imagine themselves in a certain way. *Le Jeu de Saint Nicolas* does not represent urban life as it is, but offers instead one way of imagining how it might be. The play in fact represents a miracle of St Nicholas as a festive celebration of mutual profit arising out of the containment of potential conflict. It is this valorisation of profit-making as the natural result of conflict that takes on important meaning in the context of late-twelfth-century Arras, seemingly designed to affirm for the Arrageois the worth – in more than monetary terms – of their financial activities and to convince them that their interests are indeed mutually shared.

The play creates this valorisation thematically through its focus on profit and conflict, themes that cross the two frames, unifying the play's actions and characters through the figure of St Nicholas. As even a cursory reading shows, the play is overwhelmingly preoccupied with profit in its various guises: credit, loans, and pledges, dicing and betting, advertising, robbery, and attempts at fraud fill both the Tavern and Court scenes of the play. Indeed, the whole of the play seems to be organised around patterns of loss and gain, with nearly every action motivated by the desire for increase of wealth. This impulse overtly controls the three Tavern scenes, which are all centred on the pursuit of profit: the Tavreniers loans money on interest (803–4); he tries to gain his share of the treasure (1067–8, 1175–8); and his assistant Caigneés steals from him (701–6).[9] In the main action of the Tavern scenes, the three thieves play dice, first to see who will pay the bill (821–62) and then for money (863–920). In between these games, Raouleés, the town-crier, advertises the Tavern's wine (591–3), since the Tavreniers is worried that he has not been doing enough business. The Tavern scenes drive home the point that profit dominates human action and behaviour – at work and at play.

Yet not just the Tavern scenes, where a desire for profit might be expected, but also the scenes at Court revolve around loss and gain. It is here in the Court, of course, that the thieves steal the king's treasure, providing St Nicholas with the opportunity to work his miracle by turning the king's loss into an advantage. But even where we would not anticipate seeing it, profit creeps in. For example, the battle between the crusaders and the Saracens, with which the play opens, is seen in monetary terms as a form of payment in which, as the Senescaus says, the harm done by the crusaders must be repaid (393), and in which profit and honour are closely linked (226). Tellingly, the king himself is described not as an ideal warrior or leader but as the Saracens' only salvation from loss (*perte* and *lagan* 133). His response to the battle, once he has sent for the emirs to help him, seems more mercantile than heroic: he negotiates and finally strikes a kind of bargain with his god, Tervagan, after threatening to melt down the gold statue of the god if Tervagan allows the crusaders to win (134–43). The emirs reiterate this emphasis on monetary values, boasting not, as we would expect, of their prowess in battle, but (with the exception of the Amiraus d'outre l'Arbre Sec, who is too poor) of the wealth they bring the king (355–83). In all of these instances, the conventional feudal values of fealty, leadership, courage, and strength in battle are refigured into the discourse of profit: to win the battle is to gain. The one crucial exception might seem to occur when the king lays out his treasure to test the powers of the Preudom's St Nicholas icon. But even this act, if not explicitly motivated by desire for gain, ends nevertheless in profit, with St Nicholas not only restoring but doubling the king's treasure (1392–5). Thus in both the Tavern and the Court scenes, character motivation and plot development focus on the desire for profit. Strikingly, the play does not at any point criticise the quest for wealth; even the thieves are treated sympathetically and actually come out ahead, getting off scot-free in their robbery of the king (although they have to return the treasure), paying the Tavreniers less than they owe him, and even taking his sack in the end.[10]

In spite of what would seem to be an obvious emphasis on monetary and other forms of gain, critics have been reluctant to acknowledge that profit for its own sake is such a dominant force in the play, preferring instead to see the pursuit of wealth as subsumed under other, loftier, concerns. Jean-Charles Payen, for example, describes the central miracle of the play as being 'd'ordre économique', yet insists that 'l'aspect économique du miracle est moins important que ses conséquences spirituelles.'[11] Although Payen agrees that the tavern scenes represent an obsession with gain, nevertheless he views this obsession as pejorative, arguing that the tavern is a place where 'une action dérisoire' is played out.[12] In a similar fashion Tony Hunt, although recognising the desire for gain as the main argument of the play, softens the emphasis on money by viewing it as part of a call for renewal of spiritual values intended to solicit donations from the town to support the crusade. In Hunt's reading of the play, the desire for increase of wealth, or profit, is criticised by Bodel with the result that the '*possession* of wealth may be productive ... but the *pursuit* of wealth is destructive, standing as a positive obstacle to prosperity and salvation'.[13] Neither of these interpretations accurately describes what happens in the play's overt embrace of profit for its own sake. Spiritual and material values are not opposed in the play, as Payen and Hunt suggest, but are instead allied. The crucial ideological move that the play makes is to recast material values as spiritual values and vice versa. In this way, what might appear to be separate and competing spheres of interest are in fact reshaped as mutually supportive forms of symbolic interest accruing to the overall account. Profit and salvation neatly mesh in this reformulation.

If the play's unabashed revelling in the pursuit of profit is difficult for modern critics to swallow, it was perhaps not so unsavoury for Bodel's original audience. Part of the reason can be found in the use the text makes of its central character – St Nicholas. The drama intertwines spiritual and material gain in the figure of St Nicholas, whose role develops out of but in essential ways modifies traditional versions of the Nicholas legend. Although the miracle in which St Nicholas restores lost treasure was widely known, as the Preecieres's allusion to St Nicholas's *vita* suggests (*Qu'en sa vie trouvons lisant*: 'which we find in reading his Life': 8), Bodel chose, significantly, to focus on this particular miracle out of a number of other possibilities.[14] Lynette Muir's description of a previously unknown fifteenth-century manuscript of Nicholas plays is a convenient place to see the range of possible Nicholas miracles available for representation.[15] This manuscript contains eight plays dramatising various aspects of the Nicholas legend that were all well-known stories, although the first three are found nowhere else in play form. The plays in the manuscript are as follows:

1. Nicholas is chosen as bishop of Myra.
2. Nicholas saves his former landlady's child from being boiled in a bath of water left on the fire when his landlady, hearing of Nicholas's election as bishop, runs out to celebrate.
3. A devil disguised as a damsel tricks some sailors into carrying oil to Myra. Nicholas appears to them and shows them that the oil is flammable and intended to burn down the cathedral.
4. The legend of the Jew who lends money to the Christian.
5. The legend of the Son of Gethron.
6. The *Tres filiae* legend.
7. The *Iconia* legend.
8. The *Tres clerici* legend.

The seventh play, the *Iconia* miracle, is the same as that used by Bodel. This manuscript demonstrates, as do the Fleury and Hildesheim plays, that the wide variety of miracles associated with St Nicholas were indeed played out in dramatic form. That Bodel's play focuses on one particular miracle as its central event suggests that this miracle offered a specific ideological potential not so readily found in the others.

What the *Iconia* miracle stresses that the other miracles do not is Nicholas's rôle as protector of wealth. For example, in the version of the *Iconia* miracle that Bodel's play most closely follows, that of the Fleury manuscript, the story goes like this: A rich Jew sets out on a journey, leaving his possessions in an unlocked chest under the protection of an icon of St Nicholas. Three thieves rob him. The Jew returns, laments his loss, regrets entrusting his goods to Nicholas and promises to beat the icon the next day. Nicholas visits the thieves, threatening them with punishment if they do not return the stolen goods. Two of the thieves propose keeping the treasure, but the third persuades them to give it back. His possessions restored, the Jew rejoices and calls on the bystanders to praise St Nicholas.[16]

The version found in Hilarius is similar, although it changes the Jew to a pagan, adds an actual beating of the icon, diminishes the conflict among the thieves, and ends with the pagan's conversion to Christianity: a pagan sets out on a journey, leaving a Nicholas icon to guard his treasure. Robbers steal the treasure. The pagan returns, laments his loss, and beats the icon. Nicholas then visits the robbers, threatening to disclose the crime unless they return the treasure. They do so, the pagan rejoices and thanks the icon. Nicholas appears to the pagan, telling him to thank God, whereupon the pagan renounces his past sins and declares his belief in Christ.[17]

It seems clear that these are not simply conversion stories, although conversion certainly plays a rôle. Instead, in both of these narratives the focus is on St Nicholas's ability to protect and restore wealth, even when it belongs to a non-Christian, and therefore presumably unworthy, owner. This emphasis on protecting the wealth of an ostensibly undeserving person makes an important point, one that *Le Jeu de Saint Nicholas* effectively exploits, suggesting that individual merit does not necessarily determine whether one's wealth will be protected or not. Deserving or not, one can turn to St Nicholas for help and receive it.

Having chosen to focus on the *Iconia* miracle, Bodel makes a couple of significant changes. First, in the place of the typical Jew or merchant as the object of the conversion, Bodel inserts a pagan king. As Joseph Dane points out, there is nothing socially problematic about the wealthy Jew or *barbarus* of other Nicholas stories. Rich heathens are well-known types. But when Bodel makes a pagan king his conversion-figure, he undercuts expectations by unexpectedly mixing religious (that is, the hallmark of the First Estate), militaristic (Second Estate) and monetary (Third Estate) concerns in one character.[18] Although this blurring of accepted distinctions may go unnoticed by a modern reader, it is not inconsequential for the play's message and was probably noticed by contemporary spectators.

Bodel next makes a second important change, this time in the portrayal of Nicholas himself, presenting him not just as a protector of material goods but as an increaser of wealth, or an agent of profit - both spiritual and material. When St Nicholas is first introduced to us in the Preecieres's prologue, it is as someone who not only protects wealth but also multiplies and increases it:

> Et s'est si bonne garde eslite
> Que il monteploie et pourfite
> Canque on li commande a garder.   36–8

> 'And he is such a good and excellent guardian
> That he multiplies with interest
> Whatever one gives him to look after.'

As Alfred Adler notes, Nicholas here sounds very much like *un banquier d'Arras, capitaliste et prêteur contre intérêt* ('an Arras banker, a capitalist and one who lends at interest'),[19] and his talent for increasing wealth is clearly one of his more attractive features. The Preecieres's speech, which provides a brief synopsis of the play, focuses almost entirely on this particular talent of Nicholas's, glancing only briefly at the crusaders' battle (7–16), omitting all mention of the emirs, and skipping all of the tavern scenes. Instead, the Preecieres emphasises the miracle Nicholas performs, advising the audience that the play to follow will be to their profit (*De vostre preu ne vous anuit!*: 3). Even if the Preecieres's speech is an apocryphal later addition, as has been suggested, it can still be taken as a commentary on Nicholas's rôle as an agent of profit and on the way that the play is supposed to function for its audience by giving them something they, too, can profit from. In the prologue, the figure of St Nicholas is thus presented as joining together spiritual values with material ones, highlighting from the outset that spiritual gain goes hand in hand with material profit.

After setting him up in the prologue as an agent of profit, the play further modifies the traditional portrayal of St Nicholas by stressing the way in which everyone – no matter what his religion or his socio-economic status – benefits from the pursuit of profit. This profit-for-all is achieved primarily through the handling of conflict in the play. The play's conflicts, such as the fight between the Saracens and the crusaders, the negotiations between the king and the Preudom, and the battle of wits between the tavern-goers and the Tavreniers, all seem to be motivated by the common desire to make a profit. But what is remarkable is that this common desire is resolved in common profit, with the result that the conflicts all end in mutual gain inspired by St Nicholas's actions. The play loses no time in establishing this rather surprising connection between conflict and profit-for-all, starting with the first speech, in which Auberons tells the king that his land has been invaded by crusaders intent on battle (115–21). The Saracen king's response is the expected one of raising forces to do counter-battle, thus setting up an overt crusader-Saracen conflict, a conflict that is mirrored in medieval thought by the traditional pitting of Christian against infidel. But the battle in Bodel's play is thought of less in terms of a clash of faiths than as a chance for loss or gain, as the king's choice of words when praying to Tervagan for a prophecy makes clear: *Se je doi **gaagnier**, si ri, / Et se je doi **perdre**, si pleure* ('If I am *to win*, then smile; / And if I am *to lose*, then weep' [my emphasis]: 181–2). From this opening conflict in the Court scenes, the action of the play shifts immediately to the Tavern, where Clikés and Auberons engage in the first of three conflicts that take place there – a series of games of *hasart* and dice. These games, more overtly than the crusader-Saracen battle, are motivated not just by a desire to win, but by a desire for monetary profit.

An important way in which the conflicts of both the Court and Tavern scenes are similar is that they are closely tied to chance and game-playing. Chance and play, though more explicit in the Tavern scene games, turn up in the Court scenes as well. Indeed, both the Court and the Tavern scenes involve analogous games of chance based on patterns of loss and gain, in which all of the participants take risks, attempt to outwit their opponents, and hope to come out winners. The Preudom hazards his life on his saint, the king gambles with his treasure, and the emirs and crusaders bet, at least implicitly, on winning the battle. All of these games of chance in the Court scenes are played out parallel to the more obvious game-playing in the tavern.[20] Turning conflict into a kind of game has important consequences,

73

especially in its ability to deflate the potential for harm and for serious defeat normally associated with strife. Not even the life and death conflict of the crusaders' battle with the Saracens is treated as a disastrous or tragic event. Although all of the crusaders except the Preudom die, their deaths are largely ignored; the whole battle-field scene in fact takes up only some sixty lines (394–453). Instead of glorifying or mourning the dead, the play focuses on the sole survivor among the crusaders, the Preudom, and on the bargain he makes with the king in order to save his life. The end of the dicing games makes clear the way in which everything ends to mutual advantage. Exchange as a basis for profit, rather than battle resulting in winners and losers, is the dominant metaphor in the play. As the Tavreniers says at the end of the dicing games: *Or sommes nous yevel; / Comme devant resoit communs* ('So now we are quits; / Everything in common, as before': 1175–6). In this reshaping of conflict as game, the play shifts focus, drawing attention to the winners rather than the losers and emphasising the spirit of play and potential for profit involved rather than the risk of failure and chance of defeat.

This treatment of conflict as a game whose outcome is mutual profit is central to understanding how *Le Jeu de Saint Nicolas* neutralises the larger potential conflict looming over the individual actions of the play, that is, the oppositional nature of the two cultures represented by the world of the Tavern and the world of the Court. The accepted wisdom about medieval society would lead us to expect that *Le Jeu de Saint Nicolas* would stress this cultural collision as irreconcilable conflict, as happens in a number of other medieval texts. The twelfth-century *Dialogus Salomonis et Marcolphi*, for example, uses its two speakers, Solomon and Marcolph, to fight out the clash between what Maria Corti calls two 'cultural realities, sacred the higher, profane the lower'.[21] These two opposing worlds, which represent two antithetical sets of values – high versus low, ordered versus disordered, serious versus comic, official truth versus unofficial truth, and spirit versus flesh – are presented in the *Dialogus* as antagonists, with their spokesmen, Solomon for the high, Marcolph for the low, trading arguments blow by blow. According to Corti, Marcolph is not a unique invention of the author, but is rather a general medieval type, 'the product of a socio-ideological context and of a transgressive operation', which expresses 'dissent from a culture which persists in basing itself exclusively on the *auctoritates* of the past and in paying no heed to new aspects of work and technique'.[22] Thus, Marcolph acts as a stylised challenger of the official ideology of high culture represented by Solomon.

The same thing could, of course, have happened in Bodel's play, where the split between the Court and the Tavern, high culture and low, could have been played out as a battle between two competing ideologies. The pagan court might well have been treated, like Solomon, as the *auctoritas* of high culture, with the tavern world taking on Marcolph's role of *rusticus* or villein. This would have been one way of creating a new ideology for the play's original audience – a specifically bourgeois ideology that would have been in open battle against prevailing high-culture norms.

In *Le Jeu de Saint Nicolas*, however, these two rival cultural codes, played out in different characters, different settings, even in different language and verse forms, neither clash nor end in an impasse but are ultimately joined in harmonious resolution and mutual profit. The way in which the play uses its cultural oppositions is quite different from what happens in the *Dialogus* – so different, in fact, that it offers a key to *Le Jeu de Saint Nicolas*'s use of disparate settings, social groups, and ideologies as its structural features. The play uses its structural and thematic oppositions as forces not of polarisation but of unification, encouraging its audience to synthesise the opposing sides.

Spatial distance between the court and the tavern worlds becomes the opportunity for a high/low class opposition, but that opposition is never played out as antagonism. The two are set up as opposing territories, thematically, spatially, generically, linguistically, and even metrically, but although their difference seems to be as exaggerated as possible, the two are never brought face to face in a way that would force the audience to favour one or the other. The court is not satirised or attacked nor is the tavern; nor is one privileged over the other. Instead, the two are treated as distinctly different spheres of interest that can be assimilated precisely because they are kept apart. Avoiding the vertical hierarchies that would be inevitable should the aristocrats and bourgeois mix in the same scenes allows the possibility of interpreting the social relations in the play as somehow horizontal, a spatial orientation that stresses communal unity. This unity derives chiefly from the emphasis on profit as a non-class-specific value, something that is available to everyone from kings to thieves. St Nicholas, with his defence of profit, draws an imaginative map of mutually shared values and interests.

What is striking in fact about the map offered by *Le Jeu de Saint Nicolas* is precisely its sense of alliance. Unlike the social divisiveness seen in the *Dialogus Salomonis et Marcolphi* or in Arrageois texts later in the thirteenth century, Bodel's play presents a world in which social relations are seen as harmonious and mutually dependent. This harmony is achieved, paradoxically, by that very splitting of social groups into the separate worlds of the Tavern and the Court that critics have pointed to as portraying class antagonism. Upper and lower classes, aristocrats and thieves, never meet in the play. Instead, they literally inhabit different worlds. Keeping these groups separate does not, however, polarise class interests; rather, it allows an illusion of unity and mutuality of interests that would have been more difficult to achieve had the play explicitly mingled its social groups. If Bodel had combined the two in one locale, bringing together the aristocrats of the Court with the bourgeois of the Tavern, he and his audience would have been forced to confront real social hierarchies that would necessarily have pointed up issues of dominance and subordination, as well as the divergence of social and economic interests. But by separating the two groups, playing out their scenes on separate but parallel tracks, Bodel allows the possibility of an imaginative rewriting of the social order in which different social groups can be envisioned as inhabiting separate but equal realms allied by the pursuit of profit.

This, then, is the crucial ideological force of the play: its emphasis on St Nicholas as an agent of spiritual and material profit who resolves potential conflicts to everyone's advantage offers a model for consolidating diverse socio-economic groups under one, profit-based, ideology. The values of the Court – battle, fealty, and conversion – are played out parallel to and by implication in harmony with the Tavern's values of cunning, shrewdness, quick wits, negotiation, and clever bargaining. The play subverts feudal ideology (especially the values of hierarchy and difference), without actually criticising or rejecting it, by pointing up how the world of the Court parallels the Tavern. At the same time, the play reconciles its opposing social groups under a profit-based ideology, containing submerged threats of conflicting interests.

Why would this model of the harmonious resolution of conflicts to everyone's advantage have been valuable in the context of Arras? In large part, the answer lies in the nature of twelfth-century urban life. Threats of disorder or discontent that might be expected from the shift to new economic forms and the attendant reorganisation of social groups that was taking place could have been at least partially minimised by appealing to the kind of ideology found in Bodel's play. Significantly, the ideological value of St Nicholas for urban communities seems to have been recognised, whether consciously or unconsciously, by those who lived in such communities. Charles Jones points out that many versions of the Nicholas legend date from the time of urban growth and the spread of a money-economy.[23] St Nicholas would obviously have been an appropriate and attractive patron for anyone engaged in money-based exchanges, and even more so in a situation where the potential for economic hostilities existed. For this reason, because he could so readily be portrayed as a bridge between social groups and an agent of profit for all, St Nicholas would have had a special force in the context of twelfth-century Arras. Not surprisingly, evidence suggests that there was an important cult of St Nicholas in Arras at the time.[24] Bodel's play would naturally have tapped into this vein of meanings surrounding Nicholas.

It must be acknowledged, however, that *Le Jeu de Saint Nicolas* was undoubtedly to some extent self-serving, an attempt to make someone's private interest seem like public good. What is remarkable is that it seems to have worked so well. The play unobtrusively creates a fictional space in which private, individual interests are not allowed to conflict with each other but are harmoniously reshaped as the public good. Later in the thirteenth century such an attempt would perhaps have been less possible, or would have appeared to be an act of overt ideological manipulation, as it became increasingly clear that in fact the common good was not being served by Arras's wealthy financiers and tradesmen. At the end of the twelfth century, however, the play's alliance of spiritual with material gain resulting in profit for all seems so innocent, so neutral, so natural, precisely because its ideological possibilities responded so well to the particular situation in Arras at the time. A thriving mercantile and banking centre, Arras was enjoying a period of calm and prosperity preceding a series of social and economic difficulties in the thirteenth century, including tax scandals, rebellions, and general dissatisfaction with the ruling classes.[25] In contrast to this approaching discontent, the late twelfth century seems remarkably free of discord.

There were, in fact, a number of outside forces that contributed to making internal harmony seem both more desirable and more achievable at the end of the twelfth century than it might otherwise have been. In the first place, Arras was newly aware of itself as a unified, self-governing entity. Although there are indications that the town had had a fairly long-standing tradition of self-government, including a mayor and a town council,[26] the *ville*'s communal charter, granted by Phillippe Auguste in 1194, would have solidified in writing this self-determination. The charter, which outlined the administrative, civil, and criminal rights and duties of the town, effectively placed all control of the town's affairs in the hands of the bourgeoisie themselves, providing for a group of urban magistrates (*échevins*) to serve for fourteen months and for a mayor to be chosen by them. Although this system would by the end of the thirteenth century evolve into a self-perpetuating oligarchy responsible for a great deal of animosity towards the magistrates, at the turn of the century it represented a significant move towards autonomy for the town now freed from arbitrary treatment by seigneurial lords. With the charter the balance of power clearly shifted from the lords to the bourgeois. Arras at this point was effectively, in both real and symbolic terms, independent.

A further sense of unity was encouraged by bourgeois status. The *échevins* had among their powers the right to grant bourgeois status to those who wished it and who had lived for a year and a day in Arras. Increasingly, pressure was exerted to make everyone who lived in Arras who was not a member of the nobility or the clergy become a *bourgeois*.[27] It seems probable that this coercion to become bourgeois, to become legally a member of the *ville*, contributed to a feeling of commonalty among the bourgeois residents of Arras. Finally, this perception of commonalty was propitiously cemented by forces pressing in on Arras from without. In 1191 Arras had passed from Flemish to French control, which would last until the Burgundian take-over in the late fourteenth century. Although this shift probably made little difference in the day-to-day lives of the Arrageois, nevertheless it might well have had a symbolic significance, underlining the precariousness of the town's existence and its susceptibility to the winds of fortune. The reminder of external threats might well have increased the drive for internal unity and diminished any tendencies towards divisiveness.

Le Jeu de Saint Nicolas plays into and upon these latent feelings of unity. Through its festive resolution of conflicts in mutual profit, the play presented its audience with a model of how they might have liked to think of their social and economic relations – as leading to the profit of all involved. The value such an ideology might have had for late twelfth-century Arras, undergoing rapid economic and social change that uprooted old patterns of life, seems clear. It translated self-interest into mutual good and suggested that common profit was the outcome of all conflict. In the play there are no losers, only winners – a valuable paradigm for covering up, if only for a little while, the inevitable struggles and inequities that the new economic order would bring, or had already brought. Festivity, and perhaps a festivity belonging in actuality to only one specific group – the members of the *carité Notre Dame des jogleors et des bourgois* for whom the play was probably performed – provided the occasion for the celebration of communal accord whether such accord really existed or not. The play offered a possible model for ideological production, a model in which both individual and society resolve all conflicts, win all games, and have good reason indeed to exit singing – like the actors at the end of the play – *Te Deum laudamus*.

University of Iowa

NOTES

1. As has been argued by Sheila Lindenbaum 'Rituals of Exclusion: Feasts and Plays of the English Religious Fraternities' in this collection.
2. See Arnold Arens *Untersuchungen zu Jean Bodels Mirakel 'Le Jeu de Saint Nicolas'* (Franz Steiner Verlag, Stuttgart, 1986) 27–8, for a discussion of the date and performance of the play.
3. David Raybin 'The Court and the Tavern: Bourgeois Discourse in *Li Jeus de Saint Nicolai*' *Viator* 19 (1988) 178.
4. See for example Marie Ungureanu *La bourgeoisie naissante: Société et littérature bourgeoises d'Arras aux XIIe et XIIIe siècles* (Commission des Monuments Historiques du Pas-de-Calais, Arras, 1955), and the critique of her argument by Henri Roussel 'Notes sur la littérature arrageoise du XIIIe siècle' *Revue des sciences humaines* 87 (1957) 249–86.
5. See for example Tony Hunt 'A Note on the Ideology of Bodel's *Jeu de Saint Nicolas*' *Studi francesi* 58 (1976) 67–72, who argues that the audience identifies with the pagan court; and Konrad Schoell *Das komische Theater des französischen Mittelalters: Wirklichkeit und Spiel* (Fink, Munich, 1975) 66, who sees the realism of the tavern scenes as pointing to a bourgeois audience.
6. Patrick R. Vincent *The 'Jeu de Saint Nicolas' of Jean Bodel of Arras: A Literary Analysis* (Johns Hopkins University Press, Baltimore, 1954) 66.
7. As Howard S. Robertson 'Structure and Comedy in *Le Jeu de Saint Nicolas*' *Studies in Philology* 64 (1967) 562, points out.
8. Alfred Adler 'Le Jeu de Saint Nicolas, édifiant, mais dans quel sens?' *Romania* 81 (1960) 113.
9. All quotations are taken from *Le Jeu de Saint Nicolas de Jehan Bodel* edited Albert Henry (Palais des Académies, Brussels, 3rd edition 1981).
10. See Nigel Wilkins 'Yet More Concerning the Tavern Bills in Jehan Bodel's *Jeu de Saint Nicolas*' *Zeitschrift für romanische Philologie* 82 (1966) 339–44, for a discussion of the thieves' overall success.

11. Jean-Charles Payen 'Les éléments idéologiques dans le *Jeu de Saint Nicolas*' *Romania* 94 (1973) 493.
12. Payen 498.
13. Tony Hunt 'A Note on the Ideology of Bodel's *Jeu de Saint Nicolas*' 69 (see note 5).
14. For Bodel's possible sources, see Charles Foulon 'La représentation et les sources du *Jeu de Saint Nicolas*' *Mélanges d'histoire du théâtre du Moyen-Age et de la Renaissance offerts à G. Cohen* (Librairie Nizet, Paris, 1950) 61–2.
15. Lynette Muir 'St. Nicholas: A Newly Discovered French Play Cycle' *EDAM Newsletter* 11 (1988) 1–4. The legends on which these plays are based can also be found in Wace and Hilarius, and in the Hildesheim and Fleury manuscripts.
16. See Karl Young *The Drama of the Medieval Church* 2 vols (Clarendon Press, Oxford, 1933) 2 343–51, for the text of the Fleury play.
17. Young 2 337–43.
18. Joseph A. Dane *Res/Verba: A Study in Medieval French Drama* (Brill, Leiden, 1985) 82.
19. Alfred Adler '*Le Jeu de Saint Nicolas*' 113 (see note 8).
20. Carolyn L. Dinshaw 'Dice Games and Other Games in *Le Jeu de Saint Nicolas*' *Publications of the Modern Language Association of America* 95 (1980) 802–11, has examined how the concept of game-playing underlies the whole play.
21. Maria Corti 'Models and Antimodels in Medieval Culture' *New Literary History* 10 (1979) 357.
22. Corti 358.
23. Charles Jones *Saint Nicholas of Myra, Bari, and Manhattan: Biography of a Legend* (University of Chicago Press, 1978).
24. Charles Foulon 'La représentation et les sources' 57, says that the Artois and the Arrageois in particular had a special devotion for St Nicholas, but offers no proof; further evidence is found in the importance of buildings dedicated to the saint, for example, l'hôpital St-Nicolas, built at the end of the eleventh century, and a St-Nicolas gate begun in 1214.
25. See Ursula Peters *Literatur in der Stadt: Studien zu den sozialen Voraussetzungen und kulturellen Organisationsformen städtischer Literatur im 13. und 14. Jahrhundert* (Niemeyer, Tübingen, 1983) 89–92.
26. See the *privilège* granted to Arras by Phillippe, count of Flanders (undated) in *Inventaire chronologique des chartes de la ville d'Arras* edited Adolphe H. Guesnon (Topino, Arras, 1863) 1–2.
27. Roger Berger *Littérature et société Arrageoises au XIIIe siècle: Les Chansons et dits artésiens* (Commission des Monuments Historiques du Pas-de-Calais, Arras, 1981) 74–5.

MASKS IN THE MEDIEVAL PENINSULAR THEATRE
Ronald E. Surtz

In the Iberian Peninsula, masks appear in both the liturgical and the vernacular traditions and continue to be found in sixteenth-century dramatic performances. Although documentary evidence of their use is not lacking, it is likely that masks were worn even more often than is indicated by the available written sources.

Before considering the question of masks and staging practices, it is appropriate to consider masking in a wider social context. It must be observed at the outset, however, that most information about such practices is derived from sources hostile to the wearing of masks.[1] In the sixteenth century, the custom of masking in courtly entertainments was condemned by such severe moralists as Father Pedro de Covarrubias, who, in his treatise on games, prohibits the use of masks because they are condemned by Christ Himself, they are incompatible with the noble estate, they are a means by which the devil deceives humankind, they are used as a cover for sinful activities, and they conceal and falsify the human face created in God's image.[2] Writing forty years later, Father Francisco de Alcocer, who was acquainted with Covarrubias's book, not only attests that masks were normally worn in plays and pageants, but also adopts a less intransigent stance on the question of masking in general. He states that masks may be worn in edifying and devotional plays or in order to escape death. He further specifies that even in the case of sinful plays, it is the plays themselves that are an occasion for mortal sin and not the use of masks in them.[3]

Moral prejudice against masking must also be related to the wearing of veils in the Muslim fashion by high-born Christian women. The papal nuncio (and future pope Paul V) Camillo Borghese visited Spain in 1594 and observed that Spanish women normally wore veils that covered their faces.[4] But the custom was already widespread in the Spain of the Catholic Monarchs.[5] Indeed, the practice was so pervasive in the early sixteenth century that the Castilian playwright Diego Sánchez de Badajoz (*floruit* 1525–1547) used the story of Tamar to criticise a custom that he considered pernicious to morals. In both Genesis 38:14–15 and Sánchez de Badajoz's *Farsa de Tamar* the heroine covers her face with a veil and dresses as a prostitute in order to trick Judah into having sexual relations with her. In the play's lengthy prologue (lines 1–144) and later in lines 313–60, a shepherd warns that the wearing of veils leads to shameless and sinful behaviour.[6]

But in the legislation of Church councils and synods, the ecclesiastical hierarchy had already expressed its disapproval of masking within its own ranks. Generally, the official banning of certain kinds of dramatic spectacles inside churches was due to the vulgarity or licentiousness of those performances. Occasionally, such prohibitions mention expressly the custom of masking as contributing to the offensive nature of such practices. Thus, the Synod of Avila (1481) forbids clerics to turn themselves into grotesquely disguised figures (*homarraches*) by donning faces 'other than those Our Lord saw fit to give them'.[7]

The suspicious, if not hostile, attitude towards masks and veils in other social contexts raises the logical question of the extent of their presence in the theatre. The use of masks is documented in the stage directions of various plays and in account books relating to dramatic performances; however, the extant texts are normally sparing in stage directions of any kind, and the cathedral or town council account books as a rule mention masks only when they had to be fashioned anew or repaired.

In nearly all the liturgical plays performed in the cathedral of Palma de Mallorca, the clerics wore a sort of white veil that covered their faces. Thus, in the fourteenth century at Christmas Lauds two choirboys, wearing dalmatics and veils (*velati*), with candles in their hands, stood in front of the altar of the Blessed Virgin and sang the verse *Infantem vidimus* in response to the choral exhortation *Pastores dicite*. As Donovan observes, the fact that the boys wore veils is the only visual indication that they were considered to represent the shepherds of the Nativity.[8]

The celebration of the Feast of St Stephen (26 December) actually began later on Christmas Day when at the *Magnificat* of Vespers, 'St Stephen', that is, a deacon, emerged from the sacristy. Wearing a dalmatic and a veil (*velatus facie*), a candle in one hand and a book in the other, he proceeded to the choir. Four clerics carrying a canopy escorted the deacon to the chapel of St Stephen, where he performed the rites proper to the feast-day. Then, at Matins, the deacon, wearing the same outfit, came forth from the sacristy singing a hymn in honour of the Virgin and recited the first lesson. He then returned to the sacristy only to emerge later to begin the *Te Deum*. On the following day, the deacon, still *velata facie*, took part in the farced epistle of St Stephen (Donovan 126–8).

On 27 December, the Feast of St John the Evangelist, two clerics, the one dressed as St John the Baptist, the other as St John the Evangelist, participated in both Vespers and Mass. Their costumes followed conventional modes of iconographic representation. St John the Baptist wore a hairy black mantle, a belt of esparto grass, and sandals, as well as a mask (*aportera maschare*). In his left hand he carried a lamb with a diadem and in his right hand a cross with the inscription *Ecce Agnus Dei*.[9] St John the Evangelist wore a chasuble, a diadem, and a white silk veil over his face (*un vel blanch de sede devant la cara*). He carried a palm branch and a small book in his left hand and a small lighted candle in his right hand. As Donovan observes, while these ceremonies were more pageants than plays, their relation to the liturgical drama is evident:

> It is difficult to classify the ceremonies in which the two Mallorcan ecclesiastics took part. They can hardly be said to have participated in a play;

strictly speaking, no story was presented in action, and it appears that neither had a speaking role. Perhaps the word *pageantry* best describes their activities. Still, however we define these ceremonies, they are closely allied to liturgical drama.129

Veils were also used at Palma in the liturgical plays performed at Easter-time. A fourteenth-century manuscript describes how after the ninth responsory of Matins on Good Friday, three singers performed a dramatised *planctus*. They wore black or violet dalmatics and their faces were veiled (*velati faciebus*). The manuscript does not specify the roles the singers played, but Donovan (136) surmises that the clerics represented the Virgin Mary, St John, and one of the other Maries. As the three characters proceeded through the cathedral, each one sang a stanza of the lament and, between stanzas, all three sang the refrain, *Ay, ten greus son nostras dolors*. It is not known whether the whole *planctus* or just the refrain was sung in the vernacular.

For the *Three Maries* play at Easter Matins, three clerics, each dressed in a different-coloured dalmatic (red, white, or green), emerged from the sacristy, carrying red candles and wearing a veil (*velati in facie*). Proceeding to the altar of the Virgin Mary, each cleric sang a verse of the sequence *Victimae paschali laudes* (Donovan 130–2).

The use of veils in the Mallorcan rites is a sign of some sort of dramatisation, as opposed to merely the antiphonal singing of chants. To wear a veil is thus to act a part. This is especially true in those cases (the *Shepherds* play, St Stephen's Day, the two Easter plays) where there is otherwise no attempt to costume the 'actors' in any symbolic, let alone realistic, manner. The veils would not only conceal the personality of the 'actor' as an individual but in a sense would also conceal the personality of the character he represented. By preventing any attempt at psychological interpretation, the veil underscores the role, i.e., the character's function, within the re-presentation of sacred history.

Veils were occasionally used in the liturgical drama in other parts of Europe. For example, in an Easter play from an unidentified French monastery the three Maries appear *vultibus coopertis*.[10] More normally, however, outside the Peninsula the clerics representing the three Maries either wore their normal vestments (thus identifying themselves by their function in the plays) or covered their heads in some way (thus underscoring the fact that they were representing women).[11] But as Rainer Warning observes, even the covering of the heads suggests a ceremony that remains more liturgical than representational:

> Thus the *imitatio*, for instance, does not lead to costuming, but only to cautiously symbolic utilizations of the customary vestments and ritual vessels. The Maries do conceal their heads *ad modum mulierum*, but with liturgical attire (*amicta, humerale, capitagia*) ... The clerics do not represent what they are not, but within their roles they remain clerics and as such executants of a liturgical ceremony.[12]

Thus, if the ritual nature of the medieval theatre is a commonplace of literary criticism, the use of masks confirms that ritual nature, distancing the medieval drama from representational theatre. At Palma, it is likely that the veils heightened this hieratic and ritualistic effect to the extent that they depersonalised and desexualised the participants. Because they covered the face, the veils concealed the executant's personal identity and neutralised his sexual identity: the veils neither identified the clerics as representing women (since they were worn by St Stephen and the two St Johns as well) nor did they particularly reveal the clerics' maleness (since they concealed the secondary sexual characteristics associated with the face).

With regard to vernacular plays, the account books from the cathedral of Toledo point to the wide-spread use of masks, diadems, and wigs in a variety of plays.[13] Masks were used to solve certain concrete problems of staging. Thus, in the *St Sylvester* play the Emperor Constantine wore a mask that represented his leprosy. In the play of *The Beheading of St John the Baptist*, a calf's neck was used to simulate the actual beheading and it was probably to that end that the Saint wore a mask. And in the play of *The Last Judgement* the resurrected souls wore masks and wigs, which were presumably intended to give them an otherworldly appearance.

Christ wore a wig made of hemp in the plays of *The Harrowing of Hell*, *The Last Judgement*, *The Ascension*, *The Assumption*, and *The Woman Taken in Adultery*. The apostles wore a wig, a diadem, and a false beard in the plays of *The Last Judgement*, *The Ascension*, *The Woman Taken in Adultery*, and *The Entry into Jerusalem*. Masks as such were worn mostly by the antagonists – devils, torturers, and Jews. Thus, the devils had masks in the plays of *The Last Judgement*, *Cain and Abel*, and the 'man who burst' (the *Reventado*).[14] In the play of *The Temptation in the Desert*, the devil was often disguised as a hermit and had a false beard and mask. The torturers and executioners who appeared in the plays of *The Beheading of St John the Baptist*, *Susanna* and most likely *St Catherine* also wore masks. Herod was masked in *The Beheading of St John the Baptist*. Finally, the Jews in the plays of *The Woman Taken in Adultery* and *Susanna* wore masks.[15] In the latter case, it is specified that they were 'peculiar masks' (*máscaras singulares*).[16] It is worth noting that the Jews appear to have worn masks only when functioning as antagonists, for the accounts do not indicate masks for either Abraham or Isaac in the representation of *The Sacrifice of Abraham*. However, in the play on *The Parable of the Rich Man and Lazarus*, Abraham wears a mask, but another Old Testament patriarch wears a wig.[17]

It thus appears that in the Toledo vernacular plays masks in the strictest sense, that is, devices that cover the face or even the entire head of the character, were worn only by the antagonists. The sacred protagonists (Christ, the prophets, and the apostles) normally wore diadems or wigs in imitation of the halos that surrounded the heads of sacred characters in medieval painting.[18] In addition to disguising the actors who wore them, wigs and diadems served as a sign of the sacred characters' spiritual otherness. Thus, both the actors who portrayed 'good' characters and those who played 'evil' characters wore something on the head that disguised their personal identity: the antagonists wore masks, the protagonists a wig or diadem.

Alongside this dichotomy between good and evil, it is also possible to speak of a dichotomy between characters who wore masks (or their equivalent) and those who wore none. The masks thus served to separate the 'natural' characters from the supernatural characters, be the latter diabolic or heavenly. Indeed, the mask or diadem literally de-humanises the character who wears it, signalling his participation in a higher or a lower sphere of existence. It could be argued, however, that in this respect the use of masks (as opposed to the use of wigs and diadems) is intended to elicit different audience responses. The mask, to the extent that it cancels the human personality of the actor, would have a distancing effect and thus inhibit any sort of identification with evil on the part of the spectators. On the other hand, since wigs and/or diadems would disguise the actor but not entirely conceal his human personality, in the case of 'good' characters room would be left for the possibility of some sort of identification with the role. Thus, although the character would be perceived as belonging to a higher sphere, the spectators might be encouraged to imitate the holy life that had earned the character his spiritual dimension.

In more general terms, perhaps the opposition between characters with masks and characters without them was complemented by a difference in the acting styles of the two groups of characters. Twycross and Carpenter observe the stylising effect of masking on the actors:

> When the face is hidden all expression has to come from the body, the stance and movement of the actor, and the way he tilts the mask. This clearly will tend to slow actors down. All movements become significant, so it is hard to make trivial or unnecessary gestures. The actor's gestures therefore become more emphatic, and larger ... Another important consideration for the actor is that there is less sense of personal exposure. His own personality is less directly engaged with the audience, and indeed even with the character he plays. Even more than an unmasked actor he needs to concentrate on what the audience sees, rather than on what he himself feels, because his own feelings will not be transparently reflected in his face. Because of this the whole acting process seems to move slightly nearer towards being a dance that has been learned, or a demonstration. There is a formal quality to masked acting, and a certain necessary stylisation.
>
> *Medieval English Theatre* 3:1 (1981) 34

Relevant to the question of the consequences of masking is an observation made by Sebastián de Covarrubias in his dictionary (1611) to the effect that masks amplify the sound of the human voice,[19] a phenomenon that would create yet another difference between characters with masks and those without them. It is also probable that within the group of masked characters the acting style of the 'good' differed from that of the 'evil' to the extent that masks, wigs, and diadems would create different degrees of stylisation.

The probable ugliness of the masks worn by the evil characters would underscore their diabolical nature, given the close association between ugliness and sin in the symbolic world of the Middle Ages. Indeed, such an effect would be in line with conventional modes of iconographic representation. The features of the devils that appear in medieval painting are often so distorted – so unhuman – that the figures appear to wear masks. In like vein, the pictorial arts portrayed Jews in caricature-like fashion, emphasising their long beards and curved noses.[20] Finally, the tormentors and executioners, especially those in representations of the Passion, were endowed with grotesque or distorted features.[21] It is therefore noteworthy that in the case of the Toledo *St Catherine* play, the tormentors in all probability wore masks; they also wore padding that made one hunchbacked, another potbellied, and gave the others an exaggerated chest or buttocks (*Teatro en Toledo* 64).

The wearing of masks by the antagonists in the Toledo Corpus Christi plays is a connotative marker that calls attention to the antagonistic role such characters play in the sacred dramas. To the extent that, as a means of dramatic expression, the mask participates in a system of theatrical signs whose primary element is not necessarily the written text, the Toledo plays constitute an exemplary illustration of the way in which masks form part of a vestimentary code that is in turn inserted into the larger system of theatrical signs.

Princeton University

NOTES

1. This preliminary investigation of masks in the medieval Peninsular theatre owes an obvious debt to Meg Twycross and Sarah Carpenter 'Masks in Medieval English Theatre: The Mystery Plays' *Medieval English Theatre* 3:1 (1981) 7–44; 3:2 (1981) 69–113.
2. *Remedio de jugadores* (Burgos, 1519), fols 28^v–30^v.
3. Fray Francisco de Alcocer *Tratado del juego* (Salamanca, 1559) 302–5.
4. *Le donne vestono generalmente di negro et come anco gl'huomini, et intorno alla faccia portano un velo a guisa di suore, usando in testa tutto il manto, quale portano sì fattamente nel viso, che non si vede loro la faccia; ma se non fosse la pregmatica che il Re ha fatto sopra questo, anderiano coperte del tutto, come facevano pochi anni sono* ('The women are usually dressed in black, like the men, and across their faces they wear a veil like nuns, with the cloak right over the head, which they wear in such a fashion that their faces cannot be seen; and if it had not been for the pronouncement that the King has made on this matter, they would go around completely covered, as they used to some years ago') from 'Relation du voyage en Espagne de Camillo Borghese, auditeur de la chambre apostolique en 1594', edited A. Morel-Fatio in his *L'Espagne au XVIe et au XVIIe siècle* (Heilbronn, 1878) 178. In a book published in Madrid in 1641, Antonio de León Pinelo defends the custom of covering the entire face with a veil, but views as lascivious the practice of leaving the left eye uncovered. See his *Velos antiguos y modernos en los rostros de las mujeres: sus conveniencias y daños* 2 vols (Editorial Universitaria, Santiago de Chile, 1966) 2 327–33.

5. Carmen Bernis *Trajes y modas en la España de los Reyes Católicos. I. Las mujeres* (Consejo Superior de Investigaciones Científicas, Madrid, 1978) 17.
6. See Diego Sánchez de Badajoz *Recopilación en metro* (Sevilla, 1554) edited Frida Weber de Kurlat (Universidad de Buenos Aires, Buenos Aires, 1968) 243–6, 250–1.
7. ... *pónense otras caras de las que Nuestro Señor les quiso dar, faziéndose homarraches* ... ('donning faces other than those Our Lord was pleased to give them, making themselves into grotesques ...': quoted in Angel Gómez Moreno 'Teatro religioso medieval en Avila' *El Crotalón* 1 (1984) 770). The text refers specifically to the post-Christmas celebration of the feasts of the Holy Innocents, St John the Evangelist, and St Stephen.
8. 'The word *velati* reveals that the boys were considered as representing the shepherds' (Richard B. Donovan C.S.B. *The Liturgical Drama in Medieval Spain* (Pontifical Institute of Mediaeval Studies, Toronto, 1958) 126).
9. The costume is very similar to that worn even in this century in performances of the religious dance of St John the Baptist in Mallorca. At Felanitx and Pollensa, for example, St John wore a mask, a wig, and a crown. The dance was performed in religious and civic processions at least as far back as the sixteenth century. See Gabriel Llompart 'La danza religiosa de Sant Joan Pelós en las Islas Baleares' *Revista de Dialectología y Tradiciones Populares* 23 (1967) 273–87.
10. Karl Young *The Drama of the Medieval Church* 2 vols (Clarendon Press, Oxford, 1933) 1 293. Similarly, in a *Visitatio* from the Sainte-Chapelle (Paris) the Maries appear *vultus sive facies semitecte* (1:287).
11. Thus, in a *Visitatio* from Le Mans the clerics who represent the Maries wear white dalmatics and appear *opertis capitibus candidis amictibus* (Young 1 289). Collins explains the infrequent use of veils in the liturgical plays by the need to keep the ears uncovered: 'For actors of women's roles in the plays the exposure of the ears is crucial to hearing the musical cues, which cannot be lip-read as spoken dialogue can' (Fletcher Collins Jr *The Production of Medieval Church Music-Drama* (The University Press of Virginia, Charlottesville, 1972) 284).
12. Rainer Warning 'On the Alterity of Medieval Religious Drama' *New Literary History* 10 (1978–1979) 269.
13. For a description and discussion of the properties and costumes used in the Toledo Corpus Christi plays, see Carmen Torroja Menéndez and María Rivas Palá 'Teatro en Toledo en el siglo XV: *Auto de la Pasión* de Alonso del Campo' *Boletín de la Real Academia Española* Anejo 35 (Madrid, 1977) 54–70.
14. Devils normally wore masks in the medieval religious theatre. See Allardyce Nicoll *Masks, Mimes, and Miracles: Studies in the Popular Theatre* (George Harrap, London, 1931) 190.
15. Toledo was not the only Castilian town where actors portraying Jews characteristically wore masks. Three *reales* were paid for the rental of masks and robes for the 'Jews' who participated in the Corpus Christi festivities at Salamanca in 1531. See Ricardo Espinosa Maeso 'Ensayo bibliográfico del maestro Lucas Fernández (¿1474?–1542)' *Boletín de la Real Academia Española* 10 (1923) 582.
16. *Teatro en Toledo* 69. *Máscaras singulares* were also used in the play of St Catherine, presumably by the tormentors (*Teatro en Toledo* 64).

17. These appear to be the same sort of wigs worn by the apostles, since the accounts for 1493 mention that five *reales* were paid for wigs for the apostles and patriarchs (*Teatro en Toledo* 189).
18. Twycross and Carpenter (*3:1* 17–18), quoting Durandus of Mende, observe that long, flowing hair was an iconographic convention denoting sanctity.
19. ... *porque los que representan con las carátulas dan a la voz mayor sonido* ... ('... because those who act with masks give a greater resonance to the voice ...': Sebastián de Covarrubias *Tesoro de la lengua castellana o española* (Ediciones Turner, Madrid, 1977) 299).
20. Bernhard Blumenkranz *Le Juif médiéval au miroir de l'art chrétien* (Etudes Augustiniennes, Paris, 1966) 20–39. For the identification of the Jew with the devil in the Middle Ages, see Daniel Iancu-Agou 'Le Diable et le Juif: Représentations médiévales iconographiques et écrites' in *Le Diable au Moyen Age* (Université de Provence, Aix-en-Provence, 1979) 259–76.
21. This diabolic connection is especially apparent in such paintings as Bosch's Ghent *Christ Carrying the Cross* or his Princeton *Christ Before Pilate*.

HOLY WEEK PERFORMANCES OF THE PASSION IN SPAIN:
Connections with Medieval European Drama
Rafael Portillo & Manuel J. Gomez Lara

In our article published in *Medieval English Theatre 8:2* (1986) 119–133, we made a typological study of the vestiges of dramatic performances of the Passion which we had found in Andalusia. In that article, a series of ceremonies related to scenes of the Passion were described and were found to be connected with medieval performances in England and the rest of Europe. Some of these points of contact were meetings, races, blessings, and examples of Depositions, almost all of which have no dialogue. The intention of this article is to extend the field of study to the rest of Spain and thus, following a preliminary encounter with what remains of dramatic performances of the Passion, taking a first step towards what could be a full research project on these phenomena. Here, we shall not deal with the several really theatrical performances of the Passion which exist throughout most of Spain – Valmaseda (Vizcaya), Riogordo (Malaga), Besalú (Gerona), Carvera (Lérida), Esparraguera (Barcelona), Moncada (Valencia), etc. – but with official religious quasi-liturgical ceremonies which involve numerous theatrical elements.

Several sources have been used as the basis of this study including among others and in spite of deficiencies in systematisation, Luis de Agromayor's book *España en fiestas* (Aguilar, Madrid, 1987). It should be pointed out that there is still no exhaustive and systematic study of all the folk festivals which take place in Spain, nor is there a work which studies surviving dramatic phenomena in their relation to the cycles of the calendar. This article intends to open the door to serious research into all the ceremonies which in form and communicative intention go back to the Middle Ages, above all, into those that have a direct relation with European and, in particular, English drama.

First of all, according to Agromayor's list, it is clear that the element common to the majority of these dramatic phenomena related to the Passion is the open air setting on a mountain or hill called 'Calvary' in the local toponomy. There the markers of the fourteen Stations of the *Via Crucis* (podiums with Crosses, landmarks, etc.) are still partially or totally preserved. In some towns, a church or hermitage crowns the mountain top. A makeshift or permanent pulpit or even a sepulchre are also frequent.[1] Towards such a setting, a procession leaves from a nearby church, normally with a statue of Christ Crucified or carrying the Cross and another of the Virgin. The basis of the ceremony performed on this site is a sermon of the Passion delivered by a priest and this is sometimes preceded by pious comments at precise points along the route.

As in many Andalusian villages – Alcalá de Guadaira (Sevilla), Carcabuey and Doña Mencía (Córdoba) – in places like Bercianos de Aliste (Zamora), Alcañiz and Calanda (Teruel) or Peraleda de la Mata (Cáceres), the sermon narrates the Passion, substituting for a dramatisation of the events. In the same way, we also find sermons of the Passion in big towns like Valladolid and Salamanca; in these cases they are not preached in a rural space but in a square with a clear civic importance. Hence the sermon is the central and perhaps most common element in many celebrations of the Passion in Europe, precisely because of its liturgical nature. The sermon, as a devout practice, and the Stations of the Cross in particular, must have provoked and influenced a good deal of literature in the vernacular. In the English cycles, the dramatisations of the Passion do not exclude the sermons. In fact they are integrated into particular episodes, and fulfil various functions within the dramatic text. In N. Town, the *Passion Play 1* is preceded by two 'prologues' (one by Satan and one by John the Baptist) which explain the theological significance of Christ's drama. Between *Passion Play 1* and *2*, there are 'doctors' that explain the exegesis of some of the passages to be performed:[2]

> To þe pepyl not lernyd I stonde as a techer,
> Of þis processyon to ȝeve informacion;
> And to them þat be lernyd as a ghostly precher,
> That in my rehersayl they may haue delectacyon.
>   28: 9–12 (page 294)

This dual aim, to teach and delight, is made even clearer when, after the doctors' prologue, a messenger makes his way through the crowd shouting: 'Tydyngys, tydyngys' (29.89 *sd*: page 299). His appearance speeds up the action by telling, in the past, those parts of the Passion which are not performed, thus fulfilling a role very similar to that of the commentators during the different episodes of the *Via Crucis*.

Insufficient emphasis has been placed on the importance that the *Via Crucis* has had in the shaping of Medieval European dramaturgy. Prior to continuing with a typology of surviving dramatic elements, it is essential to reflect on the *Via Crucis* itself, not only as a useful unifying element but as a representative pattern of the Passion which was familiar both to author and audience.

The *Via Crucis* was a devout practice which systematised the several expiatory rites which existed in the Late Middle Ages. The mimesis of the road to Calvary – the procession – had great dramatic possibilities, being a path through the different Stations where we find the climactic moments of the Passion. A marked area which is usually circular and divided into Stations takes us back to the beginnings of open-air theatre throughout Europe, and suggests that it was a form of sanctifying secular ground. It should be understood that the procession allows the public to take part in a ceremony whose aim is none other than the collective purgation of sin. The Cross – the central element of the Good Friday and Easter Sunday ceremonies – is the focal point of the procession and a symbol of martyrdom, and by identifying with this, the participants in the procession become the focus of the ritual. Therefore it is not surprising that Franciscans were the great promoters of the Stations of the Cross, as this Order gave great emphasis to popular religious festivals and open air preaching. In fact, it is clearly documented that the Franciscans began the Holy Week celebrations in several parts of Spain, as in Híjar (Teruel) where the parish archives make it clear that they started the processions in 1517.

There are obvious relationships between dramatic and liturgical features and the fact that the first dramatists were probably clergymen allows us to believe that they made use of an existing model which involved procession and performance. Therefore, it is possible to make use of the *Via Crucis* as a guideline for our study of these dramatic phenomena.

In the setting we have described, the statues of Jesus and the Virgin carry out a series of movements which represent the crucial moments of the road to Calvary. These are organised not only according to the Gospels but according to the apocryphal sources of the fourteen Stations of the Cross. Most of these ceremonies involve meetings between different statues which are carried on floats: Jesus and the Virgin, the central characters, as well as others, as St John and the Three Maries.

In Lorca (Murcia), on the morning of Good Friday, there is a *Via Crucis* procession during which a meeting takes place between Jesus and his Mother. This is probably a dramatisation of the fourth Station when they meet on the road to Calvary. Something similar takes place in Chinchón (Madrid) when on the Saturday night the Passion is shown by means of a series of scenes (*pasos*) performed in different parts of the town. The sixth scene shows a meeting between the Virgin and Jesus which is marked by the playing of drums. In Benetuser (Valencia), in what can be called the re-enactment of a very old and previously forgotten tradition, similar meetings take place but this time real people play the parts. A different form of these meetings is found in Alcira (Valencia) where the floats carrying the scene of Christ being lowered from the Cross meets the float that carries the Virgin. This may be associated with the passage of the *Pietà* which corresponds to the thirteenth Station of the Cross.

The main sources for these meetings are largely apocryphal.[3] In the English cycles, the influence of these is obvious; for instance, in the York Cycle, in the play known as 'The Shearmen's Play', or *The Road to Calvary*, we find St John is about to tell Mary that Christ is already on his way to death. Although the next page is lost we can assume that a meeting has taken place because what follows suggests that some kind of dialogue has been performed between Mary and Jesus. In N.Town there is no such meeting but when the Virgin has been informed by Mary Magdalene that her son is to be executed, she is given a speech which takes the form of a *planctus* or lament: a popular genre in medieval European theatre, depicted in Spanish iconography by the very popular image of the *Dolorosa*.

The second of the meetings in the *Via Crucis* is that which takes place at the sixth Station: Veronica wiping the face of Christ. The source of this is the apocryphal narration *Mors Pilati qui Iesum condenavit*. In Spain, this meeting gives rise to many dramatic possibilities: in some cases Veronica is portrayed simply as a woman carrying a cloth with Christ's image painted on it, in other cases a more complex dramatisation occurs. For instance, in Mairena del Alcor (Sevilla), a woman playing the part of Veronica climbs onto the float carrying Christ, holding a folded cloth; when she holds it up to Jesus's face, it unfolds to reveal the Saviour's image. This scene is part of the N. Town Passion, where a stage direction states: '*and sche whypyth his face with here kerchy*' (32.44 sd: page 326).

Another ceremony clearly associated with the meetings is that of the blessings, normally carried out by an articulated statue of Christ carrying the Cross. By means of a mechanical device Jesus's right hand makes the sign of the Cross before the public. This seems to be related to the third meeting of the *Via Crucis*, which appears in the eighth Station when Jesus meets the women of Jerusalem. This ceremony, with its source in the Gospels, is clearly reflected in the English cycles (Chester page 306; N.Town pages 324–5; York page 310) which reproduce Luke 23:27–31 almost exactly. In Málaga, the statue of Jesús *el Rico* has an articulated hand which not only blesses the crowd but in the past used to point at one of three convicts who would consequently be set free, thus showing Christ's divine power over human laws. In Aguilar de la Frontera (Córdoba) and Tobarra (Albacete), among many other towns, the statue of Jesus blesses those who attend the procession. The blessing not only relates to the meeting in the eighth Station of the Cross but may also be related to the medieval literary tradition of the *Improperia*; this idea may have originated in Luke 23:24, but it is also present in Psalm 66 of the Vulgate: *Deus misereatur nostri et benedicat nobis*. The idea of the blessing is related not only to the words of condemnation and consolation spoken to the women on the road to Calvary but also the ceremony of the *Adoratio Crucis* which occurs during the service on Good Friday. This includes the so-called *Improperia* ('Reproaches'). Moreover, the concept of divine mercy as present in that passage from the Gospel is clearly involved here. As Rosemary Woolf has pointed out, in English cycles the blessing is given at the moment of crucifixion.[4]

In the *Via Crucis* we also find Christ's being lowered from the Cross and his burial. This corresponds to Stations thirteen and fourteen and was known in the Middle Ages as the *Depositio Sepulchri*.[5] It gave rise to many church ceremonies and now involves an articulated statue of Christ Crucified which when lowered from the Cross is moved into a lying position. The passage which appears in the English cycles is still carried out in Spain by means of sculptures of Jesus and Mary and several human actors. In the large majority of cases the ceremony takes place on Good Friday and we find its source in the liturgical drama originated after the Benedictine Reform. This is described by bishop Æthelwold in his *Regularis Concordia*: at that time the ceremony was performed inside churches, which is still done in Peraleda de la Mata, although it is usually performed in the open air on the so-called Calvary.

There are many variants of this ceremony, almost as many as there are performances. In Bercianos de Aliste and Peraleda de la Mata it is part of the liturgy of Good Friday and the deacon and subdeacon themselves lower the figure of Christ, then place it in the arms of a statue of Mary and finally lay it out in a glass coffin. At this point, a procession is organised in which the coffin is carried and later it is either returned to the church or left in a kind of sepulchre. In Bercianos de Aliste money is collected during the procession to pay for the burial. In San Vicente de la Sonsierra (Logroño), a sepulchre has been cut out of a rock for that purpose. In other places like Híjar and Lorca, the existence of a small church which crowns the top of Calvary would seem to indicate that the burial took place there.

In the medieval English cycles this scene follows the story of the Passion according to St John (all have the figure of Nicodemus who is mentioned solely in this Gospel). In the case of N.Town, the ceremony includes the scene of the *Pietà*:

> Here Joseph and Nychodemus takyn Cryst of þe cros, on on o ledyr and þe tother on an-other leddyr. And qwan [he] is had down, Joseph leyth him in oure Ladys lappe ... 34:121 *sd* (page 311)

Considering that the Death of the Saviour (Play 32), which requires a human actor, appears in this same cycle in a different play from that of the Deposition and Burial (Play 34), it is possible that an articulated statue of Christ – like the 'puppets' employed in many Easter Sepulchre ceremonies – was used for the scene described in this stage direction. Such an arrangement would certainly facilitate the performance of other actions such as the piercing of Christ's side and the flowing of blood from his wound onto the eyes of Longinus (34:100 *sd*: page 341).[6]

Usually, the episodes of the Passion and Death of Christ are complemented with ceremonies performed on Easter Sunday. The central figure is Christ Resurrected, which is usually carried from the same place or church where the tomb is found as well as involving the Virgin and the Three Maries. This was common practice in all the important churches in Europe and in some cases a fifteenth Station was added to the *Via Crucis*, consisting of the Holy Cross being discovered by St Helen in what seems to be a vestige of the medieval *Adoratio Crucis*. This ceremony closes the celebrations of the *Via Crucis* with the symbol of Death turned into a symbol of glory.

Statues of the Virgin and the Risen Christ meet in Villanueva de la Serena (Badajoz), in Carrión de Calatrava (Ciudad Real), and in Coria del Río (Sevilla) among other places. These meetings symbolise the conversion of sorrow to joy because of the Resurrection and usually involve the change of the colour of the statues' clothes from the black of mourning to white.[7] This is what happens in Villa del Río (Córdoba), where by means of a mechanical device, Mary's black cloak is removed to reveal a white cloak underneath. There is something similar in Peraleda de la Mata, when not only the statue of the Virgin but the Maries themselves (played by human actresses) undergo a similar transformation. This type of meeting comes from apocryphal sources: the *Gospel of St Bartholomew* and other medieval traditions which tell of the encounter between Christ and his Mother following the episode of Jesus and Mary Magdalene recounted in Luke 24:10.

Another way of enacting the same meeting involves the appearance of an angel which, by means of a pulley, descends from a cloud sphere located at first in a high place. It comes down to the point where the float carrying the Virgin is found and then uncovers the face or sometimes the whole statue which has been covered in mourning. This happens in villages like Aranda de Duero (Burgos), Peñafiel (Valladolid), and Tudela (Navarra). In Finisterre (Coruña), an angel delivers a speech announcing Christ's Resurrection. The appearance of this heavenly figure is connected with the announcement of Death and Resurrection, the *psychopompos*, which must have been a general practice in the past in Spain and other European countries. In the *Mystery of Elche*, which is still performed, an angel descends from heaven inside a sphere, which represents a cloud, to announce the future death of the Virgin and her meeting with Christ in Heaven. These announcements of rejoicing because of the Resurrection also appear in the English cycles. In N.Town it is Christ's own words which make this clear:

> Now dere modyr my leve I take
> joye in hert and myrth 3e make
> Ffor deth is deed and lyff doth wake
> now I am resyn fro my graue.　　　35:117–120 (page 353)

There are other kinds of meeting which are more complicated from a theological point of view. These occur on Easter Sunday and involve a statue of Mary and allegories of Christ Triumphant. In Benacazón (Sevilla), the Virgin meets the baby Jesus who carries the emblems of the Passion whereas in Espartinas (Sevilla), she meets the Eucharist which is carried in a monstrance. In both cases the ceremony takes us back to its liturgical origin because it substitutes the actor or statue with the symbol of Christ Triumphant.

Having said all this, it would seem to be worthwhile to use the organising principle of the *Via Crucis* to help us understand the different vestiges of drama in Spanish Holy Week festivals. The Stations of the Cross may throw new light on medieval dramas of the Passion in Europe and, more particularly, in medieval English texts. At the same time a deeper understanding of the Holy Week celebrations in Spain might solve many enigmas about European religious theatre, particularly considering the many similarities between the vestiges we have listed and the existing English plays.

Universidad de Sevilla

NOTES

1. There are places called Calvary with traces of previous forms of Stations of the Cross in many towns including Alcalá de Guadaira (Sevilla), Bercianos de Aliste (Zamora), Híjar

(Teruel), Jumilla and Lorca (Murcia), Peraleda de la Mata and Valverde del la Vera (Cáceres), Puente Genil, Priego, and Torrecampo (Córdoba), Ríogordo (Málaga), and San Vicente de la Sonsierra (Logroño).
2. For N.Town, see *The N.Town Play* edited Stephen Spector *EETS SS 11* (1991). The prologues of Satan and John the Baptist are 26:1–164, pages 245–51. In Spector's edition, the procession of Apostles and its interpretation by the two Doctors is put at the end of *Passion Play 1*, though it is fairly clear from the following stage direction the Contemplacio's speech follows on directly from it. For quotations from the other plays, see *The York Mystery Plays* edited Richard Beadle (Edward Arnold, London, 1982) and *The Chester Mystery Plays* edited R.M. Lumiansky and David Mills *EETS SS 3* (1974).
3. *Los evangelios apócrifos* edited Aurelio de los Santos Otero (Biblioteca de autores cristianos, Madrid, 1985) 421; see *The Ante Nicene Fathers Volume 8: The Twelve Patriarchs ... Apocrypha ...* edited Alexander Roberts and James Donaldson (T. and T. Clark, Edinburgh: reprinted Eerdmans, Grand Rapids MI, 1986): *Gospel of Nicodemus* (Second Greek form) 429–30 for meetings; *The Death of Pilate, who Condemned Jesus* 466-7 for Veronica.
4. Rosemary Woolf *The English Mystery Plays* (Routledge and Kegan Paul, London, 1972; reprinted 1978) 261.
5. See E.K. Chambers *The Mediaeval Stage* 2 vols (Oxford University Press, London, 1903) 2 16–25 and 306–15 for details of the Deposition ceremony and the Easter Sepulchre.
6. See Margaret Aston 'Iconoclasm in England: Official and Clandestine' in *Iconoclasm vs. Art and Drama* edited Clifford Davidson and A.E. Nichols (Medieval Institute Publications, Kalamazoo, 1989) 47–91, especially 59–60. See also in the same volume, Pamela Sheingorn '"No Sepulchre on Good Friday": The Impact of the Reformation on the Easter Rites in England' 145–63, especially 153–5.
7. St Bernard in his sermons about Easter, especially in *Sermo Primus: De Opprobiis Iudeorum*, where he makes a curious reference to this colour as a symbol of the Resurrection: *Inde est quod stola candida et fulgureo vultu testis quoque resurrectionis apparet* ('For this reason the witness of the Resurrection (the angel) appeared with a white cloak and a flaming face'); *Obras completas de San Bernardo* (Biblioteca de autores cristianos, Madrid, 1986) 4 73; *PL183* Col. 277.

THE *FESTA D'ELX*:
Civic Devotion, Display and Identity
Pamela M. King

The early Catalan sung drama of the Mystery of the Assumption of the Virgin, otherwise known as the *Festa*, has been performed in the basilica of Sta Maria in Elche, complete with elaborate aerial machinery, continuously since the fifteenth century. Texts and records become more numerous in the seventeenth and eighteenth centuries, but the play is of clear medieval origins. Its self-consciously eclectic mixture of monodic song and late medieval polyphony, quasi-liturgical procession and baroque stage machinery, testifies to its almost unbroken evolution. There were years when it was not performed, of course, when the basilica of Sta Maria fell down in the eighteenth century, and during epidemics of yellow fever and cholera in the nineteenth. In 1885, performance was deferred only until October, when it was offered in thanksgiving for relief from the epidemic. Cholera has, typically, not struck Elche since. It was the Civil War of 1936–41, however, which caused a wilful and premeditated attempt to stop performance for all time. Hence, to understand the *Festa* of the late twentieth century as a civic event, whilst acknowledging its continuity, it is as important not to ignore in it dimensions of postwar reconstruction not, perhaps, too dissimilar to the York Mystery Plays' revival for the Festival of Britain in 1951. This paper will not discuss the nature or the history of the play itself,[1] but will look at aspects of its economic organisation, the personnel involved in it, and its non-mimetic festive context, in order to explore the relationship between civic-religious drama and the community.

A lack of documentary sources makes it impossible to establish how the *Festa* was formally organised and funded before the sixteenth century. Earliest records[2] indicate that the performance was the object of the patronage of one noble Elche family, the Perpinyas, the earliest documentation of this coming from 26 September 1530. At the same time there existed in the town a *Confraria de la Mare de Déu* dedicated to the celebration of Marian festivals culminating in the *Festa*. The chapel of this confraternity was the little hermitage of S. Sebastian built in 1489 and just around the corner from Sta Maria. On 11 March 1609, the municipal council took on the financing of performance out of local taxes and revenues levied from individual trades for the purpose. At this stage in its organisational evolution, the office of the honorary *cavallers* ('knights'), answerable to the municipal government for aspects of performance, was instituted. These honorary posts are still symbolically represented by the three dignitaries who sit at the end of the *andador* ('walkway') throughout the performance, coming and going to fetch each group of performers for their entrances from that same chapel of S. Sebastian, in more recent times used as dressing rooms. Over the ensuing three centuries, the organisation of the *Festa* became an established part of municipal government with various trades' associations of devotional leanings, as well as local wealthy magnates, making their own special contributions.

The church of Sta Maria itself was also involved throughout the period of the earlier records in the organisation, training, and supplying of the singers. This duality of organisation was not without its potential for friction, coming to a head in 1734 and 1740. As a result, in the 1790s a clear division was made, whereby the town was responsible for the performance of the *Festa* itself, but the church took care of the processions, Masses, and other surrounding events and also looked after the church building. This organisational arrangement is reported to have led to the slow deterioration of the authenticity and quality of performance, particularly in the late nineteenth century, for in 1924 Pere Ibarra, an Elche-born intellectual, and others formed the *Junta Protectora al Patronat Nacional* ('Committee for the Protection of the National Heritage') in an attempt to restore performance to what was then perceived to be an authentic state on the evidence of the available historical documents.[3]

Further opinion and legislation followed in 1930 concerning the rôle of the *Patronato* or guild which has traditionally attended to the organisation of the *Festa*.[4] It was suggested then that the area of the *Patronato*'s competence was in urgent need of formal demarcation, that it should not involve itself in public affairs, but that it should restrict itself to the 'artistic purity' of the *Festa* and all matters pertaining to it. As guardian of the *Festa* it required autonomy from interference from the *Ajuntamiento*, the Town Hall. It was at this time suggested that there should be three types of person recruited to the *Patronato*, categories which bear some relevance to its present day social make-up: those born in Elche, those elected from current residents, and, in addition, young and active people who are judged to be suited to the task and unlikely to renounce their traditions. In effect, the present day *Patronato* is made up of businessmen, professionals, and young artists and poets, all of whom have a long-standing connection with the town.

The following year further attention was drawn to the national significance of the *Festa* and the necessity of instituting clear measures for its conservation.[5] Singled out for emphasis was the importance of traditional sung theatre to all musical history and to folklore, particularly when the material was passed down from father to son. There was a deeply felt danger that without regulation the original would become infested with impurities and be lost little by little. Commercial tourism, now recognised as a controllable and positive force in the preservation of popular works of art, was then perceived as a risk factor. It was suggested that the way in which the *Festa* could best be protected was by declaring it a national monument. This duly took place, under the Republic, in September 1931.

It was, of course, not many years thereafter that Civil War brought an abrupt halt to all such activities. The basilica of Sta Maria was gutted by fire and then used as a garage, so that in 1941 it was in need of complete restoration. The Franco government in Madrid shouldered the burden, appointing a National Committee for the restoration of the *Festa* under the then Minister of National Education.[6] A local sub-committee was established simultaneously. This *Junta*, established as a controlling and enabling body, was transformed in 1948 into the present two-tier *Patronato* which was perceived as the means by which the *Festa* could be funded and also controlled by the state in perpetuity.[7] In the immediate post-war Franco era, there is every indication that, because of its bringing together of secular and ecclesiastical authority in the production of an intensely traditional festival, the *Festa* became tantamount to an organ of political propaganda. In any case, the channelling of energy in a community into religious rituals has been observed by anthropologists as consistently characterising societies in which the men are politically comparatively impotent.[8]

The initial brief of the *Patronato* was that it should concern itself with guaranteeing annual performance conforming to traditionally established modes, that it should see to the conservation of the church building itself, and that it should propagate information about the *Festa*. Its honorary presidents were to be the (national) Minister of Education and the Director General of Fine Arts. The first vice-president was the mayor of Elche, the second the chief priest of Sta Maria, both *ex officio*. There was then to be a third vice-president, a secretary, and eight ordinary members nominated by the Ministry of Education. This made up the national committee. As was the case with the *Junta* for restoration, a local *Patronato* was also established to deal with the actual running of the *Festa*.

The national committee was given three months, May to July 1948, to draw up its full constitution, which was further amended in December 1950, amplifying in particular upon the function of the local body. The national body gained two more honorary vice-presidents, the Bishop of Orihuela and the Civil Governor of Alicante, as well as having the number of ordinary members increased to fourteen. The local *Patronato* was led by the mayor, the chief priest of Sta Maria, and another managing president, with below them a vice-president, secretary, treasurer, archivist, and twelve ordinary members. This local body was obliged by the constitution to take on all the ongoing work to which the *Festa* gives rise, holding regular meetings on the first Wednesday of each month and Friday of the same week, with a provision for extraordinary meetings to be held on the instigation of the president or any five members. The treasurer was to be responsible for accounting to the national *Junta* for the annual expenditure of centrally supplied finance.

Also established at the same time was the *Capella* of the *Misteri*, a standing organisation of great importance intended to preserve the purity of both music and text and to prepare local people of aptitude for performance. Seventy men and thirty boys currently make up the membership of the *Capella*, allowing ample provision for understudying rôles from year to year. Each year, on 6 August, a ceremony called the *Prova de veus* is held in the Town Hall, presided over by the mayor, obviously a symbolic occasion, serious auditioning having taken place much sooner, but harking back to the era when the town governors administered the *Festa* directly. Masters of the *Capella* were charged with responsibility for musical and scenic production, and so were, and have remained, the chief aesthetic arbiters. With that, the structure which has financed and governed the *Festa* ever since was finally in place.

Since the post-war re-establishment of the *Festa* as a National Monument with direct state funding and its two-tier administrating *Patronato*, annual performances have progressed smoothly,[9] with a replacement of all costumes in 1960, the same year in which the music was first recorded, and, in 1965, the first filming of the performance for television. The constitution of the *Patronato*, though largely the same in outline, has undergone several modifications of detail. In 1974, the number of ordinary members of the local body was doubled from twelve to twenty-four, with the twelve new members to hold office for six years only, rather than for life. In 1986 the number was again increased to forty.[10]

Folques, who wrote a history of the *Patronato*, concludes by stating that the reconstruction of the *Festa* under direct state control and finance during the 1940s and beyond is tangible evidence of Spain's victory over Communism. This published attitude perhaps begins to explain some of the perceptible tensions in present-day Elche surrounding the preservation and performance of the *Festa*. Undoubtedly, in the Franco era, the *Festa d'Elx* signified by tangible and popular means the reunification of church and state. On 1 November 1950, for example, Pius XII's proclamation of the dogma of the Assumption was the subject of enthusiastic and special celebration in Elche.[11]

Since Franco's death and the shift in Spanish politics towards the secular Left, another influential lobby of opinion, which is in many ways ideologically incompatible with the immediate post-war reconstruction, has become concerned with the *Festa*. Many of those actively involved in preserving and studying the *Festa* are secular 'leftist' intellectuals, interested in the performance for its aesthetic qualities. Its potential as a tourist attraction, with all the economic benefits attendant on that, has also not escaped notice. Indeed the *Patronato*'s function in promoting the *Festa* has become a serious part of tourist publicity, and the performance and peripheral events are 'media events', with, unfortunately, many of the best vantage points being reserved for the cameras. Nonetheless, all groups unite in a desire to preserve the *Festa*, with much continuing argument about what constitutes 'purity'. There have been what might be seen as attempts to purge it of twentieth-century intrusions, but there again, it is difficult to strike a balance between the unselfconscious evolution of a popular festival event and the loss of, or contamination of, its aesthetic coherence.

The late 1980s saw another change in administration, as state control of the *Festa* was devolved to the *Generalitat Valenciana* who keep close and direct control over the financing of the event. The *Patronato* still administers, but real economic control lies elsewhere with the regional Department of Education and Science which clearly sees the way forward for the *Festa* as lying in the secular sphere. It is packaged as a facet of the distinctively Catalan culture, aimed at foreign visitors who want to do more than lie on the beach, but who are in no sense experts. It has been simultaneously brought to the notice of international scholarship, particularly with the sponsoring of the travelling exhibition, *Món i Misteri de la Festa d'Elx*, which was assembled in 1985. Administrative devolution was most evidently marked, however, by the construction of *La Casa de la Festa*, opened in 1988, a building round the corner from the basilica with the provision of exhibition and archive space, meeting rooms, costume stores and dressing rooms. Ironically, the construction of the *Casa* breaches tradition in that it removes the vestigial rôle played by the hermitage of S. Sebastian, for so long part of the history of the *Festa*. Since 1989, major repair and replacement work has been done on the scenery and aerial machinery too.[12]

A sense of the shifts and balances in the perceived rôle of the *Festa* in the post-war era is reinforced by the attitudes of participants. Fortunately the local press constantly and assiduously interviews those involved every year in special supplements devoted to the subject, so there is no shortage of accessible raw material. Certain elements clearly emerge, such as the immense status which goes with being a performer and the clear hierarchy of rôles, the continuity of performance achieved within individual careers, as boy singers become adult singers and tasks are passed down the generations of an individual family. Least clear are the answers to the often-asked question, 'And what does the *Festa* mean to you?'

There are a total of twenty-six boy singers involved in the production, all under the age of fourteen.[13] The reminiscences of Emilio Señaris, a 'young veteran', afford some access to their impressions.[14] At twenty-eight years old he already has nineteen years' experience in the *Festa*. Brought up in Brazil until he was six, he first took the part of an angel at the age of nine. He recalls vividly the impression from above when the doors of heaven first open, of the immense heat which rises from the church below, and of the huge height when you are hanging above it waiting to descend. Asked whether he ever suffered from vertigo when playing the angel in the *mangrana* ('pomegranate', the first aerial machine to appear), he replied that he simply recalls it being a great adventure and says that he began so young that it did not occur to him to worry. It was later when he was on the *araceli* that he remembers having more time to imagine possible consequences. But, he adds, as soon as you begin to sing, you forget all that. The worst moments on the aerial machines are, therefore, those which involve hanging in mid-air and doing nothing, as, for instance, when the *araceli* listens to St Thomas's solo to the Virgin, or considerably higher, when the Trinity hangs in mid-air while the Virgin is crowned. In general, however, he recalls that as a child it was the height which he enjoyed. Certainly the boys whom I spoke to in 1988, who had descended on the aerial machines, were much more concerned about how sore it was on the knees than the giddying height from which they are lowered. Señaris claims that participation for him is more than a religious or cultural experience, but has become something which he simply cannot live without.

The distinct impression that, for the performers, the music is everything, is borne out in all accounts. The machinery is something to which they become accustomed to a lesser or greater extent, usually from an age when unquestioning faith in the adults who operate it – and, who knows, in the protective powers of the Virgin – means there is mercifully little anxiety expended on being suspended on the end of a hemp rope and some primitive winching gear. The machinery is only in reality involved for one week in August, whereas the training of singers takes place in the *Capella* over several months. The master of the *Capella* has all the usual problems of those who train children, starting with mothers who wish their sons would spend their time doing 'something more practical'.[15] Antonio Berenguer Fuster describes the agonies of the cycle of preparation which begins in earnest after Easter. They are not able to do much prior to that because of the commitments which the boys have to school. The eternal problem is not only that of boys' voices breaking, but of competing with all the other distractions which attract boys of around thirteen, not least that in July they would rather be at the beach. When a boy is recruited, it is a complete lottery whether his voice will permit him to participate for one year or for four. This is particularly critical in the case of the Virgin Mary, who is, naturally, played by an older and more experienced boy singer.

More illuminating, perhaps, in terms of what the *Festa* has meant to the local populace are the reminiscences of retired performers. It seems to be the view that once an adult singer is cast in a rôle, he has a commitment for life.[16] The normal pattern is for a singer to begin in the crowd of Jews who interrupt the funeral and are then converted, from where, depending on the quality of his voice, he may move on to become an Apostle. The life of a performer then involves considerable sacrifices, of time for rehearsals and of holidays, with the constant obligation to exercise his voice. Retired performers share with the new generation the difficulty in defining what the magic of the *Festa* amounts to for them, but reach the same conclusion that it is the pure joy of the music, although in the older performers this is explicitly linked with focusing their faith in the Virgin.

The reflections of Ibarra Reyes, nicknamed 'Peny', who played second tenor amongst the Jews for thirty-seven years, are typical.[17] For him the *Festa* has been part of his whole life, as his father participated in it before the Civil War. The singers of the *Festa* were the supermen of his youth, and he describes his own admission to the *Capella* as a *sueño*, a dream come true. He cannot remember when he was not steeped in the music of the *Festa*, a great escape-valve like all the local traditional festivals in which he participated in his youth. His one regret is that he never had an exceptional solo voice. The *Capella* was for him one big family, but a traditional one which ends with his own generation. It is a source of regret that his son has showed little interest in following him in his obsession and a participation which he sees not only as a great source of pleasure but an honour.

The *Festa* also has its superstars. The rich baritone voice of Francisco Garcia Llinares,[18] in the rôle of St James, is perhaps the most memorable of all. He has been one of the elected delegates of the *Capella* on the local *Patronato* for fourteen years, but has participated in the *Festa* for thirty, having played the rôle of the Virgin, of an angel on the *araceli*, and part of the Trinity as a boy. He was, like most others, a Jew before being promoted to Apostle. He is a businessman, but his whole life and hobbies have been coloured by the *Festa*, as his chief interests are music and popular theatre. He finds the times when he feels that he has transmitted something (he does not say what) to his audience most rewarding, the most trying when there are internal divisions in the *Capella* to be resolved.

Sixto Marco claims that his St John is a very personal emotional interpretation based upon inspiration taken from art, from a conception of an apocalyptic visionary whom he compares with secular literary examples, but also infuses with something personal. The whole of the music conveys powerfully to him the sense that God, 'if he exists', is not dogmatic but welcoming. He does not see the performance bounded by the constraints either of religion or of theatre, but more than both. One of his three major occupations in life – along with football and painting – is opera, but he firmly feels that the *Misteri* is not designed for trained operatic voices, that the sound of the traditional singing of the boys especially does not appeal to the same taste as professional sopranos. The *Misteri* is for the people and of the people: there are many superb voices in Elche who are not in the *Capella* and who ought to be,[19] in his view. Others who play the rôle present slightly different views, one, notably, feeling that his obligation is to the text and to an interpretation of the rôle based on the 'real' St John, not mediated through any other art form. For him, the *Misteri* confirms his faith in the Virgin.[20] Another, Pedro Pomares, puts it even more strongly, stating that he feels sorry for those who have no faith, feeling that artistic and popular values in the *Festa* are necessarily secondary to the veneration of the Virgin.[21]

There is also a distinct category of performer, in that the rôles of St Peter, Christ on the *araceli*, and God the Father in the Coronation, must be played by priests. They must also, of course, have good voices. The Reverend Luis Lopez,[22] having played first God the Father, then St Peter, feels that although he is playing traditional priestly rôles (St Peter actually has to conduct the funeral ceremony of the Virgin) his prime responsibility remains, like the others, as a singer. For him personally it brings to life the realities of his faith. Clearly he is less coy about religious experience, and expresses himself in terms much less ambivalent than those of most of the participating laymen, who fight shy of expressions of spiritual certainty, favouring responses to the *Festa*'s qualities as a traditional cultural event.

Beyond the performers there are, of course, the many men who are involved in operating the machinery, organised by a 'stage manager' who directs operations during performance by a telephone link from the organ gallery. He is an important lay member of the local *Patronato*, but much of the setting up and superintending of prior arrangements within the church is undertaken by a sacristan. Each of the operatives has his own specific task, both within the tomb and above in the dome. These have been, in many cases, passed on from father to son. Despite a tradition of rivalries, therefore, laity and clergy continue to co-operate in bringing forth the annual production.

Most of the 'ordinary people' who are annually interviewed by the press about their reaction to the *Festa* and their assessment of its importance, have as much trouble expressing their answer as do the participants themselves. Thirteen of the fifty people interviewed[23] in one survey had never attended a performance, but still claimed that it is traditional, should never fall into the hands of professionals, and that it is in some way good for Elche to continue its tradition. The sense that it is good for the town is made more explicit by the number of people of all ages who believe that it should have more national television and radio coverage, although certain aspects seem to the outsider at least to have already become largely media events. The only interviewees who explicitly stated that the performance had chiefly a religious significance were, ironically, the young, who stayed away for this reason, and the elderly. The middle ground all prefer to use the words 'culture', 'tradition', and *'ilicitanismo'*, that is, in describing the event as peculiar to Elche – *Ilicitanos* are the people of Elche.

If one way in which the outsider can attempt to understand the nature of the *Festa* is by simply exploring the history and attitudes of those involved, another involves attempting to understand the formal semiotics presented by the event in its broader semi-mimetic festive contexts. To see the music-drama of the *Festa* on its two days of performance in the church of Sta Maria is to experience 'live' devotional theatre in every sense of the word. Anyone present in Elche for the *Festa* will observe, however, that it is impossible to delimit performance to the two halves of the play itself, played in the early evening of two consecutive days. The festival itself, as opposed to its narrowly mimetic components, begins with the symbolic *preuvas*, or tests, of the voices on 5 August, and of the angel's courage on the aerial machinery on 11 August, on which day in the Town Hall the budget of the *Festa* is formally approved. All of these events, formerly administrative, are now pure formalities, their preservation a part of the ritual enactment of the celebration of the Assumption in its widest festive sense. There again, the two halves of performance have a specific celebratory context which contributes much to the understanding of what the *Festa* actually means to the town of Elche.

After the preliminary ritualised preparations and public rehearsals, all of which carefully stoke anticipation and court considerable media interest, the beginning of the *Festa* proper, that is the public holiday, is marked by the *Nit de l'Albà*,[24] or 'white night', a firework display of impressive proportions during the official part of which a large cluster of fireworks in the shape of a palm is set off every five seconds. The display culminates at midnight with the lighting of over seven hundred rockets simultaneously on the top of the tower of the basilica, forming the shape of the biggest palm, the major agricultural crop of the city and also, of course, symbolic of the Assumption. The unanimous assent of the entire town is marked by the fact that the electricity supply is cut at the central power station so that the climax of the display can be appreciated in total darkness. After midnight the streets truly come to life with the less official, but no less traditional, fights with hand-rockets, carried on by gangs of youths until dawn.

The display involves a lot of family and commercial rivalry, with the desire to set off bigger and better fireworks. A programme[25] for the official display requests that no-one let off their fireworks until around 11.30. It includes the timetable of sponsored fireworks with the time they are to be set off at ten-, then five-second intervals from 11.15 onwards, and their location. Here the blend of the devotional, the civic, and the commercial which characterises the *Festa* is perfectly encapsulated. Most of the fireworks are listed as being sponsored by commercial companies, including Elche's many large shoe manufacturers, as well as hotels, restaurants, and insurance companies. The short line provided for a statement under each entry in the programme creates a certain sense of incongruity as, in among what amount to commercial advertisements, there are entries which show that some fireworks are sponsored by private individuals as memorials for their dead. The 1988 programme lists, for example.[26]

> 228. Calzados Pikolino's S.L.,   11.36.45
> Fabrica de Calzados,
> "Marca la moda, busca la marca"
> Desde el Banco Bilbao-Vizcaya
>
> 229. En Memoria de   11.46.40
> Manuel Peral Agullo
> Desde C.P. Candalix

Some express dedication to the Virgin, others do not. The *Patronato* of the *Festa* of course does its share of sponsoring, as does the *Ayuntamiento*, which is responsible for the last and biggest cluster on the church roof.

The references to the *Nit de L'Alba* begin in 1574. A deaf ear was turned to eighteenth-century prohibitions of fireworks pronounced by Carlos III, but the event led to the establishment of the town's very efficient fire brigade.[27] Carlos III's prohibition was founded partly on the disastrous effects which firework festivals had on a town's buildings, and even now in Elche the following day's papers are full of the night's disasters, though most of these arise from the later hand-rocket fights, which are every bit as dangerous as they look. In 1988 the fire chief hired reinforcements and mounted a four-point watch throughout the night. He advised all bars to take down canvas awnings and asked people not to go near waste ground on which there was combustible rubbish.[28] In the event, no buildings did catch light, although 253 people were reported to have been injured, seven seriously, three of whom lost fingers. At least three babies were among the injured, one, aged two months, having a lighted firework land in her perambulator.[29] Although all this is reported punctiliously and at length in the local newspapers, it seems that the toll is not thought to be either unusual or unacceptable.

The second night of the festival is very different in mood, as it involves the extended celebration of the Virgin's funeral after the performance of the *Vespra*, the first half of the play. This ends with the death of the Virgin and the *araceli's* descent to take up the soul. The second day's performance will begin with the funeral procession set within the play, interrupted most dramatically by the Jews who will be converted and assumed into the celebration. Throughout the night, the town continuously observes events which combine mourning and celebration, penance and holiday, united by procession. In the early evening, a ceramic portrait of the Virgin is set up outside the church. Young girls in traditional costume bring bunches of flowers to it. The secular entertainment continues with an invited group of musicians from overseas performing a *Serenade* to the Virgin on a platform erected outside the west door of the church. This music is always secular and light, of broad popular appeal, and has little connection with the main event beyond contiguity.

In the meantime, however, Masses are said inside the church around the statue of the Virgin which lies in state on her funeral bier in front of the high altar, and candle-sellers' stalls spring up, selling the candles which will be carried around the boundaries of the old town of Elche in the procession known as *La Roa*. Traditionally *La Roa* and the Masses were the means by which the faithful who came to Elche for the *Festa* passed the night, there being no room to accommodate them. The focus of this procession is penance and thanksgiving, and even nowadays some go barefoot, generally again the elderly who believe in the efficacy of *La Patrona*'s intervention for their sick and their dead. The whole town is united in its wakefulness as the procession of those keeping the vigil pass through streets full of revellers and stalls selling souvenirs and *churros*. The following morning the penitents are still walking but are joined by the costumed girls, members of the *Ayuntamiento*, the *Patronato*, and the entire cast, accompanied by a brass band, as the Virgin is carried around the town on her bier. Again, the mixture of civic celebration and devotion, as the bands play local folk tunes in competition with the Apostles' singing, objectifies the complexities of the meaning of the event.

A visit to Elche in August, therefore, alerts the spectator to the way in which the play not only divides into horizontal and vertical action within the church, but overflows the boundaries of both the space and time of *play* to embrace the boundaries of the old town and to occupy the intervening night. To return to Elche in December, however, is to be forced to acknowledge more radically that Elche's mimetic celebration of its patron saint in fact occupies the whole year. The celebration on 28 December of the less widely known *Venida de la Virgen*, not only contributes an additional dimension to the understanding of the main *Festa*, but has a distinct dramatic focus which is founded on local legend and which demonstrates exactly why the image of the Virgin of the *Festa* is of itself an object of veneration and is truly *La Virgen d'Elx*.

THE *FESTA D'ELX*: CIVIC DEVOTION, DISPLAY, AND IDENTITY

La Venida is a re-enactment of the legend of the arrival of the image of the Virgin in 1370, when a guard called Francisco Cantó, protecting the town from the incursions of invaders and pirates, discovered in the early hours of the morning an ark washed up on the beach bearing the words *Soc pera Elig* ('I am for Elche'). Cantó then galloped back to the town for help, the ark was collected by the townspeople, brought back with rejoicing, and enshrined in the church where the statue, or her successor, has been ever since.

The re-enactment of *La Venida* has developed as a complicated series of processions. It begins on the beach of Tamarit at dawn, where the image in the ark, already placed in the sea in a rubber inflatable boat, is 'discovered' by Cantó, a part played by an extremely accomplished horseman, in front of many citizens and the media. A Mass is said near the little hermitage which has been built on the site of the original one in which the ark was reputedly lodged while Cantó galloped to warn the citizens. The accompanying crowds then set out on foot or horseback with Cantó and the Virgin in a cart pulled by oxen, on the procession known as the *Romería*, accompanying the Virgin on the 20-kilometre journey to the town. What then happens is complex: this procession stops at another hermitage on the outskirts of the town, which stands in for the one at the beach, while Cantó executes a hazardous gallop through narrow cobbled streets, each year an attempt to break the record, to tell the townspeople to go to the beach. Another procession, a formal one including dignitaries and the usual brass bands, then sets out carrying huge palm fronds to meet the first one. Everyone then brings the Virgin into the town amid rejoicing, with fireworks being set off at every corner, church bells ringing, and streamers and balloons thrown from balconies along the route. When the Virgin arrives at the church, Mass is said, and she is serenaded, only to be brought out again the following day to be carried around the town, standing erect on a very elaborate *paso* in yet another procession led by Cantó on a fine dressage stallion and followed by ranks of dignitaries. For this procession the people lining the streets and walking with the Virgin carry red candles, the arrangement being similar to that of the *Róa*.

The details of the origins of the legend and aspects of its re-enactment have been studied in detail elsewhere,[30] but in the present context it illuminates certain points about the nature of Elche's festival which would otherwise remain obscure, even though it is in many respects a distinct event, undocumented before the eighteenth century, and organised by a separate body known as *La Sociedad Venida de la Virgen*. It is not a festival of medieval origins, therefore, but a mimetic-processional realisation of a medieval legend. What makes it particularly dramatic and incidentally characteristic of its flourishing in the nineteenth century, is the elaboration of the character of Cantó as a romantic hero. Playing opposite the actor who takes the rôle of Cantó is the statue of the Virgin Mary. If it is unclear in the *Festa* in August whether it is the 'real' Virgin Mary or the statue which is venerated by the town, the question is resolved here, for the statue in the *Venida* takes the rôle of another statue, the one found on the beach in 1370. In a sense, then, when a young boy plays the Virgin in the *Vespra*, the first half of the *Festa*, his rôle is not taken over by a special effects dummy – *he* is the special-effects dummy, or perhaps the stunt-man, by whose aegis *La Virgen d'Elx*, always and only a statue, is able to walk and to sing. The opposition of Cantó and the image of the Virgin also creates an additional narrative-historical layer of meaning to the entire *Festa*, interlaying medieval local legend between apocryphal or biblical narrative and contemporary performance. The play of the Assumption of the Virgin in Elche is then, a play within a play, the legend of Cantó forming the framing narrative, to which a further dimension is added when the Virgin again leaves the church during Holy Week to meet her Son in yet another procession.

In theatrical history, the *Festa d'Elx* may be unique, but in its local context it can be seen simply as the most impressive of many popular festivals which its home town and region celebrate annually. Some of these, though festivals with organisational structures in their own right, such as the December *Venida* and the Holy Week processions, are intimately connected with the *Festa* and part of the continuing popular tradition of linking local tradition with the universal celebrations of the Christian church calendar. Others, however, celebrate different aspects of regional identity and are in some cases recent inventions. Only when the whole pattern of contemporary festivals has been set around it, can the continuing significance and interest of the *Festa* for the late twentieth century be approached with any degree of confidence.

The constant assertion of the value of *ilicitanismo* by those interviewed about the value of the *Festa* has now at least something to do with a consciousness of the connection between tourism and prosperity in a town close to Benidorm and one of the most intensively exploited sections of Spanish *costa*, as it has to do with regional chauvinism. The town councillor with special responsibility for fiestas in general went as far as to complain that Elche now has nineteen days of *fiesta* in August, which can be disruptive. His suggested solution is, however, that they all be pushed into five or six days, turning the streets into a permanent *fiesta*, of greater benefit to the town and likely to attract more tourists.[31]

The *Patronat Provincial de Turisme* in Alicante produces monthly timetables of local festivals for the whole region, specifically aimed at the tourist market. The commonest elements are, as one might expect, processions of floats, dances, fairs, pilgrimages, floral displays, feasts of traditional dishes, costumed processions, firework displays, bonfires, battles, sports, and religious rites generally connected with a local saint. There are, of course, special events, like the 'bulls in the sea' festival in Dénia in July. In this context, the entry, '*Misterio de Elche, Nit de l'Alba, La Roa, Entierro de la Virgen*' passes almost unremarked. What is more, it occurs cheek by jowl with the very popular festival of *Moros y Cristianos*, ('Moors and Christians'), which is celebrated throughout the region in the early weeks of August.

The history of the festival of Moors and Christians in Elche is in turn connected with that of the *Venida* of the Virgin[32] in so far as, during the early nineteenth century, the *Venida* and other religious processions began to develop secular accretions. In 1806, on 29 December, various trades-guild floats took part in the *Venida* procession as well as two 'castles' of Moors and Christians which were raised up in the Plaza Mayor and the Plaza de las Barcas.[33] The special significance of the Virgin as protector of the city against invaders from the sea is, of course, a major element in the *Venida* in particular. Then in 1899 the celebration of the fiesta of Moors and Christians became a separate event in its own right, taking place in early August. In 1977 the *Asociación Festera de Moros y Cristianos* was created to have special responsibility for the event. The programme for the present-day celebration is very elaborate, consisting of processions, calls to arms, mock battles, parades of women and children, and concluding with the conversion and baptism of the defeated infidels. In that it necessitates the central involvement of a huge number of people drawn from all ranks of society, the festival of Moors and Christians is more markedly 'popular' than the *Festa*, but is not so completely divorced from it as might at first seem to be the case, either in terms of its history, or its place in the local imagination.

Much more recently, Elche has developed another August festival, also quasi-mimetic and processional in character. This is the festival of the *Pobladores*, a celebration of all the races who have contributed to Elche's history – the Iberians, Greeks, Phoenicians, Carthaginians, Romans, barbarians (Visigoths), Byzantines, Syrians and Aragonese. The festival was consciously begun in 1979 and seems to have been inspired by a wave of archaeological finds in the Elche area which took place around that time. Each *poblador* is run as a separate society having its own programme of events for the period of the festival which lasts for around four days in the first week in August, but can extend beyond that. These programmes include the establishing of a camp, processions and enactments associated with the invading race in question, as well as feasts, sports, and discotheques.[34] There are, naturally enough, few reflections as yet upon what might loosely be called the 'iconography' of the festival, all commentary concentrating on the dissemination of the actual history which the festival has evolved to celebrate.

Although the proliferation of festivals in Elche, particularly in August, might seem to rival one another for attention in physical terms, they are not so unrelated actually as aesthetic considerations might suggest. Their links are to begin with tangibly historical: the glossy brochure produced by the Association for the organisation of the Moors and Christians uses as its frontispiece a photograph of the Virgin in her shrine, just as many publications about the *Festa* show photographs of the ancient Iberian statue of *La Dama d'Elx*. It is all part of *ilicitanismo*, and the statue of the Virgin, found by Cantó during a particularly troublesome time in the town's history, has protected Elche from incursions of Moors, pirates, and other unwelcome visitors ever since. Those who were not repulsed successfully in the ages before the arrival of the Virgin were assimilated, became part of the identity of the people, and are now celebrated in their own right. All such events are now consciously developing and adapting in the common cause of drawing further varieties of *pobladores*, those who come to spend rather than to pillage, while recent secular academic and cultural interest in the *Misteri* itself ensures simultaneously that it remains central but somewhat aloof from its less self-conscious festive context.

This still leaves unanswered to some extent the question of why Elche continues to proliferate festivals at all. The nature of the *Misteri* may be largely unique, but all over Spain processional, quasi-mimetic festivals remain the tenacious form of popular holiday entertainment, tourism probably notwithstanding. In this area, recent developments and opinions about the *Misteri* itself are helpful, since its preservation has been addressed in such a self-conscious manner, owing to its being ancient, unique, religious, and aesthetically respectable. An examination of the history of its organising body strongly suggests that revivification has conformed to certain social patterns in the aftermath first of the Civil War, then of the Franco era. The Civil War also brought to an end another pan-hispanic festival which has never been revived, that of *Mardi Gras*, or Carnival. One of the most plausible local explanations I heard in Elche for the continuing enthusiastic proliferation of processions and festivals is that they are still filling the gap left in the popular imagination by the loss of Carnival, the occasion on which religion, insular chauvinism, and outright profanity became the seamless coat of popular festival at its best.

Q.M.W. (University of London)

NOTES

1. Pamela M. King and Asunción Salvador-Rabaza 'La Festa d'Elx: the Festival of the Assumption of the Virgin, Elche (Alicante)' *Medieval English Theatre* 8:1 (1986) 21–50.
2. Joan Castaño Garcia 'L'Organització de la Festa a Través dels Temps' *Món i Misteri de la Festa d'Elx* (Generalitat Valenciana, Valencia, 1986) 55–68.
3. Castaño 'L'Organització' 64–5.
4. Castaño 'L'Organització' 65–6; Alejandro Ramos Folques *Annales del Misterio de Elche* (Elche, 1974) 47–48.
5. Castaño 'L'Organització' 49–51.
6. Castaño 'L'Organització' 53–4.
7. Castaño 'L'Organització' 55–66.
8. For example, David D. Gilmore 'Sexual ideology in Andalusian oral literature: a comparative view of a Mediterranean complex' *Ethnology* 22 (July 1983) 241–52.
9. Gilmore 'Sexual ideology' 81–3.
10. Private correspondence with Joan Castaño Garcia.
11. Folques *Annales del Misterio* 67; Isabel Martinez Cerda 'El Misterio de Elche' *Cien Años de la Historia de Elche y de su Caja de Ahorros (1886–1986)* (Caja de Ahorros, Alicante, 1986) 32–39.
12. Gomez Orts 'Antonio Serrano, el Arquitecto de las restauraciones': interview in *La Verdad: Misteri-88* (August 1988) 7–9.
13. 'Misteri d'Elx' *Cuadernos de Informacion* (August 1988) 18.

14. Gomez Orts 'Emilio Señaris, un caso paradójico' *La Verdad: Misteri-88* (9 August 1988) 20–21.
15. Gomez Orts 'El Mestre de Capella se queja de las madres que prefieren que sus hijos se dediquen a cosas más *practicas*' *La Verdad: Misteri-88* (9 August 1988) 14–15.
16. Profiles of veteran performers are a favourite with the local press in their special supplements. Typical examples include: Gomez Orts 'Juan Sempre se repuso de una enfermedad que le alejaba de las representaciones' and 'La importancia de los protagonistas *anónimos*' *La Verdad: Misteri-88* (9 August 1988); 'La opinión de cinco cantores' *Cuadernas de Informacion: Misteri d'Elx* (August 1988).
17. Orts 'La importancia de los protagonistas *anónimos*'.
18. 'Cinco cantores' 13.
19. Antonio Gonzalez Beltran 'San Juan: Cuatro hombres frente a un personaje' *B.V. Periodico de Elche Comarca: Festes-85* (August 1985).
20. 'San Juan' *B.V. Periódico*.
21. 'San Juan' *B.V. Periódico*.
22. Gomez Orts 'De Padre Eterno a San Pedro' *La Verdad: Misteri-88* (August 1988) 3–5.
23. 'Encuesta Baix Vinalopó sobre el Misteri' *B.V. Periodico de Elche: Festes-85* 42–5.
24. Enrique A. Llobregat *La Festa D'Elx* (Patronato Nacional del Misterio de Elche, Elche, 1983).
25. Excmo. Ayuntamiento de Elche *Nit de L'Alba* (Elche, 1988).
26. *Nit de L'Alba*.
27. *El Periodico* (13 August 1988).
28. *La Verdad* (9 August 1988).
29. *Información* (15 August 1988).
30. Juan Castaño Garcia *Apuntes sobre la Venida de la Virgen a Elche* (Elche, 1984); Pamela M. King 'Elche Again – The *Venida* and *Semana Santa*' *Medieval English Theatre* 12:1 (1990) 4–20.
31. *El Periodico* (13 August 1988).
32. Juan Castaño Garcia 'Antecedentes de las Fiestas de Moros y Cristianos en Elche' *Fiestas de Moros y Cristianos Elche* (Asociación Festera de Moros y Cristianos, Elche, 1985) unpaginated.
33. Castaño 'Antecedentes'.
34. *Pobladores de Elche* (Pobladores, Elche, 1985) *passim*.

THE *AUTO DA FÉ* AS MEDIEVAL DRAMA
Robert Potter

In the workings of every drama, however comic or tragic, we can discern the operation of a process of justice; the characters are placed on trial, and their actions judged and eventually punished or rewarded according to some authorial scheme of enacted justice. Conversely, in the workings of every society's processes of justice, however merciful or arbitrary, we can discern the structure of a scripted human drama. As I wrote in 1983:

> The interconnections of drama and jurisprudence are as ancient as the *Oresteia* and as persistent as the ubiquitous trial scenes of television drama. In part this is because judicial processes are inherently dramatic – re-enacting past events for present purposes; moreover dramas are in some senses implicitly judicial – dedicated to reaching a determination of equity and, typically, to distributing punishments and rewards to their fictional participants. This being the case, it is entirely possible that greater cultural connections than we realize may be discerned between the structures of a given society's legal and theatrical institutions.[1]

Such considerations will help us to make better sense of one of history's most notorious judicial spectacles, devised by the Spanish Inquisition but best known to the world under its Portuguese title as the *Auto da Fé*, or 'Act of Faith'. We must first, however, set aside some lurid preconceptions – blazing images of mass executions, howling mobs and the odour of burning flesh – and look more carefully at what the *Auto da Fé*, and indeed the Spanish Inquisition, were actually about, in the context of the sixteenth and seventeenth centuries.

To reach the Inquisition in its original circumstances we must sweep aside many of the obfuscations of the so-called Black Legend, that campaign of anti-Catholic and anti-Hispanic propaganda which flourished in the eighteenth and nineteenth centuries and created our still-vivid modern image of the Inquisition.[2] Historians of many nations, including post-Franco Spain, have taken a new look at these matters in recent years. Unhampered by the need either to attack or defend the Inquisition, and armed with the extraordinarily detailed records which this institution kept of its own activities, these investigators paint for us a strikingly revised picture, in which neither the *Auto da Fé* nor its inventors appear quite so mindlessly inhuman as we might have imagined.

The *Auto da Fé* is revealed by these records to have been a unique invention of the Inquisition, a formal and highly dramatic public ceremony for the announcement of judicial sentences, during which no executions ever took place. The lengthy behind-the-scenes trials which preceded such ceremonies, while secret and unjust by modern standards (the defendant having no access to the evidence or even the names of witnesses against him), were certainly no worse than the practices of secular courts in the same era, and quite probably were more fairly administered.[3] Most of those convicted in such proceedings stood accused of relatively minor transgressions, such as oaths of blasphemy, acts of bigamy, and other violations of accepted sexual conduct. Their sentences were chiefly nothing worse than acts of public penance, or in more serious cases flogging and confiscation of goods.[4] Death sentences on the whole were pronounced sparingly, and only for what were perceived to be the most heinous offences; the best contemporary estimates are that no more than two percent of the hundreds of thousands convicted by the Inquisition were ever executed.[5] Any such executions took place at an entirely separate location following the ceremony, under the supervision and control of the civil authorities. The *Auto da Fé* itself, then, was an ecclesiastically-organised public ceremony, and its primary action involved the reconciliation and forgiveness of convicted offenders.[6]

These revisionist conclusions may help to demystify the *Auto da Fé*, but should not blind us to the darker aspects of the process. Flourishing in an age of religious fervour and conflict, and energised by expanding Royal political ambitions, the Spanish Inquisition and the *Auto da Fé* were instruments of ideological and racial persecution from their inception. Their principal targets were persecuted minorities, notably the so-called *conversos*, who were Jews who had become New Christians under pressure of institutional persecution and finally the threat of deportation, when Ferdinand and Isabella banished all Jews from Spain in 1492. Having virtually compelled these Jews to accept Christianity, under the most dubious of circumstances, the ecclesiastical and civil authorities proceeded to suspect them – often with good reason – of lingering adherences to Jewish customs and beliefs. The campaign to unmask and punish these 'Judaisers' was the pretext for the creation of the Spanish Inquisition, and the inspiration for the violent fervour of its activities in the early decades of the Inquisition, from 1480 to 1510. A similar surge of activity in the 1560s was the result of a parallel campaign to extirpate suspected Erasmians, Illuminists, Lutherans, and other reputed Protestant factions. Despite occasional signs of dissent, usually stemming from the humanitarian compunctions of the intelligentsia or the grumbling of the peasantry against strangers meddling in their affairs, the Spanish Inquisition seems to have been a deeply popular institution in its own times.[7] The *Auto da Fé*, the Inquisition's most visible public manifestation of its own purposes, can be seen both as an appeal for, and a demonstration of, unquestioning public support. Beginning in suspicion and ending in justice and forgiveness, its motives were deeply religious and political, and its message to its audience strongly penitential. As such, it is perhaps best understood not as a wanton spectacle of persecution, but as a carefully-scripted and deeply serious – if in some respects highly insidious – ritual drama.

ROBERT POTTER

An *Auto da Fé* was the public culmination of a lengthy process, beginning with the arrival of the Inquisition in a locality and the public proclamation of a grace period of forty days. During this period of grace all who were guilty of heresies, or knew of others who might be, were urged to confess what they knew to the Inquisitorial authorities. Anyone subsequently arrested, on the basis of the meticulous and secret investigations which then ensued, was presumed to be guilty and urged to confess his or her crimes before charges were disclosed. Since the defendant would have no idea of what had been said about him, or by whom, he could only guess at what he actually was accused of, and no adequate defence was possible. Acquittals were rare; once charged and condemned as guilty, the prisoner would be ordered to appear on a specified date to receive a sentence of punishment, either in private at an *Auto particular*, or at an open ceremony, an *Auto publico*. It was these latter public events, held periodically from 1481 onwards in dozens of cities in Spain, Portugal, and territories far afield under Spanish jurisdiction from Sicily to Peru, that came to be known as *Autos da Fé*.

An *Auto da Fé* was no routine matter, but a special event, carefully planned by the tribunal of the Inquisition in conjunction with local authorities, and held only when there were sufficient prisoners available, convicted, and ready for sentencing. Preparations began a month in advance of the date fixed for the *Auto*, with a public procession of Inquisitorial officials and their lay-brother subordinates through the city streets announcing the date of the forthcoming event. This is precisely the manner in which criers of Banns for religious plays would make preliminary announcements of their events, some days or weeks before the fact, in the streets of a medieval city. Characteristically *Autos da Fé* were scheduled for Sundays or Feast days, offering maximum opportunity for the populace to gather, not merely from the city itself, but also from the surrounding countryside.

During the month that followed the initial announcement, elaborate preparations would be made at the location specified for the *Auto* – generally the spacious main plaza of the city. Here scaffolding would be erected, and seating for two contrasting groups of participants, with Inquisitors and civic dignitaries on the right and convicted offenders on the left. A prominent pulpit would also be constructed for the delivery of the sermon that would form a vital part of the ceremony: generally a prominent Dominican friar would be chosen to perform this rôle. On the eve of the *Auto* the formalities would begin, with a torchlight procession of Inquisitorial lay brethren through the streets of the city, bearing the Insignia of the Inquisition, a green cross draped for the occasion with black cloth. The procession halted at the location bordering the plaza, and here an all-night vigil would be held, with public prayers, culminating in Mass at daybreak, with breakfast afterward for all participants.[8]

The *Auto da Fé* proper began with a procession of prisoners, marked by elaborate visual symbolism designed to proclaim, differentiate, specify, and vilify the transgressions of the accused. Strong dramatic elements of surprise were implicit in the proceedings, since the identities of the accused were kept secret until the last moment. Moreover the prisoners themselves would not in most cases be aware of the precise outcomes of their cases until the time came, when their punishments were revealed to them and they were clothed in garments symbolic of their sentences. Each prisoner wore a special penitential garment called a *sanbenito* made of yellow sackcloth, named for the austere Saint Benedict. Each carried an unlit green candle, in token of his need for enlightenment. Those convicted of lesser offences (oaths of blasphemy, for example) wore plain *sanbenitos*, while more serious offenders were accorded proportionally more highly decorated garments, such as one stripe of a red cross, or the full red cross. Convicted heretics who had repented of their sins wore a cross front and back, and a mitre-like hat called a *corazo*. The final two categories of prisoner, destined for capital punishment, were relapsed heretics. But even at this level of infamy there were visible gradations. Those relapsed heretics who had repented wore *sanbenitos* decorated with images of devils, signifying their damnation, but also flames pointing downward, indicating that they would be spared burning, though executed by strangulation. Unrepentant relapsed heretics, however, were clothed in *sanbenitos* painted with devils and *upward*-pointing flames, signifying that they would be burned at the stake.[9]

These penitential garments were no temporary costume, but a badge of shame that would be worn by the surviving prisoners (that is, the great majority of those sentenced) for lengthy periods thereafter, and then hung up for the public memorials within the offender's parish church for generations to come. In this sense the *Auto* ceremony was not merely a present shame for the prisoners, but a prophecy of a penitential (one might almost say purgatorial) future to come. In another striking visual feature the *Auto* also manifested its supremacy over the dimension of past time as well. As contemporary depictions of the processions clearly show, effigies of those convicted *in absentia* were carried in on poles by Inquisitorial functionaries; others carried coffins containing the disinterred remains of deceased offenders, which were being expelled from hallowed ground.

Persons condemned to death received special penitential treatment. They were always informed of the sentence the night before, in order to give them time for soul-searching and repentance. Friars were in attendance on them from that time until the moment of their execution, offering them a chance to repent at any moment – even during the *Auto* itself. Last-minute confessions were urgently sought and not infrequently achieved, adding a further element of macabre suspense to the proceedings.[10] Those deemed likely to disrupt the ceremony, however, were gagged to prevent their uttering blasphemies or denunciations.

Once in the plaza, the procession of condemned prisoners and their attendants made its way to the raised scaffold on the left. It was followed by a very differently-clothed procession of ecclesiastical and civic officials, who took seats on the opposing scaffold to the right. The ultimate position of honour was reserved for the highest official of the Inquisition, who led the assembled crowd in an oath of fidelity to the

Holy Office of the Inquisition. Following this came an open-air celebration of Mass, including a lengthy and detailed sermon castigating the sins of the convicted prisoners, and warning other transgressors to mend their ways and repent, before they suffered a similar fate. Then, as if to demonstrate these admonitions in the most unmistakable terms, the prisoners were called one by one to account. Their crimes and sentences were announced, beginning with those tried *in absentia* and continuing through all those present.

There is ample testimony, from both sympathetic and hostile witnesses, of the dramatic emotional effect which these events had on the multitude of spectators. But what was the effect of this drama on those who participated in it? In a recent article, Mariá Victoria González de Caldas points out that taking part in this public humiliation became, for most prisoners, an act of penitence in itself. In enduring the public exposure, they were in effect participating in a public ritual of justice, a public reconciliation which offered them 'the chance to abjure their errors and be readmitted to the bosom of the Church'.[11]

Nevertheless, the culmination of the accusatory phase of the *Auto* (and, one must candidly admit, its dramatic climax), was the 'relaxation' of prisoners condemned to death – that is, their formal release from ecclesiastical custody into the hands of the civil authorities, who alone had the right to carry out executions. On a human level these actions must have engendered a strong measure of fear and pity in the hearts of the audience, whose disposition according to contemporary accounts was to hope for a last-minute repentance.[12] From a distance we can observe that the action of these 'relaxations' is remarkably similar to a familiar episode in the medieval Passion Plays. In dramatisations of the Passion, of which Spain has a rich tradition, the authority figures who disclaim responsibility for a forthcoming execution are the villains Annas, Caiaphas, and Pilate. Whether this irony was lost on the original audience, or taken to heart, we can only speculate; in any event it is safe to say that the handing over of a heretic condemned to death would be a terrifying moment.

The *Auto da Fé* reached its formal conclusion in a highly theatrical action, the separation of the prisoners into the quick and the dead. The 'relaxed' prisoners were taken off under guard to an open space beyond the city walls, the *quemadero*, or 'burning place'. The remaining prisoners, all penitents, fell to their knees in thanks for their forgiveness. Receiving absolution from censure and excommunication, they abjured their errors, professed their faith, and returned in procession to their place of incarceration, to begin their punishments immediately.[13]

But though the *Auto* ended on this note of forgiveness and reconciliation, it seems evident that the bulk of the witnesses to the Act of Faith did not follow the path of the penitents, but chose to accompany the condemned prisoners to the place of execution, to see justice done. Inquisitorial records give strong indications that executions were an expected part of the proceedings, however legally and physically detached from the formal ceremony. There are reports of vocal public disappointment when executions did not take place, and opinions that *Autos* without executions were failures, scarcely worth attending.[14]

In all of its actions the *Auto da Fé* embodied both a conscious didactic purpose and a dramatic method; it is no coincidence that the word *Auto* was also used in Spain in this period to denote the frankly theatrical religious plays (*Autos Sacramentales*) performed on festive occasions such as Corpus Christi. As public ritual dramas of justice, the *Autos da Fé* were similarly performed on festive occasions, often on an important Sunday, and even in some cases (to the horror of foreign observers) in honour of Royal events, including weddings and celebrations of the birth of Princes.[15]

The visual pageantry, costuming, and symbolic use of theatre space in the *Auto da Fé* were crafted to create an overwhelming dramatic effect on its audience. Contemporary records refer quite freely to the scaffolding constructions as *teatros*, and make a point of emphasising the necessity for good sightlines and acoustics in ensuring the success of the ceremony. And the comfort of the audience was not neglected: in summer huge awnings were provided to shade spectators from the heat of the sun. The settings in the plaza, with an audience in the windows and balconies of the buildings that faced on the square, was suggestive of multi-tiered Spanish Golden Age public theatres, the *corrales*.[16] In all these respects the *Auto da Fé* is a particularly fascinating example of what Michael Foucault wryly termed 'The Art of Punishing'.[17]

I want to emphasise the traditional dramatic artistry of the *Auto da Fé* both as an individual experience and as a collective act. Its approach to the individual participant or spectator bears comparison to that variety of medieval penitential drama we call the morality play, which shows us individual human life as sinful by nature, but redeemable through human action, in the conjoining of personal conscience with institutional remedies of repentance and forgiveness.[18] Like a real-life morality play, the *Auto da Fé* summons humanity to a general accounting, and compels the individual sinner to acknowledge and repent his or her sins. This process begins with the initial public pronouncement of a period of grace, and continues with a certain dramaturgical inevitability. The grace period gives way to the actuality of arrests and accusations, and eventually to a public revelation and acknowledgement of the hidden crimes, followed swiftly by their sure and severe punishment. The ordeal of the prisoners, and their conversion from sinners into penitents, is the external drama – artfully and horrifically designed to set in motion an inner drama in the conscience of the individual spectator, contemplating the eventual price of his yet-undivulged misdeeds.

In this respect there is no doubt that the *Auto da Fé* may be accurately compared, as it often has been, to a rehearsal for the Last Judgement.[19] Artistic representations of this future but promised event form one of the central concerns of Christian iconography, from the great West windows of Gothic cathedrals to Michaelangelo's Sistine Chapel ceilings, and always for a present purpose – to catch the conscience of the spectator, while there is still time. Dramatising the Last Judgement serves the same urgent penitential purpose in the medieval dramatic traditions of all European countries. Those familiar with the medieval drama will observe that the *Auto da Fé*'s dramatic action unfolds in consonance with the best theatrical traditions for representing this event – a *mise en scène* which unearths the deepest-hidden crimes and criminals, and separates the righteous from the wicked definitively and inexorably, with realistic threats of torture and hellfire, an all-knowing judge, and an exemplary process of rewards and punishments. In an unsettling way, such symbolism goes well beyond the figurative in the *Auto da Fé*, with its real-life actors and its motif of conversion. It is worth remembering that dubiously converted Jews were the favourite target of these ceremonial trials, and the Patristic tradition held that Jews were predestined to be converted to Christianity in the last days.[20]

It was this theatrical literalism and ideological fervour which so astonished the foreign visitors who witnessed these events. Pageantry, rhetoric, and spectacle were fused to present an unarguable demonstration of Catholicism triumphant,[21] in a ritual act of propaganda affirming the power of the Monarchy, Church, and Inquisition. In this sense the *Auto* used typological trappings to glorify its own supremacy, comparing its own judicial sway to the final justice of God at the end of time.

Like all merely human institutions, however, the *Auto da Fé* had an historical inception and development, and eventually a demise. In its earliest manifestations, the *Auto* was a stark and urgent event. The mass ceremonies of the 1480s were more remarkable for numbers than theatricality: a Toledo *Auto* of 1486 dealt with seven hundred and fifty cases in a single morning.[22] The once-simple ceremonies flourished and expanded in the Counter-Reformation climate of religious persecution in the sixteenth century; there were twenty-three *Autos* in Seville alone in the years 1549–1599.[23] But as the *Auto* grew more theatrically embellished, it became increasingly expensive, to the point where smaller tribunals could no longer afford to mount such events. By the seventeenth century, whether because of such lavishness or the lack of suitable transgressors, *Autos da Fé* had become rare occurrences.

However the grandiose descriptions and depictions of the magnificent *Auto* held in 1680 in the Plaza Mayor in Madrid give vivid proof that the institution was by no means extinct. The grand procession included one hundred coal merchants bearing fuel for the fires of justice, with the King and his court in attendance, and twenty relapsed heretics to be sentenced to death. Such was the pomp and pageantry of this *Auto* that the ceremony lasted from early morning until nine o'clock in the evening, and the executions did not take place until midnight.[24] The end, nevertheless, was in sight. The *Auto* came to oblivion in the early nineteenth century together with the Inquisition itself, but not before it had become one of the favourite targets for Enlightenment denunciations of Medieval Superstition, lampooned by Moratin and immortalised by Goya's brush and pen.[25]

THE *AUTO DA FÉ* AS MEDIEVAL DRAMA

That the *Auto da Fé* is so well remembered, albeit somewhat inaccurately, is due to its passionate vilifiers. But credit must also be given to the authors of the hundreds of meticulously detailed official accounts of these ceremonies. Their efforts have created what has recently been described as a unique historical data bank of vast proportions, through which we may investigate the Inquisition as meticulously as it once intruded into the lives of its victims. Such documentation also allows us to observe in fine detail the workings of a ritual drama, of whose beauty and efficacy the pious compilers seem to have had no doubts whatsoever, and of whose human dramaturgical logic they were manifestly proud. We who live far enough away in time to recognise both the enormity and the artistry of these events may also discern in them the roots of some of our own century's Acts of Faith, in this great age of show trials, televised inquisitions, and public scapegoats.

University of California, Santa Barbara

NOTES

1. Robert Potter 'Divine and Human Justice' in *Aspects of Early English Drama* edited Paula Neuss (D.S. Brewer, Cambridge, 1983) 134.
2. See Edward Peters *Inquisition* (Free Press, New York, 1988).
3. Edward Burman *The Inquisition: The Hammer of Heresy* (Aquarian Press, Wellingborough, 1984) 151.
4. Henry Kamen *Inquisition and Society in Spain* (Weidenfeld and Nicolson, London, 1985) 178–97.
5. Jaime Contreras and Gustav Henningsen 'Forty-Four Thousand Cases of the Spanish Inquisition (1540–1700): Analysis of a Historical Data Bank' in *The Inquisition in Early Modern Europe* edited Gustav Henningsen and John Tedeschi (Northern Illinois University Press, DeKalb, Illinois, 1986) 113.
6. Maria Victoria González de Caldas 'Nuevas Imagines del Santo Oficio en Sevilla: El Auto de Fé' in *Inquisición Española y Mentalidad Inquisitorial* edited Angel Alcalá (Ariel, Barcelona, 1984) 239.
7. Bernardino Llorca *La Inquisición en España* (Editorial Labor, Barcelona, 1954) 166–7.
8. Kamen (note 4) 190.
9. Jean Plaidy *The Spanish Inquisition: its Rise, Growth and End* (Citadel, New York, 1967: from 3 vol. edition by Hale, London, 1960) 153–4.
10. H.C. Lea *History of the Inquisition of Spain* 4 vols (Macmillan, New York, 1906–1907) 2 586.
11. González de Caldas (see note 6) 238–9 (my translation).
12. Pedro Rubio Merino 'Autos de Fé de la Inquisición de Cordoba durante el Siglo XVII a través de la documentación del Archivo de la Santa Iglesia Catedral de Sevilla' in *La Inquisición Española* edited Joaquin Perez-Villanueva (Siglo XX, Madrid, 1980) 347.
13. González de Caldas (see note 6) 260.
14. Lea (see note 10) 4 526.

15. Juan Antonio Llorente *Historia Crítica de la Inquisición de España* 10 vols (Madrid, 1822) translated as *Histoire critique de l'Inquisition d'Espagne* traduit par Alexis Pellier, 4 vols (Treuttel et Wurtz, Paris, 1817–1818) 4 3.
16. Miguel Jimenez Monteserin *Introducción a la Inquisición Española* (Editorial Nacional, Madrid, 1980) 654–64.
17. 'The art of punishing, then, must rest on a whole technology of representation ... To find the suitable punishment for a crime is to find the disadvantage whose idea is such that it robs for ever the idea of a crime of any attraction': Michel Foucault *Discipline and Punish* translated Alan Sheridan (Penguin, Harmondsworth, 1979) 104. The connection of the *Auto de Fé* with Foucault's theories is noted by González de Caldas (see note 6) 237–41.
18. Robert Potter *The English Morality Play* (Routledge and Kegan Paul, London, 1975) 6–10.
19. See, for example, Plaidy (see note 9) 148.
20. Peters (see note 2) 77.
21. González de Caldas (see note 6) 239.
22. Kamen (see note 4) 191.
23. González de Caldas (see note 6) 240.
24. Kamen (see note 4) 192–4. The pomp and circumstance of this event are vividly captured in Francisco Rizi's 1683 painting 'Auto de Fé in Madrid 1680' (Museo del Prado, Madrid), which encapsulates events which would have occurred separately over a twelve-hour period into a single artistic composition. See *Carreno, Rizi, Herrera y la Pintura Madrileña de su Tiempo* (Exhibition Catalogue, Museo del Prado, Madrid, 1986).
25. See Peters (see note 2) plates 1–26. For other artistic representations of the *Auto de Fé* see Angel Alcalá *Inquisición Española y Mentalidad Inquisitorial* (Ariel, Barcelona, 1984); *La Inquisició* (Generalitat Valenciana, Valencia, 1985) and Llorca (see note 7).

FORMS AND THEIR USES:
The Antwerp *Ommegangen*, 1550–1700
John Cartwright

In the course of the thirteenth century, the level of the North Sea began to rise perceptibly, a process which, on the whole, has continued since. By the late fifteenth century this had the consequence of making Antwerp accessible by sea and river by a shorter and more economical route than previously, and also, through erosion of the coastal dunes, of silting up the river Zwin which leads from the sea to the city of Bruges.

In 1482, the Emperor Maximilian had all foreign merchants expelled from Bruges in retaliation for the leading role which the town had played in agitating for increased independence from imperial control. In 1488 he went even further, transferring from Bruges to Antwerp the privileges and protection enjoyed by those same merchants. In 1499, Portugal officially recognised Antwerp as the European depot for the spice trade which the Portuguese effectively controlled, and in 1501 the Venetian Senate transferred their galley trade from Bruges to Antwerp.

And so, while Bruges, despite the pleas and efforts of its burghers, declined to the status of a picturesque provincial town, Antwerp became in the following century a centre of international trade and commerce, a manufacturing town, and an essential stopping place for artists and intellectuals such as Dürer, Erasmus, and Sir Thomas More. As a recent writer puts it, 'Early 16th-century Antwerp was truly one of history's remarkable urban settings',[1] while a Spanish visitor to the city in 1549 commented that 'The rich and densely populated city of Antwerp could rightly be called the metropolis of the world'.[2]

Antwerp's prosperity, its geographical situation, its relative autonomy, and its commanding position in the printing industry in this period made it inevitable that it would feel very directly the shocks and changes of the Reformation and the Counter-Reformation and the effects of continual interdynastic tensions. The peace of Cateau-Cambrensis in 1559, which ended a series of Franco-Hapsburg struggles, led to a renewed boom in Antwerp: in 1561–1562, thirty-eight new warehouses were built for the *Engelse Natie* ('the English Nation', the association of English merchants in the city), and in about 1568 the population within the city walls reached a peak of about 105,000 persons.

About that time, however, Protestant-Catholic hostility broke out more violently and widely than before, causing Spain to send in the Duke of Alba to restore their authority. In 1576 the city was sacked by Spanish and mercenary troops,[3] and in 1579 Antwerp became officially Protestant for several years, with all but a few Catholic chapels being closed and all religious processions being banned. In 1585, however, Antwerp submitted to Philip II, and the modern border with the predominantly Protestant Netherlands was established, putting Antwerp on a cultural and economic periphery rather than in a centre. Although there was a revival of trade and industry in Antwerp in the early seventeenth century, the centre of gravity of the Dutch-speaking Netherlands had moved North.

A study of the Antwerp *ommegangen* – or regular annual processions – of this period, while of course, having a relevance of its own for those interested in late medieval drama, may also enable one to draw some tentative conclusions concerning possible relations between political and social change and the forms of popular culture. In this preliminary study I focus on those aspects of the *ommegangen* for which the fullest and most accessible documentation survives, namely, on the frequently-changing contributions of the Chambers of Rhetoric, described in a number of printed pamphlets and one manuscript, with a particular concentration in the 1560s – that period of late bloom and great apparent confidence[4] – and with less frequent publications up to the late seventeenth century.

I shall describe the main features of the *ommegangen* and attempt to show how over the course of less than a century some of the older pageants or tableaux – either scriptural/anecdotal or allegorical/explicatory – became adapted, and new ones were devised, in order to serve the changing needs of the Antwerp merchant class or *Sinjoren*. A study of these processions, indeed, provides us with a microcosm of the broader shift in paradigm from medieval to modern.

First, though, I should like to recall the difference between occasional processions and regular ones, which, although they have many elements in common, and may even use in one kind of procession a figure or pageant which was originally designed for the other, nevertheless tend to serve different ideological functions.

Among the former – that is, occasional events – are processions celebrating the end of a war, the wedding of a member of the reigning house, the return of a monarch from abroad, or the visit of an important foreigner. These 'occasional' events take the form of an entry into the town, and usually centre upon one individual (king, prince, or visiting dignitary), who is the centre-point of the procession; the route itself is adorned with stationary features such as fountains of wine, tapestries hung from windows, decorated arches, or costumed personages, often allegorical, standing on platforms and bearing scrolls addressed to the important person in the procession and containing words of welcome or advice.

Entries of this kind, while they do involve the whole populace in a shared celebration, have the function of re-affirming a strongly hierarchical paradigm of social interdependence – as in a court masque, the one person honoured has the best view of all, and is indeed probably the only person who can fully see or hear all the elements of the formal celebration.[5]

Regular annual processions, on the other hand, celebrated either patronal festivals or the presence of a holy relic, which was publicly exhibited through the town on such an occasion. In addition, the feast of Corpus Christi, instituted in the early thirteenth century, had soon acquired its own annual procession, an event which became widespread in Western Europe in the course of the fourteenth century.

While annual processions of this kind had much in common with those of the 'occasional' type (indeed, a pageant or image from a regular festival could be pressed into service on another special occasion and vice versa), their emphasis was different: the occasional procession has, roughly speaking, a double focus – the people look at the prince and the prince looks from his privileged point of view at the triumphal archways over his route, the allegorical personages waiting to address him, and the crowd who are looking at him.

In the regular processions, on the other hand, the whole procession is the focus, and its deliberate fostering of communality is stressed both by the presence in it of representatives of the town and by its slow circular journey through the streets from and back to the church.

Let us now consider the regular processions of Antwerp. In the course of the thirteenth century, a rather unusual relic, the Holy Foreskin, had been brought to Antwerp from the Holy Land, and a procession to commemorate the Holy Circumcision seems to have been well established by 1324, held on Trinity Sunday, the eighth Sunday after Easter.

At about that time Corpus Christi processions (which took place on the Thursday after Trinity Sunday) are recorded as having been established for the first time in several Flemish towns, and Antwerp's may probably be dated from before 1350. At any rate, the *ommegangen* of the Circumcision and of Corpus Christi were in 1398 referred to as *de twee processien die men hier jaarlijk doet* ('the two processions which are annually held here').

In the following year, however, there was established an annual procession of the Blessed Virgin Mary (taking place on the Sunday after the Feast of the Assumption, 15th August), in honour of the patron saint of Antwerp's main church. You will have noted that all three processions take place during the summer, when there can be a reasonable expectation of suitable weather.

All three *ommegangen* had much the same overall arrangement: first came lay people of the town, grouped by craft; then there were a series of waggons bearing *puncten* or tableaux, some of them being scenes from the Scriptures and others illustrating particular points or matters of spiritual or moral importance; after these *puncten* came a representation of the Last Judgement; then groups of the religious orders (in the order of their foundation), and secular and regular clergy; then members of the *schuttersgilden* or shooting clubs, the *lakengilde* or cloth-merchants' guild – recognised as the senior guild in Antwerp – and the city officers and dignitaries; then the prelates, including the heads of local abbeys; and finally a scene, object, or image particular to that feast: a scene representing the Circumcision, or the Holy Sacrament in a vessel, or a statue of the Virgin.

JOHN CARTWRIGHT

The fourteenth and fifteenth centuries, the period during which the *ommegangen* established their regular form, were the Golden Age of the Flemish 'Chambers of Rhetoric', cultural and social clubs – usually with links to religious confraternities – whose members met to drink, gossip, and compose poetry and plays in a variety of conventional forms, including medieval and folk elements, but increasingly showing humanistic influence in both form and subject matter.

By the middle of the sixteenth century, Chambers of Rhetoric had been given the responsibility of devising and presenting new *puncten* for the annual *ommegangen*. This appears to have had two main effects: the religious emphasis, already weakened by the presence of folklore elements such as the Antwerp Giant, was further diluted by a mixture of images and ideas drawn from classical mythology, and the tendency to allegorise became intensified, both in the design of new *puncten*, and in the interpretation of traditional ones. Also, as we shall see, the earlier highly creative literary and dramatic function of the Chambers of Rhetoric had by now increasingly given way to their function as, in effect, chambers of commerce, with consequent changes in emphasis.

The Peace of Cateau-Cambresis in 1559 brought to an end a long period of warfare in Western Europe, and for the following few years we have records of what appears to have been an outburst of communal creative activity in Antwerp. There are, first, from 1561 to 1566 a series of printed *ordinancies* or officially encouraged descriptions and interpretations of the regular processions of these years; there are texts and descriptions relating to the famous Antwerp *Landjuweel*, or regional cultural competition, of 1561;[6] and there is an apparently eyewitness account, surviving in manuscript, of the procession of the Holy Sacrament in 1562, written by a visiting Scot.[7]

In 1561 an *ordinancie* was published for the procession of the Circumcision,[8] describing and interpreting in detail a new series of *puncten* in addition to the traditional scenes and images chiefly drawn from the Scriptures and local folklore: this new sequence of seven waggons dealt with *De geheele loop des werelds* ('the whole way of the world'), in a way which blends old and new.

In front of the group walked two pages bearing a banner inscribed with a five-line stanza, pointing out that the earth turns continually without beginning, end, or foundation, and is known as *een zee vol turbacie* ('a sea full of trouble'), an image that, of course, goes back many centuries, being drawn upon, in English, in poems such as the Old English *Wanderer* and *Seafarer*, and Chaucer's *Man of Law's Tale*.

Thereafter follows a great turning world with seven figures upon it: Riches, Pride, Envy, War, Poverty, Humility, and Peace. Then came the seven waggons of the new set, each representing a stage in a circular process: the first depicts how riches brings forth pride; then pride causes envy, envy leads to war, war brings poverty, poverty brings about humility, humility makes peace possible, and peace brings riches.

After the waggons there rides a woman whose horse is hung about with books and other signs of the arts; then follow farm-workers with their implements, and the artisans of the town. This group is called *Geschikte behendigheid* ('proper' – or 'fine' – 'skilfulness') or Industria. One may perhaps ask the question – which is certainly not posed in the *ommegang* – *Geschik* for whom? Whose interests were served by the presence of labourers and artisans in this context? We shall return to this question later.

There are banners borne before each of the waggons, and one final one, with another five-line stanza, which compares the way of the world to *een wankelbaer riet* ('an unsteady reed') and thanks God who makes everything good in His time. Thereafter comes the Last Judgement at the end of the *puncten*, as usual.

A certain conceptual strain is apparent both within this sequence and in its relation to its context. On the one hand, there is an accumulation of traditional images stressing the mutability of life in the world and the vanity of human wishes, with echoes of the Wheel of Fortune, and with the Last Judgement following close behind; on the other hand, it is surely no accident that the cycle of worldly life begins and ends in this sequence with Riches, rather than with any other point in the circle such as War, Poverty, or Humility. This emphasis is continued in the procession of labourers and artisans, a necessary and far from allegorical element in the production of riches. Finally, the optimism of the closing stanza, that God *Alle dinghen in sijnen tijt goet ghemaekt* ('makes everything good in His time'), while a comfortable thought for the prosperous burghers who are responsible for the design and presentation of this sequence, may have been harder to swallow for many of their employees and dependants, who were at this time feeling the impact of the scarcity of basic goods and of sharply rising prices. The overall moralisation of this sequence, therefore, although using traditional elements, is, in its context, unresolved, even ambivalent.

The next surviving description is that of the visiting Scotsman who observed the procession of the Holy Sacrament in June 1562. He describes the whole *ommegang*, not only the new *puncten*, but very much through the eyes of an outsider, and has not grasped the full implications of all the pageants, perhaps because he was not fluent in Dutch.

The first waggon depicted an elephant (ten fathoms high), with what the writer describes as 'ane goddes' standing on its back, holding in her hand 'ane apill of gold'. All later references to this *punct* by other observers identify her as the Lady Fortune with her wheel.

Then a 'dromedary', presumably also an artefact, bearing soldiers shooting fireballs. No commentator attempts to invest this exotic image with any moral or economic significance – a writer in 1649,[9] in the spirit of the new philosophical enquiries of the period, asserts rather vaguely that it 'had previously been on view in Antwerp, brought from Persia, Media, Assyria, or some such lands', but others seem to have been content to accept it as sheer spectacle, even in a procession with an ostensibly religious purpose.

JOHN CARTWRIGHT

Thereafter comes a giant, eight fathoms high and five broad, with a beard two ells long, and his head looking about from side to side. A later writer[10] informs us that this giant was made by Pieter Coeck of Aalst, the master of Pieter Brueghel the Elder, especially for the *Blijde Inkomst* or Royal Entry of Charles V. He has twenty-four young giants accompanying him, 'all monstrous to behold and look upon'. The Scots observer calls this image 'Golyas', presumably assuming from the context that it was a biblical reference, but it appears that the giant was actually a figure from local folklore who, like the dromedary, and like the sixteenth-century giants in the processions of Norwich, Chester, and London, has simply been incorporated into the annual religious processions for its entertainment value.

Then comes a ship with sails and a crew, moving 'as it had bene in valter, without þe persaving of men'. This too had been made for the Royal Entry of Charles V, supposedly to celebrate the renewal of the shipmen's privileges, and had become a permanent part of the regular *ommegangen*, and it too was later pressed into the service of neat but new interpretations.

After several scenes from the life of Christ and the Virgin Mary, come a series of waggons which appear to be the sequence on 'the way of the world', which had been new the previous year. It begins with the globe of the world, 'þe men being within þe samyn, turnand ay about þe said gloib without þe persaving of ony body' – in the Scots observer's view this represents 'þe vanitie of þe world, as it had bene þe quhill of Fortoun, sum tymes vp and sum tymes doun'.

After recognisable descriptions of the waggons of Riches and Pride, the previous year's order of seven stages appears to break down somewhat, either because it has genuinely become confused in the mean time, or because the writer is not clear as to the significance of what he is seeing. Indeed, his rather uncertain description of these complex allegorical presentations may confirm the need for printed *ordinancies* to help the spectators. He may, however, be drawing on his own experience of North British pageants when he identifies two of the figures accompanying Pride as 'David Dispit and Willie Wanrest'.

At any rate, there appear to be sufficient similarities between this sequence of *puncten* and that of the Circumcision *ommegang* of the previous year to suggest that the two processions of the Circumcision and the Holy Sacrament, held four days apart, are still virtually identical at this stage, as had been earlier noted in an item in the city records of 1494.

If the Scotsman is less accurate than the local observers, he gives in some instances a far more vivid and immediate impression of the procession than they tend to do, concerned as they are more with the niceties of interpretation. His description of the waggon of the Last Judgement, for example, is as follows:

Item, þair wes þe pictour of Crist sittand on ane bow with angellis blawand þair trumpatis, representand þe Day of Iugement, with þe deid bodyis risand in sindry partis of þe erth ... and þe dewillis on þe said cairt resawand þe condampnit creatouris with greit lamentationis, ʒowlling and ʒowting, quhilk vas ane intollorable thyng to behald.

The iconography is directly in the traditional line represented, for example, by Roger van der Weyden's famous painting. This 'intolerable' performance was not, apparently, too much for the citizenry of Antwerp, for from seventeenth-century descriptions of the *ommegangen* we find that by then there had been added, immediately after the Last Judgement, another waggon devoted entirely to the torments of Hell. Again, we see how spectacle takes on a life and justification of its own, going well beyond, in this case, the requirements of the original homiletic purpose.

The Scots observer concludes by noting that 'þair mes beand donne, all þe artailʒorie of þe toun schot, greit and smal, to þe nomer of xx^m pece, as honest men of þe toun did report and as honest Scottis men can verifie þat ves þair present'. Mass is almost, but not quite, the climax of the occasion.

The *ordinancies* of 1564 and 1566,[11] describing the procession of the Blessed Virgin Mary, concentrate on the new *puncten* in each, with the 1564 publication noting that waggons are changed and new ones introduced *naer de gelegenheyt des tyts* ('as it suits the time'). One should remember, however, that the old *puncten*, some of them possibly more than two hundred years old by this stage, remain part of the *ommegangen* – scenes such as the Annunciation, the Nativity, the Seven Sorrows of Mary, and, of course, the Last Judgement.

There are brief references in the 1564 *ordinantie* to a series of waggons with a maritime theme, including the ship we previously heard of, now with Aeolus on board; the Giant, now called *Een groote reus van Antwerpen* ('a great Antwerp giant'), with the *Reuskens* ('little giants') dancing about him; and a waggon which was to become particularly prominent in the next century, namely, the Maid of Antwerp, accompanied by Scaldis, god of the River Scheldt, together with Mercury (god of trade) and Copia ('Plenty').

There are six new *puncten* in the 1564 procession, beginning with *de theater der werelt* ('the theatre of the world'), which may perhaps be a recycled version of the turning globe first seen in 1561. The interpretation of this picture of the world, however, has nothing to do with mutability: the accompanying verses note that

> deen lant sonder dander niet en mach
> want elck heeft syn gave ...
> welck behooren vry te syne, sonder tyt of dach,
> tot ghemeynen orboor, met een redelyck verdrach.

> 'One land can do nothing without another,
> for each has its special gift ...
> which ought to be free, without constraint,

to the common profit, with a reasonable mutual understanding.'

This emphasis on the economic interdependence of nations with varying resources and products and the desirability of unrestricted trade is continued on the next waggon, which showed *het paleys der nacien* ('the court of the nations'): Mercury is surrounded by twelve nymphs, representing the principal nations of Europe that are represented in Antwerp, including England and Scotland.

In the third *punct*, the course of Antwerp's prosperity and the nature of its products is shown by *Het Huis des Hantwerks* ('The House of the Trades') decorated with signs and badges of the City trades. In the house is *Lands Welvaert* ('The Land's Prosperity').

The fourth scene departs from allegory to show a specific and important local example of a trade, namely, *Der Vrouwen Spinninghe* ('Women's Spinning'), with associated activities.

In the next *punct*, classically influenced generalised allegory returns with *Het Dal der Vruchtbaerheyt* ('The Vale of Fruitfulness'). Next to a horn of plenty, naiads and virtues welcome all nations.

The sixth and last in the set shows *Der Throon van Justicie* ('The Throne of Justice'). At her feet lie Riguer and Favuer (excessive rigour and excessive slackness, or corruption), and on her right stands Wisdom with a Bible in one hand and a burning light (*het licht der Waarheid*, 'the light of Truth') in the other.

The final *tafel* comments that when Justice is governed by Wisdom and not corrupted by Rigour or Favour, the common welfare (*ghemeyn welvaert*) will remain firmly founded in love without envy. This 'love', however, is clearly not the kind demonstrated elsewhere in the *ommegang* in, for example, the Nativity, but refers to the amicable relationship of trading partners, to their mutual economic benefit. The Bible in Wisdom's hand appears in this context to be a traditional and now rather misleading 'prop'.

This sequence of *puncten*, therefore, devised when Antwerp was recovering its economic position – or attempting to do so – six years after the peace of 1558, puts forward a carefully thought-out mercantile philosophy with only the smallest of nods to the supposedly religious content of the procession: after a general statement on the interdependence of nations, it names Antwerp's chief trading partners, points out the basis of the city's prosperity, and ends with an assurance that it is a place of stability and fair dealing.

The *ordinantie* then lists the seven remaining scenes, from the Annunciation to the Last Judgement, with the specific comment that these are *de geestelyke poincten* ('the religious/spiritual pageants'). The division between Church and commerce, between holy days and other days, is becoming apparent.

Two years later, on 18 August 1566, the procession of the Virgin took place under very different circumstances, in an atmosphere of considerable political tension. Indeed, two days after the procession, there took place the event known as the *beeldstormerij* or 'smashing of images', when a Protestant faction rushed into the chief church of Antwerp and attacked the altars and images.

The new *puncten* of 1566, as described in the *ordinancie* of that year, reflect this tension – they consist of a group of four very elaborate waggons on the theme of *Den Tijt Present* ('The Present Age'). The set begins with the 'Theatre of the World', presumably recycled yet again, but with a very different message: 'the present time' is in an confused state, as are the four chief regions of the world, with every nation being oppressed by *quade suspicie* ('wicked suspicion'); three horsemen preceding the first waggon represent *Aerdtsche Ghiericheyt* ('Earthly Greed'), *Ongheregelde Nature* ('Unbridled Nature'), and *Tyrranighe Wreetheyt* ('Tyrannical Cruelty'). The second waggon represents the Cave of Discord, with discordant music being played by Unreasonable Worry, Evil Suspicion, Mistaken Understanding, and Obstinacy.

This is contrasted with the next waggon, of 'God's Providence', preceded by Wise Advice, Careful Investigation, and Unified Community, and showing *Gods Ordonantie* supported by the Spiritual State, with her sword the Word of God and her book of the Gospel Teachings, and the Secular Authority, with the sword of Justice, and numerous other figures.

The last of the four shows 'the Throne of Mercy', and includes such figures as Peace, Truth, Reason, and Control of the Flesh.

The confidence of the 1564 *puncten* has vanished in the face of possible social and economic disruption, and Antwerp's anxious *Cooplieden* ('tradespeople') have turned again to moral and religious ideas – expressed in characteristically complex allegorical forms – in order to impress upon their audience in the streets that social disorder is evil and unnatural and arises largely out of misunderstanding the true nature of things, and that the secular authority is part of God's plan and is properly to be associated with peace and goodwill.

In the course of the seventeenth century there were four relevant descriptions printed, now as commercial publishing ventures rather than officially encouraged *ordinancies*.

The 1609 booklet printed by Abraham Verhoeven[12] comes after another period of warfare and the new *puncten* of the year concentrate on the return to peaceful activities, including trade and the arts. The Giant is preceded by a couplet announcing that he has changed his garments and laid down his *gheweer* ('arms'), while the Ship has been transformed into an *oorlogschip* ('warship'), but contains sailors from various countries; after them come two trumpeters dressed as sailors, and then crewmen from various countries carrying samples of their wares – the Spaniards, for example, carry oranges and canaries, while the Scots have *couffoiren* ('coffers'? 'coifs'? tam-o'-shanters?).

After the Elephant and Fortune – perhaps more pointedly appropriate than usual on this occasion – comes the mountain of Parnassus: Phoebus and Pallas have overcome Mars and Bellona, and the Muses are awakening from their enforced sleep.

JOHN CARTWRIGHT

The last waggon before the *gheestelijcke puncten* ('spiritual scenes') shows farmworkers and artisans again, now rejoicing in the establishment of peace.

The overall message of this sequence, then, might be roughly summed up as 'Business as usual', with a strong hint to the workers of Antwerp that their interests are essentially the same as their employers', the devisors of these pageants.

Christopher van Essen's booklet of 1649[13] is notable for its elaborate and consistent interpretation of some of the well-established images. Fortune, for example, is said to represent good and bad luck, gain and loss; as often in this period, she is associated with Opportunity, whose lock of hair must be grasped with *Snelligheydt, vlijtigheydt, moeyte, en aerbeydt* ('quickness, skilfulness, effort, and hard work') so that one may come to *de rechte haven des ghewins* ('the proper haven of profit'). The Elephant which supports her is the *rechte uytbeeldinghe der ghewinsoeckeren* ('the appropriate representation of the profit-seeker'), upon whom Fortune gladly stands firm.

Fortune still represents the mutability of life in this world, but this notion is here entirely devoid of its traditional moral or spiritual associations. Mutability is now seen as providing opportunities for the entrepreneur – without ups and downs there can be no profits.

The selection of sinners specifically referred to in the description of the Hell pageant on this occasion is equally illuminating in its emphasis: those singled out in this account are *tyrannighe oberhoofden* ('tyrannical rulers'), the *woeckeraer* ('usurer'), who is having molten gold poured down his throat,[14] the bankrupt, whose skin is being pulled off by his creditors, the drunkard, and the frequenter of brothels – all these particular representatives of sin are either hindrances to free and effective trading (the tyrant and the usurer), a source of embarrassment and loss (the bankrupt), or (the drunk and the libertine) useless burdens on those others who are gainfully employed.

Jacob Mesens' book of 1661[15] is a detailed description and commentary with a strong antiquarian and classical tendency, but with the continuing emphasis on praise of Antwerp as a centre of trade and culture. There has been yet another war, and Neptune, for example, is now said to have come 'to congratulate us in this peace', while the young giants are dancing to show their joy that war is over, and are dressed in various national costumes to indicate *een vast verbondt* ('a firm alliance').

The Parnassus waggon is now said to indicate that Antwerp is as outstanding among cities in the Seven Arts 'as the moon among the stars', while the Maid of Antwerp has a silvered laurel branch, and will uphold 'all rules and laws in their proper state'.

The religious scenes follow, with the camel now coming between the Nativity and the Visit of the Three Kings, perhaps a sign of increased interest in geographical authenticity.

By the end of the seventeenth century, the Antwerp *ommegangen* had eventually – and symbolically – split into two separate events, one stream of which, the *processie*, continued the popular devotional tradition, with the emphasis on a relic or a saint, while the other, the *stoet* ('cortege'), was an avowedly secular occasion, often with a strong commercial-cum-political purpose.

What conclusions may we draw from this brief overview of a period in the history of the Antwerp *ommegangen*?

First, cultural artefacts are not inherently stable, with only one possible meaning or set of meanings – they may be adapted in quite unpredictable ways.

Secondly, this process of adaptation is not necessarily revolutionary in appearance, but may proceed incrementally and as it were, from 'inside'. The resultant tensions may be accommodated up to a point, but there comes a time when it has to be explicitly recognised that the ways have parted.

Specifically, in the first two centuries of the Antwerp *ommegangen*, no significant strains or deviations are noticeable in the overall presentation of popular piety and communal solidarity; from the late sixteenth century, however, the occasion itself and some of the particular forms in it are being used to promote a quite different view of the world, a distinctively modern moral, social, and economic paradigm.

It is only in retrospect that one can see the irrevocable decline in the course of this period in Antwerp's position as a European centre of trade; the beginnings of this slow decline coincide exactly with the increasingly explicit mercantilist emphasis of the new *puncten* incorporated in the annual processions and the unashamedly materialist reinterpretations of the older pageants and images. As the *Cooplieden* sensed a slipping away of the prosperity which they had come to take for granted, they turned to the *ommegangen* in the hope of shoring up their position, seeing them as a powerful means of disseminating their values and their socio-economic programme. To outsiders, they extended a message of welcome and reassurance, emphasising the fairness and probity of their commercial and legal institutions; to the less prosperous Antwerpenaars watching or taking part in the procession, the repeated message is that what is good for the *Cooplieden* is good for Antwerp and all its inhabitants, and that dissension and unrest are sinful and against nature.

In general, we may observe that by the mid seventeenth century, the new and reinterpreted elements of the Antwerp *ommegangen* reflect a fundamental secularisation of values, involving changes in attitudes to both the individual and the common profit. The governing assumptions of the Middle Ages have been quietly displaced – the modern world has arrived, advertising and all.

University of Cape Town

NOTES

For a discussion of the Antwerp, Brussels, and Leuven *ommegangen* from the point of view of theatre and religious iconography, with a bibliography of primary and secondary sources, see Meg Twycross 'The Flemish *Ommegang* and its Pageant Cars' *Medieval English Theatre 2:1* and *2:1* (1980) 15–41 and 80–98.

JOHN CARTWRIGHT
1. Larry Silver *The Paintings of Quinten Massys, with Catalogue Raisonné* (Montclair, New Jersey, 1984), 5.
2. Juan Calvete de Estrella, cited (in translation) from *Antwerp: Twelve Centuries of History and Culture* edited Karel van Isacker and Raymond van Uytven (Mercator, Antwerp, 1986) 84.
3. George Gascoigne has left an eloquent eye-witness account of this event: *The Spoile Of Antwerpe* (London, 1576: facsimile edition Da Capo Press, Amsterdam and New York, 1969).
4. One may note that the most confident, even bombastic, expressions of the centrality and importance of Antwerp in trade and culture were expressed – partly through the *ommegangen* – in the 1560s, when we may see in retrospect that the city's true peak had already passed. The same phenomenon may be observed in the cultural expressions of the British and American empires.
5. Sir Roy Strong, in *Art and Power: Renaissance Festivals* (Boydell Press, Woodbridge, 1984) has brilliantly documented and analysed the political agenda of Royal Entries and related shows in the Renaissance, especially in Italy.
6. *Landjuweel* was the term used in Brabant to refer to an occasional regional gathering of Chambers of Rhetoric, in which valuable prizes were offered in a variety of competitions. The Antwerp *Landjuweel* of 1561 was, by all accounts, the largest and most comprehensive such festival ever held. The competitions and allied festivities lasted for nineteen days; the texts of the poems and plays show an unselfconscious mixture of traditional piety, devotion to *Retorica* as the foremost of the Seven Liberal Arts, and concern for the corporate welfare of the merchant class, the *Cooplieden*. See C. Kruyskamp *Het Antwerpse Landjuweel van 1561* (De Nederlandsche Boekhandel, Antwerp, 1962); E. van Autenboer *Het Brabants Landjuweel der Rederijkers (1515–1561)* (Uitgeverij Merlijn, Middelburg, 1981); John Cartwright 'The Politics of Rhetoric: Three Plays by Willem van Haecht' *Comparative Drama* 26 (1992) 334–42, and 'The Antwerp Landjuweel of 1561 – a survey of the texts' in *The Centre and the Compass: Studies in Medieval Literature in Honor of Professor John Leyerle* edited Robert Taylor (Medieval Institute Publications, Kalamazoo, 1993) 68–84.
7. I am producing an edition of this manuscript for publication in article form. This description appears on fol. 130 of Sir Gilbert Hay's Prose MS, previously in the Abbotsford Library and now in the keeping of the National Library of Scotland – see *Gilbert of the Haye's Prose Manuscript* edited J.H. Stevenson (Scottish Text Society 44: Edinburgh, 1901) viii.
8. *Ordinancie, Inhoudende de Poincten vanden Heylighen Besnijdenis Ommeganck der Stadt van Antwerpen, geschiet inden Iare M.D.LXI* (Hans de Laet, Antwerp, 1561).

   For a discussion of the 1564 engravings by Cornelis Cort after Maarten van Heemskerk entitled *Circulus vicissitudinis rerum humanarum* ('Cycle of the vicissitudes of human affairs'), which apparently represent or are based on the 1561 *puncten* described here, see Ilja M. Veldman *Maarten van Heemskerk and Dutch Humanism in the Sixteenth Century* (Schwartz, Maarssen, 1977) 133–141.
9. Christopher van Essen *Antwerpsche Omme-gangh ofte Lvst-Trivmphe* (Jacob van Ghelen, Antwerp, 1649).
10. Gasper Bouttats *Verbeeldinghe vanden Triumphanten Ommeganck van Antwerpen...* (Bouttats, Antwerp, 1685).

11. *Nieuwe ende Poetijsche Inuentuien figuerlijcken vvtgestelt tot den Ommegangck van der stadt van Antwerpen ... 1564* (Hans de Laet, Antwerp, 1564); *Ordonantie inhoudende de nieuw Poincten van den Ommeganck hallf Oogst Anno 1566* (Hans de Laet, Antwerp, 1566).
12. *Cort Verhael van t'Ghene is ghepresenteert ghevveest in den Ommeganck die men tot Antvverpen ghehouden heeft op den xiiij. Iunij Anno 1609* (Abraham Verhoeven, Antwerp, 1609).
13. Van Essen *Antwerpsche Omme-gangh* (1649).
14. In representations of Hell or the Last Judgement, this punishment is traditionally reserved for Avarice: the particular application in this case to Usury reflects, once more, the specifically mercantile interpretation of these traditional images.
15. *Verbeldinghe van der Jaerlijckxen Trivmphanten Ommeganck van Antwerpen* (Jacob Mesens, Antwerp, 1661).

CHESTER'S MIDSUMMER SHOW:
Creation and Adaptation
David Mills

Background and Sources

Many English medieval towns celebrated Midsummer with civic ceremonial. The most frequent form of celebration – as, for example, at York[1] – was the marching Watch or Show, a civic procession accompanied by men in armour bearing weapons. But spectacular 'pageants', often in the form of large carnival figures such as giants or dragons, were frequently incorporated into such shows. London, perhaps inevitably, seems to offer an early model for such occasions, as Stow's famous description indicates,[2] but towns such as Newcastle with its Gogmagog Show[3] and Coventry with its male and female wicker giants[4] produced provincial examples of the same carnival activity.

The Midsummer Show at Chester, however, proved a peculiarly enduring example of the genre. Begun perhaps in the late fifteenth century or even much earlier, it remained an annual spectacle in the streets of Chester – with occasional disruptions in plague-time and for other factors – until 1641. Moreover, it was subsequently revived after the Restoration and continued until 1676, and attempts to re-establish it continued into the 1680s. Unfortunately, Chester's records, particularly for the fifteenth century and earlier, are very sparse. But from the mid sixteenth century onwards, the Show is fairly well documented, not only in the treasury and company accounts and the Assembly records of the city, but also by Chester's numerous antiquarians who valued the Show as part of the City's glorious past. Its alleged origin is noted in the various Mayors' Lists in the city, which were authoritatively revised in 1594 by the antiquarian William Aldersey.[5] It found a place in the notes of another Chester antiquarian, Archdeacon Robert Rogers (*obit* 1595), which formed the basis of the *Breviary of Chester History* that his son David compiled from them on several occasions from 1609 in memory of his father.[6] And a number of interesting supplementary documents are preserved among those Harley manuscripts which came from the collection of the Randle Holme family, Chester heralds and painters, who were closely involved in the arrangements for the Show.[7] Most of these records and accounts have been gathered and transcribed by L.M. Clopper in his *REED* volume, but a few were not available to him, and others, which relate to performances later than the REED cut-off date of 1642, have not yet been published in a systematic form.[8]

The older historians of Chester, such as Hemingway or Morris, were fascinated by the Show as a great popular festival, and tended to pour scorn by contrast on the absurdities of Chester's other great civic event, enacted only sporadically during the sixteenth century, its Whitsun Plays.⁹ More recent critics, such as Salter or Nelson, have focused on the textually controlled Whitsun Plays and have treated the Show as an interesting part of the surrounding cultural context.[10] That the Show and Plays were linked in the minds of his contemporaries is attested by David Rogers, who, in the 1609 version of his *Breviary of Chester History*, discusses the Plays and Show serially, with the statement that when the Plays 'went', the Show did not – and vice-versa. Both were splendid occasions for extravagant display at which the city's companies processed in their traditional order. The two festive actions also shared a number of characters. And on the last occasion on which the plays were performed, in 1575 after a plague-scare had passed, the performance occupied a four-day period at Midsummer when a carefully vetted selection of the Plays – omitting those held to contain 'superstition' – was put on. During the sixteenth century, both Show and Plays were valued as traditional activities publicly proclaiming a continuity from the distant past to the present – a past by then irretrievable because of the virtual absence of authentic documentation for the city's early history.

The assimilation of the Plays to this purpose has already received considerable attention.[11] Briefly, some time between 1471/2 and 1521 the cycle was separated from the Corpus Christi procession and moved to Whitsun, where it appears in 1521, under the control of the Mayor and Assembly. It expanded into a three-day performance by the 1530s at the latest. Possibly the system of waggon-performance at stations in the streets was introduced during this transition. Simultaneously, theories of the Plays' antique origin were proclaimed officially. In 1531/2 a Proclamation was describing the plays as 'ancient', and attributing their authorship to an otherwise unknown monk of Chester Abbey in the 1370s–80s, Henry Francis, and their production to the enterprise of Chester's reputed first mayor, Sir John Arneway, whose mayoralty was erroneously ascribed to the early fourteenth century until Aldersey corrected the city's Mayoral Lists. After the Reformation, the Banns attributed the Plays to Ranulf Higden, a monk-historian of Chester's Abbey in 1299–1364, and asserted both the antiquity of the enterprise – evidenced in the archaic language and crude production-methods – and its generic innovation as the first English cycle.

But the Show held a comparable importance in the eyes of the City, for it not only served the same function of proudly displaying contemporary civic hierarchy and establishing a solidarity between the present and past. It also proved the more powerful and adaptable vehicle for those purposes. By the end of the sixteenth century it was considered to be at least as old as the Plays, and possibly older. In Rogers' words: 'The showe or watche. on midsomer eaue called midsommer showe. yearelye now vsed within the Cittie of Chester. was vsed in the tyme of those whitson playes. and *before so farre as I canne vnderstande*'.[12] Not being subject to the same theological-political suspicion as the Plays, it was more frequently seen in the city's streets in the sixteenth century than the Plays, and it continued long after the Plays had been abolished in Chester, and long after similar Shows had been abolished

DAVID MILLS

in London, Coventry, Newcastle, and elsewhere. The purpose of this paper is to suggest the changing functions of, and attitudes towards, the Show which ensured that survival.

The Shape of the Show

Though discussed by others before, it may be helpful to envisage the particular form that the marching Watch took in later-sixteenth-century Chester, always recognising the dangers of arguing generally from sporadic records and accounts that date only from the mid-sixteenth century onwards. The Show fell into two parts – one provided by the city authorities and the other by the city companies. The show provided by the city authorities, first mentioned unambiguously in the Treasurers' Account Roll of 1554/5,[13] was carnivalesque. The Painters' Company was responsible to the City for providing or renovating its huge figures, for arranging their transport in the Show, and for storing them. The Company was reimbursed somewhat by the City but never adequately, so it also bore some of the material costs. We get a clear idea of the character of the properties it supplied from a commission dated 21 April 1564, apparently seeking to renew the pageants, by which the Mayor, Aldermen and Council of Chester contracted with Thomas Poole and Robert Halwood of the Painters' Company,

> to bring ffurth repare & have in redines for the wache afforeseid all suche ornamente*s* as hereafter ensueth according as the seid wache here to fore hathe ben set furth, withall furnytures thervnto belongeng v*i*d*elicet* ffoure Ieans, won vnicorne won drombandarye, won Luce, won Camell, won Asse, won dragon, sixe hobby horses & sixtene naked boyes, And the same being in A Redines shall bere & carie or cause to be borne & caried during the seid wache from place to place according as the same have ben vsed vpon their proper cost*es* & charges.[14]

Another record, undated, in British Library MS Harley 2150, clarifies the financial responsibility for these displays.[15] The City Treasury paid for the four giants. The Mayor had formerly paid for 'the Citty or Maior's Mount till mr. Edwards tyme', but this expense had been offloaded on to the Treasury. The Mayor continued to pay for 'his 6 mens garlaits and balls for his burches', together with the wages of the man who carried his mount and of the attendants, who also received 'new gloues', and all entertainment expenses. The Sheriffs paid for their show, the Elephant and Castle – another undated item in MS Harley 2150 refers to the 'Elephant & Castell & Cupitt to sute out of it' and indicates that two men carried it. They too had to pay for garlands and gloves and other equipment for their attendants. Chester's Leavelookers paid for four beasts – the unicorn, antelope, 'Flowerdeluce' and Camel, carried by eight men – and the four hobby horses and the boys to carry them and dance alongside them. The Painters supplied a dragon, six naked boys to beat at it, and morris dancers and music. Additionally, there was a feature called 'the marchant mount' 'with a shipp to turne', requiring further boys and five men to carry it.[16]

The second part of the Show consisted of the individual 'shows' provided by the companies. It is in this part that we find mention in the companies' records of characters in costume who are familiar from the Plays. Order 21 of the Barber Surgeons' Register Book provides for 'one to Ride abraham and a younge stripleinge or boy to Ride Isaacke and they to be sett fourth according to Auncient custome';[17] the Company was responsible for the play that included the Sacrifice of Isaac. The Linendrapers, Bricklayers and Brickmakers provided Balaam and his ass (1601, 1620), which appear in the play for which they were responsible.[18] The Painters' Accounts for 1576 include 'Item, to the ij shepertes for going vppon the Syltes xxd',[19] which is usually taken to be an allusion to the *Shepherds' Play* for which that company was responsible. The Smiths' Accounts of 1566/7 include payments 'for gloues for the docters' and 'little god' and for 'gilding Gods face' on Midsummer Eve, probably referring to the episode of the boy Jesus before the Doctors in their play.[20] The Shoemakers' Accounts for 1561/2 record 'more for the gyldynge of godes fase on medsomare heue x d', for 1562/3 'Item spend in settyng out of mare modelan on mydsomar even xxd', and for 1563/4 'Item payd vpon mydsomer yeven ffor the setynge ffowrthe of marye modeand and Iudas the some of xvjd' – all characters being from their play of the Betrayal.[21] In a marginal note on later reforms, David Rogers mentions 'the Diuell Ridinge in fethers before the butchars' who were responsible for the play containing the Temptation of Christ, and 'A man in womans apparell with a diuel waytinge on his horse called cappes & canes'. The Innkeepers' Accounts suggest a woman with an iron-bound cane who rode with two devils in costume and used the cane to break 'goddertes' as she rode. The 1589/90 account specifies 'two dosen of goddertes' at xvjd.[22] This figure was evidently the Ale-wife who appears at the end of the Innkeepers' play of *The Harrowing of Hell* in four of the manuscripts.[23]

These characters must have been recognisable to the audience, and were perhaps the most readily available 'costumed contribution', since in a play-year each company seems to have provided one or more costumed characters from its play to accompany the crier on St George's Day when the Banns were read.[24] Nor was the direction of influence necessarily from Plays to Show. If the Shepherds did walk on stilts in the Painters' play (and there seems little evidence to support that, though they walked on stilts at the reading of the Banns), it would hardly be for the contingencies of the biblical narrative; and the 'ale-wife scene' appears to offer a virtuoso role for an already familiar character – perhaps the revision for the 1575 Midsummer performance? But, as we shall see, an alternative to the Play-figures was available by the time of these records, and may have been there from the beginnings of the Show.

These two interconnected shows were contained in a great civic procession which assembled at the Northgate Bar and moved through the streets of the town to the beat of the city's drummer, presenting largesse to the prisoners at the Northgate and Castle gaols, and ending at St Oswald's Church. The companies processed in their traditional hierarchy – the same order as in the Plays – with their members in full livery and with their banners borne with them. In the Painters' Minute Book for 1640 it was reported that 'the [Painters'] Company banners being spoyled last midsomer Eue by Rayne', they had been inspected and repairs agreed.[25] As a Watch, the procession was escorted by armed men – in 1632, by four men, 'with halbards to keepe the Compennys in order at the show' and 'Edward parry and ... his mate' to lead and keep the armed guard in order.[26]

Like all public ceremonial, Chester's Show was multi-functional. It was political in its display of the civic hierarchy in all its order and splendour. It was popular in its appeal – Rogers notes with disdain in 1609 the popular outcry against moves at the end of the previous century to reform it.[27] The two aspects are reflected in its alternative titles, for officially it was know as 'The Midsummer Watch' and the name 'Midsummer Show' is frequently qualified in official records as the popular or vulgar appellation. The Show was also commercial, for it took place on the occasion of Chester's annual Midsummer Fair and became one of the attractions – along with the licensing of minstrels at the Minstrels' Court of the Dutton family[28] – which accompanied that great three-day commercial enterprise. But the Show also fed the 'past-consciousness' of the city in its alleged antiquity which was proclaimed by the herald at the start as he issued a general summons to all the aldermen and stewards of the companies to appear 'accordinge to Ancient Custome' and then called up each company in turn to 'Come forth with your shewes accordinge to Ancient Custome', much as the herald called up the companies in the reading of the Play-Banns.[29] It was claimed of the Show 'a particular profite to eich one & honor to the Citty to preserue theis auntient Customs'.[30]

The Beginnings of the Show

Despite belief in the Show's antique origin, the Mayors' Lists in Chester circulating in the sixteenth century give a precise and comparatively recent date for its institution. Under the entry for the mayoralty of Richard Goodman in 1498/9 is a record which in the admirably cautious words of William Aldersey in 1594 reads: 'In this yeare it appeareth the watche vpon mydsomer euen begune'.[31] This claim may reflect only an interest in the origins of the Show akin to that which we find with the Whitsun Plays; but, unlike Arneway and Higden, Goodman was not a figure of the remote past. If the ostensibly contradictory statements about the Show's origins are to be reconciled, it might be that Goodman institutionalised an already established local custom as a great civic occasion, or significantly changed an existing procession, perhaps on the model of similar celebrations elsewhere. London's Midsummer Show which, according to Stow, included giants and morris-dancers provided by the City and a limited number of pageants provided by the companies, *may* have begun in the early fifteenth century.

Some indication of the significance of the Show is, however possibly indicated in the remainder of the entry under Goodman's mayoralty:

> also the northsyde of the pentize buylded, prince Arthure came to chester aboute the fourth of august, the assumption of our ladie played before the prince at the .Abbaye gate, the xxvth august the prince made mr goodman esquier [word lost] the xix daye of September he departed from chester.'[32]

Clopper has pointed out some of the difficulties in reconciling the date of the Prince's visit with midsummer in Goodman's mayoralty,[33] but the entry is less important as historical record (though it may well be accurate) than as an indication of a nexus of significant events to which the Show's origins are appropriately related.

The completion of the Pentice, Chester's major administrative building, at the High Cross where the four Roman streets met, must itself have been a significant achievement. While its opening was an occasion for celebration, the new Pentice can be regarded also as a symbol of civic authority and a sign of a growing civic confidence which the new Midsummer Show could reflect and promote. Chester was now embarking on the most powerful period of its post-Roman history, which would culminate in the palatinate status accorded to the city in the 'Great Charter' granted to it by Henry VII in 1506. The visit of Prince Arthur, Prince of Wales and Earl of Chester, was also a great event which was marked by the performance of one of the religious plays, no longer extant. R.V.H. Burne has connected this event circumstantially with the completion of the great West Front of St Werburgh's Abbey,[34] and though this link is highly speculative, there seems no doubt that a major building programme was at least under way in the city when the play was performed and that both the statuary on the present West Front and the dedication of the present cathedral suggest a particular devotion to the Virgin Mary. The honour done to Goodman, and through him to the town, provided annalists with the connecting point between Show, Pentice, and royal visit.

But we can now only speculate on the possible political significance of the Show's institution. The Midsummer Show does seem to have become regarded as a celebration of the city and its government, perhaps to be considered as Chester's Mayor's Show, and it is certainly plausible to associate its origins with the confident establishment of Chester's administration at the centre of its city. Perhaps there was also a desire to emulate London's Midsummer Show and those of other towns with which Chester wished to be compared. Possibly also the route and content of the Show signalled different priorities from those signalled by the city's Corpus Christi Play, whose procession from St Mary's-on-the-Hill beside the castle of the Earls of Chester, through the town and out to the old Norman church and former cathedral of St John's-without-the-Walls, linked older seats of political and ecclesiastical power. It is tempting to speculate that the events associated with 1498–9 were somehow connected with the transfer of the Plays from the Corpus Christi procession to Whitsun, under the closer jurisdiction of the City. Or perhaps the

Show's institution was in some way related to the ongoing dispute between the City and the Abbey about St Werburgh's Fair, the great three-day Midsummer Fair whose control had been vested in the Abbey in 1093 by its founder, Hugh Lupus, Earl of Chester, and which would finally pass into the control of the City by the Great Charter of 1506, despite the appeals of the Abbot. Would a great civic ceremonial on the eve of the Fair make some sort of political statement?

What is certain is that later annalists assigned the historical foundation of the Show to the 'time when civic spirit was consolidated in Chester, when mayor, sheriffs, aldermen, and councillors seemed to be developing into a fairly closely-knit oligarchy, proud of the city and jealous of its (and their) privileges'.[35]

The Decorum of Civic Ceremonial

The later sixteenth century suggests a different mood in Chester from that early confidence. Many of the privileges granted by the Great Charter were whittled away under the influence of Tudor centralism, and in part the City responded by seeking solidarity with its past. The antiquarian writings and investigations and the concern with the origins of the Plays are two manifestations of this insecurity. The Show is drawn into the same movement as it is similarly adapted to the needs of the times rather than rejected as an outdated and expensive activity.

The changes in the Show are often attributed to the influence of the growing Puritan element in the city and the surrounding area which felt offended by its conjunction of the carnival and the religious. In his *Breviary* of 1609 Rogers speaks of abuses in the Show 'that the watchmen of oure soules <or Deuines> spake againste as thinges not fitt to be vsed',[36] suggesting opposition from the pulpit, and praises the reforms of the Puritan Mayor of 1599/1600, Henry Hardware, who courted unpopularity from the populace in effecting them. As a Mayors' List says:

> he caused the Gyanntes, in the Mydsomer show to be put downe <and broken> and not to goe, The devill in his fethers <to ride for the buchers but a boy <as others had>> he put Awaye. and the Cuppes and Cannes. And dragon and Naked boyes. <but caused a man in complet Armor to goe before the show in their steed>[37]

But the City figures were reconstructed the following year by order of Mayor John Radcliffe[38] and the carnival figures continued.

It is notable that Hardware did not attempt to suppress the celebration but rather to reshape it as a more decorous civic occasion. Rogers thinks of the kind of continuity the Protestants sought in the Reformation when he says that those opposing the changes did not know 'that Antiante sinnes oughte to haue new Reformation' and his side-note indicates that Hardware particularly objected to the representation of the devil and to the man dressing up as a woman,[39] and in this aspect of his reforms, Hardware was successful. The reference to the Butchers having to substitute a boy 'as others did' suggests that most companies had, in any case, already been moving from the Play-characters in their shows towards young boys in rich costume on horseback, so that the survival of 'Cups and Cannes' must have seemed out of keeping with the developing format. The Play-characters in the Show were always a sort of visual shorthand for their fuller rôle in the Cycle, and as performances became less frequent and finally ceased, these figures would progressively lose their associative significance. Moreover, when companies no longer had to prepare for play-productions, it made good sense to direct their resources exclusively to an appropriate display for Midsummer. The inevitable separation of the Show from the Plays led to a greater sense of it as an autonomous form.

We can see this transition reflected in the Painters' Accounts. In 1570/1 their Show-accounts include: 'Item for towe men goyng on the styltes xijd' but in 1573/4 this becomes: 'Item spent at the dressyng [A] of the chyld vppon mydsomer euen ijd', though a further iiijd had to be paid out to Thomas Poole's child 'bycose he plednot our god'![40] It seems unlikely that this change was occasioned by religious pressure, but rather by convenience, economics, and a desire to conform to a growing pattern. It met many contemporary objections. In his *Breviary* of 1618/19 Rogers speaks unequivocally of the Show: 'Bot for the decensie of it now, it is most Comendable, rich, and beautifull, The like in few Cities of this lande',[41] praise reminiscent of the proud boast in the Post-Reformation Banns to the Plays which Rogers had transcribed in his preceding entry:

> And then dare I compare that, this lande throughout,
> none had the like nor the like darste set out   40–1

By the seventeenth century the Companies' Show had attained a fixed and uniform format, varying only in the extravagance of display. The Mercers' and the Ironmongers' Companies solved a possible conflict of interests in their merger by the Company Ordinances, confirmed in their accounts from 1606 to the last pre-Commonwealth Show of 1641[42] which provide for both a Lord and a Lady:

> some comely striplinge or boye. to Ride before the same companye, and also to get some other childe, to Ride as agentelwoman or ladye ... and the saide boye and ladye to Ride vpon two seuerall horses by them selves, and the saide Stewardes for the tyme beinge, to bye for eyther of said children, at the companyes charge. eyther of them a suit of apparill fyttinge for the said shew. not exceedinge aboue the some of five poundes of Currant money, and soe the same sutes of apparill to contynue to the companyes vse, from tyme <to tyme> at theire pleasures.

So the 1641/2 accounts include 'paid for the lords, gloues hose rosses and shooes 00–10–00' and 'payd for the Lady shooes, ribbins, roses and stockinges 00–10–00'. The interesting mélange which distinguished individual companies has, however, been lost in the quest for the picturesque. The Show has become a civic duty rather than a celebration and can develop no further. The Commonwealth period simply closes a form that had, by 1641, already outlasted its usefulness as a communal art-form.

The Marketing of Heritage

The Restoration movement to revive the Show may have owed something to a nostalgic determination to return to the Royalist past in the hope of restoring 'normality' after the disruptions of the time. Chester, as a Royalist stronghold in a countryside predominantly Parliamentarian in sympathies, had been badly damaged both morally and physically by its prolonged siege and surrender in the Civil War. While the Restoration was a boost to morale, the city faced the problem of re-establishing its commerce and reviving its fortunes in order to rebuild. Memories of the 1630s, 'a time of unprecedented prosperity in Chester', must have intensified the sense of recession in the 1650s, though that recession owed more to long-term changes in the social and political order than to short-term crisis.[43]

It was against this background that in the Assembly of 19 March 1657:

> It was declared by the worshipfull Richard Mynshull Esquire Maior of this Cittie that it was the desire of the greatest part of the companyes within this Cittie that the Auncient custome of the said companyes Attending vpon Mr. Maior in their gownes vpon Midsomers eve (vulgarly called Midsomer Shew) haveing layne dorment for many yeares now last past should bee revived and observed alledging it to tend much to the promocion of trading and other advantages to the said Cittie.

The resolution was passed on a majority vote.[44] But this decision was evidently not implemented, for a call for its implementation was made at the Assembly of 22 March 1661, stating that 'as to the manner how the same shall bee performed It is referred to the Maior and Justices of the peace of this Cittie to order and determine the same as in theire discretions shall seeme most meet and convenient'.[45] Whatever measures were taken seem to have been inadequate for, in an order of 8 June 1666, regulations were tightened because 'seuerall misdemeanors and disorders haue of Late yeares past beene done and committed Att the tyme of the Show commonly called Midsummer Show'.[46]

City and company accounts confirm that the Show resumed in its familiar form. The civic figures were restored, for the 1663/4 Treasurers' Roll includes: 'paid for painting ye Giants & Majors mount & ye stakes at ye Rood eye 3–15–04'; and phrases in an undated bill of account transcribed in BL MS Harley 2150, such as that the giants are 'to be made as neere as may be like as the were before', and the merchants' mount 'as auntiently as it was', suggest a nostalgic desire to recreate the old Show accurately.[47] The Painters were again in charge of preparing the great figures (see below). And the boy-riders returned in the Companies' Procession. The Glovers' Accounts for 1661 are typical:[48]

Item paid to Mr Maior toward Midsomer Shoe	01–00–00
Item paid for Match and Pouder	00–06–10

Item paid to Gloues for the Ald: and stewardes	00–10–10
Item spent at the shoe	00–03–00
Item paid to the Musicke	00–10–00
Item paid to the Cryer	00–01–00
....	
Item for Gloues for 3 men	00–03–00
Item for Ribins for hors and men	00–07–02
Item paid for 3 yards of Cotten tape to tye vp ye hors tayl	00–00–07
Item paid for Mending the Collors agt: Mid: show	00–02–06
Item paid for Carieing the Collors	00–01–00
Item paid for bear bread and Tobacoe on Mid: Eue	01–02–00
Item paid for the boyes hose shoose and hat	00–10–00

and an Assembly resolution of 1671 includes a penalty of £5 for 'every company that shall neglect or faile to putt forth theire boy and horse in usuall manner'.[49] Company records continue to list expenditure on the Show until 1676, after which it was discontinued, though a production must have been contemplated in 1677 because the painter Randle Holme was paid £20 in 1679,

> in full satisfaccion of all his disbursements and other charges about the Gyants and other Pageants for the Midsummer shew intended to haue beene obserued in the yeare one thousand six hundred seaventy seaven And whereof a noate of particulers was produced and read in this Assembly, and also in full recompence and satisfaccion of all his other demands touching or concerneing the said shew.[50]

The reason for the pressure to revive the Show is found in an Assembly decision of 12 May 1671: 'That the Shew commonly called Midsummer shew, may bee observed upon tuesday in Whitson weeke next'.[51] As the Plays in their final production had moved to Midsummer, now the Show in its final years moved to Whitsun. The actual occasion of celebration no longer had significance. The priorities behind this move are stated with disarming honesty. First, the transfer would boost trade 'by attracting very many (if not a multitude of people) therevnto, specially vpon this occasion to see the shew att that tyme, by whom noe little mony may bee expended within the said Citty'. Second, 'not onely how inconvenient, but alsoe how preiudiciall it was (as hee [the Mayor] conceived) to the Cittizens to haue the said shew att Midsumer in the faire tyme, in that it did cause many of them to shutt in theire shopps (haueing noe apprentices) and the rest to l[...]e their shopps and busine[....]'. Behind these lines we see the desperate desire to increase trade by spreading the city's attractions across the calendar, and also the sign of decline in the claim that many now had no apprentices to look after their shop while they processed and so lost the benefit of the Midsummer crowds. Chester was truly trading on its past.

Evidently the Show did not provide the returns envisaged. After the cancellation in 1677, someone must have asked about future plans, and a resolution was put

DAVID MILLS

before the Assembly on 7 June 1678 'whether the show commonly called Midsummer Shew shall bee ever hereafter, or never obserued within this Citty'.[52] The decision was 'never hereafter'. Unfortunately, the record is considerably more reticent than that of 1671 and gives no indication of the considerations that led to the decision. Despite this resolution, on 30 April 1680 the Assembly was asked 'whether the shew commonly called the Midsummer Shew shall bee obserued this yeare, or not'; but the answer was 'That the said Shew shall not bee obserued nor kept this yeare'.[53]

University of Liverpool

NOTES

1. *REED: York* edited Alexandra F. Johnston and Margaret Rogerson, 2 vols (University of Toronto Press, 1979) *1* 399, line 34 – 400, line 7: 1582 House Books (13 June).
2. *A Survey of London by John Stow* edited Charles Lethbridge Kingsford, 2 vols (Clarendon Press, Oxford, 1908) *1* 101–104 under 'Of watches in this Citie, and other <matters> commanded, and the cause why'. For the relation of the London Midsummer Show to the Lord Mayor's Show, see Sheila Williams 'The Lord Mayor's Show in Tudor and Stuart Times' *The Guildhall Miscellany* 10 (1959) 3–18, especially 3–6.
3. *REED: Newcastle Upon Tyne* edited J.J. Anderson (University of Toronto Press, 1982) xv.
4. *REED: Coventry* edited R.W. Ingram (University of Toronto Press, 1981) xxiii–xxiv; Thomas Sharp *A Dissertation on the Pageants or Dramatic Mysteries Anciently Performed at Coventry* (Merridew and Son, Coventry, 1825: facsimile reprint EP Publishing Ltd, Wakefield, 1973) 174–206.
5. Aldersey's book, containing his original revised Mayors' List, was deposited in the Chester City Record Office in 1985 (Ref. CRO 469/592) but was not available to L.M. Clopper for the REED volume (see note 8 below). I offer a description of the manuscript, together with transcripts of entries relevant to drama, in 'William Aldersey's "History of the Mayors of Chester"' *REED Newsletter 14:2* (1989) 2-10. On the importance of Aldersey's revision, see *REED: Chester* edited L.M. Clopper (University of Toronto Press, 1979: hereafter *REED: Chester*) xxv–xxvi.
6. On Robert and David Rogers and the versions of the *Breviary*, see *REED: Chester* xxiii–xxxvi, and Steven E. Hart and Margaret M. Knapp *'The Aunchant and Famous Cittie': David Rogers and the Chester Mystery Plays* (Peter Lang, New York, 1988). References to the *Breviary*, unless otherwise stated, are to the selected transcripts from the 1609 version in *REED: Chester* 232–54. The reference here is to page 252, lines 16–26.
7. On the four generations of the Randle Home family, see J.P. Earwaker *The Four Randle Holmes* (1892), reprinted from the *Journal of the Chester Archaeological and Historical Society* (1891).
8. I have drawn extensively upon the *REED: Chester* transcripts in this paper. Records of Chester drama to 1642 not included in *REED: Chester* will be published in *REED: Cheshire* edited by Elizabeth Baldwin and myself (in progress). It is hoped that the appendices of the volume will include the Restoration civic records and company accounts relating to the Show. They are to be available on the database of Cheshire drama records held at the University of Liverpool.

9. Joseph Hemingway *History of the City of Chester* 2 vols (J. Fletcher, Chester, 1831) *1* 199–206; Rupert H. Morris *Chester in the Plantagenet and Tudor Reigns* (privately published, Chester, n.d.) 323–30.
10. F.M. Salter *Medieval Drama in Chester* (University of Toronto Press, 1955) 22 and 28; Alan H. Nelson *The Medieval English Stage: Corpus Christi Pageants and Plays* (Chicago University Press, Chicago and London, 1974) 165–9.
11. See Salter *Chester* 29–53, 'Town and Gown'; L.M. Clopper 'The History and Development of the Chester Cycle' *Modern Philology* 75 (1978) 219–46; R.M. Lumiansky and David Mills *The Chester Mystery Cycle: Essays and Documents* (University of North Carolina Press, Chapel Hill, 1983) 165–202, 'The Development of the Cycle'.
12. *REED: Chester* 252, lines 17–20 (*Rogers' Breviary*: 1609): my italics.
13. *REED: Chester* 55 (*Treasurers' Account Rolls*, mb 4): 'Item payde for mydsomer wache for the Caredge of the pagions and paynters xviijs vjd'.
14. *REED: Chester* 71, line 34 – 72, line 26 (*Midsummer Giants*); the quotation is from 72, lines 5–14.
15. *REED: Chester* 477, line 14 – 478, line 20 (*Midsummer Show*).
16. *REED: Chester* 481, line 9 – 482, line 24 (*Midsummer Show*). The 'Elephant' quotation is from 481, lines 24–25; the 'marchant mount' from 481, lines 22–3.
17. *REED: Chester* 469, lines 17–19 (*Barber Surgeons' Records*).
18. *REED: Chester* 206, line 5 (*Linendrapers' Order for Midsummer*); 485, lines 6–8 (*Cappers, Pinners, Wiredrawers, and Linendrapers' Company Minute Book*, 1603). This company Order Book, which was not available to Clopper who therefore relied upon printed sources, is now deposited in Chester City Record Office (Ref. CRO G6/1). The order, reprinted by *REED: Chester* on 206 from Morris *Chester in the Plantagenet and Tudor Reigns*, is on fol. 16^V (numbered page 27) of the book. It differs in some minor respects from Morris's version; that in *REED: Chester* 385 is closer.
19. *REED: Chester* 120, line 3 (*Painters, Glaziers, Embroiderers, and Stationers' Records*).
20. *REED: Chester* 75, lines 26–9 (*Smiths, Cutlers, and Plumbers' Records*).
21. *REED: Chester* 68; line 27; 69, lines 27–8; and 71, lines 17–18 (*Cordwainers and Shoemakers' Records*).
22. *REED: Chester* 253, margins (*Rogers' Breviary*, 1609); *REED: Chester* 158, line 38 (*Innkeepers' Records*).
23. *The Chester Mystery Cycle* edited by R.M. Lumiansky and David Mills EETS SS 3 (1974) play 17, lines 277–336.
24. See *REED: Chester* 325, lines 26–33 (*Rogers' Breviary*, 1618/19).
25. *REED: Chester* 452, lines 29–41 (*Painters, Glaziers, Embroiderers, and Stationers' Records*).
26. *REED: Chester* 408, lines 18–21 (*City Treasurer's Accounts*).
27. *REED: Chester* 253, lines 11–15 (*Breviary*, 1609).
28. *REED: Chester* li–lii.
29. *REED: Chester* 474–6 (*Midsummer Proclamation*, undated); quotation from 474, lines 35–6.
30. *REED: Chester* 478, lines 40–2 (*Midsummer Show*, undated).
31. Aldersey: CRO 469/542, fol. 26^V.
32. Aldersey: fol. 26^V; compare *REED: Chester* 21, line 18 – 22, line 9.
33. *REED: Chester* xliii–xliv.

DAVID MILLS

34. R.V.H. Burne *The Monks of Chester: the History of St Werburgh's Abbey* (SPCK, London, 1962) 142–3.
35. J.T.P. Driver *Cheshire in the Later Middle Ages, 1399–1540* (Cheshire Community Council, Chester, 1971) 38.
36. *REED: Chester* 253, lines 8–10 (*Breviary*, 1609).
37. *REED: Chester* 198, lines 14–19 (*Mayors' List 5*). The words between <> are interlineated in the MS. See also similar entries in *Mayors' Lists* 8 and 15 on 198–9.
38. *REED: Chester* 206, lines 22–23 (*Mayors' List 5*).
39. *REED: Chester* 253, lines 12–13 and margin (*Breviary*, 1609).
40. *REED: Chester* 90, line 14, and 100, lines 17–18, 34 (*Painters, Glaziers, Embroiderers, and Stationers' Records*).
41. *REED: Chester* 323, lines 35–7 (*Breviary*, 1618/19).
42. *REED: Chester* 471, lines 15–17 (*Mercers, Ironmongers, Grocers, and Apothecaries' Records*: undated order), and 214–216.
43. On Chester's declining fortunes, see Nick Alldridge 'The Mechanics of Decline: Population, Migration and Economy in Early Modern Chester' in *English Towns in Decline 1350 to 1800* edited by Michael Reed (Centre for Urban History, University of Leicester, 1986) unpaginated: the quotation is from page 12 of essay 3.
44. *Assembly Book 2, 1624–1684* (Chester City Record Office, Ref. AB/2) fol. 119^r.
45. *Assembly Book 2, 1624–1684* fol. 132^r.
46. *Assembly Book 2, 1624–1684* fol. 155^r.
47. *Treasurers' Rolls, 1663–1664* (Chester City Record Office Ref. TAR 3/54) mb. 5; *REED: Chester* 481, lines 15–16, 22 (*Midsummer Show*).
48. *Wet and Dry Glovers' Company Book 1629–1948* 154. This book is now on temporary deposit at the Chester City Record Office, catalogue G11/1.
49. *Assembly Book 2* fol.171^v, 12 May 1671.
50. *Assembly Book 2* fol.190^v, 15 July 1679.
51. *Assembly Book 2* fol.171^r, 12 May 1671.
52. *Assembly Book 2* fol.188^r, 7 June 1678.
53. *Assembly Book 2* fol.192^r, 30 April 1680.

THE WELLS SHOWS OF 1607
James Stokes

In the summer of 1607, a major controversy erupted in the city of Wells, Somerset, when a large group of its citizens – supported by the Mayor, several officials of the Cathedral Chapter, five of the city's six craft guilds, and several of the local gentry – organised an elaborate series of ales, shows and other entertainments spanning a two-month period. Opponents, claiming that the shows libelled them and violated laws against playing on the Sabbath, sued the players, the organisers, and the supporters, thereby precipitating a two-year legal war between the two sides.

Copious records of the case, including numerous witness statements, survive in documents at the PRO and elsewhere.[1] In 1936, C.J. Sisson included a popularised summary of the controversy in his *Lost Plays of Shakespeare's Age*.[2] His purpose was not to provide a close scholarly analysis of the events in the context of the Somerset entertainment tradition, but to present the controversy as part of the cultural backdrop to Shakespeare, and as a comic misadventure mainly illustrative of the rustic humour to be found in Elizabethan/Jacobean provincial life. Typically, his summary blends description of the events with bits of dialogue from Shakespeare and Marlowe, and quoted material from the Puritan writer Stubbes. Though colourful and useful, Sisson's treatment, as does that of those who subsequently cite him,[3] unduly emphasises one of the events (the May Game), conflates several others, and generally ignores numerous instructive features of the documents. Records of the case preserve, for example, uniquely detailed descriptions of civic and craft-guild entertainments in a county for which almost no other such guild records survive; festive activities encompassing all the playing days traditionally associated with late spring and summer entertainment in Somerset; local minstrelsy and ballad-making; and information about the nature of civic sponsorship of entertainments in Somerset. Such features, and others in documents related to the case, have never been studied in a thorough, systematic way.

This article proposes that the above shows and activities related to them between 30 April and 25 June 1607 were not merely an incidental, self-generating chain of events, but a concerted attempt to re-establish traditional festive summer entertainments, as held in Wells for centuries, but suppressed during the late sixteenth and early seventeenth centuries. From that perspective, the records of the case offer an opportunity for valuable new understanding of the playing tradition in Somerset's cathedral city.

JAMES STOKES

Background

Starting in the late sixteenth century, justices periodically issued or renewed quarter sessions and assize orders suppressing church ales, bear-baiting, minstrelsy, and other traditional entertainments in Somerset. The first such order for which there is a record was issued at Michaelmas 1594, followed by a second in 1596;[4] a third, in January 1608, six months after the Wells Shows, reaffirmed an order made by 'the late Lord Cheife Justice of England' and twenty-two Justices of the Peace for Somerset.[5] Yet in 1607 supporters of the shows in Wells defended them on the grounds that they were traditional there. One 35-year-old resident testified in 1609 that it was 'an auncyent Custome' for the Mayor and inhabitants to hold ales at the church-house of St Cuthbert's Parish Church during May and June, with pageants, May Games, and morris dances to raise funds for the parish;[6] the shows, he testified, had been performed 'thrice' in his lifetime (thus at least three times since 1572). But a former Mayor testified that an order suppressing the shows had been 'kepte and observed' in Wells (fol. 231ᵛ) for '13. or .14. yeares after [the suppression orders]'. Thus, though perceived as traditional, it may be that no shows had been held in Wells between c.1596 and 1607.

The trouble in 1607 seems to have been the culmination of a long-term struggle between two factions within the city. The first was a large group, including the Mayor, the Dean of Wells Cathedral, Sir John Rodney, the vicar, and numerous burgesses, guildsmen, and parishioners. Because they wished to re-establish church ales along with other parish and civic entertainments, these traditionalists were accused of being 'popishlie affected' (fol. 49). Their opponents, whom they in turn described as a 'factious' group who kept company with 'professional puritans' (fol. 156ᵛ), were led by a wealthy clothier named John Hole (constable in 1607). Hole had generated enmity as early as 1598 when, serving as churchwarden, he attempted to remove an altar from the parish church. Opposition to that move was led by several persons who were later involved in the shows.[7] A number of nuisance suits grew out of the feud between 1598 and 1607. By granting the traditionalists permission to hold an ale in 1607 to repair a church bell (fols 12ʳ⁻ᵛ), Benjamin Hayden, Dean of Wells Cathedral, was reasserting the increasingly explosive view that parish entertainments were matters for diocesan authorities not laymen (or apparently civil courts) to decide. Hole, then constable, directly challenged the Dean by arresting the show-makers. The incident involving the shows, thus, needs to be seen within the context of the larger struggle for control of the religious, political, and social culture in Wells and throughout the county. Because the shows derived their legitimacy in part from the argument that they were an ancient custom, the structure and pattern they followed provides useful information about the playing tradition in Wells (as perceived by its residents in 1607).

The following summaries extract a chronology and brief descriptions of the entertainments from the mass of evidence (212 folios of charges, interrogatories, and

THE WELLS SHOWS OF 1607

depositions by fifty witnesses) surviving in the Star Chamber case. Then follows a discussion of some implications arising from the evidence.

30 April 1607 (Thursday)

Summoning to the maypole. Between dawn and 8 a.m. about twenty men, women, and children, led by a boy drummer, paraded through the streets 'in sporte and merryment to fetch in May & to sett vpp the May Poole ... in the high streete of the said City [Wells]' (fol. 172).[8]

3 May 1607 (Sunday Easter 4)

Church ale and May revel with street dancing. About 7 a.m., shoemaker Thomas Peters (see note 8), with drumming, summoned numerous people into the street for May revels, but John Hole, being constable, ordered him not to drum on the Sabbath. Later, following a dinner in the church-house, the revellers defiantly elected a May Lady (Thomasina White, 35–45, a barber's wife), and a May Lord (George Greenstreet, 26, gentleman), named 'by a generall voyce of many people' (fol. 215) and 'lifted vp above the ground to kisse togeather' (fol. 215^v). Then, led by the May royalty, some 30 or 40 married couples danced long dances (hand in hand) twice – once before and once after evening prayers (fols 41^{r-v}) – moving from the church-house toward the George Inn, then to East Wells, stopping to drink before the doors of several houses including the constable's (fol. 215^v). Leading them were two local minstrels (fol. 9^v), a drummer, a taborer (fol. 41^v), and a boy drummer (fol. 173) 'playenge before them in twoe or three seuerall Companyes' (fol. 41^v). Hole had earlier arrested the two minstrels for missing prayers, but the Mayor, Alexander Towse, released them in time to play again. One gets the impression that the royalty were to 'rule' for the entire month of May.

10 May 1607 (Rogation Sunday)

Street show by a troupe of morris dancers. This show was designed to parody a woman (Mistress Yard) who had complained that the painted maypole standing between her house 'in the open Markett place' (fol. 52) and the church was a 'paynted caulf' preventing her from going to services (fol. 40). In this show, an armed troupe said to number about 100 young men (fols 40, 52) led by their 'Captayne', Edward Cary, gentleman (fol. 40), carried a board bearing the picture of the calf, which they several times ceremoniously shot and killed in front of Mistress Yard's door and elsewhere (fol. 40). The troupe danced up and down the street 'with naked rapyers and daggers in theire handes' (fol. 40). The calf itself was painted with white and red spots similar in colour to the maypole. It had been painted by Walter Smythe, a local painter (fol. 159). One of the company, dressed in satyr skins, cried like a calf (fol. 52), suggesting that the show may have unfolded as a kind of mock bullbaiting. While the show parodied one of the town's Puritan-leaning wives, the morris Captain himself seems to have been a traditional 'officer' of the May Games, similar in status to the May Lord and Lady, with the duties extending throughout the month, and in that sense, part of the traditional structure of the May Games in

JAMES STOKES

Wells. One witness said that other pageants and shows were also held this day (fol. 159), but no clear evidence survives.

14 May (Thursday, Ascension Day)

May Games and morris dancing on Ascension Day. Details are sketchy, but witnesses agree that many people (between 600 and 700: fol. 40), from town and country, watched and participated in shows which included the May Queen and Lord, the morris troupe (fol. 40) led by Edward Cary (fol. 31^v), and the children, specially dressed to 'goe [and make a show]' (crossed out by scribe: fol. 6). Some 'vnder ye age of 8 years' were dressed as virgins and 'carried or led about with others in ye street' (fol. 140^a). According to one woman whose child took part, the use of children was 'in suche honest and Civill manner as hath ben heretofore vsed to see' (fol. 6). Such use of children was common among guilds in Wells, but the clear connection to the Feast of the Ascension would have inflamed the Puritans. The shows ran from noon to evening prayer, then continued until 8 or 9 p.m. (fol. 40).

17 May (Sunday, Ascension 1)

Ale in Croscombe; street revel in Wells. The morris troupe led by its Captain, Edward Cary, and his lieutenant, William Peter, attended an ale in Croscombe (3 miles from Wells) held to aid a poor weaver.[9] Upon return about 6 p.m., led by a taborer and two trumpeters (retainers of Thomas Hughes, Esquire, of Wells, a Somerset Justice of the Peace, fol. 170), they paraded through Wells, dancing and sporting before about a hundred persons (fol. 1). A scuffle broke out when the Constable, John Hole, attempted to arrest them near the High Cross for profaning the Sabbath (fol. 29). The troupe then paraded into the grounds of the Bishop's Palace, where they continued revelling for about an hour, then dispersed (fol. 29). The event shows the sustained role of the morris troupe in the May Games, the range and charitable dimension of its activities, and the extent of the support it enjoyed, from Justice of the Peace and bishop alike. No other entertainment is recorded this Sunday, perhaps because it follows so closely after the Ascension Day activities.

24 May (Whit Sunday)

More May Games. Led by the May Lord and Lady, many people danced near the High Cross (presumably near the maypole) and sang songs mocking Hole who, a day earlier, had posted the King's proclamation prohibiting unlawful games and pastimes on the Sabbath (the Mayor rejected Hole's interpretations of the proclamation: fol. 41).

31 May (Trinity Sunday)

Shows, sports and merriments. Summoned by drummers, many persons crowded the market place after dinner and again after evening prayer (fol. 29^v) where they danced and made shows. A Robin Hood is mentioned for the first time. He was Robert Prinne, yeoman (no age given); his man (to carry arrows) was Steven Myllard, 43, a tailor (fol. 211). The morris troupe may have performed, given the presence of 'ensigne shott & other munition': fol. 211). No May Lord is mentioned, though one of the drummers was servant to Edmund White, husband of the May Queen.

The Mayor covertly watched the shows from inside John Yard's house (fol. 29^v).

Thus, the parishioners held games of one kind or another on every Sunday and major feast day during May. The Pinner of Wakefield and his men 'singing a song of wakfeeld green' is mentioned in Gamage's ballad (fol. 120^v) as having come between the morris troupe and Robin Hood (perhaps between 17 and 31 May), but is not mentioned by any other witnesses. Also taking part were men bearing a 'cavil staff' and 'eye between them' (fol. 120), apparently a skimmington. No shows are recorded on Thursday, 4 June (Corpus Christi Day) or Sunday, 7 June. Then begins a new series of shows co-ordinated by guilds, city officials, and parish.

14 June (Sunday, Trinity 2)

A breakfast. The churchwardens and 10–12 others met with the curate, presumably (but not provably) to discuss Guild shows that began next day (fol. 209^v).

15 June (Monday)

The show for Tucker Street. No details have survived, except that the show included a procession to the church-house (fol. 72). Tucker Street was the 'presence of the cloth industry',[10] and in 1613 the Shearmen and Tuckers' Company would provide a small show – a streamer and their arms – during the Queen's visit.[11] If this show was by the Tuckers, it may have been a modest one (but see 16 June below). The productions by each street seem to have had processional shows and a church ale, all designed to raise money for the parish.

16 June (Tuesday)

The show for High Street. It progressed from the market place (at the top of High Street) to an ale at 'Saint Cuthbertes Churcheyeard', then returned by the same route and was seen by many people (fol. 60). Cathedral choristers, singing and dressed in white habits, accompanied the shows (fol. 60). Some of the company 'cryed Hey for heigh streete', but no other certain details survive. One witness said that the shows for 15 and 16 June had the same elements (fols 25^{r-v}). Cordwainer Vertue Hunte (see note 8) was involved in the show for High Street, but there is no other evidence that the Cordwainers' Guild produced this show.

17 June (Wednesday)

The show of the Mercers for Chamberlain Street. This elaborate show progressed from Chamberlain Street to an ale at the church-house (fol. 209), then back to Chamberlain Street, via the market place (thus took a circular route). The event 'was begun by the Mayor' who with other dignitaries accompanied the show on its entire circuit (fols 23^v, 52^v); at least 600 persons from town and country watched (fol. 52^v). The elements of this 'Shewe of Diana' (fol. 52^v) were the same as those later used by the Mercers in 1613 (fol. 376).[12] They included: four choristers dressed in white vestments and singing (perhaps the Psalms), going before a person (perhaps a chorister) representing Diana, who was carried in a coach or on men's shoulders; men (or women) carrying a pageant bearing 'plate of all sortes'; a tent, also carried (by men or women), with a man inside playing a sackbut; two giants (representing a man and woman); a dragon (with a man inside) and St George on horseback (St George and about twenty 'knights' – many also on horseback – acted the fight of St George with the dragon in the market place before a large crowd after the church supper: fols 25^{r-v}, 69); and perhaps other pageants. The show lasted until 9 or 10 p.m. (fol. 155). The Dean of Wells Cathedral had given permission for the choristers to take part. The Dean, as well as a Justice of the Peace and a local knight, was present.

18 June (Tuesday)

The show for South Street (fol. 25^v). This explosive show progressed from South Street (fols 4, 25^v) to the church-house, then to the market place, and was viewed by 300–1000 persons (fols 25^v, 47^v). Considerable evidence suggests that the show was made by the Tanners, Chandlers, and Butchers. Elements were similar to their show in 1613, though modified for satiric purposes. It used riders on at least five horses. On one rode a man (representing John Hole) holding a spinning-wheel and wearing a red petticoat, kerchief, and muffler and apparently singing 'Holes woole' as he rode (fol. 4). On the second rode two men face to face, one wearing a gown and playing a usurer with a bag of tile-stones representing money, the other playing a scrivener. Between them they held a desk, pen, and ink, and dispensed money from a bag (fol. 127), as if lending money to the show's opponents. A third rider, dressed as a haberdasher (John Yard), and wearing a beard and flaxen hair supplied by the Dean of the Cathedral, together with other props, bartered hats with the crowd so as to mock Yard (fols 17–18). The scrivener, in turn, tried to extort high interest from the haberdasher as the show progressed (fol. 18). A fourth rider, disguised as pewterer Hugh Meade (fol. 69^v), also made libellous transactions. Finally, two riders on a single horse carried a merchant's scale and cast grain from a basket onto spectators (fol. 161), mocking the grocers Humphrey and Palmer. Further: the show of 1607 was described as the 'shewes of Tradesmen' (fols 32, 38^v); it originated at the house of a chandler (fol. 127); William Atwell, a tanner, supplied a horse (fol. 128v); John Atwell rode in the show (fols 31–32), as did James Liddyard (fol.161^v), a butcher; one of the players in the church-house was a Richard Tanner; Richard Gorway, a chandler, was called to testify (fol. 47^v). In the 1613 Tanners', Chandlers', and Butchers' Show, St Clement and a friar would ride, dispensing grain from bags. It seems obvious that the players had inverted the meaning of their traditional show, so that it illustrated not the traditional beneficence and charity of their patron but the greed and self-interest with which they charged their opponents.

The evidence makes it clear that this particular show involved three separate kinds of performances: (1) at the church-house supper, two women (one the wife of a Justice of the Peace) and three men (different persons than the riders) played a parody of haberdashers, grocers and worsted makers (fols 38^v, 155); (2) in the streets, players and the crowd exchanged speeches parodying the shows' opponents (fol. 127), as the procession advanced; (3) and finally, the assembled dignitaries followed the shows to the market place where a performance before a large crowd took place (fols 32, 43^v).

19 June (Friday)

Arrests. Constable John Hole arrested some of the performers from the 18 June shows, but Sir Edward Wadham, a supporter, ordered them to be released (fol. 209).

25 June (Thursday following Midsummer Day)

The show for East Wells (later St Thomas Street). Described as 'a great company' with 'many shews' (fol. 54), it progressed about 4 p.m. from East Wells Street to an ale at the church-house (fols 18^{r-v}, 54), by way of either High Street or Chamberlain Street. At least 400–500 persons watched in the streets (fol. 54).

The evidence seems overwhelming that this show was produced by elements of the Hammermen's Company (carpenters, joiners, coopers, masons, tilers, and blacksmiths). The three identifiable participants all lived in East Wells Street and/or were miners (fols 133^v, 18^{r-v}). The show used cleverly devised pieces of carpentry, painting, and joining. One rider carried a yard-long painted board, attached and painted on either side with pictures of two men (John Hole and John Yard) and a woman (Ann Yard); at the bottom of the board were nine holes through which a person trundled a small ball on another board fastened to the main boards (fols 142-3). The purpose of the show, in response to the Puritan self-righteousness, was to accuse Hole of adultery with Yard's wife, who dwelled at the Sign of the Crown (fol. 23). Thus, the players in this and other pageants sang suggestive lyrics such as 'hee holes or holes not for a Crowne, but for xijd, & xs he sayed he holed' (fol. 142), and 'he holed her in the meade' (for Hugh Meade, fol. 143), and similar wordplay. The 'holing game' eventually became notoriously spread throughout the county. The boards (as well as the spotted calf) had been prepared a month earlier (fols 159^v–160) by Walter Smythe, variously described as a joiner and carpenter (fol. 132^v), but identified by himself as a painter (fols 159^{r-v}). A rider on a second horse carried a large paper book, desk, and pen (fol. 18^v); a third carried a noddy board and pair of cards, the meaning of which is unclear. Connection with the Guild's traditional show is not immediately apparent, except for its display of guild-related skills.

Late June 1607

A proposed oration. John Atwell, alias Tanner, a Wells Court Proctor, was goaded into writing an oration by the Wells schoolmaster, who argued that Atwell's street (unidentified), where many tanners lived, had not yet done a show, and that a learned speech would bring honour to tanners (fol. 72). Atwell wrote a Latin oration and proposed, until dissuaded, to deliver it at the High Cross, sitting on an ass, and wearing a bishop's habit (fols 55, 58). The Dean of Wells Cathedral supplied Atwell with a costume for his show (fol. 73).

Between July 1607 and May 1608

Libellous ballads. Following the shows, William Gamage (who had carried the holing-game board) and William Williams, alias Morgan the Younger, both of Wells, wrote ballads about the shows and their opponents, and circulated them in alehouses, homes, businesses, cathedral offices, a church ale in Pill (near Wells), and in London. Both ballads survive. For his efforts, Gamage was jailed in the Fleet Prison.

What was the nature of the shows in 1607?

The games and shows began as a charitable religious activity (an ale to raise funds in the traditional pre-Reformation way for a church bell) and were opposed on Reformist religious grounds (that they violated the Sabbath) by five former constables with evident Puritan leanings. Eventually the entertainments became a two-month series of shows encompassing every major feast between May Day and Midsummer's Day.

The entertainments fall into two distinct but related groups: first, the May sports, including a maypole, street dancing, sports, shows, church ales, morris dancing, and a Robin Hood Show; and second, five June Guild Shows presented by residents of particular streets.

The May Games occurred on every Sunday in May, plus May Day and Ascension Day, and followed a typical pattern. People danced or watched shows before and after evening prayers, attended a dinner in the church-house, and contributed such funds as they could afford. The May Lord and Lady, the morris Captain, or the Robin Hood variously 'ruled' the proceedings. Because they were parish activities, the games attracted the participation of many in the community from labourers to gentry, from curate to mayor. The playful 'usurpation' of authority, good order, and the Sabbath enraged those who opposed it, especially John Hole who was increasingly parodied in the shows. The principal mimetic elements were the roles played by the 'royalty', but the populace took part in their fictive rule.

In the June Shows, on the other hand, people assembled to watch more formal performances staged by particular streets and guilds on five separate days between 15–25 June, culminating just after Midsummer (the Feast of St John the Baptist). These shows were essentially mimetic, involving each guild's traditional plays, props, costumes, and pageants. Each show followed a circular route similar to the May Game, travelling from its own street to the church-house, then to the market place, with performances at all three points. A certain amount of competition among streets existed. As with the May Games, the principal purpose of the Guild shows was charitable - to gather offerings for the parish church - and officials of the parish, town, Cathedral Chapter, and the gentry took part. Their participation and the pattern of movement reflects the historically close formal relationship among all those elements within the town. Officials, for example, greeted the performers at the church-house, shared a dinner there with them, then walked with the shows to a performance in the market place. Elements in the shows of 1607 closely resemble those in 1613, though satirical topical elements are present in 1607.

How traditional were they?

The earliest reference to a parish (as opposed to a cathedral or guild) entertainment in Wells is an enquiry by the Mayor of the town in 1497 concerning funds raised by a Robin Hood entertainment, girls' dancing, and a church ale.[13] So the similar activities during May in 1607 do seem to have been part of a much older tradition in Wells. Even earlier, a Robin Hood play and dancings are recorded in nearby Croscombe.[14]

For Guild Shows, only three evidences survive: a directive in 1556 setting forth the order of crafts in the King's and Queen's Watch on Midsummer Night;[15] court records discussed in this article concerning the shows of 1607; and a description of shows set forth in 1613 during a visit by Queen Anne.[16] All three indicate continuity in the structure of the guilds and their approach to entertainments. In 1556, Wells had seven companies. Their order for the watch was: Hammermen, Mercers, Butchers, Cordwainers, Weavers, Tuckers, and Tailors. In 1607, the town had six companies (representing fourteen trades and occupations) and the order in which their shows were given was: Tuckers, (?)Cordwainers, Mercers, Tanners/Chandlers/Butchers, and Hammermen. (The Tailors, some of whose members were being parodied, seem not to have taken part.) In 1613, the order was: Hammermen, Shearmen and Tuckers, Tanners/Butchers/Chandlers, Cordwainers, Tailors, and Mercers. Between 1556 and 1613 the only company to have significantly changed its place seems to have been the Mercers, who moved forward in the Show for Queen Anne. But in fact all three types of evidence reflect different occasions, from which it seems rash to draw conclusions other than to say that order could be modified to suit the performance situation.

Each company had its own 'show', comprised of streamers and arms, music, dance, and, in some cases, pageants and plays dramatising patron saints and biblical or mythological themes traditionally associated with that guild. In fact, some of the shows look very much like traditional saint's plays, at a time when such plays were supposed to be forbidden. There is nothing in the records or history of the town to suggest that the six shows had evolved from a single cycle play. Rather, the multi-day pattern, the independence of the guilds and the iconic nature of their plays, suggest the opposite: that Wells had always had several separate playing days and several distinct guild plays. However, though separate and distinct, the shows functioned as elements in a larger, unified, civic entertainment spanning the entire Midsummer week.

JAMES STOKES

Who participated?

The impetus for the shows in 1607 came from a group of parishioners (average age 35), including the churchwardens, who wished to raise money for the parish in the traditional way – by holding entertainments. They received approval from the Dean of the Cathedral, and support from city, guild, and parish officials, as well as local gentry.

We have no clear evidence of who participated during the sixteenth century and earlier. But in 1607, the ales and May Games were communal events in which every segment of the community could take part if it wished (in fact, there was pressure *to* participate): for that month, the May royalty ruled; middle-aged couples danced in the streets; children summoned the revellers, helped fetch the maypole, and participated in shows; young men mustered and danced; dignitaries attended ales, dinners, and processions with the showmakers. The purpose was to make giving painless by means of entertainments. These activities were simultaneously festive, religious, communal, and charitable.

The Guild Shows in 1607 had many of the same qualities. Every segment of the community could contribute to its respective show: children rode on pageants; choristers sang; churchwardens' assistants went house to house gathering money for the church bell; young men rode on horseback; others went disguised as giants or dragons, or played the part of St George and his knights; two women and three men put on a play in the church-house; some men carried pageants on their shoulders; musicians and drummers led the processions and the dancers; the Mayor and Cathedral officials marched in the shows. In short, every segment in the community, except the Reformist faction, took part. The shows in 1613 had the same broad participation and support. According to witnesses, at least four of the shows attracted between 500 and 1,000 spectators from town and country, suggesting that the shows were widely advertised.

What playing gear did they use?

The records do not mention a great deal of playing gear for the May Games. Robin Hood's bow and arrows and his garments might have been part of a permanent stock of playing gear, as occurred in other parishes, but no proof exists. The muskets, daggers, rapiers, and pikes used by the morris dancers might have come from the militia's stores. Otherwise the gear mentioned in the records includes a painted maypole; special dress for children playing virgins on the Feast of the Ascension; drums, trumpets, and musical instruments including a bass viol; an ensign; a painted board; and animal skins. Only the painted board and skins were non-traditional elements – added for the killing of the calf.

Gear for the Guild Shows in June was much more elaborate (one opponent complained that many women missed church services because they were in their gardens preparing shows), and can be put into two categories:

1. *Properties traditionally used in Guild Shows.*
a. Pageants, either carried or rolling: one bearing Diana; one (carried by men) bearing guild plate; a tent (carried) inside which a man played a sackbut; one (carried by six men) bearing Noah building an Ark; one for Cupid; other pageants not identifiable.
b. Creatures: dragon with a man inside; two giants (men and women) later repaired by the churchwardens at a cost of ten shillings contributed by parishioners.
c. Costumes: for traditional emblematic guild figures such as St George, the Goddess Diana, and St George's knights; choristers' vestments; virgins' garments for the children.
d. Other: a cavil staff and a large eye (purpose unspecified).
2. *Items apparently unique to 1607.*
a. Costumes: a red petticoat, kerchief, and muffler; a long gown; a grey beard, flaxen hair (both given by the Dean of Wells Cathedral), brush and hat; three old hats and a cap to hang from a girdle; a black petticoat; a man's coat; a velvet coat, square cap, and satin hose (also supplied by the Dean); a canvas apron.
b. Wooden devices and related paraphernalia: a spinning wheel and worsted wool upon a staff; a writing desk, pen, and ink; two yard-long boards attached at the top, painted with pictures of two men and a woman, and having nine holes at the bottom, with a second board for trundling a ball through the holes; a large paper book; a noddy board and a pair of cards.
c. Horses: several.
d. Other: a bag filled with tiles representing money; a piece of paper representing a bond; two hammers and saucers representing pewter; a small pair of brass scales, and weights of lead and brass; a frail with grain in it; and a wheel barrow.

The great array of *ad hoc* playing gear illustrates both the strong topical elements that the showmakers introduced into their traditional play, and a clever theatrical sensibility.

The controversy growing out of the shows in 1607 did not kill the traditions of the May Games and Midsummer Guild Shows in Wells. The city presented its Guild Shows again when Queen Anne visited in 1613. A Cuckoo Lord and maypole controversy on Chamberlain Street are recorded in an ecclesiastical court deposition book in 1611.[17] The Cordwainers' Company records payments to refurbish its streamer and arms as late as 1640.[18] However, by the mid seventeenth century, having endured the cumulative effect of suppression orders and increasing factionalism, both the May Games and Midsummer Shows seem to have disappeared as annual sponsored events. In the shows of 1607 one can see not 'rough ridings' but a uniquely concerted effort to preserve traditional cultural practices in a society whose culture was already fracturing.

University of Wisconsin, Stevens Point

JAMES STOKES

NOTES

1. Records of these Shows, together with all other dramatic records from the City of Wells and Wells Cathedral will appear in the REED volume for Somerset, forthcoming 1995.
2. (Cambridge University Press, 1936) 162–77, 205.
3. For example, Martin Ingram 'Riding, Rough Music and Mocking Rymes in Early Modern England' 171 in *Popular Culture in Seventeenth-Century England* edited Barry Reay (Croom Helm, London, 1985). Ingram briefly describes the events only as 'a series of spectacular ridings' (171), citing Sisson as his source (194, note 11).
4. See Thomas G. Barnes 'County Politics and a Puritan *Cause Célèbre*: Somerset Church Ales, 1633' *Transactions of the Royal Historical Society*, 5th Series, 9 (1959) 109, note 1, for a list of suppression orders.
5. Somerset Record Office: QSR/2, Quarter Session Rolls (1607/1608): an order signed by John Still, Bishop of Bath and Wells, and eleven Justices of the Peace.
6. PRO: STAC 8/161/1, fol. 155. Unless otherwise stated, all references to the Shows are cited from this case.
7. A complete list of Wells churchwardens can be found in Thomas Serel *Historical Notes on the Church of Saint Cuthbert in Wells* (J.M. Atkins, Wells, 1875) 49–54.
8. One of the organisers was Thomas Peters, journeyman shoemaker and servant to master shoemaker Virtue Hunte. Hunte organised Shows in 1613, when Queen Anne visited the city, and he was a future Mayor of Wells. See James Stokes 'The Wells Cordwainers' show: New Evidence Concerning Guild Entertainments in Somerset' *Comparative Drama* 19.4 (1985–1986) 332–46.
9. In c.1586–1587, a cathedral clerk was brought into the Bishop's Court for wearing a vizard and going with others to Croscombe and Pilton for a purpose similar to that in 1607. See Wells Cathedral Library: Chapter Act Book H (1571–1599), fol. 40.
10. Michael Aston and Roger Leech *Historic Towns in Somerset* (Committee for Rescue Archaeology, Bristol, 1977) 149.
11. Wells, Town Hall: Mayor's Convocation Book (1553–1623), fol. 376.
12. See note 8.
13. Wells: Mayor's Convocation Book (1450–1553), page 203.
14. 'Church-Wardens' Accounts of Croscombe, Pilton, Yatton, Tintinhull, Morebath, and St Michael's, Bath, Ranging from A.D. 1349 to 1560' edited [Edmund] Hobhouse *Somerset Record Society* 4 (1890) 1–48.
15. Wells: Mayor's Convocation Book (1553–1623), fol. 19. Three earlier references to the Midsummer Watch (but not to the craft guilds) occur in 1552 (page 533); and in 1555 (fols 12 and 18^V).
16. Wells: Mayor's Convocation Book (1553–1623), fol. 375.
17. Somerset Record Office: D/D/Cd 44, fols [149^V and 155^V–156], Ecclesiastical Court Deposition Book (1610–1612).
18. Somerset Record Office: DD/SAS/ SE 50/1, fol. [73v], Cordwainers' Account Book (1606–1720).

THE BISHOP OF FOOLS AND HIS FEASTS IN LILLE
Alan E. Knight

The Feast of Fools was a burlesque celebration of the New Year by the inferior clergy of cathedrals and collegiate churches, which seems to have originated in the twelfth century. It was ultimately adopted in many parts of Europe, but nowhere was its observance more firmly entrenched than in France. Though many bishops, popes, and councils fulminated against what they saw as a profanation of the liturgy, the practice continued in some places well into the Renaissance and beyond. In most churches the feast was celebrated on the first of January; in a few, however, it was postponed until Epiphany. The festivities began at Vespers on the eve of the feast during the chanting of the *Magnificat*. As the choir repeatedly sang the verse, *Deposuit potentes de sede et exaltavit humiles* ('He hath put down the mighty from their seat: and hath exalted the humble and meek'), one of the lower clergy was invested as Bishop of Fools. This was the signal for the carnivalesque celebrations and parodies of the liturgy to begin. Though practices differed from one church to another, a condemnation of the feast in 1445 by the Faculty of Theology in Paris excoriates clerics who wear monstrous masks during the divine office, who dance in the choir dressed as women, who eat sausages and play dice at the altar during Mass, and who burn old shoe soles in the censers.[1]

In the city of Lille in Flanders, the collegiate church of St Peter celebrated the Feast of Fools throughout most of the fourteenth and fifteenth centuries. Each year the new Bishop of Fools was elected by the lower clergy and enthroned at Vespers on Twelfth Night (5 January). The feast lasted until the Octave of the Epiphany (13 January), at which time a sumptuous banquet terminated the burlesque festivities. We do not know what forms the rejoicing took at Lille, since the documents relevant to the event are terse in the extreme. A typical item in the accounts of the Duke of Burgundy records a subsidy paid to *l'Evesque des Fols de l'eglise saint Pierre ... pour aydier a soustenir les despens de la folye par lui et ses gens entretenu[e] ceste saison en la maniere acoustumee* ('the Bishop of Fools at the church of St Peter ... to assist [him] to help defray the expenses of the folly undertaken by himself and his people in this season in the accustomed manner').[2] This is dated 1469 (Old Style). There must have been more folly than usual that year, however, because only a few months later the chapter of St Peter's completely suppressed the Bishop of Fools and all his activities. One of the documents from the church archives complains that the clerics *dabant multa scandala in vilipendium capituli, a vigilia Epiphanie usque ad octavas* ('did many offensive things, bringing the Chapter into disrepute, from the Eve of the Epiphany to its Octave').[3] But festivities of this kind, being deeply rooted in folk customs, are virtually impossible to eradicate. Five years later the Bishop of Fools again appears in the account books.

In Lille the Bishop's tenure of office was a full year, and his duties extended beyond the week of merry-making that followed his investiture. He was also responsible for organising dramatic performances and contests at the annual procession in honour of Mary and at occasional princely Entries. It was only in Lille, moreover, that the Bishop of Fools assumed such responsibilities. We do not know exactly when he began to organise entertainments, but the first reference to this function is found in the church accounts for the year 1430, at which time he helped prepare for the Entry of the Duke of Burgundy and his bride. The first reference to his awarding prizes at the procession appears in the church records for the following year, when he received a subsidy *pro jocalibus dandis in processione Insulensi* ('for giving prizes at the Lille procession').[4] We are not told what the prizes were for, but if we may judge from subsequent practice, it is likely they were given for the best play. The first clear reference to awarding prizes to groups staging plays at the procession is found in the municipal accounts for 1438, when the Duc du Lac, the leader of a neighbourhood group, made the awards.[5] Though the Bishop of Fools did not organise the contest every year at this period, he again received subsidies for the prizes in 1440, 1446, and 1447.[6] From 1450 on, however, he is mentioned virtually every year in the municipal account books as the one who gave the prizes for the best plays staged at the procession.

The *Grande Procession de Lille* took place every year in the month of June on the Octave of Trinity Sunday. It was founded in 1270 by Countess Margaret of Flanders in honour of the special devotion paid to a statue of the Virgin, called Notre Dame de la Treille because of a trellis that decorated its base. The statue, which belonged to the collegiate church of St Peter, had earlier survived a fire and had become associated with a series of miracles. In the beginning the procession was entirely religious, centring on the statue of Mary that was carried through the streets and around the city walls. As time passed, however, the parish clergy were joined by deputations of the trade guilds, carrying their insignia, and by units of the city guards.[7] The addition of these civic elements to the procession apparently took place in the fourteenth century. An ordinance of 1402 concerning the peaceful assembly of the guilds on the day of the procession implies that there had been disorder in the past. The ordinance also mentions those who intend to perform *aucuns jeux ou representacions de vies de sains ou autrement* ('any plays or representations of saints' lives or other plays').[8] There is, however, earlier evidence of the staging of plays at the procession. An ordinance of 1382 forbids the playing of plays by neighbourhood groups for any occasion *excepté le porchession de Lille* ('except for the procession of Lille').[9] This too implies a pre-existing tradition of staging plays both at the procession and during other, perhaps unauthorised, neighbourhood festivities. In any case, by the time the Bishop of Fools began to organise the dramatic contest, the procession had become an important event in the cultural and economic life of the city. Moreover, it continued to play a significant rôle in municipal affairs until it was finally abolished at the time of the Revolution. We should note that the Lille procession was established almost a century before the Corpus Christi procession was introduced into that city. As a result, the older local procession always took precedence over the newer Church-wide observance, especially since the two events fell only three days apart.[10]

We may infer from the archival evidence that the staging of plays and the dramatic contest gradually became more important features of the procession during the first half of the fifteenth century. We have already noted that during the same period the Bishop of Fools was involved with increasing frequency in these events and that by mid-century he had become their regular organiser. In 1463 the Bishop issued a proclamation in which he called upon the established neighbourhood associations to prepare new plays for the *decoracion* of the procession that year. It is likely that he issued such proclamations annually, since an entry in the municipal account book for 1461 makes reference to a similar *publicacion*.[11] Only this one has survived, however. The document also describes the prizes to be awarded for the best plays and explains the procedures for entering the contest. The call for plays is phrased as follows:

> Nous, Prelat des Folz ... avons intencion a l'aide de Dieu de donner les pris et joieulx cy dessoubz declariéz a ceulx qui tous d'unne place, sans nullui emprunter, vendront au jour de ladite procession sur cars, carettes, esclans, ou escaffaulx portatifs remoustrer au matin par signes, tandis que ladite procession passera, es places par nous ou noz commis a eulx ordonnés, et le apres disner devant nous, et la ou il nous plaira, aucunnes histoires de la Bible, tant du Viel Testament comme du Nouvel, vie ou passion de saint ou de sainte approuvee par nostre mere sainte Eglise, ou aultres histoires rommaines contenues en anchiennes croniques, contenant iii^c lingnes du moins et du plus a volenté, en bonne et vraie retorique, non jouees en ceste ditc ville depuis l'espace de seze ans encha.[12]

> 'We, Prelate of Fools ... intend to award, with God's help, the prizes listed below to groups formed in one neighbourhood with no outsiders, who come on the day of the procession on large or small waggons, wains, or portable scaffolds to present histories from the Bible, both Old and New Testaments, saints' lives or passions approved by our Mother Holy Church, or Roman histories from ancient chronicles, each containing at least 300 lines and at most as you will. In the morning as the procession passes, the plays are to be mimed in the squares designated by us or our deputies, and in the afternoon to be played before us, wherever we wish in good and true rhetoric. They must not have been played in this city within the last sixteen years.'

We should note that, even though the staging on pageant waggons parallels the practice in England, the requirement for new plays each year precluded the development of fixed historical cycles. Moreover, the plays in Lille were staged by neighbourhood associations rather than by trade guilds as in England. Apparently it was the exclusive prerogative of the neighbourhood groups to stage plays at the procession, since the trade guilds traditionally participated as groups parading with their torches and insignia. A municipal ordinance of 1422, for example, directs *tous marchans et gens de mestier* ('all merchants and craftsmen') to assemble in an orderly fashion prior to marching in the procession.[13] Jacques Heers has pointed out that late medieval social life was based less on class distinctions than on concrete daily contacts in such groups as trade guilds, neighbourhood associations, parishes, and religious confraternities.[14] In this context feast days were occasions for the members of such groups to reaffirm their solidarity by participating in the observances as groups rather than as individuals. Therefore, the Bishop's stipulation that the neighbourhood troupes were not to include outsiders had the effect not only of avoiding unfair competition, but also of reinforcing group solidarity and pride.

The proclamation further states that the Bishop of Fools would award silver statuettes as first and second prizes for the best history plays. There would also be a special prize for the company whose waggon was the most richly and appropriately decorated according to the play presented. In addition, there would be two prizes for the best farces, which must not have been played in the city within the last ninety-nine years. The time-limitation is clearly a joke, which makes one wonder if the sixteen-year limitation on the history plays was also an exaggeration. Still, it stresses the fact that new plays were desired each year. This is also borne out by some of the entries in the account books, where money is given to players to help cover the costs of new productions. In one such case in 1469 the Compagnons de la Place de Petit Fret petitioned the Chambre des Comptes of the Duke of Burgundy for financial assistance because they had undertaken to play *une haulte et sumptueuse matere de l'Ancien Testament* ('a costly and sumptuous matter from the Old Testament').[15] We know, however, that only two years earlier the same group had staged the Parable of the Workers in the Vineyard. The Old Testament play was therefore an entirely new production. One deeply regrets, of course, that the 1469 petition failed to reveal the title or the nature of the 'sumptuous matter' they chose to dramatise.

The Bishop's proclamation continues with instructions for entering the competition:

Et sera tenu chascun veullant gaignier lesdis pris de venir le jour du Sacrement entre trois et quatre heures apres disner en nostre palaix des clers jetter lotz et aporter par escript l'istore qu'i volra jouer et l'enseigne de son seigneur ou de sa place. Et ne pora on gaignier aucun des pris dessusdis qui ne s'enploira tant esdis jeux de folie comme esdites histoires.

'Anyone wishing to compete for the said prizes must come to our palace of clerics on Corpus Christi Day between three and four o'clock in the afternoon, where lots will be drawn. He must bring the script of the history he wants to play and the banner of his leader or his neighbourhood. No one can win any of the above prizes who does not compete in both categories: farces and history plays.'

The Bishop's 'palace' was nothing more than the house in which the lower clergy lived at the church of St Peter. It is not clear what the drawing of lots was for, though we may surmise that it had to do with the order in which the plays were to be presented. The examination of the texts was apparently the first stage of the judging, the second being the observation of the performances. This is suggested by an entry in the municipal account book for 1470, after the Bishop of Fools had been temporarily suppressed. In that year the city took over the responsibility of judging the plays and awarding the prizes. The municipality paid the expenses of two Dominicans and two Franciscans who spent an entire day *ceulx qui les avoient gaignie* ('in order justly to give the said prizes to those who had won them').[16] The day is not specified, but if this is the same examination that the proclamation refers to, the new examiners took much longer than the Bishop to approve the texts. The same entry names another group of men commissioned by the aldermen to award the prizes and to listen during the performances for any faults they might find in the plays. It was no doubt these judges who also determined which group was to receive the prize for the best decorated stage. Because the item appears in the account book as an extraordinary expense, one may infer that these judging functions had previously been carried out by the Bishop of Fools and his companions.

The organisation of the dramatic contest at the procession was not the only function of the Bishop of Fools in the fifteenth century. In 1432 and again in 1446 he received subsidies from the city to lead a troupe of players to perform in nearby towns.[17] In 1458 he awarded prizes to the groups who provided the best entertainments at the Entry of the Comte de Nevers and his wife.[18] Still, the dramatic contest at the annual *Grande Procession* seems to have been his principal activity after the festivities of his enthronement in January. We noted earlier that the suppression of his office in 1470 lasted only a few years. One reason for the quick restoration may have been the valuable service that he performed in organising and judging the dramatic presentations. The plays in addition to the procession must have drawn a large number of visitors to Lille each year, adding to the economic vigour of the city. In any case, beginning again in 1475, we find the Bishop of Fools in charge of the dramatic contest, a duty that he exercised with few interruptions until 1526.

Having examined the function of the Bishop of Fools in regard to the plays staged at the annual procession, let us now compare what we have learned from the archival records with the collection of fifteenth-century plays from Lille now in the Herzog August Bibliothek in Wolfenbüttel, Germany.[19] The manuscript contains 72 different plays written for production at the procession, each of which is preceded by a painting. Although the manuscript is undated, the styles of dress and armour in the paintings suggest that it was made in the 1480s. It is not known when the individual plays were written, with the exception of the one based on the parable of the workers in the vineyard, which, as we have seen, was first staged in 1467. Since the Bishop's call for new plays precluded the formation of an historical cycle that would be repeated each year, it seems likely that the plays were written and collected over a number of years prior to the time they were copied in the manuscript.

The types of plays that we find in the manuscript accurately reflect the kinds that the Bishop called for in his proclamation, i.e. plays from the Bible, Roman history, and the lives of the saints. Of the 72 plays, 64 are based on events in the Bible; 43 of these come from the Old Testament and 21 from the New Testament. In addition, there are 4 Roman history plays based on the works of Livy and Valerius Maximus and a play of Octavian and the Sibyl, which may have been considered Roman history by the playwright. There is only one saint's life, that of St Euphrosyne. We find, however, one example each of two genres that the Bishop did not mention: a miracle play about a pregnant abbess who is saved from shame by the intervention of the Virgin Mary, and a morality play on the Assumption of Mary.

One of the striking characteristics of the Lille plays is their consistent use of prologues and epilogues to frame the dramatic action. The character who speaks these parts introduces the play, provides historical background, asks for silence among the spectators, and draws a moral lesson at the end. The prologues contain much other information as well. Ten of them, for example, inform us that the play is being presented to *decorer une feste*. Two of the ten specify that the feast involves a procession and one of these locates the procession in the city of Lille. Four of the prologues insist that the play is new, reflecting the Bishop's request for new works. Finally, the Bishop of Fools himself is directly addressed in five of the prologues. The most informative of these introductory speeches is the prologue to the play called *Le Juge d'Athenes*, the story of an unjust judge condemned to death by the Roman Senate. The Prologue addresses the spectators as follows:

> Le Filz de Dieu omnipotent
> veulle garder generalment
> tous ceulx qui sont chy assamblez
> devant, derriere et a tous lez,
> et principalment le Prelat
> des Folz et son joieulx estat,
> qui, pour la decoration
> de la sainte prochession
> qui aujourd'hui se fait a Lille,
> a envoiet avant le ville
> ses lettres et ses mandemens,
> en requerant a toutes gens
> de faire nouvelles histoires
> contenans euvres meritoires,
> qui soient aux gens exemplaires
> du mal fuïr et du bien faire.

> Sy viengnent cy a celle fin
> ceulx de la plache saint Martin,
> requerant a tous humblement
> que on leur laise paisiblement
> ung exemple cy [re]moustrer,
> qui haultement fait anotter,
> pour justice en son cours tenir. fol. 293

'May the Son of God omnipotent protect all who are here assembled, before, behind, and on all sides, and especially the Prelate of Fools and his joyful followers, who, for the embellishment of the holy procession that is taking place today in Lille, issued his letters and proclamations to the city, requesting all to write new history plays containing meritorious works that are examples to people of doing good and avoiding evil. To that end we of St Martin's Place come before you, humbly requesting silence of all, that we may here show you a notable example of keeping justice in its course.'

We saw that the Bishop of Fools in his proclamation required that the plays for the procession contain 'at least 300 lines and at most as you will'. The plays in the manuscript range in length from 200 to 1900 mostly octosyllabic lines of verse. Five of them, however, fall short of the 300-line minimum set by the proclamation. Still, only a few are at the extremes, with most falling in the range of 500 to 600 lines. The two longest plays are those that dramatise the stories of Joseph and his brothers and the famine in Egypt, which may have been played together as a single work in two parts.

Five playing companies are named in the prologues: Les Compagnons de la Place de Petit Fret, Les Compagnons de la Place Saint Martin, Les Galants de Fannain, Les Galants de la Sotte Tresque, and Les Guingans. An entry in the municipal account book for 1463 names twelve companies or neighbourhood groups that presented plays (both *histoires* – 'history plays' – and *jeux de folie* – 'farces') at the Entry of Philip the Good in July of that year. All but the Sotte Tresque are in the list. The latter group, however, is mentioned in an item from the 1457 account book as one of several companies that presented plays on another festive occasion.[20]

It is not known who chose the plays that were copied in the manuscript or for what purpose they were collected. But if the selection is typical of what was staged at the procession, then it is surprising that there are no plays dealing with the Passion and Death of Christ. This was, after all, the central act of late medieval drama, as well as one of the principal objects of religious devotion. A series of entries in the municipal account books, however, may provide the reason for this omission. Beginning in 1434, payments were made periodically to the Compagnons de Saint Sauveur for *histoires* represented during the procession. From 1466 on, their plays are identified as dealing with the Passion. The entry for 1470, however, is even more specific, stating that this group presented, as was their custom, several episodes from the Passion *au devant de ladite fiertre Nostre Dame, mouvant depuis ladite eglise saint Pierre jusques a le porte saint Sauveur* ('in front of the said reliquary of Our Lady, moving from the said church of St Peter as far as St Saviour's Gate').[21] Here we have a representation of the Passion staged, one presumes, on waggons, moving in the procession at a point just ahead of the reliquary containing the Virgin's milk and a strand of her hair, which was the central focus of the event. Since the other plays, stationed along the route of march, were mimed as the procession passed, it is likely that the Passion plays were also mimed as they moved through the streets. Because the same company always played the Passion plays, it is probable that they had exclusive rights to the subject, as did the Confraternity of the Passion in Paris. If that was the case, their plays may not have fallen under the aegis of the Bishop of Fools and would not, therefore, have been played *en bonne et vraie retorique* as part of the competition.

Whatever the case regarding the Passion plays, it is clear that the other plays were written with the contest in mind. We do not know who wrote them, but several prologues make reference to clerics who chose the topics and translated them from their Latin sources. Since the procession was sponsored by the collegiate church of St. Peter, it seems most probable that some of the canons of that institution wrote the plays for performance by the neighbourhood associations. This would be an example of the 'type of play and production in which the Church supplied the script and then encouraged the civic authorities to accept responsibility for almost every aspect of its theatrical representation'.[22] The selection of events to be dramatised reveals a thorough knowledge of the Bible and an almost infallible sense of the dramatic possibilities of the stories. We noted earlier that 43 of the plays in the manuscript are drawn from the Old Testament, but they seem to have been selected, not on the basis of their familiarity to the spectators, but rather for the stimulating action of their plots. We can judge the degree of excitement that the playwrights wished to convey to the spectators if we recall that St Benedict forbade his monks to read from the Heptateuch or the four Books of Kings immediately before going to bed.[23] Of the 43 Old Testament plays in the Lille collection, 35 are from those very books.

If the contest organised by the Bishop of Fools influenced the choice of topics, the urban context of the performances also played a rôle in that choice. Because the procession proceeded not only through the streets of Lille, but also around its walls, the city itself was the focal point of the festivity. Just as feast days provided occasions for small groups to reaffirm their solidarity, they also enabled an entire city to reinforce its communal bonds. In Lille, the annual procession, which included representatives of every important aspect of city life, was a symbolic re-creation of the ideal city with its order and hierarchy. Five of the plays in the Wolfenbüttel manuscript serve to reinforce urban values by portraying cities under siege that are saved by the heroic deeds of both kings and ordinary citizens. Saul, for example saves the city of Jabesh from Nahash, king of the Ammonites, who had threatened to put out the right eye of every male citizen. In one of the Roman plays, Mucius Scaevola saves the city of Rome from the siege of Porsenna. In an age when the security of a city depended not only on the strength of its walls, but also on the mutual cooperation of every citizen, plays of this kind could stir deep feelings of patriotism and communal pride. Here too the contest may have been a factor, since playwrights and players alike must have counted on such patriotic emotions to influence the judges in their favour.

We may conclude, then, that the contest organised by the Bishop of Fools exerted a powerful influence on the kind and quality of plays presented at the *Grande Procession de Lille*. We do not know which of the plays in the manuscript, if any, were awarded prizes. But given the high dramatic quality of so many of them, it is perhaps not too far fetched to think that these plays have survived because someone five centuries ago made a collection of prize-winning plays.

Pennsylvania State University

NOTES

1. E.K. Chambers *The Mediaeval Stage* 2 vols (Oxford University Press, London, 1903) 1 294.
2. Archives Départementales du Nord (*ADN*) B 93 (Chambre des comptes de Lille).
3. E. Hautcoeur *Histoire de l'église collégiale et du chapitre de Saint-Pierre de Lille* 3 vols (L.Quarré, Lille/A. Picard, Paris, 1896–1899) 2 221.
4. Hautcoeur 2 216–17.
5. Archives Municipales de Lille (*AML*) 881 (Comptes de la ville).
6. AML 16181, 16187, 16188 (Comptes de la ville). See also Léon Lefebvre *Histoire du théâtre de Lille de ses origines à nos jours* 5 vols (Lefebvre-Ducrocq, Lille, 1901–1907) 1 7.
7. Victor Derode *Histoire de Lille* 4 vols (Vanackere, Lille (1–3)/Leleu (4), 1848–1877) 4 90.
8. AML 374 (Ordonnances du Magistrat).
9. AML 373 (Ordonnances du Magistrat).
10. Henri Platelle 'La Vie religieuse à Lille' in *Histoire de Lille, I: Des origines à l'avènement de Charles Quint* edited Louis Trenard (Faculté des Lettres et Sciences Humaines, Lille, 1970) 355–6.
11. AML 16200 (Comptes de la ville).
12. ADN B 93 (Chambre des comptes). See Lefebvre 1 8–9.
13. AML 376 (Ordonnances du Magistrat).
14. Jacques Heers *Fêtes, jeux et joutes dans les sociétés d'occident à la fin du Moyen Age* (Institut d'Études Médiévales, Montréal; J. Vrin, Paris, 1971) 77–9.
15. ADN B 93 (Chambre des comptes).
16. AML 888 (Comptes de la ville).
17. AML 16174, 16187 (Comptes de la ville).
18. AML 16199 (Comptes de la ville.)
19. Codex Guelf. 9 Blankenburgensis. I am currently preparing a critical edition of the plays in this manuscript.
20. AML 16202, 16198 (Comptes de la ville).
21. AML 16209 (Comptes de la ville).

ALAN E. KNIGHT

22. Glynne Wickham *The Medieval Theatre* (Cambridge University Press, 3rd edition 1987) 69.
23. St Benedict *Benedicti Regula* edited Rudolphus Hanslik (Corpus Scriptorum Ecclesiasticorum Latinorum 75: Vienna, 1960) 105; chapter 42.

BATTLES AND BOTTLES:
Shrovetide Performances in the Low Countries (c.1350 – c.1550)
Marjoke de Roos

On Shrove Tuesday 1441 the inhabitants of the cathedral city of Utrecht in the Northern Netherlands witnessed a rather unusual Shrovetide performance. The local authorities had asked at least ten noblemen to participate in a tournament. Up to now the only trace of this *steecspuel* ('joust') is to be found in the town accounts.[1] They do not mention any special reason for organising such a manifestation of chivalric civilisation there at that particular moment. In comparison with other towns in the Low Countries these records do not contain a lot of information about urban festivities. Moreover some of the municipal accounts are lacking. So it might be possible that it is totally wrong to conclude that a pre-Lent tournament was an extra-ordinary event in Utrecht in the fifteenth century. However, there is only one other item in the accounts which mentions a Shrovetide tournament, in 1478–1479.[2] The 1441 joust could have been a personal initiative of one of the most prominent members of the aristocracy in the Low Countries, Jacob van Gaasbeek (died 1459),[3] for in the account it is registered that the town government paid for an enormous quantity of wine as a gift to the Lord of Gaasbeek for *his* tournament.[4] Perhaps he had to be in Utrecht for a reunion of the Three Estates or for some other formal occasion. I am not able to answer that question. However, it seems much more important that we have a few specific details on the Utrecht tournament.

Jousting was of course a favourite activity in the aristocratic set, and Shrovetide was an excellent occasion for the organisation of tournaments. According to Richard Barber and Juliet Barker in their survey of tournaments, jousts, chivalry, and pageants in medieval Europe, Shrovetide was the most common single date for tournaments of any size.[5] In her book on *Edward III and Chivalry* Juliet Vale refers among others to a series of jousts and tournaments at the English court during the days before Ash Wednesday of the year 1329.[6] The author suggests that in England there had been something of the same sort of social integration between the urban patriciate and the knightly classes as she had observed in an earlier chapter on civic *festes* and society in the Low Countries and Northern France.[7] The evidence for this assumption comes from the well-known towns in the Southern Netherlands (Ghent, Bruges, Douai, Lille, etc.). In this kind of comparative inquiry concerning the later Middle Ages, the Northern Netherlands are always lacking. And that is a pity. Even if they were territorially and politically a cluttered and insignificant part of Western Europe, several rather flourishing towns existed there. Certainly, they were of no great importance compared with Ghent or Bruges, but seen in their own context (some of them belonged to the Hanseatic League) they are quite interesting. As we have noticed in the above-mentioned example of the Shrovetide tournament in Utrecht in 1441, nobles came over to that town for their pre-Lent festivities.

Because of the concomitance of certain Shrovetide activities of the nobility with pre-Lent festivals in the towns, it seems useful to me not only to investigate the Shrovetide performances in the urban context, but also to analyse what people did to amuse themselves during the days preceding Ash Wednesday at a princely court in the period about 1400. Presumably it will not be possible to verify Juliet Vale's thesis concerning the social integration of princes and nobles with the urban patriciate, for Shrovetide is, of course, not at all a representative event. At that particular moment, everybody might behave in a very unusual way, since at Shrovetide it was permitted to turn the world upside-down. But perhaps it may give us some information about the entertainments they liked. The most obvious choice in the Northern Netherlands is the well-documented Dutch court of Duke Albert of Bavaria (1336–1404), who ruled in Holland, Zeeland, and in Hainault from 1358 until his death in 1404.[8]

I will try to compare, in brief of course, these courtly festivities with what was happening during the Carnival days in towns like Arnhem, Deventer, Zwolle, and Kampen in the eastern regions of the Low Countries, and with other towns if there are any relevant data. It will be clear that I have a special interest in dramatic performances, but in my opinion one has to study the whole complex of Shrovetide performances. Drama is only one of the means of expression. It goes together with other manifestations such as tournaments, parodic jousts, pageantry, masquerades, and dancing. The ultimate goal of this investigation is to get an idea of the ideological framework in which people with different social backgrounds organised their festivities before Lent. The period in view runs from the second half of the fourteenth century up to the middle of the sixteenth century, with an accent around 1400.[9]

In 1395 Duke Albert of Bavaria organised a magnificent Shrovetide tournament in his residence in the county of Holland, The Hague.[10] He invited knights from all over the Holy Roman Empire to participate in the feasting. Servants brought Albert's special suit of jousting-armour over from Hainault to Holland. He ordered lots of equipment to make it a very spectacular performance. Velvet and helmets were bought in Paris, the goldsmith in The Hague gold-plated letters to decorate the Duke's jerkin, and a painter had to make an appropriate design for a cloth. They even altered a rowing-boat into a 'jousting-boat' for a water-tournament. Possibly Albert had an underlying intention in setting up this festive meeting of quite a number of more or less important princes and lords. He was planning a kind of crusade against the Frisians in the North, and perhaps he wanted to gain the support of other nobles for this project. Besides this particular motivation and the extraordinary pomp and circumstance, the 1395 Shrovetide festival was not very different from the others during Duke Albert's reign.

Already in the early years of his government Albert was tilting at Shrovetide. It is noticeable that up to 1383 the family used to pass the days before Ash Wednesday in Brussels or in towns in Hainault. From that year on (with the exception of 1385) they stayed in The Hague and the surrounding area. Apparently, it was more attractive to participate in an urban festival than to stay in the rather rural ambience of The Hague. In 1361 Albert jousted a few days before Shrove Tuesday in Mons with the Count of Flanders and the Duke of Brabant.[11] For the real Shrovetide festivities he went to Brussels, and his tournament armour was taken there too.[12] One year later the Duke and the Duchess met each other in Brussels *ter feesten* ('for the feast').[13] And in 1363 they were in Mons, in company with the Queen of Hungary, for a *fieste de joustes et behourt as quaresmiaus* ('a feast of jousting and the tilt at Shrovetide'). On this occasion the Duke paid 100 guilders to the minstrels, the heralds, and several others 'of the tournament'.[14] The last Shrovetide joust to be mentioned here is the one in Quesnoy in 1366.[15] Not every year is well documented, but sometimes a Shrovetide festival comes up in the accounts. In 1384 the pre-Lent festivities were cancelled, because of an illness of the Duchess, Margaret of Brieg.[16] After her death in 1386 the Duke did not leave Holland at Shrovetide any more.

Albert left The Hague in 1387 to take part *inder feeste die tot Leyde was tot vastenavont* ('in the feast which was at Leiden at Shrovetide') and spent £87 11s. 6d. gr. on food, drinks, and the like, at this Shrovetide festival in Leiden, the nearest town at hand.[17] After 1388 the festivities took place in The Hague. In that year the Duke had sent invitations to a whole range of ladies in the county of Holland, asking them to accompany him at Shrovetide in dancing, banqueting, and feasting.[18] On Shrove Monday the Duke paid a gift to *alrehande ghesellen ende joncvrouwen uter Hage die an minen heer cokerelden*, young people from The Hague who sang for him.[19] In these years there are regular payments to musicians, singers, poets, or story-tellers, who came to amuse the feasting company. Sometimes there was a woman or a child among the artists.[20] A few years after the famous jousting-party of 1395 a story-teller told at Shrovetide the story of the Frisian 'crusade' which had been undertaken by Albert and his son William from 1396 on.[21]

In this paper, I cannot deal with all the Shrovetide tournaments and other 'mock battles' at the Dutch court in the days before Lent, nor with all the bottles that were emptied and the food that was dispatched by the Duke and his guests. I want to find out if there were some real theatrical performances. During the period in question I know only one clear reference to a play being performed at Shrove Tuesday in the court-hall in The Hague. In 1399 the Duke and Duchess paid a lump sum of 20 guilders as a gratuity from which the players could buy themselves drinks:

upten vastenavont den gesellen die inden Hage inder zalen voir mijnen heren ende minre vrouwen .i. spil gespeelt hadden bi horen bevelen gegeven te verdrincken .xx. ny gulden.[22]

'on Shrove Tuesday the companions who played a play in The Hague in the hall before my Lord and Lady were by their command given 20 new guilders as drink-money.'

The word *gesellen* means 'companions' (in a different context, also 'journeymen'). All over the Netherlands performers of plays and that sort of thing in the fifteenth and early sixteenth centuries are called *gesellen vanden spele* ('playing-companions'), when they are operating as a (small) group. In my view, they are certainly not professional actors. At the end of the fifteenth century the designation *gesellen vanden spele* was a common name given to the Rhetoricians in the Northern Netherlands. But about 1400 the existence of societies like the Chambers of Rhetoric cannot yet be proved, even though we know that in the Southern Netherlands they already existed in the first half of the fifteenth century. The chambers of Middelburg and Gouda are said to have been founded about 1430. In that case, they belong to the earliest creations.[23] Already in 1359 the Count of Holland paid a small gift to *den gesellen ... die up houten paerden staken* ('the companions ... who jousted on wooden horses'),[24] i.e. on hobbyhorses. With regard to activities involving disguised persons, identification is a great problem, not only in the literal but also in the figurative sense, for there was a non-dramatic form of playing that was called *mommen* ('mumming') and which meant 'dicing in disguise'. Even the Duke took part in these games.[25] With that knowledge, it becomes difficult to think of drama without any reservations, when you find that the mistress of Duke Albert, or later on the wife of Albert's son, received money for 'mumming'.[26] About Shrovetide 1415, there came 'different persons, men and women, as mummers to play at court', *die alsse mommekens quamen spelen*.[27] This entry has been misinterpreted. The transcription that circulated had *monnekene* ('monks'), instead of *mommekens*. Therefore people have thought of actors who came playing in monks' robes.[28] It is perfectly possible, however, that they only came for a masked game of gambling, though the verb *spelen* ('play') could indeed refer to a dramatic performance.

In the urban context this kind of mumming was also a favourite pastime. Town governments took measures to canalise gambling. In some towns it was only permitted during fairs and at Shrovetide. To prevent excesses most towns tried to regulate mumming: the ban on all sorts of disguises is a recurring item in statute books. In 1394 the town of Kampen imposed a £10 fine on 'each person who walks around after sunset with a masked face and dressed otherwise than during the day, that is to say, that no man will wear woman's clothes nor a woman man's clothes'. Moreover it was forbidden to disguise oneself in coarse furs or sleeping sheets and the like.[29] In Malines, in 1471, a few weeks before Shrovetide, an extra ban was put on masquerading and public dancing, by day and by night; only at wedding parties was dancing permitted.[30] The authorities feared long knives hidden in the outfits of unrecognisably disguised persons. Only the official guards had permission to bear arms. Sometimes these statutes show something more about urban Shrovetide revels. When dancing in disguise is forbidden, we may conclude that people used to do so. A ban on the wearing of a devil's outfit also raises a corner of the veil.

Shrove Tuesday was the perfect occasion for copious meals with lots of wine and beer. At the Shrovetide tournament in Utrecht in 1441, the Town Council had dinner with the Lord of Gaasbeek, the Margrave of Antwerp, and more gentlemen, in the tavern named 'Rutenberch'. Some of the lords who came over for the joust brought along their own wine, but in general the town paid for the food and the drinks.[31] In most of the towns the municipality had a festive dinner before Ash Wednesday, even when there was no tournament. They invited important persons such as the bailiff, the doctor, the apothecary and the parish priest,[32] or the local aristocracy. And very often the ladies of the diners were invited too. In 1418 the Deventer magistrate dined at the town hall to avoid the 'wild company',[33] which they might find in the taverns. Presumably, the festivities got out of hand now and again, for the authorities often paid for extra guards. During the Utrecht tournament two men had to keep watch on top of the church-tower of the Buurkerk.[34]

Among the persons who received special gifts for their performances at jousts and other Shrovetide festivities, there were of course musicians and heralds (maybe even in their quality of story-tellers?). Also interesting is the acrobat, the *tumelair*, who appeared in the tournament of 1441,[35] and the fact that dancing (often by women!) was one of the special attractions during the Shrovetide parties. In Arnhem the municipality ordered the building of a special dance-house when the court of the Duke of Guelders visited the Shrovetide festivities there in 1426.[36] As a matter of fact, Arnhem was a town with a regular Shrovetide tournament in the market place in front of the Town Hall.[37] Some of the dances which were performed at this time of year showed a certain similarity with jousting. References to sword and morris dances are frequent. This kind of dancing was often the privilege of the young journeymen of the Smiths' Guilds.[38] Between 1515 and 1540 the sword dance by the *smedeknechten* or *smeetsgesellen* in front of the Town Hall was a current spectacle at Shrovetide in Kampen.[39] Actually, it seems to be quite a common exercise, for in Arnhem there were children who danced and fenced at night.[40] It is interesting to note that these children might have something in common with the *gesellen* on their hobbyhorses we have already met in the year 1359, for there is some iconographic evidence which could signify that schoolboys amused themselves, and their audience, by jousting with mock lances (a sort of windmill) on hobbyhorses.[41]

Another mock fight was organised in Arnhem at the first Monday after Epiphany, but at the Dutch court in The Hague it took place as a kind of Shrovetide performance: a rather cruel one, I should say, for the battle was between six blind men and a pig.[42] The 'actors' received a recompense for their participation in the fight and we have to conclude that a spectacle like this must have been organised to amuse the audience. This medieval 'pig corrida' was also known in France: the well-known *Bourgeois de Paris* tells in his *Journal* that on a Sunday in the summer of 1425 there had been a parade of the four blind men who were to beat the pig:

Item, le dernier dimanche du mois d'août, fut fait un ébatement en l'hôtel nommé d'Armagnac, en la rue Saint-Honoré, qu'on mit quatre aveugles tous armés en un [parc], chacun un bâton en sa main, et en ce lieu [y] avait un fort pourcel, lequel ils devaient avoir, s'ils le pouvaient tuer. Ainsi fut fait, et firent cette bataille si étrange, car ils se donnèrent tant de grands coups de ces bâtons, que de pis leur en fut, car quand [le mieux] cuidaient frapper le pourcel, ils frappaient l'un sur l'autre, car s'ils eussent été armés pour vrai, ils s'eussent tués l'un l'autre.

Item, le samedi vigile du dimanche devant dit, furent menés lesdits aveugles parmi Paris, tous armés, une grande bannière devant, ou il avait un pourcel portrait, et devant eux un homme jouant du bedon.[43]

'Also, on the last Sunday of August, an entertainment was organised in the Hotel d'Armagnac in the rue Saint-Honoré. Four blind men, each armed with a stave, were led into a 'ring' where there was a fat pig which would belong to them if they succeeded in killing it. And so it was done, and it was a very peculiar battle, because they gave each other so many blows with the staves that it was the worse for them, for when they were absolutely sure that they were beating the pig, they hit each other, so that if they had been armed for real, they would have killed each other.

Also, the day before Sunday, on the Saturday, these same blind men had been led through Paris, armed, and preceded by a great banner on which was painted a pig, and in front of them a man playing a drum.'

We find a representation of a similarly horrendous scene, where the protagonists are beating each other instead of the pig, in the richly decorated fourteenth-century Flemish manuscript of the *Romance of Alexander* in the Bodleian Library.[44] A painting by Jherome Bosch on this subject is lost. There is anyhow enough circumstantial evidence to prove that the mock fight between blind men and a pig was often related to Shrovetide festivals in the fourteenth and fifteenth centuries.[45]

In the case of other Shrovetide gifts it is not always possible to know if it was just a yearly bonus, or if the receivers had to do something special for it. The Count of Holland, as well as the town governments, paid Shrovetide money to the schoolchildren. Sometimes there appear fees paid to young people who were called 'bachelors' (rather well-to-do males and females). I do not have any evidence for it, but I guess that they might have been the members of some religious youth fellowship. Occasionally it is plain that they were remunerated for dancing or playing.[46] Unfortunately, most of the time it is not evident that 'playing' meant acting. Without a doubt, the schoolmaster and his pupils were the right persons to rehearse and to perform a play. Now and again the schoolchildren gave a real dramatic performance at a festival in the pre-Lent period, namely at Candlemas. In Kampen the schoolboys performed a comedy in Latin in 1517. It is not clear if this show was given at Shrovetide. In the same period, however, they were playing regularly at the Shrovetide banquets given for the town magistrates in the Hall, *opten huys*.⁴⁷ But when in the town accounts Shrovetide plays are mentioned, the performers are mostly called *gesellen*, just like the players at the court of Albert of Bavaria. An exception to this rule are the members of the citizens' militia, the *schutterij* ('shooting association'), who at Shrovetide in 1403 performed a play of St George in their home town Zwolle.⁴⁸

The rather early references to Shrovetide plays in the Northern Netherlands, to begin with the 'Neidhart-play' in Arnhem in 1395, have already been discussed by different scholars.⁴⁹ Actually, the number of plays to be found in fifteenth-century documents is limited. I have the impression that the references become richer from the last quarter of that century on. The reason for this must be the existence of more drama groups, presumably a kind of Chambers of Rhetoric. In Arnhem the Rhetoricians are mentioned from 1506. It is noteworthy that in Zwolle, as well as in Arnhem, painters played a prominent role in these societies.⁵⁰ Interesting too is the fact that in the years around 1480 it becomes clear that the *gesellen van Rethorike* used a pageant waggon for their performances.⁵¹ In Middelburg in Zeeland their waggon had to be repainted and decorated on repeated occasions, a job of course to be done by a painter.⁵² For the time being I suppose that the guilds of St Luke were of considerable importance as organisers of dramatic performances in Dutch towns about 1500.

As to the plays performed at Shrovetide, one is inclined to believe that the repertoire was made up of farcical plays. The 'Neidhart-play' in Arnhem, mentioned in 1395, 1419, 1432, and perhaps in 1448, but that time not at Shrovetide, which could also have been performed by the *speelluyde van Nyttert* ('players of Nyttert') in 1521 and 1523,⁵³ pre-dates the German *Neidhartspiel* as it has been edited by von Keller.⁵⁴ If the Arnhem play was like the German *Fastnachtspiel*, then it must have been a burlesque. As a matter of fact, this play has a rather moralist reference to the beginning of Lent in its closing words. Within the context of this paper, the circumstance that the characters in the play, knights and peasants, want to fight against each, other deserves attention. Not infrequently the name of a play makes one think that a confrontation of two extremes must be going on, a kind of combat, in the drama in question. In the sixteenth century the Smiths' Guild in Deventer regularly gave a performance at Shrovetide that showed the transformation of an old woman into a young one.⁵⁵ In this play something old is defeated and replaced by something new. Is not that the essence too of plays about 'the winter and the summer'? Such dramas were performed in Arnhem in 1404, in Zwolle in 1517, and in 's-Hertogenbosch in 1525, 1539, and 1546.⁵⁶ Of course this title makes us think of one of the four *abele spelen* ('fine plays') from about 1350 which were written down in the famous Hulthem manuscript at the beginning of the fifteenth century. That play *Vanden Winter ende vanden Somer* ('Concerning Winter and Summer') fits easily into the ideological framework of Shrovetide as a festival on the edge of two seasons.⁵⁷ And evidently winter is fighting a losing battle.

In the fragment of a Dutch summer-and-winter play from about 1436, discovered in an account book of the church of St Jacob in Ghent, there is a dispute going on between the Bailiff of the Snow, who represents his cousin Winter, and the Summer. The other characters are a fool, a poor man, a rich but stingy man, Mercy, Truth, Avarice, and Lent.[58] Even though this play is only known as a *membrum disiectum*, it is the perfect illustration of the meaning and the background of all sorts of Shrovetide performances. It is a kind of morality play that seems to warn all people, but especially the rich, that God will be merciful to those who have suffered on earth as He has. Mercy warns the miser that he should know where his soul will go to when he is not willing to give something to the poor. But in the end, Scrooge hits back. For he has got a brother, whose name is *Vast houden* ('Fasting' or Lent), and, playing on that word, he makes clear that fasting means frugality and meagreness.

So we might conclude that Shrovetide festivities had something to do with the inescapable cycle of the seasons. They are at least intended to mark the end of the period before Lent, during which term all people, the nobles as well as the townsfolk, should observe the fast. The well-known painting 'The Battle between Carnival and Lent' (1559) of Pieter Bruegel the Elder in the Kunsthistorisches Museum in Vienna is obviously the best and clearest evidence for the fact that people in the sixteenth century could think, or were used to think, of Shrovetide as a combat between two characters, who impersonated on the one hand the period before Ash Wednesday, and on the other the Lenten period. I do not have to argue here that this theme is to be found elsewhere in literature and drama as well.[59]

It is impossible to know if the 'king' and the 'emperor', who acted in the play that was performed in Arnhem in 1411,[60] had a real combat with each other. But it seems natural that they took opposite positions in relation to each other. And the play might have included a fight or a joust. Yet not all the Shrovetide plays were burlesques or mock battles. In 1436 the 'companions' in Deventer played *Teofeles spull*, i.e. a play after Rutebuef's *Miracle de Théophile* (c. 1261), for which they received a large gift.[61] The play was certainly known in these northern regions. It was staged in Bocholt in 1459; in Deinze in 1483 a play of *Thehouffelluse* is mentioned.[62] The Hulthem manuscript contains a Theophilus-text, and there is a rather curious reference to a gift to *Theophilus volck* ('the people of Theophilus') in the Kampen account of 1516.[63]

From the end of the fifteenth century the groups of players performed religious plays as well as farces. Probably Shrovetide had become a real urban (drama) festival where several guilds, confraternities, or Chambers of Rhetoric staged both serious and comic plays, where all sorts of people amused themselves and enjoyed the music, the (ritual) dancing and the dicing, not, of course, forgetting the food and the drinks. And sometimes there was a tournament or a water-joust organised, mostly on occasions when the towns had noble or princely guests. For, like all the other Shrovetide performances, the tournament could act as a temporary relaxation of discipline and self-control, a sort of 'safety valve' or, in the words of Umberto Eco, 'an authorised transgression'.[64] Shrovetide manifestations surely had an important social function in the period in view. Thanks to the bottles and the jugs of wine and beer offered by the town governments and the noble hosts to the performers of all sorts of battles and plays, it is possible to get an impression of the Shrovetide festivities in the Low Countries during the later Middle Ages.

Koninklijke Vereniging van Archivarissen in Nederland

NOTES

Abbreviations
Gemeentearchief Utrecht (Municipal Archives):   GAU
Archives of the Counts of Holland: AGH
The Hague, Algemeen Rijksarchief: ARA

1. GAU Stadsarchief 1 587 (1439–1440) fol. 81^{r-v}, for the invitations.
2. GAU Stadsarchief 1 626 (1478–1479) fol. 12^v.
3. Jacob van Gaasbeek was Marshal of Hainault and belonged to the nobility in the Duchy of Brabant, the County of Holland, as well as in Utrecht. Bram van den Hoven van Genderen *Het kapittel-generaal en de staten van het Nedersticht in de 15^e eeuw* (Walburg Pers, Zutphen, 1987) has a portrait of Jacob van Gaasbeek on page 98.
4. Some 500 litres of wine *'opten vastelavont ... tot sinen steecspuell'*: GAU Stadsarchief 1 587 (1441–1442) fol. 72^r.
5. Richard Barber and Juliet Barker *Tournaments: Jousts, Chivalry and Pageants in the Middle Ages* (Boydell Press, Woodbridge, 1989) 173.
6. Juliet Vale *Edward III and Chivalry: Chivalric Society and its Context, 1270–1350* (Boydell Press, Woodbridge, 1982) 63. In Appendix 12 there are some other pre-Lent festivities.
7. Vale (note 6) 25–41 and 111–122 for the notes (chapter 2). Barber and Barker (note 5) also enter into details concerning the history of tourneying and jousts as civic festivals in the Low Countries, by which they mean Flanders, Hainault, and Brabant (45–7).
8. I do not enter into political details. I would like to thank prof. dr D.E.H. de Boer (University of Groningen), who is preparing a biography of Albert of Bavaria, and dr J.G. Smit (Institute for Netherlands History, The Hague) for their very kind permission to go through some of the documentary information they gathered for their own research.
9. This paper is only an interim report of a much larger and more detailed investigation. See e.g. Marjoke de Roos 'Carnival Traditions in the Low Countries' in *Custom, Culture and Community in the Later Middle Ages* edited Thomas Pettitt and Leif Søndergaard (Odense University Press, 1994) 17–36. I am grateful to the small group of students of the University of Utrecht who studied Shrovetide festivities in an European context with me for some time.
10. The jousts took place in the Hague on the first Sunday of Lent, *Invocavit*. In the Low Countries this day was called *Grote Vastenavond*, Shrove Tuesday was *Kleine Vastenavond*. In this paper events on *Invocavit* Sunday are considered as Shrovetide festivities without any comment. All the details on the feast of 1395 are to be found in the archives of the Counts of Holland (*AGH*) in the Algemeen Rijksarchief (*ARA*) in The Hague, mostly in

inv. no. 1250. See also: D.E.H. de Boer 'Vorst tussen twee werelden: Het hof van Albrecht van Beieren' *Fibula* 27:2 (1986) 4–11 and F.P. van Oostrom *Het woord van eer: Literatuur aan het Hollandse hof omstreeks 1400* (Meulenhoff, Amsterdam, 1987) 171, 176: English translation: *Court and Culture: Dutch Literature 1350–1450* (University of California Press, Berkeley, 1992). On water-jousts: A. Viaene 'Watertornooien op Vlaamse rivieren' *Biekorf* 77 (1977) 5–12.

11. *Cartulaire des comtes de Hainaut, de l'avènement de Guillaume II à la mort de Jacqueline de Bavière (1337–1436)* Vol. 5 edited L. Devillers (Académie Royale des Sciences, des Lettres et des Beaux-Arts de Belgique, Commission Royale d'Histoire, Brussels, 1892) 554–5. See also: J.G. Smit 'De graven van Holland en Zeeland op reis. Het grafelijk itinerarium van het begin van de veertiende eeuw tot 1425' in *Holland in wording. De ontstaansgeschiedenis van het graafschap Holland tot het begin van de vijftiende eeuw* edited D.E.H. de Boer and others (Verloren, Hilversum, 1991) 91–124.
12. *Cartulaire* V 556.
13. ARA: AGH 1380 fol. 16^{r-v}, 17^r; *Cartulaire* V 562.
14. 'Cent florins au mouton de Flandres', *Cartulaire* V 572–5, 577.
15. By mistake this mention figures on 20 January, *Cartulaire* V 592.
16. ARA: AGH 1238 fols 119^v, 139^r.
17. ARA: AGH 1241 fol. 30^v, 32^v, 35^r, 75^r.
18. ARA: AGH 1242 fol. 116^{r-v}; Van Oostrom (note 10) 130 makes a mistake in situating this feast in 1387. He refers to an anonymously published article, ' 's-Gravenhage onder de regering der graven uit de huizen van Holland, Henegouwen en Beijeren' *Mededeelingen van de Vereeniging ter Beoefening der Geschiedenis van 's-Gravenhage* 1 (1863) 207–342.
19. ARA: AGH 1242 fol. 143^r.
20. A lot of information from the archival sources is collected in C. Lingbeek-Schalekamp *Overheid en muziek in Holland tot 1672* (Blok en Flohr, [Rotterdam], 1984).
21. ARA: AGH 1400 fol. 57^v (1399); Lingbeek-Schalekamp 185.
22. ARA: AGH 1253 fol. 43^v; see H. van Wijn *Historische en letterkundige avondstonden* (Johannes Allart, Amsterdam, 1800) 355 and *'s-Gravenhage* 1 (see note 18) 316; also cited in J.M. Hollaar and E.W.F. van den Elzen 'Het vroegste toneelleven in enkele Noordnederlandse plaatsen' *De nieuwe taalgids* 73 (1980) 302–324, see 315–316.
23. A. Van Elslander 'Lijst der Nederlandse rederijkerskamers uit de XVe en XVIe eeuw' *Jaarboek 'De Fonteine'* 18 (Gent, 1968) 41, 50.
24. 12 gr., mentioned by W.J.A. Jonckbloet *Geschiedenis der middennederlandsche dichtkunst* 3 (Van Kampen, Amsterdam, 1855) 600.
25. E.g. about Shrovetide in 1399, a certain amount '... die mijn heer tDordrecht (in the town of Dordrecht) *vermommede*', ARA: AGH 1400 fol. 31^r.
26. *'s-Gravenhage* 1 (see note 18) 331 and 319.
27. ARA: AGH 1268 fol. 54^r (a small gift of 3s. 4d. gr.).
28. Hollaar and Van den Elzen (see note 22) 315; Van Oostrom (see note 10) 44, 276. They refer to Jonckbloet (see note 24) 616. In the original document, this item is unmistakable.
29. *Overijsselsche Stad-, Dijk- en Markeregten. Eerste deel: Stadregten* (Tjeenk Willink, Zwolle, 1875) first part: *Boeck van Rechten der Stad Kampen* 18–19.
30. E. Van Autenboer 'Vastenavondviering te Mechelen' *Volkskunde* 49 (1948) 171–2.

31. GAU Stadsarchief 1 587 (1441–1442) fols 39^v, 45^v (other lords had to eat in other taverns) and fol. 41^v for the wine.
32. E.g. Zwolle 1426, *Maandrekening van Zwolle: 1426* edited F.C. Berkenvelder (Gemeentelijke Archiefdienst, Zwolle, 1984) 70 and *Maandrekening van Zwolle: 1430* (Gemeentelijke Archiefdienst, Zwolle, 1985) 39–40 (for the parish priest) as well as *Maandrekening van Zwolle: 1431* (Gemeentelijke Archiefdienst, Zwolle, 1986) 64.
33. 'omme wilde gheselschap te schiwen', *De stadsrekeningen van Deventer 4* edited G.M. de Meyer (Tjeenk Willink, Groningen, 1976) 65.
34. GAU Stadsarchief 1 587 (1441–1442) fol. 39^v.
35. GAU Stadsarchief 1 587 fol. 40^r.
36. *De stadsrekeningen van Arnhem 4* edited W.J. Alberts (Wolters-Noordhoff, Groningen, 1978) 384–6.
37. See G.J.M. Nijsten 'Openbare feesten, toneel en "volksvermaak" in Arnhem ca.1430 – ca.1500' *Bijdragen en Mededelingen Gelre* 79 (1988) 29–47 (this article is based on archival documents which were not used by Hollaar and Van den Elzen - see note 22), H. Leloux 'Schauspiel, Schauspieler und Musikanten im Geldrischen Arnhem um 1400' *Rheinische Vierteljahrsblätter* 39 (1975) 342–57 and B. Neumann 'Mittelälterliches Schauspiel am Niederrhein' *Zeitschrift für deutsche Philologie* 94 Sonderheft (1975) 148–94. More details about court and culture in Guelders are to be found in Gerard Nijsten *Het hof van Gelre. Cultuur ten tijde van de hertogen uit het Gulikse en Egmondse huis (1371–1473)* (Kok Agora, Kampen, 1992). See also Gerard Nijsten 'The Duke and his Towns: the power of ceremonies, feasts, and public amusement in the Duchy of Guelders (East Netherlands) in the fourteenth and fifteenth centuries' in *City and Spectacle in Medieval Europe* edited Barbara A. Hanawalt and Kathryn L. Reyerson (University of Minnesota Press, Minneapolis, 1994) 235–70.
38. In Deventer the *smedenknechten* got a special gift in 1426, probably for dancing a sword dance: *Stadsrekeningen Deventer 5* edited G.M. de Meyer (Wolters-Noordhoff, Groningen, 1979) 61. See also e.g. J.M. Hollaar and E.W.F. van den Elzen 'Toneelleven in Deventer in de vijftiende en zestiende eeuw' *De nieuwe taalgids* 73 (1980) 412–425, especially 413 and 415; S. Elte 'Sprekers, tooneelvoorstellingen en rederijkerij in de 15^e en 16^e eeuw in Zwolle' *Verslagen en Mededeelingen Overijsselsch Regt en Geschiedenis* 50 (1934) 11; Nijsten (see note 37) 30–31.
39. *De kameraars- en rentmeestersrekeningen der stad Kampen van 1515–1540* edited J. Nanninga Uitterdijk (Van Hulst, Kampen, 1875) *passim*.
40. In 1480: Nijsten (note 37) 32 and note 24.
41. E.g. misericords from the beginning of the sixteenth century at the choir stalls of St Catharine's Church in Hoogstraten and the Great Church in Dordrecht.
42. Arnhem 1440 and 1441: Nijsten (see note 37) 30 and note 8. The Hague 1414: ARA: AGH 1267 fol. 87^v.
43. *Journal d'un Bourgeois de Paris de 1405 à 1449* edited Colette Beaune (Livre de Poche, Librairie Générale Française, Paris, 1990) 221.
44. Bodleian Library, Oxford: MS Bodley 264 fol. 74^r.
45. See Paul Vandenbroeck *Jheronimus Bosch tussen volksleven en stadscultuur* (EPO, Berchem, 1987) 306, 310–311.
46. E.g. Zwolle 1450: '*voir den scoelres, die voir den rade speelden des Dinxdages in den Vastelavent*', Elte (see note 38) 8.

47. *Kameraarsrekeningen* (see note 39) 20, 61, 64, 70, 75.
48. *Maandrekening van Zwolle 1403* edited F.C. Berkenvelder (Gemeentelijke Archiefdienst, Zwolle, 1975) 28.
49. See note 37 for the references.
50. Elte (see note 38) 11–13; Nijsten (see note 37). The references concerning drama in the Arnhem accounts during the sixteenth century have been examined by H.Chr. van Bemmel 'Toneel in Arnhem van 1500 tot 1565' in *'Wat duikers vent is dit!' Opstellen voor W.M.H. Hummelen* edited G.R.W. Dibbets and P.W.M. Wackers (Quarto, Wijhe, 1989) 121–38.
51. In Oudenburg, a town between Bruges and Ostend, a pageant waggon is mentioned as early as 1434. See R. de Wolf 'Bijdrage tot de kennis van ons middeleeuwsch tooneel' *Tijdschrift voor Nederlandsche Taal- en Letterkunde* 14 (1895) 303.
52. *De stadsrekeningen van Middelburg 2* edited H.M. Kesteloo (Altorffer, Middelburg, 1885) 63–4.
53. Nijsten (note 37) 31 and Van Bemmel (note 50) 123.
54. *Fastnachtspiele aus dem fünfzehnten Jahrhundert 1* edited Heinrich Adalbert von Keller (Wissenschaftliche Buchgesellschaft, Darmstadt, 1965; reprint of the Stuttgart edition, 1853) 191–8 (no. 21).
55. Hollaar and Van den Elzen (see note 38: Deventer) 421. See also Vandenbroeck (see note 45) 299–300.
56. For Arnhem, see Hollaar and Van den Elzen (note 22) 311; for Zwolle, see Elte (note 38) 14; for 's-Hertogenbosch, see M. Heyer 'Iets over middeleeuws toneel' *Tijdschrift voor Taal en Letteren* 29 (1941) 127–8, 130–1.
57. Among other editions: *Het abel spel Vanden Winter ende Vanden Somer* edited G. Stellinga (Pantheon: Thieme, Zutphen, s.d.). See Marie Ramondt 'Van jaarspel tot abel spel' *De Gids* 106 (1942) 165–84; this article also seems to be slightly influenced by a specific ideological framework (namely, of the German *Volkskunde*). I leave some recent articles on the play aside for this moment, for they do not influence my argument.
58. In the cast list Summer is not mentioned, but a character named Justice figures there who does not appear in the fragment: *Middelnederlandsche dramatische poëzie* edited P. Leendertz (Sijthoff, Leiden, 1907) 436–41.
59. See Claude Gaignebet 'Le combat de Carnaval et de Carême' *Annales, Economies, Societés, Civilisations* 27:2 (1972) 313–45; Martine Grinberg and Sam Kinser 'Les combats de Carnaval et de Carême: Trajets d'une métaphore' *Annales, Economies, Societés, Civilisations* 38:1 (1983) 65–98; Anthony Gash 'Carnival against Lent: the ambivalence of medieval drama' in *Medieval Literature: Criticism, Ideology and History* edited David Aers (Harvester, Brighton, 1986) 74–98; Wim Hüsken 'Streitgedicht-influences in comic dialogues in the Netherlands' in *Atti del IV colloquio della Société Internationale pour l'Etude du Théâtre Médiéval (Viterbo 10–15 luglio 1983)* edited M. Chiabo, F. Doglio, and M. Maymone (Centro Studi sul Teatro Medioevale e Rinascimentale, Viterbo, 1984) 65–74.
60. 'Der coning ende keyser speel'. See Hollaar and Van den Elzen (note 22) 311.
61. Hollaar and Van den Elzen (see note 38: Deventer) 413. The editor of the town accounts of Deventer, Mrs. G.M. de Meyer, has been so kind as to verify this item for me. It looks as if the clerk did not know what he was writing down: *teofilus spull* might have been *teufelen* or *teofelen* in the original draft. In that case the play was about a devil!

62. Bocholt: Neumann (see note 37) 171; Deinze: J.A. Worp *Geschiedenis van het drama en van het tooneel in Nederland 1* (Langerveld, Rotterdam, 1904) 34.
63. *Kameraarsrekeningen* (see note 39) 10.
64. Umberto Eco 'The frames of comic freedom' in *Carnival!* edited U. Eco, V.V. Ivanov, and M. Rector (Mouton, Berlin, 1984) 6.

WHY A PEASANT IS TAUGHT HOW TO 'SHOOT'
Rhetoricians, Militiamen, and a Late Medieval Dutch Farce[1]

Femke Kramer

In August 1615 in a small Dutch town called Kethel, near Rotterdam, a festival of Rhetoric took place. Chambers of Rhetoric from all over the Low Countries congregated on occasions such as this in order to compete in performing plays. At the Rhetoricians' feast in Kethel the company *De Koorenbloem* ('The Cornflower') from The Hague performed a farce entitled *Een boerdige cluchte van een boer die wil leeren schieten* ('A comical farce of a peasant who wants to learn how to shoot'), the text of which, stating place, date, and name of the performing company, is included in an early seventeenth-century repertory-book[2] that most likely belonged to a famous Rhetorician, P.C. van der Morsch, member of the Leiden Chamber of Rhetoric *De Witte Acoleijen* ('The White Columbine').[3] It is unlikely that the production from The Hague at the Kethel festival was a first staging of the piece. Rhetoricians used to copy plays from one another and inserted successes of other Chambers in their own repertory.[4] Elements in the text of the play performed at Kethel by the *Koorenbloemen* indicate that it originated in early-sixteenth-century Mechelen.

The farce can be summarised as follows:[5] a peasant, suffering from a severe sense of inferiority, goes into town with the intention of learning how to shoot. By becoming a militiaman he expects to acquire admiration and prestige. The two militiamen whom he approaches simulate willingness to help him. They take him to the tavern of the *doelen*, the place used by militia-guilds for target-practice. Here they give him instructions. The most important thing is for him to get acquainted with *'t cruijt* (meaning either *kruit*, 'gun-powder', or *kruid*, 'herb'), but first of all he must get himself a suit of armour and buy all sorts of militia necessaries. After he has provided himself with everything, he returns to the tavern, looking ridiculous in his outfit. The militiamen take him to the pharmacy, where he is administered the *poijer* ('powder') *quod retro exit* (F138R): *schietkruit* ('gun-powder'), the peasant thinks, *schijtkruid* ('laxative'), the audience knows. On the shooting-range of the *doelen* the medicine takes effect. At the moment when the peasant thinks he is about to fire his rifle, his bowels give way: *hij laet een veest* (F140R, 'he farts'), according to the stage-direction. The peasant's initial disappointment is cleverly counteracted by the militiamen who praise the performance in flattering terms. Elated, proud, and with dirty trousers he goes home. At home the peasant's wife punishes her husband, enforcing him to take an oath in which he promises never to undertake anything this foolish again: a peasant should remain a peasant.

The central feature in the farce is formed by a pun concerning *schieten* ('to shoot') and *schijten* ('to shit'), words that sound nearly similar in the medieval Dutch language. In an early stage of the play the audience already realises that the peasant is about to shit instead of to learn how to shoot, something of which he himself, unballasted by intellect, is unconscious. In fact during the whole play the audience is advantaged in being better informed than the hero, as a result of the peasant's ignorance and the numerous asides of the two militiamen. This culminates in the scene in which the peasant assumes that he has accomplished a marvellous achievement, whereas his actual state is ridiculous and pathetic: dramatic irony. Apparently, however, making a fool of the peasant is not enough. It seems as if the playwright begrudges his protagonist even the happiness of imagining that he has learned how to shoot, because after the dramatic climax a new plot is developed, which results in the beating the peasant gets from his wife. She, moreover, addresses herself to the audience at the end of the play, explicating the moral of what has gone before. The didactic tone of this explanation indicates that the farce is not purely aimed at amusement. Closer investigation of the social context in which the farce came about reveals that it may contain strong satirical elements and that its function may have been more complex than it seems at first sight.

Rhetoricians[6]

During the late Middle Ages a significant shift took place in the social constellation in the Low Countries. The growth of the city and its population saw the rise of a class which no longer recognised itself as a part of the traditional feudal system. Townspeople, mainly engaged in trade and industry, associated on a relatively equal footing. The search of the newly-emancipated class for a fitting identity and appropriate values is reflected in the literary texts that survive from this period. Well-to-do citizens in the Low Countries united in *rederijkerskamers* ('Chambers of Rhetoric' or Rhetoricians' Guilds) which were organised like guilds, partly drama companies, partly schools of oratory and poetry. They were of important cultural and social significance in late medieval urban society. The quantity of texts that have survived gives evidence of great activity. As for drama, only one of the genres they practised, almost 600 plays have survived or are known to have existed, titles and descriptions of which are recorded in Hummelen's *Repertorium van het rederijkersdrama*.

With the Rhetoricians' services to the city community, their activities were part of a tradition of town festivities.[7] They seized every opportunity to entertain and edify the citizenry. For this purpose they were financially supported by the city authorities who thus made sure that the Rhetoricians acted according to their wishes: they were to create the desired atmosphere and advocate the proper opinions. Obviously the city rulers recognised the potential influence of these bearers of culture on public opinion, politics, and even economics.[8] The Rhetoricians considered the stage a platform on which they could exhibit, illustrate, and advocate their private opinions or those of their (indirect) principals. Rhetorical competitions like the feast at Kethel were not only important festive occasions but also an opportunity for discussing ethical problems by means of theatre. The plays were to give an answer to a moral question posed by the Chamber acting as host. The companies that appeared at Kethel, for example, were invited to solve in their *sinnespelen* ('moralities') the problem *waerdoor de werelt meest heyloos en blindich dwaelt* ('what is the main reason for the world's fatal and blind erring?').[9] Closer examination of the farce of the 'shooting' peasant demonstrates that, like the serious *sinnespelen*, the comical plays, however trivial they may seem, nevertheless reflect a viewpoint and carry a more or less ideological message.

The moral with which the peasant's wife concludes the play, directly addressing herself to the audience, states that the peasant should remain a peasant, and should he still dare to aspire to a higher status, then he will quite rightly be punished. Considering the social background of the audience aimed at, which consisted in the first place of townspeople, this 'lesson' may be interpreted as the expression of an affirmation of the new-found identity of this new class which needed to be protected against infiltration from people thought of as inferior.

This tendency is firmly connected with a more profound intention which is perceptible between the lines though it is not explicitly presented in the play. Closer examination of the way in which the protagonist in the farce is pictured demonstrates that this peasant is nothing but the embodiment of a series of unpleasant traits, the personification of several forms of misbehaviour. In the opening scene the peasant reveals his motive for longing to become a militiaman: vanity. When he meets the two militiamen, their politeness contrasts with his insolence and rudeness. The scenes in the tavern give the peasant the opportunity to demonstrate his lack of civilisation and his immodesty. Despite his ignorance in matters concerning the town and the militia-guild, he is conceited. The peasant's stupidity, in fact a thread throughout the whole play, is very evident from the way he reports on the events to his wife: the story he tells her about what happened makes no sense at all.

In attributing to the peasant all sorts of unacceptable conduct, the play places itself in a tradition of peasant characterisation in which the complete peasant population is invariably ridiculed. Works of art which are representative of this genre have the underlying intention of holding a mirror in reverse to the audience. Under the surface of satire against peasants lies a message with the tenor that 'we' (the townspeople) are not, and above all, should not be like 'them', those filthy, stupid, rude (etc.) peasants.[10] Thus the farce, against the background of a newly-emancipated, searching group of the population, may be interpreted as a set of guidelines presented in reverse, through which the playwright indirectly (and possibly unconsciously) imparted a code of behaviour.

We may ask ourselves if the characterisation of the co-starring characters, the two militiamen, also contains a similar homily in disguise, a question all the more interesting because of the assumed connection between the medieval militia-guilds and the Chambers of Rhetoric. There are apparent similarities in the way these two associations were organised and presented themselves, and these have led many to conclude that the Chambers originated from the militia-guilds: another typical exponent of the emerging class of townspeople.

Militiamen[11]

The civic oath which townspeople took when they obtained their rights and privileges under the title of freedom bound them to defend the place in which they lived and to accompany the local sovereign power on military expeditions, for which they were equipped with weapons. The earliest militia-guilds were formed in wartorn Flanders in the thirteenth century: the use of bow and arrow as a professional weapon of war required a high degree of skill which in turn made a sufficient amount of practice necessary. Communal target-practice eventually led to the formation of volunteer municipal target-practice clubs which were recognised by the city fathers or the local lord. Though in principle militia service was rendered voluntarily and unpaid, the members of the militias enjoyed privileges, and the city governors tried to secure their loyalty by means of financial support. Following the Flemish example, militia-guilds soon formed in other parts of Europe. The oldest guilds were equipped with the cross-bow. Younger guilds specialised in the use of the long-bow, and when firearms began to gain in popularity during the sixteenth century, *kloveniersgilden* came into existence as well, the members of which were equipped with arquebuses.

Militiamen came from a second-rank élite, just below the class of the city rulers. The membership of a militia-guild was usually considered honourable, and it was reserved for free, independent, and irreproachable inhabitants who could afford the expenses it entailed (clothes, weapons, entrance-fee) and the time for target-practice. The status and the popularity, however, decreased in times of tension and war, and under such circumstances militiamen had to pay for resigning. For fear of undesirable activities by the armed force within the city walls, the rulers tried to control the appointment of militiamen, apparently not always with the intended effect. Even in cities in which, as a result of a carefully considered appointment policy, close ties were developed between the authorities and the men who had leading positions in the guilds, the militiamen's loyalty was not guaranteed. Although the official militia-decrees required them to come to the aid of the city authorities at times of unrest, the guilds did not always allow themselves to be used by the city rulers. Often they took upon themselves the rôle of passive onlookers and as such rather contributed to the disturbances than suppressed them. Sometimes they turned against the government, siding with the troublemakers or even assuming their leadership.

Unlike their reliability and adequacy in military matters and their loyalty to the city government, the militiamen's concern with the social and cultural life of the medieval city is beyond doubt. The militiamen formed a clearly visible group within urban society, with their colourful appearance which symbolised the glory of the city which they served. Even in times of peace city governments presented their corps at full strength in order to convince everyone of their power. The militiamen added pomp and circumstance to processions, celebrations, and 'Joyous Entries', and had a rich club-life of their own with feasts, parades, and shooting competitions which were important festive occasions that saw the annual crowning of a 'shooters' king'. The occupations of the militia became more and more dominated by a festive element which originally accompanied the military aspect, but eventually became a substitute for it. The militiamen were engaged in affairs which had nothing to do with target-practice, for instance performing plays, occasionally with a competitive element. Often they staged plays themselves, but at times the local Rhetoricians did this for them.

This indicates close connections between militiamen and Rhetoricians, which is confirmed by the fact that some Rhetoricians are known to have been members of the civic militia as well. The members of both the Chambers of Rhetoric and militia-guilds were part of the well-to-do (upper) middle class. Moreover, the Rhetoricians' festivals were organised in the same way as, and may have followed the example of the militia feasts, in that the militia-guilds and the Chambers of Rhetoric show a great resemblance in their rôle in urban society. All these facts have led many to conclude that the Chambers originate from the militia-guilds, or from a literary section within the guilds.[12]

A 'militia-piece'

The farce in which a peasant is tricked by two militiamen might originally have been a militia piece: performed for an audience of militiamen, maybe even by militiamen. This might be assumed from the use of a terminology which was possibly particularly comprehensible for militiamen. But there are more indications. The first one can be found on the title page in the collection. The full text reads as follows:

> Een boerdige cluchte
> van een boer die wil leeren
> schieten inden doelen
> Gespeelt inden dorpe van kethel
> bijde koorenbloemen van 'sgravenhage
> op den IV en augustii 1615   fol. 131^r

'A comical farce of a peasant who wants to learn how to shoot at the *doelen*; performed at the village of Kethel by the Koorenbloemen from The Hague on the fourth of August 1615.'

The compiler of the Leiden collection apparently interpreted *inden doelen* as an indication of the scene of the action, as witness also the addition *Gespeelt inden dorpe van Kethel* ... This is not surprising, in the first place because on occasions such as the Kethel festival it was usual to stage plays in the open air, and the *schuttershof* ('shooting-range' at the *doelen*) is indeed the place where the peasant is taught to 'shoot'. Since the version in the Leiden collection is likely to be a copy, the original sense of *inden doelen*, however, might have been slightly different. The reference may be interpreted as an indication of the space in which the show was performed, and *Gespeelt inden dorpe van Kethel* ... as an addition. *Doelen*-buildings were not uncommonly used as playhouses.[13]

Another element in the text indicates that the performance originally took place in a *doelen*-building and for an audience consisting of militiamen. One of the stage-directions reads:

> De coning sal ergens in een venster leggen, sonder spreken, altemets eens knickende. fol. 133^v
>
> 'The king will lie somewhere in a window, not speaking, now and then nodding.'

Undoubtedly *coning* refers to the shooters' king, he who shot the wooden parrot and as such was the winner of the annual shooting contest. The list of characters does not mention this king, nor has he any lines in the text, but, however superfluous his rôle in the play, the other characters refer more than once to his presence, and he is expected to show his agreement with the course of events by nodding. Any person, irrespective of any talent for acting, would have been able to play the king's part, but probably originally it was not just anyone. It is likely that the actual king of the militia-guild was invited to join in the play, by just being there among the audience, non-verbally responding to the action, an excellent way of involving the audience to the performance.

The suggestion of an intimate, indoor performance provides an attractive explanation for the somewhat unusual place in which the break is inserted. Although the scene of the action before the break (the pharmacy) is different from the one after it (the shooting-range), there is no actual need for an intermission. Moreover, the break is not signalled by the common interruption of the linking of speeches by rhyme.[14] Perhaps during this 'intermission' the actors, while performing, made their way with the audience from the actual tavern of the *doelen* to the actual shooting-range where the rest of the piece was performed: a performance on location.

The reconstruction of the original setting of the play as suggested above might throw a new light on the meaning of the farce. If indeed the play was meant to be performed in a *doelen*-house and for militiamen only, it might carry a message specifically aimed at this more particular audience: a hypothesis that creates more questions than can be answered in this context. In the following some possibilities will be discussed without jumping to conclusions. First of all it is necessary to have a closer look at the characterisation of the militiamen in the farce.

With a protagonist craving for membership of a militia-guild, the farce appears to set the militiaman on a pedestal. Considering, however, the social position of this character, it is doubtful whether the audience was supposed to agree with him. Perhaps, on the contrary, they were expected to conclude that only a peasant wants to become a militiaman ... Being typical deceivers who play a dirty trick on their victim, the militiamen seem to be negative characters. On the other hand, this trick is not really malicious, and they make a fool of the peasant because he practically asks for it by talking and acting the way he does. The joke, moreover, is justified in the final words of the farce in which the moral is expressed. The militiamen give an over-ambitious member of an inferior class a treatment which would have been considered right by any citizen. From the audience's point of view the militiamen play the rôle of heroes rather than of villains. It is however hard to judge whether their characterisation is completely positive.

Their performance shows numerous subtle traces of self-conceit. They virtually compete in being smart, speaking (pseudo-)French and (dog-)Latin and exhibiting their intellectual baggage. Real contemporary militiamen possibly derived from their status a feeling of superiority which manifested itself in a certain arrogance in respect of provincials as well as towards their fellow townsmen. Indeed, the way in which the militiamen are typified, and their self-satisfied conduct in the farce, creates the impression that it is satirising an exaggerated sense of self-esteem. This could be evidence against the interpretation of the farce as a militia play: the real militiaman would not want to be satirised by a farce. Considering, however, the arguments in favour, and the harmless character of the mockery, it can hardly be interpreted as a fundamental rejection of the behaviour of militiamen. Paradoxically some moderate self-irony is all the more evidence for the reconstruction of a setting in a *doelen*-house. Within the militia-guild, criticism could safely be expressed, because it stayed within doors. Some self-irony among peers, in the knowledge that the image existing in the outside world will not be affected, may even have consolidated and stimulated the sense of unanimity and solidarity within the guild. In a way we may compare this effect with the function attributed to the militia portraits, such as the painting generally known as *De nachtwacht*. These portraits appear to show self-complacency rather than heroism. In spite of this they were meant to decorate a *doelen*-house, and therefore they must have represented an acceptable view of the guild. Art-historians indeed ascribe to the pieces a harmonising, fraternising function.[15]

Rhetoricians versus militiamen

As yet no assertions have been made about the actual performers. The play might have been an exclusive militia production, considering the fact that the militiamen occupied themselves with performing arts during their pseudo-military feasts. The Rhetoricians, however, are known to have rendered all kinds of cultural services to the militia-guilds. It is recorded that they appeared in performances on festive militia occasions.

The name given to the inn-keeper figuring in the play, Jan van Kruijbeke, suggests that the farce originally was indeed a Rhetoricians' production. A man called Jan van Cruybeke lived in Mechelen, the city which is mentioned in the text as the scene of part of the action (fol. 141ᵛ). He was a member of the Mechelen Chamber *De Peoene* ('The Peony'), and died in 1513.[16] It seems that members of the Mechelen *Peoene* staged the farce as a special occasion for a Mechelen militia-guild. If this was indeed the case, an even more complex message might be hidden in the play.

The history of Mechelen shows that at a certain moment there was serious friction between Rhetoricians and militiamen. In the middle of the sixteenth century Rhetoricians in this city made efforts to be exempted from militia duties, which they vainly fought up to the highest levels of the city government. The origins and the exact nature of the conflict are obscure, but the existence of troubles in those days is beyond doubt.[17] If the play indeed is an early-sixteenth-century Mechelen Rhetoricians' product, aimed at an audience of militiamen, it might be showing us a picture of the Rhetoricians beginning to put themselves at a distance from their armed brothers, illustrating a process in which the Rhetoricians and the militia guilds were growing apart. Thus the farce might after all contain a reaction against militia conduct, still an innocent and harmless one, but with a more serious undertone.

I hope that I have pointed out that in the farce of the 'shooting' peasant, though on the surface it is obviously meant as sheer entertainment, lies a more profound significance consisting of several layers, the most evident of which is formed by a rejection of the infiltration of over-ambitious members of a group thought of as inferior into the urban (upper) middle class. Furthermore we may distinguish the affirmation of a new-found identity of this social class, and the prescription of a code of behaviour for townspeople in general. The assumption that the play was originally aimed at an audience of militiamen, moreover, leads to the conclusion that the farce contains an even more specific message, as is discussed above.

The connotations of texts such as this farce probably varied with the occasion and the audience aimed at. In view of the character of this genre of drama, and the fact that this farce in any case still was considered presentable more than a century after its first staging, this is not an unreasonable notion. The staging in early sixteenth-century Mechelen undoubtedly reflected a common urban opinion of peasants and of desirable conduct. Presupposing that Rhetoricians staged the farce for an audience of militiamen, and considering that later in that century the Rhetoricians were on very bad terms with the militia-guilds, we might suspect the author of the text of passing criticism on militiamen as well as on peasants. The performance at Kethel in 1615, by the *Koorenbloemen* from The Hague may have been less satirical in their interpretation of the rôle of the two militiamen. In riots during the Twelve Year's Truce (1609–1621) militiamen usually sided with the population against the wish of the authorities, who in substitution for the rebellious local militias engaged paid soldiers. In comparison with these mercenaries from elsewhere, the militiamen undoubtedly played the rôle of the good guys.[18]

University of Groningen

NOTES

1. I wish to thank the Fonds Dr. Catharine van Tussenbroek for the support which made it possible for me to contribute to the SITM Colloquium.
2. Verzameling Van der Morsch, Gemeente-archief Leiden 72421, fols 131^r–144^r.
3. W.M.H. Hummelen *Repertorium van het rederijkersdrama 1500 – ca.1620* (Van Gorcum and Co, Assen, 1968) 256. N. van der Laan 'Rederijkersspelen in de bibliotheek van het Leidsche gemeente-archief' *Tijdschrift voor Nederlandse Taal- en Letterkunde* 49 (1930) 127. J.C. Overvoorde *Archieven van de Gilden, de Beurzen en van de Rederijkerskamers uit het Gemeente-Archief Leiden* (Drukkerij Hermandad, Leiden, 1921) 169, 172.
4. C.G.N. de Vooys 'Rederijkersspelen in het archief van "Trou moet blijcken"' *Tijdschrift voor Nederlandse Taal- en Letterkunde* 45 (1920) 265.
5. The text of the play is not yet available in an edition.
6. Detailed information on Rhetoricians: J.J. Mak *De rederijkers* (Van Kampen, Amsterdam, 1944); D. Coigneau 'Rederijkersliteratuur' *Historische letterkunde* edited M. Spies (Wolters-Noordhoff, Groningen, 1984) 35–57; A. van Elslander 'Letterkundig leven in de Bourgondische tijd, De rederijkers' *Jaarboek De Fonteine* 18 (Koninklijke Soevereine Hoofdkamer 'De Fonteine', Gent, 1968) 61–78; E. van Autenboer *Volksfeesten en rederijkers te Mechelen (1400–1600)* (Koninklijke Vlaamse Academie voor Taal- en Letterkunde, Gent, 1962).
7. Coigneau 35.
8. Autenboer 96, 144; J. and L. van Boeckel 'Landjuwelen en haagspelen in de XVe en XVIe eeuw' *Jaarboek De Fonteine* 18 (Gent, 1968) 13–14; Coigneau *passim*; H. Pleij 'De sociale funktie van humor en trivialiteit op het rederijkerstoneel' *Spektator* 5 (1975–1976) 108–27.
9. Hummelen 265.
10. P. Vandenbroeck *Over wilden en narren, boeren en bedelaars, Beeld van de andere, vertoog over het zelf* (Koninklijk Museum voor schone Kunsten, Antwerpen, 1987) 63–113; H.-J. Raupp *Bauernsatiren, Entstehung und Entwicklung des bäuerlichen Genres in der deutschen und niederländischen Kunst ca. 1470–1570* (Lukassen, Niederzier, 1986).
11. Detailed information on militia-guilds: *Schutters in Holland, Kracht en zenuwen van de stad* edited M. Carasso-Kok and J. Levy-van Halm (Waanders, Zwolle / Frans Halsmuseum, Haarlem, 1988); C.J. Sickesz *De schutterijen in Nederland* (Dissertation: De Bruyn, Utrecht 1864); A.M.C. van Asch van Wijck 'De schut- of schuttengilde in Nederland' *Berigten van het Historisch Gezelschap te Utrecht* 1:2 (Kemink en Zoon, Utrecht, 1848) 92–202; 3:2 (1851) 1–170; Autenboer (1962); Autenboer 'Rederijkers en schutters in de branding van de zestiende eeuw' *Noordgouw* 18 (1978) 85–106; J.C. Grayson 'The Civic Militia in the County of Holland 1560–81' *Bijdragen en mededelingen betreffende de geschiedenis der Nederlanden* 95:1 (1980) 35–63; G. Marnef *Het Calvinistisch bewind te Mechelen 1580–85* (UGA, Kortrijk-Heule, 1987).

12. For the assumed connection between rhetoricians and militiamen: Autenboer (1962) 79–85; Boeckel *passim*; Elslander 64–5; Mak 11; *Spelen van Cornelis Everaert* edited J.W. Muller and L. Scharpe (Brill, Leiden, 1920) 598–600.
13. Hummelen 111; *Spelen van Cornelis Everaert* 598.
14. *Een esbattement van smenschen sin en verganckelijcke schoonheit* edited Nederlands Instituut der Rijksuniversiteit Groningen (Tjeenk Willink, Zwolle, 1967) 61.
15. J. Levy-van Halm 'De Haarlemse schuttersstukken' *Schutters in Holland* 105.
16. Autenboer (1962) 169–70.
17. Autenboer (1962) 102–103.
18. *Schutters in Holland* 45.

MANKIND: AN ENGLISH FASTNACHTSPIEL?
Tom Pettitt

Few medieval English plays have experienced as radical a critical reassessment in recent years as the fifteenth-century morality, Mankind. Dismissed by Hardin Craig as 'a play of the utmost crudity', 'ignorant, corrupt ... and vulgar to the point of obscenity',[1] Mankind has emerged from more recent literary appreciations as a quite sophisticated handling of moral themes in which the vulgarity and obscenity have a carefully controlled function,[2] and the dramatic skills of its author have been emphatically underlined by numerous successful productions.[3] With very few exceptions, however, both admirers and detractors are agreed on the play's auspices and performance context: while for Craig Mankind had been corrupted from something perhaps resembling the more acceptable Castle of Perseverance 'by the necessities of staging with a small troupe and by a comic appeal to the yokels and the toughs of small towns', it was precisely to these necessities that David Bevington considered the play a successful response.[4]

However none of the features of the play habitually appealed to necessarily or exclusively points to the orthodox scenario of a company of itinerant professionals performing before a popular, paying audience on a booth stage erected in an inn-yard.[5] While it may be generally true of moralities that 'it is possible ... to deduce the social standing of the audience from the social standing of the protagonist',[6] this is not necessarily the case when the latter is so basic a representative of mankind as a peasant (witness Langland's Piers Plowman). To the objection that Mankind motivates one of his exits by saying to the audience, 'I wyll into þi ʒerde' (561),[7] an odd remark if he is in the yard as he says it, Bevington responded by moving his players and their booth stage into a room inside the inn,[8] only to prompt the further objection, to which I have not seen a response, that fifteenth-century provincial inns are unlikely to have provided a room large enough to facilitate such an arrangement, particularly if the audience is to be sufficiently numerous to make performance a worthwhile proposition for professionals.[9] Equally problematic is the collection taken from the audience in the course of the play as a pre-condition for the entry of the devil-figure, Titivillus (457–70). Claimed as the earliest instance of a 'gate' taken from the audience, it would take considerable time (professionals would presumably expect a contribution from everyone) and seriously disrupt the continuity of the action. And if the performance context were indeed an innyard (or a room inside an inn) then the audience would have been charged as they entered this is precisely the main financial advantage of such a venue for professionals. It is just as likely that the collection was made from a few members of the audience primed in advance.[10] Even a genuine collection would not demonstrate conclusively professional auspices: in recent tradition mummers similarly extract contributions from their audience and sometimes, as here, within the fiction of the dramatic action (for example to pay the fee of the Quack Doctor). The repeated use of the term 'gather' in connection with the collection (457, 460) suggests that the Vices see themselves as undertaking one of those 'gatherings' of money and provisions by which medieval parishes financed their community feasts (and from which the recent mummers' plays probably derive).

Such difficulties, together with the play's witty use of Latin (not all of which is translated for the audience's benefit) have prompted some to what is still probably a minority view associating the play with indoor, private auspices,[11] and I would suggest specifically the Shrovetide revels of a domestic (i.e. noble) or institutional household (e.g. a Cambridge college).[12] A further possibility of the same kind would be the revels of the conglomerate household formed by a craft or religious guild, celebrated at the guild-hall or at the residence of the master.[13] A play with a small cast and minimal scenic requirements would be equally appropriate to the limited resources available under such circumstances, and larger households could as much as an inn provide the 'mynstrellys' (72), the 'goodeman of þis house' (467) and the 'ostlere' (732) referred to as (or as if) present. Even taking such references to suggest an inn or tavern need not inevitably involve reverting to the orthodox booth-stage in innyard scenario; a guild lacking a hall might very well hire a room in such an establishment for its revels.

Reference in the play to 'þis house' (209) and an exit at a 'dore' (159) suggest indoor performance, perhaps in the Great Hall of a domestic or institutional residence, and the crowding of the audience around the acting-area usually envisaged in such a context (where a booth stage would not be used) explains the frequent demands for 'room' or 'space' made by the Vices as they enter (331, 474, 612) or exit (701). Mercy's appeal in his opening address to 'souerens þat sytt' and 'brothern þat stonde ryght wppe' (29), usually taken to refer to the arrangements for an audience paying different prices, would apply equally well to a householder and his guests of varying status, or to the elders of a guild and its less exalted 'brethren'.[14] The play's many references to local people and places,[15] which would take considerable research and metrical ingenuity to replace for each new locality, suggest it would be unsuitable for the repertoire of a travelling company, and this is also the implication of *Mankind*'s extraordinarily specific seasonal affiliations. The sophisticated London audiences of the late sixteenth century who could go to a play on almost any weekday throughout the year may have appreciated *A Midsummer Night's Dream* as much on 6 January as they did *Twelfth Night* on 23 June (although both may have originated as occasional plays for particular festivities), but in late-fifteenth-century East Anglia, when most drama was associated with household or community celebration of seasonal festivals, performance of a play with as intense seasonal affiliations as *Mankind* would be effectively restricted to the season concerned.

And that season, as already suggested, is the day or two immediately preceding the beginning of Lent on Ash Wednesday, the Carnival of Mediterranean countries, the *Fastnacht* or *fastelavn* of Germany and Scandinavia, the English Shrovetide. For in *Mankind* the usual morality struggle of agents of damnation and redemption for control over the soul and body of the Mankind-figure is presented with seasonal action and imagery of a detail and complexity which match, and which can be usefully compared to, the celebrated depiction by Pieter Brueghel the Elder of 'The Combat between Carnival and Lent'.[16] As the (confused) etymologies and associations of the English and European terms for the festival suggest, it is delicately poised between the season of Christmas revels of which it is the climax, and the period of Lenten fast for which it prepares. Correspondingly, in its calendrical rendition of its morality theme, *Mankind* has its agent of redemption, Mercy, persistently endeavour to draw Mankind (and the audience) in mind and spirit out of the revels season and forward into Lent and on to Easter. He has appealed to the Crucifixion by the fourth line of his opening address and goes on to urge the audience to qualify themselves (through repentance) for the grace it made possible. In this context his warning, 'Dyverte not yowrsylffe in tyme of temtacyon' (19), would seem to refer specifically to the special dangers of the Carnival period. In traditional terms Mercy is the 'Jack of Lent' of the play; the symbolic figure who, according to William Elderton's ballad, 'Lenton Stuff',

> ... comes justlynge in,
> With the hedpeece of a herynge,
> And saythe, 'repent yowe of yower syn,
> For shame, syrs, leve yower sweringe'.[17]

The warning is balanced by the recommendation that the audience purify their souls by good works (25–6), an activity which (as Brueghel was evidently also aware) was particularly appropriate to Lent. Mercy's later insistence on the shortness of 'þe tyme of contynuance' and the necessity of using it well (233–5) could refer to Lent as much as to the life of man. He is seconded by the as yet innocent Mankind, who likewise recommends his hearers to 'mortyfye' their 'carnall condycyon' (190), almost an etymological explication of *carnival*, and who on parting from Mercy strengthens his resolve by citing a line from the liturgy for Ash Wednesday: *Memento, homo, quod cinis es et in cinerem reuerteris* ('Remember that thou art ash, and to ash thou shalt return', 321).[18] Even the agricultural work he goes about 'To eschew ydullnes' (228–9) fits the season as the spring or 'Lent' tilth.[19] Appropriately for Shrovetide (in its moral aspect), his concluding conversation with Mercy (811–902) takes very much the form of a confession, and this time it is Mercy who quotes from the Ash Wednesday liturgy: *Ecce nunc tempus acceptabile, ecce nunc dies salutaris* ('Behold, now is the acceptable time; boheold, now is the day of salvation', 866).[20]

The calendrical exactness of the play is suggested by Mankind's initial rejection of Mercy when he returns to upbraid him (726): 'I xall speke wyth þe anoþer tyme, to-morn, or þe next day'; it is Shrove Tuesday, repentance can wait until Ash

MANKIND: AN ENGLISH FASTNACHTSPIEL?

Wednesday. For conversely, the aim of the Vices is clearly to keep Mankind (and the audience) within the season of revels extending from Christmas to Shrovetide and to prevent him from turning the page in the calendar which would usher in Lent.[21] As if appreciating the calendrical implications of Mercy's opening homily with its anticipations of Easter, Mischief interrupts it with a reference to the threshing which was precisely the main agricultural labour of the mid-winter season (50–62).[22] The action which follows with the irruption of the minor Vices, Newguise, Nowadays, and Nought, contains a good deal of dance, song, and ribald repartee appropriate to the revels season, and which is characterised as such by the use of terms like *game* (69), *sporte* (78), *reu[e]ll* (83), *pley* (84), *rewelynge* (85), and *dysporte* (167). And despite the loss of a manuscript leaf at this point in the text it is possible to identify this sequence as a specific form of revels activity, a customary house-visit or mumming in which the Vices offer their show to a householder who is somewhat reluctant to receive them.[23] Mischief functions as the Presenter whose job it is to knock on the door and enter first to prepare for the show to follow; the figure is familiar in the mummers' plays and, as the *Vorlaufer* – 'he who comes before' – in the German *Fastnachtspiele*. Accordingly he asks Mankind to open his door and have his money ready (52),[24] and announces the purpose of the visit: 'I am cumme hedyr to make yow game' (69). Mercy's response is very much that of the pious housekeeper disturbed by mummers: 'Why com ȝe hethyr, broþer? ȝe were not dysyryde' (53). When the text resumes after the lost leaf the other three Vices are making their entry with a confusing but evidently highly spectacular show. Minstrels are instructed to play and Nought to 'Leppe about lyuely'; so much so he fears breaking his neck (71–8), and then all dance (81 *sd*). In the manner of modern mummers they introduce themselves individually to the housekeeper (113–115), and the visit ends with a formal leave-taking and a song as they go out (149–61 and *sd*). While not matching the scale of the modern mummers' plays, the behaviour of the Vices and its implied context resembles in general terms a host of recent subdramatic house-visit customs, many of which must have had medieval antecedents, and which with very few exceptions belong to the Christmas-to-Shrovetide revels season. Most involve the presentation of a show, prefaced as here by a Presentation, in the course of seasonal house-visits, and there are some hints in *Mankind* of the specific kind of show involved (in addition to the usual music, dance, and song).

Prompted by a line (73) which may imply that the dancing Nought is urged on by others wielding sticks or whips, Glynne Wickham has suggested that they are parodying the show of a bearward and his dancing bear,[25] which is appropriate enough to Christmas revelry, but since the 'bear' is represented by Nought, and in the specific context of house-visit customs, the reference is more likely to be to a figure like the 'Straw Bear', a man swathed in a straw-costume and straw-mask, still taken from house to house around Twelfth Night in East Anglia; the corresponding German custom, interestingly, belongs more usually to Shrovetide.[26] But many other beast-figures from similar customs – called and vaguely resembling a ram ('tup'), bull,

TOM PETTITT

horse, etc. – provide equally appropriate analogues: in each instance one mummer is encased in a beast-costume, and may be made to dance or leap about by others, some wielding sticks or whips.[27] That something of the kind is going on here may be suggested not merely by Nought's evidently violent locomotion (and the possible use of whips) but equally by his complaint (97) that 'yt ys a narow space' – that is, inside the beast-costume, rather than in the room as usually supposed. This may also explain why he instructs Mercy, whom he suggests might care to take his place, to take off his clothes before doing so (86–9). Perhaps a horse-figure is suggested by Newguise's threat to make Mercy 'prawnce' (91); the modern horse-figures often involve a man stooping under a cloth and supporting himself by grasping a pole topped by a horse's head: hence both the narrow space and the possibility of a quick change of performer. This teasing of Mercy, which extends to tripping him up or pushing him over (113), may reflect the traditional mistreatment of the 'Jack of Lent' to which I have already compared him,[28] but in context also links the action to those varieties of the mumming involving some mischievous interaction between the visitors and the householder on whom they impose themselves with seasonal licence; whatever the theological reasons for the choice of identity for the main Vice-character, it may be significant that Shrove Monday is one of the 'Mischief Nights' of the traditional calendar.[29] And again Mercy's reaction when they have gone is appropriate to the circumstances of an unwelcome house-visit: 'Thankyde be Gode, we haue a fayer dylyuerance / Of þes thre onthryfty gestys' (162).

On a later occasion the Vices invite the audience to join them in what turns out to be a filthy 'Crystemes songe' (332; see 335–43 for the song itself). This has caused some perplexity about the precise seasonal affiliations of *Mankind*, but as already suggested the conflict in the play (as in Brueghel) is not between two days (Shrove Tuesday and Ash Wednesday) but two extended periods: the Christmas revels season and Lent-to-Easter, with Shrovetide as disputed territory between them. Indeed some Shrovetide customs (one of which will be referred to below) included a figure representing Christmas, whose rule ends at precisely (or rather roughly) this time. The dramaturgy here too may be that of the mumming, only now with the audience (and *Mankind*) as the recipients of the Vices' visit; the situation parallels closely that depicted in a late-fifteenth-century carol which announces the arrival of a visitor representing Christmas revelry who will invite the audience to join in a Christmas (and not inevitably religious) song:

> Now ys comyn a messyngere
> Of yore lorde, Ser Nu Yere,
> Byddes vs all be mere here
>   And as mere as we may.
> Therefore euery mon that ys here
> Synge a carol on hys manere;
> If he con non we schall hym lere,
>   So that we be mere allway.[30]

MANKIND: AN ENGLISH FASTNACHTSPIEL?

These inserted revels, together with other sporadic seasonal references[31] are contextually more significant than those many features of the words and actions of the Vices which echo the Christmas mummers' plays of recent tradition, in particular the sequence of action involving the fight of the three minor Vices with Mankind, in which he wounds them with his spade in various parts of their anatomy (respectively arm, head, and testicles), and their subsequent 'cure' by Mischief, which may have involved the chopping off and re-affixing the part concerned.[32] The mummers' plays never involve a beheading (let alone a castration) as a form of cure (although the Doctor or his assistant may claim to know a cure by these means), and it is rare (confined to the so-called Sword Dance Plays) as a means of slaying, but the general parallel to the frequent combat – slaying – cure sequence in the mummers' plays is striking enough, and reinforced by occasional verbal echoes as well. The history of the mummers' plays prior to the eighteenth century is too obscure to admit confident assertions, but it is possible that the action in Mankind here does reflect semi-dramatic games performed at household winter revels, be it by residents or guests or visiting mummers, and that this reinforces its seasonal affiliations.

The likelihood that *Mankind* was indeed intended for performance under the specific auspices of the Shrovetide revels of a household, institution (educational or ecclesiastical), or guild would be greatly enhanced by identifying a tradition of plays and performances to which it might belong, and models are readily available in roughly contemporary continental drama and custom. In a highly perceptive analysis which anticipates much of my discussion on the Carnival versus Lent theme in the play, Sandra Billington has pointed to *Mankind*'s parallels with the French *sotties*, also performed at Shrovetide, although there is some awkwardness in the necessity (since all characters in *sotties* are *sots*) of making a fool (if a holy one) of Mercy.[33] A more promising option is provided by the *Fastnachtspiele* of a number of provincial towns in the German-speaking areas of Europe – notably Lübeck, Sterzing, and (above all) Nüremberg – and (coming closer to East Anglia) the derivative tradition of *fastelavnsspil* of late-medieval Denmark.[34] As the name suggests, the *Fastnachtspiel* is created for and performed only at Shrovetide, but within this calendrical limitation encompasses a wide range of social auspices and performance contexts. Least significant for present purposes are the fairly massive civic productions on outdoor scaffolds or waggons in a manner similar to some forms of the English mystery cycles. More relevant is the pre-Reformation tradition at Nüremberg, where performance was in the context of the shrovetide banquets of the guilds, who also supplied the performers and in some cases the authors of the plays. Such *Fastnachtspiele* bear the impress of their auspices in frequent references to the season and its distinct ethos, the spiritual and bodily licence characteristic of Carnival, and as in *Mankind* this seasonal affiliation can be dramaturgically reinforced by the insertion of other, simpler customs associated with the season.[35] Several share with *Mankind*, the English mummers' plays, and Irish wake-games the combat –wounding/slaying – cure sequence of action which seems to have been a favourite of many types of festive performance.³⁶ The Nüremberg *Fastnachtspiele* range in size and dramatic complexity from fully-fledged plays of the format of *Mankind* itself (*Handlungsspiele*) to sub-dramatic displays (speech-sequences and dances) similar to the mumming performed by the Vices in it; *Mankind* may be a *Fastnachtspiel* (a dramatic custom) and it may also contain one (a dramatised custom).

Mankind's generic status as a morality is not necessarily incompatible with its *contextual* status as a *Fastnachtspiel*. While the German plays are generally characterised by scurrility and obscenity the fact that a couple of them present overtly the confrontation between Carnival and Lent implicit in *Mankind*'s morality structure suggests an awareness of the season's moral ambivalence,³⁷ and others introduce more solid and serious matter such as the Old Testament versus the New, the Dialogue of Solomon and Marcolf, Antichrist and the Emperor Constantine.³⁸ We should be aware of the ability of medieval (and traditional) culture to juxtapose the religious and the profane in ways surprising to post-Reformation élite sensibilities; relevant in this connection is a Shrovetide custom reported from the Black Forest region of Germany in the early nineteenth century involving professional shows, accompanied by music and beast-figures, of people got up to represent the Seven Deadly Sins.³⁹

With the exception of odd survivals (or more often revivals), Shrovetide has virtually disappeared as a major seasonal festival in England, and even in the early-modern period it is overshadowed by the more vigorous traditions of Christmasproper and by the summer games of May Day and Whitsun. It is however an East Anglian city, Norwich, which provides one of the most striking late-medieval reports of dramatic or semi-dramatic displays at Shrovetide, in the 1444 parade of John Gladman, who

> on fastyngong tuesday made a disporte wᵗ his neighburghs having his hors trapped with tyneseyle and otherwyse dysgysyn things crowned as King of Kristmesse in token that all merthe shuld end, with ye twelve monthes of ye yer afore hym eche moneth disgysd after ye seson yerof, and Lenten cladde in white with redde herrings skinnes and his hors trapped with oyster shelles after him in token yt sadnesse and abstinence of merth shulde followe and an holy tyme; and so rode in diuerse stretes of ye ite wᵗ other peple wᵗ hym disgysed making merthe and disporte and playes.⁴⁰

It is not suggested that Gladman and his company performed *Mankind* or anything like it in the course of this display, but the record is extremely valuable in confirming that in England too the Christmas revels could be conceived of as ending at Shrovetide or 'fastyngong',⁴¹ and that this ending could be symbolised in the juxtaposition (and very likely the confrontation) of figures respectively representing the Christmas season and Lent (and similar semi-dramatic confrontations may lie behind Brueghel's pictorial representation of the theme). Comparison with the Nüremberg evidence also suggests that Gladman and Co. on their progress through 'diuerse stretes' may have made occasional forays into houses with their (probably sub-dramatic) 'merthe and disporte and playes' in the kind of mumming imposed by the Vices of Mankind on the reluctant Mercy.

Occasional references to 'shrovings' suggest that the season was indeed marked by some specific form of revelry,[42] and there is some evidence of Shrovetide themes and/or auspices in connection with the two early dramatic genres most closely associated with household revels, the masque and the interlude. The records of the Revels Office and its predecessors suggest that Shrovetide remained an occasion for court revelry, including disguisings, masques, and plays, throughout the Tudor and Stuart periods,[43] and the royal court, the Inns of Court, and some noble households seem to have operated with the 'continental' extended season of revels lasting until Shrovetide. The conflict between Christmas revels and Lent suggested as a formative structure in Mankind features in some masques: Thomas Salusbury's *Knowsley Masque* (1641) includes an antimasque in which the emaciated fasting days carry off the fat 'gambolls' representing Christmas,[44] and Middleton's *Inner Temple Masque* (1619) has a similar confrontation between Plumporridge (personifying Christmas indulgence) and Fasting Day.[45] William Dunbar's poem, 'The Dance of the Sevin Deidly Synnis', while ostensibly a vision, seems to be based on a Shrovetide disguising, similar to the first show of the Vices in Mankind in which the Devil leads a dance of the Seven Deadly Sins, each followed by appropriate representatives of those 'that wer nevir schrevin, / Aganis the feist of Fasternis evin' (7–8).[46]

These are sub-dramatic shows, however, analogous to the simplest of the German *Fastnachtspiele* (and the inserted mummings in Mankind). A more substantial and dramatic performance with specific seasonal affiliations may be represented by the *Apollo Shroving*, reportedly written by a schoolmaster in Sussex and performed by his pupils on Shrove Tuesday 1627, an interesting parallel to sixteenth-century Denmark, where the *fastelavnsspil* were performed (at guild feasts) by grammar-school pupils as a means of earning money.[47] Among the surviving English interludes of the late fifteenth and early sixteenth centuries, a couple may be placed alongside Mankind as particularly or exclusively appropriate for household or guild Shrovetide revels. *Good Order*, although surviving only as a three-page fragment from a 1533 printed edition, shows every sign of being an explicit rendition of the confrontation of Christmas and Lent which is merely subsumed in Mankind. One sequence has Old Christmas banishing Riot and Gluttony at the behest of Good Order who has been greatly troubled by them for some time past, although they have now been beaten and captured; in this light allegory of the seasonal transition from Christmas festivity to Lent, Old Christmas himself seems to represent a postulated purer form of the festival, before it was contaminated by excessive carnival revelry. The surviving text fortunately includes part of the epilogue, in which Prayer clearly specifies the seasonal affiliations of performance: 'thys wyse good peple this lent tyme shold pray'.[48] The second candidate is *Youth*, which like Mankind contains a good deal of festive revelry and numerous intriguing parallels to the mummers' plays.[49] And as

TOM PETTITT

Ian Lancashire notes, the revelry of the vices confronts the moral message of the chief virtue, Charity, in a manner appropriate to the transitional season of Shrovetide. As in *Mankind*, the agent of redemption looks forward to Lent and Easter with appeals to the Passion, and the play ends with the protagonist going to shrift (lines 733-41). The treatment of Charity by the chief vice, Riot (also the symbol of revelry in *Good Order*), likewise has some similarities to a Shrovetide game.[50]

Youth may well belong to the household of the Earls of Northumberland, whose Chapel and other servants are recorded as performing plays at Christmas, Easter, and Shrovetide.[51] In the first two instances the matter (Nativity and Resurrection respectively) was appropriate to the festival concerned and we may suppose the same applies to the Shrovetide play; *Youth* would fit the bill adequately, and if some institution or household in East Anglia had a similar programme of festival plays *Mankind* would do even better as its *Fastnachtspiel*.

Odense Universitet

NOTES

1. Hardin Craig *English Religious Drama in the Middle Ages* (1955; reprinted Clarendon Press, Oxford, 1964) 350-1.
2. Kathleen M. Ashley 'Titivillus and the Battle of Words in *Mankind*' *Annuale Medievale* 16 (1975) 128-50; Paula Neuss 'Active and Idle Language: Dramatic Images in *Mankind*' in *Medieval Drama* edited Neville Denny (Stratford-upon-Avon Studies 16: Edward Arnold, London, 1973) 41-67; Lorraine K. Stock 'The Thematic and Structural Unity of *Mankind*' *Studies in Philology* 72 (1975) 386-407. See also the earlier study of Sister M.P. Coogan *An Interpretation of the Moral Play, 'Mankind'* (Catholic University of America Press, Washington D.C., 1947).
3. Robert Potter *The English Morality Play* (Routledge and Kegan Paul, London, 1975) 232; *English Moral Interludes* edited Glynne Wickham (Dent, London, 1976) 1; Pamela King and Jacqueline Wright 'The Poculi Ludique Societas of Toronto in England: *Mankind* at York, 4th May 1981' *Medieval English Theatre* 3 (1981) 58-60; John R. Elliott Jr 'Census of Medieval Drama Productions' *Research Opportunities in Renaissance Drama* 19 (1976) 83; 20 (1977) 102-103; 23 (1980) 85-6; 24 (1981) 193-4.
4. Craig *English Religious Drama* 351; David Bevington *From 'Mankind' to Marlowe* (Harvard University Press, Cambridge, Mass., 1962) 15-18.
5. See also Potter *English Morality Play* 55; Stanley J. Kahrl *Traditions of Medieval English Drama* (Hutchinson, London, 1974) 106 and 114; William Tydeman *English Medieval Theatre 1400-1500* (Routledge and Kegan Paul, London, 1986), part 2, chapter 1, 'The Booth Stage: *Mankind*'.
6. Alexandra F. Johnston 'The Audience of the English Moral Play' in *Le Théâtre et la cité dans l'europe médiévale (Fifteenth-Century Studies* 13) edited Jean-Claude Aubailly and Edelgard E. DuBruck (Hans-Dieter Heinz Akademischer Verlag, Stuttgart, 1988) 291-7, at page 292, leading to the conclusion (293) that since *Mankind* is 'a farmer, a ploughman', *Mankind* was 'written for a company to tour in the countryside'.

7. *The Macro Plays* edited Mark Eccles EETS OS 262 (1969); all further references will be to this edition.
8. David Bevington 'Popular and Courtly Traditions on the Early Tudor Stage' in *Medieval Drama* edited Neville Denny (Stratford-upon-Avon Studies 16: Edward Arnold, London, 1973) 97–8. A similar shift occurs between Glynne Wickham's *Early English Stages 1* (Routledge and Kegan Paul, London, 1959) 5, and *2.i* (Routledge and Kegan Paul, London, 1963) 186–96.
9. Sumiko Miyajima *The Theatre of Man, Dramatic Technique and Stagecraft in the English Medieval Moral Plays* (The author, Clevedon, 1977) 75 and note 2.
10. These objections are raised by Lawrence M. Clopper 'Mankind and its Audience' *Comparative Drama* 8 (1974–1975) 347–55, particularly 347–9.
11. Clopper 'Mankind and its Audience' 349–54: Richard Axton *European Drama of the Early Middle Ages* (Hutchinson, London, 1974) 199–203. Axton reverts to the orthodox position in 'The Morality Tradition' in *Chaucer and the Alliterative Tradition* edited Boris Ford (The New Pelican Guide to English Literature 1.i: Penguin, Harmondsworth, 1982) 347.
12. In her study of 'Sixteenth-Century Drama in St John's College, Cambridge' *Review of English Studies* 29 (1978) 1–10, Sandra Billington notes in some fifteenth-century lists of costumes and properties held by Cambridge colleges a few items which might have been used in *Mankind*, but she does not press the point.
13. On guilds and their feasts see Barbara A. Hanawalt 'Keepers of the Lights: Late Medieval English Parish Guilds' *Journal of Medieval and Renaissance Studies* 14 (1984) 21–37, and Charles Phythian-Adams *Desolation of a City* (Cambridge University Press, 1979) chapters 7 and 8.
14. In a very close analysis of the play Richard Southern concludes that it was designed for indoor performance before the screen of a Great Hall, but retains the connection with travelling professionals: *The Staging of Plays Before Shakespeare* (Faber, London, 1973) 21–43 and 143–4.
15. Walter K. Smart 'Some Notes on *Mankind*' *Studies in Philology* 72 (1975) 217–32; Thomas J. Jambeck and Reuben R. Lee '"Pope Pokett" and the Date of *Mankind*' *Medieval Studies* 39 (1977) 511–53.
16 Kulturhistorisches Museum, Vienna. The picture's relationship to seasonal customs has been extensively discussed by Claude Gaignebet 'Le combat de Carnaval et de Carême de P. Bruegel (1559)' *Annales, Economies, Sociétés, Civilisations* 27 (1972) 313–45, and Elke M. Schuttkehm *Pieter Bruegels d. A 'Kammpf des Karnevals gegen die Fasten' als Quellevolkskundlicher Forschung* (Peter Lang, Frankfurt a.M., 1983), both of which include reproductions.
17. Quoted by E.K. Chambers *The English Folk-Play* (1933; reprinted Clarendon Press, Oxford, 1969) 113.
18. Smart 'Some notes on *Mankind*' 46. Ashley 'Titivillus and the Battle of Words in *Mankind*' (see note 2), particularly 142–50, finds many additional echoes of the liturgy and homilies of the Lenten and pre-Lenten period. The line is a conflation of Genesis 3:19 and Job 34:15.
19. G.C. Homans *English Villagers of the Thirteenth Century* (Harvard University Press, Cambridge, Mass., 1941) 363–4; confirmed by Mankind's later decision to postpone the work and 'sow my corn at winter' (546), i.e. at the next (autumn) sowing.

20. 2 Corinthians 6:2; Eccles *Macro Plays* note to line 866.
21. For discussion of the possibly subversive and anticlerical perspectives of this carnivalesque element in the play see Anthony Gash, 'Carnival against Lent: The Ambivalence of Medieval Drama' *Medieval Literature, Criticism, Ideology, History* edited David Aers (Harvester Press, Brighton, 1986) 74–98, particularly 82–96.
22. Homans *English Villagers of the Thirteenth Century* 355.
23. Brueghel similarly places identifiable festive customs (including folk plays) specific to the revels season within the sphere of Carnival.
24. 'Onschett yowr lokke and take an halpenye'; in his note to this line Eccles, *Macro Plays* 217, concurs, without enlarging on the implied context.
25. *English Moral Interludes* edited Glynne Wickham (Everyman Library: Dent, London, 1976), note to *Mankind*, line 70 sd, and Introduction, 5.
26. A.R. Wright *British Calendar Customs, England, Volume 2: Fixed Festivals, January – May* (Publications of the Folklore Society, London, 1938) 103–4; Paul Sartori *Sitte und Brauch, Vol. 3: Zeiten und feste des Jahres* (Wilhelm Heims, Leipzig, 1914) 120–21.
27. E.C. Cawte *Ritual Animal Disguise* (D.S. Brewer, Cambridge, 1978).
28. A.R. Wright *British Calendar Customs, England, Volume 1: Movable Feasts* (Publications of the Folklore Society 97, London, 1936) 39.
29. Wright *British Calendar Customs* 5–6; Iona and Peter Opie *The Lore and Language of Schoolchildren* (Oxford University Press, London, 1959; reprinted 1970) 239.
30. *The Early English Carols* edited R.L. Greene (Clarendon Press, Oxford, 2nd edition 1977) no. 10, stanzas 2–3, and see Greene's Introduction, page clvii.
31. E.g. to February (691) and the Shrovetide sport of football (732).
32. Lines 376–81 (confrontation, combat, and wounding); 435–47 (cure). These features and their similarities to the mummers' plays are examined in detail by Walter K. Smart '*Mankind* and the Mumming Plays' *Modern Language Notes* 32 (1917) 21–5. See also the perceptive discussion by Neville Denny 'Aspects of the Staging of *Mankind*' *Medium Ævum* 43 (1974) 252–63, for whom the folk-play features of *Mankind* provoke serious questions about its professional auspices.
33. Sandra Billington '"Suffer Fools Gladly": The Fool in Medieval England and the Play *Mankind*' in *The Fool and the Trickster* edited Paul V.A. Williams (D.S. Brewer, Cambridge, 1979) 36–54.
34. Like *The Unfaithful Wife* discussed elsewhere in this collection by Leif Søndergaard.
35. Useful reviews of the genre include Eckehard Catholy *Fastnachtspiel* (Metzler, Stuttgart, 1966) and *Das Fastnachtspiel des Spätmittelalters: Gestalt und Funktion* (Max Niemeyer Verlag, Tübingen, 1961); Joël Lefebvre 'Le Jeu du Carnaval de Nuremberg au xve siècle et au xvie' in *Le Lieu théâtral à la Renaissance* edited J. Jacquot (Centre National de la Recherche Scientifique, Paris, 1964) 183–90; Dieter Wuttke 'Zum Fastnachtspiel des Spätmittelalters' *Zeitschrift für deutsche Philologie* 84 (1965) 247–67. The major collection of texts (particularly for the Nüremberg tradition) is still *Fastnachtspiele aus dem 15. Jahrhundert* edited [Heinrich] Adelbert von Keller, 4 vols (Bibliothek des litterarischen Vereins in Stuttgart 28–30, 46: Stuttgart, 1853–1858; reprinted Wissenschaftliche Buchgesellschaft, Darmstadt, 1965–1966); for Sterzing (Tyrol) see *De weltlichen Spiele des Sterzinger Spielarchivs* edited Werner M. Bauer (Österreichischer Bundesverlag, Vienna, 1982), and for Lübeck *Mittelniederdeutsche Fastnachtspiele* edited W. Seelmann (Vereins für niederdeutsche Sprachforschung, Bremen, 1885).

36. For the first three see T. Pettitt 'English Folk Drama and the Early German *Fastnachtspiele*' *Renaissance Drama* NS 13 (1982) 1–34, particularly 6–7; for the wake-games, W.S. Clark *The Early Irish Stage* (Clarendon Press, Oxford, 1955) 3.
37. Edited Keller nos 51 and 73. This too is a pan-European motif in both literature and traditional drama; for discussions see Eva Kimminich 'The Way of Vice and Virtue in European Carnival Plays: The Battle of Carnival and Lent: Textuality and Popular Culture' *Fifteenth-Century Studies* 15 (1989) 183–208; Martine Grinberg and Sam Kinser 'Combats de Carnaval et de Carême: Trajets d'une metaphore' *Annales, Economies, Societés, Civilisations* 38 (1983) 65–98; Siegfried Wagner *Der Dampf der Fasten Gegen die Fastnacht. Studien zu Form, Funktion und Entwicklung des Systems van Fastnacht und Fasten im Spätmittelalter und der Frühen Neuzeit* (Tuduv, Munich, 1986).
38. Serious plays are more common outside Nüremberg, although this may reflect (as at Lübeck) contextual differences.
39. Cited in Dietz-Rudiger Moser 'Perikopenforschung und Volkskunde' *Jahrbuch für Volkskunde* NS 6 (1983) 7–52, at page 44.
40. *The Records of the City of Norwich* edited W. Hudson and J.C. Tingley (Jarrold, London and Norwich, 1906) *1* 345–6. I have added a comma after 'schuld end' and removed one after 'of ye yer' to clarify the order of the procession. For the civic celebration of Shrovetide at Carlisle in the seventeenth century see Audrey W. Douglas 'Research in Progress (Cumbria)' *Records of Early English Drama Newsletter* 4.1 (1979) 13–16, at page 15.
41. This is also implied in the custom reported from Kent in the late eighteenth century of burning a 'Holly-boy' and 'Ivy-girl' (evidently the 'holly and ivy' of Christmas) the week prior to Shrovetide: see Bob Pegg *Rites and Riots* (Blandford Press, Poole, 1981) 24.
42. For example in the list of 'honest pastime[s]' enjoyed by the Franklin in Overbury's *Characters* (1614), quoted in *Life in Shakespeare's England* edited J. Dover Wilson (1911; reprinted Penguin, Harmondsworth, 1968) 32–3.
43. E.K. Chambers *The Elizabethan Stage* 4 vols (1923; reprinted Clarendon Press, Oxford, 1967) 4 Appendix A and B; C.E. McGee and John C. Meagher 'Preliminary Checklist of Tudor and Stuart Entertainments, 1485–1558' *Research Opportunities in Renaissance Drama* 25 (1982) 31–114, and 'Preliminary Checklist of Tudor and Stuart Entertainments, 1558–1603' *Research Opportunities in Renaissance Drama* 24 (1981) 51–156.
44. Described in James Turner *The Politics of Landscape* (Blackwell, Oxford, 1979) 146.
45. Thomas Middleton *The Inner Temple Masque or Masque of Heroes* edited R.C. Bald, lines 15–119, in *A Book of Masques in Honour of Allardyce Nicholl* edited T.J.B. Spencer and S.W. Wells (Cambridge University Press, 1967). For discussion of the seasonal appropriateness of Shrovetide masques performed at court in the Jacobean and Caroline periods, see R.C. Hassell Jr *Renaissance Drama and the English Church Year* (University of Nebraska Press, Lincoln, Nebraska, 1979) chapter 6.
46. *The Poems of William Dunbar* edited W. Mackay Mackenzie (1932; reprinted Faber, London, 1966) no. 57. For a remark on the poem's background see Enid Welsford *The Court Masque* (Cambridge University Press, 1927) 75.
47. G.E. Bentley *The Profession of Dramatist in Shakespeare's Time, 1590–1642* (Princeton University Press, 1971) 18; Leif Søndergaard *Fastelavnsspillet i Danmarks senmiddelalder* (Odense University Press, 1989) 42–55.

48. For text and discussion of its provenance see George L. Frost and Ray Nash 'Good Order: A Morality Fragment' *Studies in Philology 41* (1944) 483–91.
49. Richard Axton 'Folk Play in Tudor Interludes' in *English Drama: Forms and Development* edited Marie Axton and Raymond Williams (Cambridge University Press, 1977) 1–23, at 8–9.
50. *Two Tudor Interludes* edited Ian Lancashire (Manchester University Press, 1980) Introduction, 21.
51. *Two Tudor Interludes* 27.

TWO CARNIVAL PLAYS
From Late-Medieval Denmark
Leif Søndergaard

There survive from the later Middle Ages only two Danish plays which qualify as *fastelavnsspil*, that is designed for performance in close association with the celebration of Carnival, or (in the more usual English expression) Shrovetide, analogous to the German *Fastnachtspiele* of the same period. Both these 'Shrovetide interludes', *The Unfaithful Wife* (*Den utro hustru*) and *The Judgement of Paris* (*Paris dom*), are preserved in the so-called Odense manuscript, an edition of which was published by the scholar S. Birket Smith in 1874.[1] Following the third play in the manuscript, the saint's play *Comoedia de sancta virgine Dorothea*, is a brief colophon which mentions the year 1531 and the name Christiern Hansen. Birket Smith and later commentators have taken this to mean that he was also the author of *The Unfaithful Wife*, which is the best of the two Shrovetide interludes.

However a closer examination of the three gatherings of which the manuscript is comprised reveals such differences between them in terms of watermarks, handwriting, and wear and tear that it must be seen as a composite whose three gatherings were used separately before being brought together.[2] This in turn means of course that the note following the St Dorothy play cannot be appealed to in claiming that Christiern Hansen also wrote the Shrovetide interludes. The section of the manuscript containing *The Unfaithful Wife* is characterised by a considerable number of errors compatible with the transcription of the text from an earlier Danish original, and this, together with the wear and tear, suggests that the play had been performed a number of times before incorporation into the composite manuscript.

In the form we have it *The Unfaithful Wife* belongs in all likelihood to the first decade of the sixteenth century. The play shows no symptoms of the Reformation controversy which got under way in Denmark in the mid-1520s, nor does the moralistic trend which manifested itself from about 1515 find any echo in the play, which is characterised by a distinctly amoral attitude to secular morality: its message seems to be that if you're having trouble seducing a married woman, apply to your friendly neighbourhood witch for help. The presentation of the characters by the Prologue (Preco), the *argumentum*, is a good deal longer than usual in Shrovetide interludes, and suggests influence from school drama, in which presentations are generally more comprehensive and systematic. Together with linguistic criteria, these factors point to the beginning of the sixteenth century.[3]

It may seem odd that a religious play like the *Comoedia de sancta virgine Dorothea* (together with the *Ludus de sancto Canuto duce*, the only surviving pre-Reformation play on a Danish saint) should be found in a manuscript anthology alongside two emphatically secular Shrovetide interludes. But with the exception of those few years when Shrovetide falls extremely early, St Dorothy's Day, 6 February, would be in or very close to the week of carnival folly preceding Lent, or at least within the extended Carnival season commencing at Epiphany; and performance of this saint's play, which is characterised by a good deal of violent action, may not have been entirely incompatible with Shrovetide revels. The collection also includes a small fragment of a Danish translation of the first school play, *Henno* (performed in Heidelberg in 1497).

The collection was probably compiled in Catholic circles after 1531 but before 1536, the date of the Reformation in Denmark. Together with *The Judgement of Paris* and the *Comoedia de sancta virgine Dorothea*, *The Unfaithful Wife* may well have comprised the dramatic repertoire of the pupils of Our Lady's School in Odense, which is referred to in the manuscript note mentioned above, or of a similar institution. For it is characteristic of Danish Shrovetide interludes that they were written by teachers connected with church schools, and performed by the pupils as a means of acquiring food, drink, or money at a time of year when supplies were running low. There is documentary evidence for this as early as 1447 in an accord agreed to by two priors in Odense, and academic auspices for at least the composition of *The Unfaithful Wife* are suggested by the Latin stage directions of the manuscript text.[4]

It has hitherto been assumed that in Denmark the Shrovetide interludes were performed in the context of a round of visits during the Carnival season from one (private) household to another – i.e. a *quête* in the manner of the English mummings, pace-eggings, soulings, and other house-visit customs. But in the later Middle Ages, and particularly in towns, seasonal festivity was invariably of a social character, and the presence of both men and women in the audience – clearly signalled by Preco's greeting in the prologue to *The Unfaithful Wife* – indicates that the Danish Shrovetide interludes were performed in the context of the feasts of the craft and perhaps merchants' guilds; be it, in the case of the wealthier guilds, in the guild hall, in the house of the master of the guild or of another member, or, in the case of journeymen's associations, at a tavern. Preco's address begins:

> Wassail! Good day, beloved friends,
> To you that are herein;
> Respects and honour to one and all,
> The menfolk and the women. [5]

The Unfaithful Wife starts in the classic manner of the Shrovetide interlude (also familiar from the later English mummers' plays) with the entry of a Presenter, here designated Preco, who greets the assembled company, asks for room and attention, and describes the action and the major characters of the play to follow. The play-proper, like some of the Wooing Plays of the English mummers and the farce in the Cupar Banns of Lindsay's *Satire of the Three Estates*, comprises a sequence of wooings, in this case of a woman whose husband (in the first scene) has left her to go on a pilgrimage; she is subjected to the amorous advances, in turn, of a peasant, a monk, and a nobleman.

The peasant is emphatically repulsed and told that he is both vulgar and filthy. His reception is no better when he returns after an episode in which he visits a bathhouse and has his beard singed and his face smeared in ordure by an unsympathetic attendant. He is eventually fetched by his shrewish wife, who gives him a good dressing-down and compares his present lustfulness unfavourably with the total lack of sexual prowess he displays at home. He is succeeded by the monk, interestingly described as dancing what may be a kind of morris, who offers to throw away his cowl if it should put the woman off accepting him. But he is also rejected, and is beaten back to his monastery by the nobleman, who now intervenes and takes over the role of wooer.

The nobleman in turn is rejected, but he then enlists the help of an old hag who is clearly something of a witch. On the promise of a generous reward she conjures up a devil who is sent to implant lascivious thoughts into the woman's mind. This failing, the devil is beaten back to hell, and the witch, urged by her dissatisfied customer to try again, deploys the familiar trick of the 'weeping bitch'. She visits the woman accompanied by a weeping dog whom she claims is her daughter, transformed by a nobleman whose sexual advances she had resisted. The woman is duly impressed, and when the nobleman resumes his wooing she agrees to submit to his desires. The Presenter's concluding remarks recommend anyone in the audience who needs the same kind of help to apply to the old witch, and he ends the show by requesting a drink before the performers go on their way.

As we have it *The Judgement of Paris* dates from after the emergence of the stricter moral code mentioned earlier, but before the Reformation conflict becomes acute in the mid 1520s; the watermark in the paper can also be dated to this period.[6] As a narrative motif the Judgement of Paris can be traced through most of the Middle Ages, and its earliest occurrence among the surviving *Fastnachtspiele* is in *Das fasnacht spill Troya* (1464) and *Das spill mit den dreven nacketten gottin von Troya* ('The Interlude of the Three Naked Goddesses of Troy', 1468), although neither of these is the immediate source of the Danish play.[7]

In *The Judgement of Paris* Juno, Pallas, and Venus recommend themselves in turn to Prince Paris, Juno offering wealth, Pallas wisdom, and Venus love. In accordance with both the legend and the spirit of the Shrovetide interlude tradition, Paris assigns greatest significance to matters of the flesh, and requests the three goddesses to undress so that he can better evaluate them. He concludes by presenting to the winner, Venus, the apple which at the beginning of the play he had received from Bellona, the goddess of war: the result is accordingly a good deal of trouble and strife among the womenfolk.

The author (or reviser) has framed the action within a sternly moralising prologue and epilogue, and concludes the play with an ode, ending with a prayer to

Christ to take us under his protection and give us his peace. He laments that virtue and wisdom are neglected, while every man gives himself to immorality. On the authority of Andrilinus – Professor of Poetry, Rhetoric, and Metaphysics at the University of Paris at the end of the fifteenth century and beginning of the sixteenth – he justifies the moral function of the play as *negative didaxe*: 'In this fable and many others men can teach themselves ... what to do, and what to flee'. In other words *The Judgement of Paris* displays the immorality one is supposed to avoid.

If we excise these added didactic moralisings, we are left with the original play, with a quite different moral. Now it is Venus who has the last word, and she places both herself and Helen at Paris's disposal should he care for any pleasure with them in bed, and if it should lead to a pregnancy then that is just Nature's will: in other words an acknowledgement of sexual needs with no admonitory finger-wagging, just as in *The Unfaithful Wife*.

If we can clearly distinguish two layers in *The Judgement of Paris*, it is possible to resolve *The Unfaithful Wife* into no less than five distinct units:

1) a core play in which representatives of the Three Estates – a peasant, a monk and a nobleman – attempt to seduce a woman whose husband is away on a journey. This core play concerns a *faithful* wife, who repulses all temptations to commit adultery – in the spirit of the moral *Fastnachtspiele* of the Lübeck tradition. In the Act Book of the Lübeck *Zirkelgesellschaft* there is reference in 1471 to a play about *eyner erliken fruwen, de hade vele anlaghe unde bleff dock stanthafftlish in eren* ('an honest woman, who had many offers but yet remained true to her marriage').[8] Significantly the Prologue to the Danish play refers only to the persons and action of this central item;

2) a bathhouse scene, inserted into the core play, taken from the rich fund of such scenes in medieval farce tradition;

3) in continuation of this insertion, an episode in which the peasant is fetched by his wife, who refers to his lack of sexual prowess at home in terms which it is impossible to imagine used in the moral plays of the Lübeck tradition;

4) a conjuration scene of a type familiar in a number of medieval vernacular cultures. That the old witch beats the Devil back to hell fits well with popular notions of the sorceress being stronger and more evil than the Evil One himself;

5) the scene with the weeping dog, a migratory European legend, which can be traced back in the first instance to Steinhöwel's *Aesop* (Latin/German, 1475).[9] The first scene of the play in which the husband takes leave of his wife to go on a pilgrimage also occurs in Steinhöwel, and probably derives from this source.

The weeping-dog motif had been given dramatic rendition in England as early as about 1300 in *Dame Siriz* (which is more likely to be an interlude than a purely narrative *fabliau*) and probably also in the *Interludium de clerico et puella*, the surviving fragment of which suggests an exactly analogous plot. They may be antecedents of the German *Fastnachtspiele* which probably provided the immediate source of this episode in the Danish play. *Dame Siriz* certainly evinces a number of features characteristic of Shrovetide interludes: it ends with a request for money (i.e. a *quête*) and Dame Siriz is provided with refreshment in the course of the action. In the latter connection there are specific references to meat and to Christ's forty days' fast in the desert. And *Dame Siriz* ends with precisely the same advice to the audience (i.e. on where to find a good bawd) as *The Unfaithful Wife*.[10] There is, however, unlikely to be any direct connection between the two plays, which simply deploy the same floating motif.

On the basis of these two plays, as thus resolved into their constituent units, and with some guidance from German tradition, it is possible to sketch the outlines, but no more, of the Danish tradition of Shrovetide interludes.

Both *The Judgement of Paris* and the core-play in *The Unfaithful Wife* are speech-sequences (*Reihenspiele*) in the manner of the earliest surviving German *Fastnachtspiele* from the mid fifteenth century. In the German plays up to twelve or more peasants, fools or Estates' representatives woo a woman – often Frau Venus – who invariably chooses the last one to present himself.

In *The Unfaithful Wife* the Estates' representatives are a peasant, a monk, and a nobleman, who together with the craftsmen/merchants (of whom our husband may be a representative) are the major Estates in late-medieval society. In *The Judgement of Paris* it is the rôle of the women to woo the man, and Venus ends by winning the apple – the apple which in her rôle of Frau Venus she holds in many a German Wooing Play, and as depicted by Israel van Meckenem in an engraving of c.1480.

While the *Reihenspiele* have a structure comparable to pearls on a string, the *Handlungsspiele* ('plays-with-plots') introduce a progression towards a climactic moment. As we have it *The Unfaithful Wife* is a typical instance of the latter, in which one action prompts the next, and one episode leads on to another in a climactic sequence.[11]

Both *The Unfaithful Wife* and *The Judgement of Paris* (leaving aside the latter's Prologue and Epilogue) operate within a late-medieval secular universe. Here the manifestation of bodily needs, pleasures, and sensuality is dominant. Paris's desire to enjoy Venus and Helen provokes no moralising commentary in the original *Judgement*, and the 'moral' of *The Unfaithful Wife* is precisely the need to acknowledge the demands of sexuality.

In both plays the woman is the object of the man's desires, but the sexual needs of the woman are accorded equal legitimacy, and the woman in *The Unfaithful Wife* decides herself to whom she will give her favours. It is the *Devil* who tempts her by whispering in her ear, and the *man* who does the wooing, but it is the *woman* who says yes – exactly as Mathias Ripensis explains in his sermon collection.[12]

It was apparently necessary to revise the original, highly moral, play, suitable for the patricians of Lübeck's *Zirkelgesellschaft*, into something appropriate for performance before Danish craftsmen, with an ethos much closer to the

Fastnachtspiele of Nüremberg. So the episodes involving the conjuration of the devil and the device of the weeping bitch were integrated into the play (by luck or more likely judgement reversing its outcome), and the same probably applies to the peasant's visit to the bathhouse.

Correspondingly other episodes in the Danish play deploy motifs familiar from various German *Fastnachtspiele*: the peasant who woos the lady but is rejected on account of his coarse and dirty appearance; the domestic altercation between peasant and wife; the visit to the bathhouse; the monk who is willing to discard his cowl to get the woman; the old woman who conjures up the Devil. This impressive collection of correspondences places *The Unfaithful Wife* firmly in the tradition of the *Fastnachtspiele* of the German linguistic and cultural sphere.

The Church had no power directly to prohibit the Shrovetide revels of the craft guilds or the carnival perambulations of young people in the towns, since these fell under the jurisdiction of the city authorities. On the other hand the Church could exert severe moral pressure to tone down, limit, or prevent such Shrovetide activities. A mid-fifteenth-century sermon-collection condemns with moral indignation 'those who now fill themselves with rich food, and over-indulge in drink at feasts, sin in drunkenness and other foul sins ...' in its sermon for Shrove Sunday, clearly aimed at Carnival revelry.[13] Christiern Pedersen's collection of *miracula* from 1515 includes an *exemplum* of a butcher of Koblenz, who together with a comrade persists with his carnival drinking into Ash Wednesday and mocks the religious ritual by throwing around the ashes, only to be suffocated in them.[14]

Until the beginning of the sixteenth century the secular authorities maintained an indulgent attitude towards Shrovetide and its revelry. During his stay in Kalundborg in 1490 Duke Frederik of Slesvig-Holstein spent more than 5 marks on cloth for 'carnival costumes' and a further 6 shillings went to the servants of Hans Schrøder for making them; in 1509 Queen Christine gave 'one shilling for a staff for a scholar to go around with at Shrovetide'.[15] About 1520 the prohibitions and constraints begin with Christian II's draft Ordinance for Schools: 'Hereafter shall no priest, deacon, or scholar disguise himself at Shrovetide in the likeness of a monk or a mummer in order to go around begging or indulging in other folly as has been done heretofore. Whoever contravenes this must lose his hood'.[16]

Internationally the Catholic church sometimes permits the celebration of Shrovetide among the lower clergy, at the same time ensuring that it does not get out of hand, and the Church endeavours to incorporate Carnival into its overall cosmological system. But despite the efforts of the Church at some periods to provide it with a socio-psychological and didactic moral function, it is evident that both the origin and the native habitat of Carnival were outside the religious sphere, most plausibly in the ambience of urban companies and guilds. The carnival displays were a feature of the culture of the artisans and an expression of their identity as a social class. The Shrovetide interlude has a unique function as a vehicle for an aesthetic vision of the way of life and thought of the emerging artisan-bourgeoisie.

In the aesthetics of the Church, order, harmony, and proportion play a dominant role as manifestations of God's blueprint for mankind and the world. The function of art, literature, and drama is therefore didactic and moralising, either positively or, in more outward-looking forms, through *negative didaxe*, as when the carnival fool holds up his bauble as a mirror in which he can see his follies and so correct them.[17]

The Shrovetide interlude, in contrast, is an integral part of the revels of the craft guild and it built on an aesthetic which functions within that context: it must entertain and divert. But at the same time the ethics of the craftsmen achieve expression: rather than the Church's spiritual demands and its denial of material and bodily needs, it is precisely the material and the bodily which are given pride of place by the Shrovetide interlude.[18]

The Shrovetide interludes are full of obscene and grotesque episodes. Obscenity, comprising both sexual and scatological references as well as anything else which gives offence in more general terms, together with the grotesque, which revolts against ideal forms, provokes a laughter which challenges authority and so communicates insubordinate attitudes.[19]

Instead of a unified Christian culture we encounter a cultural conflict between two fundamentally opposed ethical systems. Of course the two tendencies cannot exist side by side without interacting. Many craft guilds supported chapels or altars in churches dedicated to their patron saint, and the festival of Corpus Christi (established by the fourth Lateran Council of 1215) is a manifestation of religious-secular co-operation, in which religious plays, produced by the various guilds, come together with fairground trading and entertainment.

In conformity with other Shrovetide interludes, *The Unfaithful Wife* is simultaneously a vehicle for Estates-satire, in which the three 'old' Estates – the nobility, the clergy (here the religious orders), and the peasantry – are laughed to scorn from the point of view of the new Estate, the craftsmen. Concurrently the moral and ethical system of the craftsmen themselves is reinforced, and behaviour incompatible with it is corrected.

The cultural ethos of the craftsmen manifests itself in the Carnival period, during which the craftsmen are liberated not merely from the regulation imposed by religious and secular authorities but also from the constraints of the guild system itself, which controlled so much of everyday life at other times. During Carnival the artisans seek to establish for themselves a free space in which to display and satisfy their bodily needs in the material (food and drink), physical (dance and song), and not least sexual spheres. This free space should be seen not so much as a contrast to the everyday way of life of the craftsmen as an extension and intensification of that way of life under the special conditions provided by Carnival.

At the time when *The Unfaithful Wife* was written and performed, the aspirations of craftsmen were still characterised by the pursuit of pleasure; the modern work-ethic and disciplined sense of time had yet to establish themselves.[20] The play accepts the sexual needs of both men and women without offering moral extenuations, and the sexual interplay between the woman and her wooers is presented with a sensuality which the audience is evidently intended to appreciate. At the same time, the implied criticism of the husband's pilgrimage anticipates the work-ethic, and the insistence on the importance of domestic commitments which were later to dominate bourgeois attitudes.

The woman is presented as an active participant in the action with her own opinions and her own needs – not least sexual – which she has every right to take account of. The late-medieval view of woman, which makes sexuality a sin and ascribes the sin exclusively to her, has yet to manifest itself at the time to which *The Unfaithful Wife* and *The Judgement of Paris* (before the addition of Prologue and Epilogue) belong. The tightening of morality which occurs in Germany in the 1470s does not manifest itself in Denmark until about 1520.

The Unfaithful Wife and – to a lesser degree – *The Judgement of Paris* have an emphatically central place in the history of Danish literature and drama as the earliest known and the best examples of a tradition of Shrovetide interludes which (to judge from numerous historical records) had a greater significance than the paucity of surviving texts might otherwise suggest: it is quite up to the standard of the best that the vastly more numerous German *Fastnachtspiele* have to offer.

Odense Universitet
(Translated by Tom Pettitt)

NOTES

1. Royal Library, Copenhagen: Thott's Folio MS 780. *De tre ældste danske Skuespil* edited S. Birket Smith (Louis Kleins Bogtrykkeri, Copenhagen, 1874).
2. Leif Søndergaard *Fastelavnsspillet i Danmarks middelalder – om 'Den utro hustru' og fastelavnsspillets tradition* (Odense University Press, 1989) 11–24.
3. Johannes Brondum-Nielsen *Sproglig forfatterbestemmmelse: Studier over danske Sprog i det 16. Aarhundredes Begyndelse* (Gyldendals Boghandel, Nordisk Forlag, Copenhagen, 1914) 109 and 125, note 1.
4. *De tre ældste danske Skuespil* 12: the new school in Odense undertakes not to *cum scolaribus ... choreas et ludos carnipriviales publice ... celebrari.*
5. Søndergaard *Fastelavnsspillet i Danmarks middelalder* 102:
    Helsel go dagh wenner kiære
    j alle som her er innæ
    edher reth alle heder och ære
    bode mendt och quinnæ.
6. C.M. Briquet *Les Filigranes: dictionnaire historique des marques de papier des leur apparition vers 1282 jusqu'en 1600* 4 vols (A. Picard et fils, Paris, 1907: reprinted 1968) 3, no. 9284 and 4, no. 9740/41.
7. F. Schnorr von Carolsfeld 'Vier ungedruckte Fastnachtspiele des 15. Jahrhunderts' *Archiv für Literaturgeschichte* 3 (1874) 5–13 and 17–25.

8. C. Wehrmann 'Fastnachtspiele der Patrizier in Lübeck' *Jahrbuch des Vereins für niederdeutsche Sprachforschung* 3 (1881 for 1880) 4.
9. *Steinhöwels Äsop* edited Herman Österley (Bibliothek der literarischen Vereins in Stuttgart 117: Tübingen, 1873) 614.
10. 'Dame Sirith' in *Early Middle English Verse and Prose* edited J.A.W. Bennett and G.V. Smithers (Clarendon Press, Oxford, 1968) 77–95.
11. On *Reihenspiele* and *Handlungsspiele* see Eckehard Catholy *Das Fastnachtspiel des Spätmittelalters: Gestalt und Funktion* (Max Niemeyer Verlag, Tübingen, 1961) 142–63.
12. Mathias Ripensis *Sermones de tempore* (c.1300), Codex Ups. S 343 and C 346 (fifteenth century), cited Anne Riising *Danmarks middelalderlige Prædiken* (G.E.C. Gad, Copenhagen, 1969) 354.
13. *Klosterlæsning fra Middelalderen* 3: *Kirkeårets Søndags-Evangelier med Udlæggelse fra Advent til Langfredag* edited C.J. Brandt (G.E.C. Gad, Copenhagen, 1865) 98.
14. Christiern Pedersen *Jærtegns Postil* in *Danske Skrifter* edited C.J. Brandt and R.T. Fenger (Gyldendals Boghandel, Copenhagen, 1850) 280–1.
15. *Danske Middelalderlige Regnskaber*, 1st series, vol. 1: *Hof og Centralstyre* edited Georg Galster (G.E.C. Gad, Copenhagen, 1953) 298; *Dronning Christine's Hofholdningsregnskaber* edited William Christensen (Nordisk Forlag, Copenhagen, 1904) 312.
16. Birket Smith *De tre ældste danske Skuespil* 13.
17. Dietz-Rudiger Moser *Fastnacht – Fasching – Karneval: Das Fest der 'Verkehrten Welt'* (Verlag Styria, Köln, 1986) 98–108.
18. On the carnival revels of craft and trade guilds see *Danmarks Lavs- og Gildeskraaer fra Middelalderen* edited C. Nyrop, vols 1–2 (1895–1904; reprinted Dansk Historisk Håndbogsforlag, Copenhagen, 1977).
19. Rüdiger Krohn *Der unanständige Burger: Untersuchungen zum Obszönen in den Nürnberger Fastnachtspielen des 15. Jahrhunderts* (Scriptor Verlag, Kronberg Taunus, 1974); Hagen Bastian *Mummenschanz: Sinneslust und Gefülsbeherrschung im Fastnachtspiel des 15. Jahrhunderts* (Syndikat Verlag, Frankfurt a. M., 1983).
20. Jacques Le Goff *Time, Work, and Culture in the Middle Ages* (University of Chicago Press, Chicago, 1982) 29–52.

ANALYSING FRENCH FARCE AND DUTCH PRE-RENAISSANCE COMIC DRAMA
Some adjustments and additions to B. Rey-Flaud's analytic model
Wim Hüsken

1. Introduction

Bernadette Rey-Flaud's study *La farce ou la machine à rire: Théorie d'un genre dramatique, 1450–1550*,[1] has justifiably earned its favourable reception.[2] E. DuBruck calls the book 'a treasure of information' (175), G. Runnalls considers it a 'well-documented and well-argued thesis' (319), while the late J.-C. Aubailly went so far as to see it as 'un ouvrage fondamental que tout spécialiste de théâtre médiéval se doit de lire' (22). However, with regard to Rey-Flaud's analytic model for the structure of French medieval farce (see chapter 4 in the second part of her study), most critics are somewhat cautious. N. Lacy, for example, observes: 'Readers are likely to wonder about the utility of proposing a mathematical formula to indicate simply that the effect of a ruse is to transform a situation into a different situation' (253). G. Runnalls thinks it conceivable too that some readers will not be able to agree easily with Rey-Flaud's 'attempt to reduce medieval farces to mathematical formulae' (320). J.-C. Aubailly, without questioning Rey-Flaud's formalistic approach as such, concentrated more intensively than other critics on her method of analysis. In his opinion the French scholar failed to present a proper genre theory. As a consequence, Rey-Flaud is said to be unable to draw a line between farce and *fabliau*. To achieve this Aubailly believes, among other things, that she should have concerned herself with more specifically theatrical conventions.

A few years ago I took Rey-Flaud's analytic model as one of the starting points for my dissertation on pre-Renaissance comic drama in the Netherlands.[3] Analysing these Dutch plays I had to make a number of adjustments and additions to Rey-Flaud's model which may also be of interest to scholars of French medieval drama.

Before summarising Rey-Flaud's theory and supplementing it with a number of necessary corrections, we should ask ourselves, of course, why one should devise a complicated formalistic model in the first place. After all, is not medieval farce a relatively simple literary genre? However, both recent and old research show that, while abstracting from texts in order to discuss structure, many scholars are inclined to make rather imprecise statements. Barbara Bowen, for example, discriminates in her *Les caractéristiques essentielles de la farce française et leur survivance dans les années 1550–1620* (Urbana 1964), next to '*simples parades*' and '*débats*', a most disputable category labelled 'pièces construites de façon véritablement dramatique'. As late as 1975, the eminent French scholar Jean-Claude Aubailly regarded the category of 'farces d'intrigue' in his *Le théâtre médiéval, profane et comique* as the summit of the genre without defining, however, what he means by the concept of 'intrigue'. So both Bowen and Aubailly clearly introduce subjective criteria in their observations as well. In my opinion, it should be obvious that any subjectivity in analysing the structure of farce must be avoided. A most appropriate means to achieve this consists of following strictly formalistic guidelines out of which categories of plays automatically evolve. Bernadette Rey-Flaud has taken the trouble to devise such a theory. However, as I claimed earlier, it needs certain adjustments and additions. This article aims to discuss various corrections and improvements to the original theoretical concepts. Apart from some occasional Dutch material I shall refer mainly to examples from French farces taken from the famous *Recueil Cohen* (hereafter abbreviated to *RC*).[4]

2. Synopsis of Rey-Flaud's model

The gist of Bernadette Rey-Flaud's analytic model is as follows: each farce is composed of one or more actions, called *sequences*, in which the relationships between two or more characters of a play change: one person's position of power passes to that of another person. Unsteady relationships between them can also become stabilised. Thus Rey-Flaud distinguishes four *developments* (as I will term them throughout this article) represented schematically as follows (see page 230):

Etat +	/ Action	=	tromperie /	Etat -
Etat -	/ Action	=	tromperie /	Etat +
Etat (+)	/ Action	=	tromperie /	Etat +
Etat (-)	/ Action	=	tromperie /	Etat -

Consequently, each development comprises three steps or *segments*: in the middle the actual change of position between the characters takes place. Hence Rey-Flaud labels this segment *dynamic*, whereas the segments on either side of it are called *static*. The dynamic segment can manifest itself in three different ways: as a *deception* (in its literal sense, for the French scholar regards deceit as pre-eminently characteristic of the genre: 'toute farce est la mise en œuvre d'une tromperie'; 226); as a *misunderstanding*, or as a *coup de théâtre*. The symbols the author assigns to these segments are F (for 'farce'), Q (for 'quid pro quo'), and Z.[5] The concept of the so-called static segment embraces victory (∨ or *victoire*), defeat (∧ or *défaite*), conflict (x or *conflit*) and reconciliation (Ø or *résolution*).[6]

3. The concepts of héros, sujet, objet, and agent

The elements mentioned in the previous paragraph form the starting-point for Rey-Flaud's further observations. Most of the other concepts in her theory are related to extensions and modifications of this basic model, in general closely linked with earlier remarks in her dissertation. Thus, the notion of two consecutive sequences, together forming one *section*, resembles the distinction, previously made by her (see 206), between *facéties* and *farceries:* the former 'présentent un bon tour dans un déroulement simple', the latter 'offrent une imbrication savante de ruses dans un déroulement complexe'.

More important for the model, but, as will be shown further on, the reason why the author gets entangled in an extremely intricate web, are her notes on *héros, sujet, objet,* and *agent,* the forces responsible for the creation of the already mentioned dynamic segments, and the ensuing distinction between active and passive sequences. After all, the notions of *victoire* (∨) and *défaite* (∧) presuppose a perspective from which the events in a farce are approached. When Rey-Flaud, for example, analyses the first sequence of *Maistre Pierre Pathelin,* her sympathy lies entirely with the person in the title, whom she then labels *héros*. Hence she speaks of: 'misère de Pathelin (∧) / vol du drap (F) / triomphe de Pathelin (∨)' (248). Following the same line she declares: 'quelqu'un "farce" ou "est farcé"' (251) and goes on to say: 'Le héros peut être défini comme le sujet de ce verbe' (251). If the *sujet* (or the *héros,* because as long as this character is on stage *héros* and *sujet* are synonymous) inflicts a defeat on his opponent, the *objet,* we can speak of an *active* dynamic segment (represented by the symbol '+'); if the opposite is the case (when the *sujet* is outwitted by his adversary), the segment is *passive* (indicated by the symbol '-'). In the latter case, according to Rey-Flaud, the opponent no longer functions as an *objet,* but instead develops into an *agent*.

Complex as the model may have become with these refinements, its application should not cause many problems. However, it is the French scholar's attempt to introduce more order into the gradually more complicated model which threatens to throw some of its aspects off balance. Thus, she tries to connect the concepts of *sujet* and *objet/agent* to the notions of *active* and *passive* in dynamic segments. On page 254 of her book we consequently find: 'L'objet est toujours la victime d'une farce positive et l'agent représente toujours l'auteur d'une farce négative'. A couple of paragraphs down, on pages 256–7, we find a similar remark, confirming this point of view: 'si le verbe est actif, le segment qui le suit recouvre nécessairement une fonction de victoire (∨), si le verbe est passif, ce dernier segment recouvre une fonction de défaite (∧)'. The author even adds to these observations: 'cette succession logique s'impose comme règle absolu' (257). However, the following study of the *Farce de Celuy qui se confesse* (RC, no. 2) will show that this absolute rule is untenable. Rey-Flaud's summary of the play, on pages 186–7 of her dissertation, reads as follows:

> Le mari, par sa gaieté, éveille des soupçons de sa femme qui décide, avec la complicité d'une voisine qui se déguisera en prêtre, de le confesser pour savoir ce qu'il en est. Le mari se fait prier car en dépit des affirmations de sa femme, il ne se sent pas malade, et encore moins disposé à recevoir un prêtre. Il finit pourtant par céder et avoue au faux confesseur qu'il est l'amant de sa fille. La confession déclenche alors une volée de coups de bâtons que les deux femmes assènent sur l'infidèle.

'The husband, through his cheerfulness, arouses the suspicions of his wife, who decides, with the connivance of a neighbour who disguises herself as a priest, to confess him to see what he is up to. The husband begs off this, because, despite his wife's insistence, he doesn't feel ill, and is even less willing to see a priest. However, he finally gives in and confesses to the false confessor that he is her daughter's lover. The confession provokes a rain of blows with cudgels which the two women launch on the unfaithful husband.'

In the first sequence we see a husband submit to his spouse's insistence that he should go to confession. Crucially important for the farce, however, is the fact that the two wives' subsequent ruse fails. Rey-Flaud interprets the ensuing events in the same way: 'Croyant tromper, les deux commères sont prises à leur propre piège et trompées par la ruse qu'elles ont élaborée' (157). In terms of Rey-Flaud's analytic model, we could label the husband as *sujet*; the two women then act as *agents* for it is they who try to eliminate their opponent. So here we seem to be dealing with a passive (-) sequence. Still it is the husband who scores a victory (∨). In order to keep within the boundaries of the French theory, we would now be obliged, in view of the sequence's outcome, to regard the women as (passive) *objets*. It is quite obvious that this interpretation is entirely unsatisfactory. After all, the initiative is theirs. So Rey-Flaud's 'absolute rule' as formulated above (a passive sequence is necessarily followed by ∧, a positive one by ∨) no longer seems acceptable: there is no reason why a passive dynamic segment cannot be followed by a *victoire*. In other words: deceptions can fail.

Of course, the reverse situation also occurs: a *sujet*'s enterprise may equally result in a fiasco. The *Farce du Clerc qui refuse à estre prestre* (RC, no. 11) provides us with an excellent example of this. At his entrance examination for the priesthood Jenin had to remain silent when he was asked who was the father of Aimon's four children. His teacher tries to make him see through this catch by reminding Jenin of Collart le Fèvre's family whom he knows well:

>   Le Maistre   Et viens ça, qui te demanderoit
>   Qui est le père des enfants
>   Collard le Fèvre, sot meschant,
>   Que repondrois-tu?
>   Jenin   G'y voys voir,
>   C'est Collard le Fèvre,
>   Car je cog[n]ais ses enfans cy,
>   Aussi leur père nourrisier.[7]

When, during a second test, the question about Aimon's four children is put to the boy again, he answers, of course: 'Collard le Fèvre'.

Although Rey-Flaud describes Jenin's activities as 'presque une auto-tromperie', and although she notes of his schoolmaster that he 'ne cherche qu'à aider son élève' (262), she nevertheless characterises the sequence of which this dialogue is part as

Q-. In other words, her own strong rule forces her to regard Le Maistre as *agent*, Jenin as his passive victim.

In conclusion, both the *Farce de Celuy qui se confesse* and the *Farce du Clerc qui refuse à estre prestre* contain examples of sequences in which a *sujet* or an *agent* fails to hit his target. Rey-Flaud's attempt, using some rather rigid rules, to link the specific parts of her theory is therefore unsuccessful.

4. Active vs. passive and a multiform interpretation of the dynamic segment

Apart from the above 'corrections', Rey-Flaud's distinction between *active* and *passive* sequences is also problematic in itself. A certain action frequently succeeds only after the victim has proved to be susceptible to deception. The sequence in which such a development takes place not only presumes an action from the initiator but it also requires a reaction from the victim. In Dutch *cluchten* and *esbatementen* relationships between characters like these occur repeatedly. Thus, in the *belachelijcke kluchte* ('ridiculous farce') of *Crimpert oom*, a play which has a theme similar to that of the French farce *Les deux Savetiers*, we have a miser on stage who plans to amuse himself at the expense of his servant, Simpel Schalck. For some time the latter has been to church more often than usual. There he has been begging the Holy Virgin to give him one hundred ducats. Simpel Schalck refuses to accept less. One day, hiding behind the altarpiece, Crimpert Oom throws a purse with ninety-nine ducats in the direction of the boy. Contrary to his earlier assertions Simpel Schalck accepts the money; for the remaining ducat he takes a rain check from his heavenly benefactress. So the *sujet*'s (Crimpert Oom) enterprise fails as a result of Simpel Schalck's counter-action: in this part of the farce both characters clearly fulfil an active role. Should we have limited ourselves to pointing out the servant's deception we would not have done justice to Crimpert Oom's failure. The reverse would not be satisfactory either, because the failure of Crimpert Oom's ruse is mainly due to Simpel Schalck's counter-move.

The *Farce de Mahuet* (RC, no. 39) contains another example of this double-sided action. Mahuet has been told by his mother to peddle their eggs 'au pris du marché' (line 53). At the Paris Halles he refuses to sell them to a woman who happens to be passing by. After having heard the reason for this, she suggests to a certain Gaultier that he introduce himself to Mahuet as *Pris du Marché*. To him the boy happily gives his eggs for nothing. So in this case we see a deception (F) coupled with a misunderstanding (Q). It is true, Mahuet is the victim of an unscrupulous swindler, but not without inflicting defeat on himself at the same time. The success of Gaultier's deception, therefore, largely depends on Mahuet's naive mistake.

These two examples, both the Dutch and the French one, illustrate the impossibility of speaking categorically of active or passive sequences. In many cases the outcome of a certain development will be the result of a combined, albeit contrastive, action of *sujet* and *agent*. Adding a plus (+) or a minus (-) to the letter symbolising the nature of a sequence's development then becomes more and more pointless. Should we nevertheless choose to maintain these symbols, we suggest regarding them as indications of the favourable or unfavourable outcome of the events seen from the *sujet*'s point of view.[8]

Elsewhere in her book (see page 280), when she discusses farces 'à pôles dédoublés', Rey-Flaud uses groups of symbols such as (α→ω) and (α←ω) to indicate the precise relationship between certain characters. Thus the formula F-(α←ω) means: *agent* ω deceives *sujet* α by means of a ruse (F). If, as we saw in the above examples, the action of one character cannot be isolated from a counter action by another, we could indicate this with a double-headed arrow: F-(α↔ω). An account of both characters' share in the dynamic segment can be given, as was the case in the *Farce de Mahuet*, by including in the formula both the symbols F and Q. By giving the one a capital letter and the other a small letter we can even indicate which action ultimately leads to success. The sequence from the *Farce de Mahuet*, discussed above, would then read: qF-(α↔ω), that is: Mahuet (α) is the victim of a misunderstanding (q), which Gaultier (ω)[9] uses to deceive him (F).

5. *Two new dynamic segments: P and C*

Rey-Flaud's definition of a *coup de théâtre* appears to be less unambiguous than she leads us to believe, since its application to the various plays she discusses is not always appropriate. On page 243 of her book, for example, she says of this dynamic segment: 'son auteur est le sort'. The unexpected toppling over of a scarecrow in *Le Franc Archier de Baignollet* and the equally unforeseen falling into a washtub by a bossy woman in *Le cuvier* fit the definition perfectly. But how is one to apply it to the events in the *Farce d'ung Savetier nommé Calbain* and in the *Farce de Mahuet*, which the author summarises on pages 266 and 272–3? From Rey-Flaud's discussion of these plays we learn that unexpected initiatives and certain mistakes can fall within the category of *coup de théâtre* as well.

With regard to the dynamic segment F the analysis of the farce *L'obstination des femmes* (its version in the *Recueil Cohen* (no. 48) is called *La mauvaistié des femmes*) forces the French scholar to admit that here it is a question of 'une série de défis qui ont raison de l'adversaire' (page 237) rather than of a '*tromperie*'.

In our opinion Rey-Flaud's view that a play can only be called 'farce' when F or at least Q is its central element not only underlies the vagueness which characterises her definition of the various dynamic segments, but also causes unnecessary complications. After all, there are many examples of farces in which relationships between characters develop, without our being able to describe them with the elements F, Q, or Z. Rey-Flaud's summary of the *Farce de Celuy qui se confesse* (see above) shows, for instance, how a husband ultimately submits to his wife's wishes. In Rey-Flaud's phrase: 'Il finit pourtant par *céder* ...' (page 186; my italics). In other words: the man allows himself to be out-talked and persuaded by his spouse. We can designate this change of situation by means of the symbol x for 'persuasion'.

By way of further illustration of this new dynamic segment I suggest the following example. Resjouy d'Amours, the main character (α) in the farce of the same name (RC, no. 18), tries to gain the favour of Tendrette (ω), whom he dearly loves. A first attempt remains unsuccessful. Consequently, he openly admits to his friend Gaultier Guillome (Tendrette's husband): 'On m'a baillié d'ung plat reffus' (line 147). His second attempt appears to be more rewarding. On the condition that he will not tell anybody, the woman grants him a rendezvous. Resjouy does not owe the favourable situation he now enjoys to either a 'tromperie' (F) or a 'quid pro quo' (Q). The man has simply 'convinced' Tendrette of his affection. The two succeeding sequences can be rendered as follows: first $\wedge.x\text{-}(\alpha\rightarrow\omega).\wedge.$, next $\wedge.x\text{+}(\alpha\rightarrow\omega).\vee.$

A change in position of power between characters can also come about by means of a physical conflict. As the result of a certain development in personal relationships we are already aware of this element in its static form, represented by the symbol x. Thus, four out of six Dutch *sottemieën*, handed down to us from the early-fifteenth-century 'van Hulthem' manuscript, end with the stage direction *Hier vechten si* ('Here they fight'). But a physical conflict can also take place in the shape of a dynamic segment. (It goes without saying that the subsequent static segment cannot then be x.) I suggest representing this new segment with the symbol C. In the *Farce nouvelle des femmes qui font baster leurs maris aux corneilles* (RC, no. 29) two women, Guillemette and Phelipote, dispatch their husbands (Pierre Tinette and Dando) to pick some medicinal herbs and watch crows on the wing. Engaged in these tasks and discussing the reason which led to them the men start growing suspicious. After their return home they accidentally overhear the women delighting in their cunning intent. A sound thrashing cures the women of their planned adultery and restores the hierarchic relationships in both families at the same time. So here the physical punishment itself causes a change of position. Consequently, it is not a static segment but a dynamic one. The farce, not surprisingly, ends with the defeat of the two women ($\wedge$).

To summarise, we may say that, next to the dynamic segments F, Q, and Z, the elements P and C are now at our disposal as well.

6. *Two new static segments:* # *and* =

With respect to the static segments Rey-Flaud's analytic model also needs some amendment. Yet unlike the above mentioned additions they seem to be less imperative.

In many cases, from the very beginning one of the characters of a farce is in an under-dog position. If he or she functions as the *sujet* the play opens with the static segment $\wedge$. Only very exceptionally (in the case of the *Farce des femmes qui font accroire à leurs maris de vecies que ce sont lanternes* (RC, no. 15) for example) will it start with a conflict (x). By definition an opening segment in the shape of a reconciliation ($\emptyset$) is not possible. Not uncommonly, however, a situation occurs where two characters, who will be fighting later on, at first live together in perfect harmony. We could render this opening segment with the symbol #.

As we have already seen, the main character in the *Farce de Mahuet* sets off with a basket full of eggs for the Parisian Halles. The boy is beaming with self-confidence since nothing as yet indicates the imminent humiliation to which he will be subjected shortly: 'je vous dis que sans doubtance / La besogne très bien feray' (lines 64–5). Therefore, Rey-Flaud has the play in her analysis begin with the segment v. However, it is not the character's mood that is decisive for the question as to whether a certain segment has to be considered as a *défaite* (∧) or as a *victoire* (∨), but rather the actual position in which he finds himself.[9] When Mahuet leaves his parental home it is still fairly neutral: #. *Cautelleux, Barat et le villain* (RC, no. 12) and *Le pourpoint rétréci* (RC, no. 44) may serve as two more examples of the neutral start referred to here. In the first of the two plays from the very outset the Villager, it is true, does not give the impression of being too bright a person, but compared with the two rogues Cautelleux and Barat he need not be regarded as inferior. In *Le pourpoint rétréci* the planning of the hoax which Richard and Gaultier intend to play on their victim extends over almost two hundred lines of text. Whether their attempt to make Thierry believe that his belly is inflating because of dropsy will be successful or not is, at least for a considerable amount of time, highly questionable.

Under the influence of a dynamic segment, positions of power between characters sometimes develop without reaching a (new) static result. As we saw earlier Rey-Flaud does observe (see page 230) the stabilisation of uncertain relationships, but she fails to draw attention to the *de*stabilisation of steady positions. For next to a development 'Etat (+) / Action = tromperie / Etat +' a sequence like 'Etat + / Action = tromperie / Etat (+)' is equally conceivable. Although situations like these probably do not occur frequently, we should bear the possibility as such definitely in mind. So what it amounts to here, is that the dislocation of existing positions of power in an attempt to unbalance the scales does not lead to a new (or perhaps even confirms the old) static segment. Henceforth I will designate these situations by means of the symbol =.

Although a further refinement of Rey-Flaud's theory, to which I shall return later, will cause a change in its analysis, the start of the *Farce de drois de la Porte Bodès* (RC, no. 20) may serve as an example of the phenomenon. A cobbler orders his wife to shut the door but she refuses to do so. A long dispute leads nowhere; therefore they agree to a silent wager and whoever breaks it will have to close the door. Any attempt at persuasion fails; the silent wager between the two persons does not imply a reconciliation (∅), nor that either party involved gains a victory or suffers a defeat. The resulting relationship cannot be labelled a conflict (x) either. Using a chess term we could call it a 'stalemate' (=).

7. *Two new character types:* iudex *and* catalyst

The apparently difficult problem in the *Farce de drois de la Porte Bodès* of who should shut a cobbler's front door is solved by a judge who happens to be passing by and asks the way to Saint Lorens, one of Paris' churches. The shoemaker merely makes some vague gestures. When the judge starts flirting with his wife, it is she who breaks the silent wager: she reproaches her husband for not protesting against the lawyer's impudence. Of course the man sees this as a victory over his wife and consequently directs her to close the door. Outraged by her spouse's behaviour she refuses; a conflict (x) results. Asked for professional arbitration the judge, of all people, decides in the woman's favour.

At the beginning of the farce it appears to be sheer coincidence that the individual who forces a breakthrough in the marital silent wager is a lawyer by profession. His presence makes the continuation of the farce easier in that it requires a 'judge' who resolves the ensuing quarrel between husband and wife. However, both the act by which the judge brings the silent wager to an end and the act by which he finally puts the wife in the right are meant to force resolutions. He does not really take part in the conflict between the two sides. His action is purely mediatory. The judge decides in favour of one party without siding with either of the antagonists. In other words as a *iudex* he takes up his own position between *sujet* and *objet/agent*. Should we want to incorporate the judge's action in the first sequence of the *Farce de drois de la Porte Bodès* (rendering it by the symbol κ) then its formula would read: #.P(α←κ→ω).x. Put into words: a neutral (#) start is followed by the attempt of a cobbler (α) and his wife (ω) to persuade (P) each other to shut the door, forced to a solution by a *iudex* (κ), who by his unacceptable behaviour elicits a conflict (x) between the spouses. It should be noted, by the way, that in the above formula after the P, the symbol to indicate the nature of the dynamic segment, a plus (+) or a minus (-) has no further function, and is therefore omitted. (See note 8.)

The way in which a catalyst in a farce acts resembles that of a *iudex*, but nonetheless it does differ from the latter. For whereas a *iudex* makes decisions in a conflict between two or more characters, a catalyst, without interfering actively, merely enables one of them to get hold of a 'weapon' with which to eliminate an opponent. The activities of a manservant in one of the funniest Dutch farces from the early sixteenth century, Cornelis Everaert's *esbatement*, *De Vigelie*, is an example of a catalyst's influence. Under the pretext of having to obey the religious prescriptions pertaining to the vigil of a church festival, one day when the faithful have to refrain from enjoying 'flesh', a cabinet-maker refuses to make love to his wife. Early next morning his spouse takes revenge by behaving as if it is indeed a Sunday: she dresses in her best clothes and sends her husband's servant home with his daily wage. When the man discovers this, he realises his mistake and knows he is defeated by his own ruse. The point here is that the manservant, without really being on either side and completely unaware of the ultimate effect of his actions, enables the woman to gain a victory.

Compared with the Dutch play, Maistre Aliborum's role in the *Farce des queues trousees* (RC, no. 6) is somewhat more explicit. Still, he functions as a catalyst in finding a resolution to the conflict between the lamplighter Macé, the cobbler

Michault, and both their spouses. Following the fashion of the times, the two women are wearing extremely long trains. The men ridicule them for this and even threaten to beat them. Therefore the women appeal to Maistre Aliborum who, not without unambigious intentions, fixes mirrors to their skirts. When Macé and Michault subsequently look at themselves in these mirrors they discover they are less handsome than they had imagined. Underneath their caps there are even calf's ears showing. This causes the two women to regain their self-confidence.

To summarise, Rey-Flaud's model needs to be thoroughly revised in its concept of the active and passive voice in dynamic segments. Other adjustments and additions are advisable to a greater or lesser degree. Indeed, we have limited ourselves in the above survey only to the more basic notions of the theory. I have not touched on the way in which the French scholar applied these concepts, in chapter 5 of the second part of her study, to the overall structures of farces, resulting in an analysis of the so-called 'sequential organisation'. Furthermore, differences between French farces and Dutch *sotternieën*, *esbatementen*, and *cluchten* will probably become clearer precisely in this area. However, describing divergences between Dutch and French farces has not been the purpose of this article. The aim I intended to pursue here was to improve, with all due respect to Rey-Flaud's starting-points, on a theory, which is in itself already workable but which, because of its originality, really should be elaborated upon. It is to be hoped that the above remarks will contribute to future discussions on both the structure of French farce and Dutch pre-Renaissance comic drama.

University of Melbourne

NOTES

I would like to express my gratitude to Dr Denise Ryan (Librarian in the Department of Germanic Studies and Russian at the University of Melbourne) for assistance in the preparation of this paper.

1. After being submitted in 1982 as a *thèse de troisième cycle* to the Université Paul Valéry of Montpellier, the book was published in 1984 by E. Droz in Geneva.
2. See the reviews by Jean-Claude Aubailly in *Bulletin de l'Association d'Etude sur l'Humanisme, la Réforme et la Renaissance* 11:20 (1985) 12–22; Edelgard Dubruck in *Fifteenth-Century Studies* 7 (1985) 170–5; J. Koopmans in *Bibliothèque d'Humanisme et Renaissance* 47 (1985) 506–507; Norris J. Lacy in *The French Review* 60 (1986–1987) 252–3; Graham A. Runnalls in *French Studies* 40 (1986) 319–321; Martijn Rus in *Rapports: het Franse boek* 56 (1986) 132–4; and Donald Stone Jr in *Renaissance Quarterly* 38 (1985) 749–51.
3. See W.N.M. Hüsken *Noyt meerder Vreucht: Compositie en structuur van het komische toneel in de Nederlanden voor de Renaissance* (Sub Rosa, Deventer, 1987). In the Netherlands

WIM HÜSKEN

    pre-Renaissance comic drama is either labelled *sottemie* (early fifteenth century), *clucht* or *esbatement* (sixteenth century), yet all three refer to the same genre: farce.
4. *Recueil de farces françaises inédites du XVe siècle* edited Gustave Cohen (Mediaeval Academy of America, Cambridge, Mass., 1949).
5. Rey-Flaud's observations do not make clear what the symbol **Z** stands for.
6. Instead of Rey-Flaud's *'résolution'* I would prefer to use the word 'reconciliation'. Not only does this term better describe the essence of what she wants to express with it, but the symbols ∨, ∧ and **x** to a certain extent are 'resolutions' too.
7. See Cohen *RC no.* 85, or Rey-Flaud *La farce ou la machine à rire* 262.
8. Combined with the symbol for the second static segment (∨ or ∧) the signs **+** and **-** do indeed result in a doubling (just as it was the case in Rey-Flaud's theory), but on the other hand the ultimate formula of the structure of a farce becomes more readable with it. As a consequence of this change it is self-evident that when a sequence ends with a conflict (**x**) or with a reconciliation (**Ø**) the **+** or **-** after the symbol indicating the dynamic segment is not applicable any longer.
9. The Dutch *sottemie* of *De buskenblaser* strikingly illustrates this. In the play a *homme à tout faire* deludes one of his colleagues with the prospect of looking fresh and young again after blowing, on payment of course, into a tin that is dangled in front of him. Since it is filled with soot the simpleton acquires a black face. So, although the man thinks he has gained a marvellous triumph, in reality he has been downright swindled (∧).

FASTNACHTSPIEL ET RECIT BREF:
L'Interférence de deux genres littéraires en Allemagne aux 15ᵉ et 16ᵉ siècles
Jean-Marc Pastré

Pour beaucoup d'entre eux, les fabliaux allemands, que nous appellerons *maere* pour des raisons de commodité, ont été probablement mimés comme le furent par les jongleurs les fabliaux français. Par ailleurs, les *Fastnachtspiele* et particulièrement les premiers d'entre eux, apparus à Nüremberg vers 1430, étaient des jeux faits pour l'ambiance festive de la liesse carnavalesque et n'avaient pas encore la forme théâtrale que leur donnèrent les poètes du 16ᵉ siècle. Les deux genres littéraires ont en fait beaucoup plus de points communs qu'on ne pourrait le supposer, ce que montre bien la comparaison des *maere* et des *Fastnachtspiele* à thème identique et, plus précisément encore, la comparaison des nouvelles de Boccace et des Jeux de Carnaval de Hans Sachs. Il reste enfin que certains *maere* sont étrangement proches des Jeux et en prennent parfois fidèlement la forme, et ce sous l'angle dramaturgique qui définit les Jeux par l'emploi du style direct, des indications scéniques et par les solutions qu'ils apportent au problème des contraintes spatio-temporelles dues à toute mise en scène.

La proximité des deux genres apparaît d'abord dans l'emploi commun du style direct ou dans le passage du style indirect au style direct tel qu'on le voit dans l'adaptation que firent de récits brefs des auteurs de *Fastnachtspiele*. Hans Sachs, dont on sait qu'il rédigea beaucoup de ses Jeux à partir des nouvelles de Boccace telles qu'il les connaissait par la traduction dite de Steinhöwel,[1] est à cet égard le meilleur témoin et le plus sûr garant. Dans *Der schwanger Pawer*, adapté de la troisième nouvelle de la neuvième journée des *Cent Nouvelles*,[2] trois compères font accroire à un quatrième, devenu riche par héritage, qu'il est malade et parviennent ainsi à lui extorquer l'argent d'un bon repas. Hormis l'introduction, qui sert chez Boccace d'exposition, la quasi-totalité de la nouvelle est en style direct, si bien que Sachs n'a pas de peine à mettre en scène la nouvelle dont il reprend fidèlement non seulement les répliques mais encore leur ordre de succession. Hans Sachs, en outre, invente certes en style direct le dialogue des trois compères qui sert au Jeu d'exposition, mais le fait à partir des quelques lignes qui résument chez Boccace l'évocation de leurs conversations et de leur dessein,[3] comme il le fait encore dans le *Jeu du jaloux qui veut piéger sa femme à confesse*[4] et dans le *Jeu de l'évocation du diable*.[5] Tout aussi naturellement, les monologues intérieurs des pièces narratives deviennent les monologues parlés des Jeux. Dans *Die alt verschlagen Kupplerin mit dem Thumherrn*, proche du fabliau *Alten Weibes List*,[6] trois petits monologues intérieurs de l'entremetteuse, qui successivement se demande quelle affaire elle pourrait bien organiser (vers 27-31), qui jauge la jeune femme à la sortie de la messe et la juge bonne pour son entreprise (vers 95–103), enfin fait de même pour le bel homme qui n'est autre que le mari de la belle (vers 383–8), deviennent trois monologues plus ou moins en aparté dans le Jeu de Sachs (vers 1–32, 129–35 et 259–64). Dans *Der jung Kauffman Nicola mit seiner Sophia*, Sachs reprend ainsi systématiquement les passages de style direct de la nouvelle de Boccace[7] et met tout autant en style direct ce qui était en style indirect chez son modèle.

Dans ces questions dramatiques de mise en scène d'un récit bref, il était plus difficile de faire passer sur la scène les parties narratives de la nouvelle. Deux procédés le permettent: la création de monologues ou de dialogues et les indications scéniques. Chez Sachs, la pratique la plus courante consiste à reprendre l'introduction narrative de Boccace sous la forme de monologues, parfois même de dialogues d'exposition, manière que le poète adopte pour les charnières narratives du récit: dans *Das Weib im Brunnen*, jeu adapté de *La noyée*,[8] Sachs s'y emploie de manière systématique.

Sachs exploite à cet effet avec tout autant de constance le procédé dramatique de l'indication scénique. Nous en prendrons d'abord quelques exemples dans *Die jung witfrau Francisca, so durch ein List zwayer pueler abkom*, jeu emprunté par Sachs à *Dos à dos* de Boccace.[9] Chez ce dernier, Rinuccio, qui croit apporter à sa belle un cadavre tiré de sa tombe, rencontre une ronde de police:

> Les gendarmes entendent le pas lourd de Rinuccio. Ils projettent brusquement un rai de lumière pour voir ce qui en est, et dans quelle direction on marche. Ils empoignent lances et boucliers en criant 'qui vive?'.

Ce sont là pour la scène de véritables indications scéniques, et Sachs en retient de fait l'essentiel après le vers 365:

> *Die zwen wechter laufen herfur, und Hirnschrot schreit: 'Wer pist?'.*

Le jeune homme n'insiste pas et prend la fuite:

> Il laisse choir Alexandre, prend ses jambes à son cou et disparaît ...

ce que Sachs reprend après le vers 367:

> *Rinuccio wirft den doten von im und fleucht.*

Alexandre n'en demande pas son reste:

> Alexandre se lève d'un bond et, malgré les longs vêtements du mort qui flottent sur son dos, il s'éloigne à la même allure ...

ce que Sachs scinde en deux indications scéniques, l'une après le vers 368:

> *Alexander, der dot, stet auf ...*

l'autre après le vers 377:

> *Er lauft im dotenclaid ab ...*

FASTNACHTSPIEL ET RECIT BREF: L'INTERFÉRENCE DE DEUX GENRES

Rinuccio revient alors à son cadavre:

> Quand le guêt eut disparu, il revint où il avait jeté Alexandre, et, pour achever sa besogne, commença de chercher à tâtons le cadavre.

Sachs en fait encore deux indications après les vers 369 et 378:

> *Sie laufen im nach hinaus ...*

et

> *Rinuczo kumbt wider und suechet den doten.*

Toute la fin narrative de l'histoire passe ainsi chez Sachs en indications scéniques.

Ce même parallélisme apparaît tout autant entre le *Jeu de l'entremetteuse* déjà cité et le *maere* qui lui est largement antérieur, *Alten Weibes List*. Dans ce dernier, l'entremetteuse s'approche du chanoine et l'aborde (vers 51–3), ce que Sachs reprend après le vers 60:

> *Sie tritt zu im, redt in an und spricht.*

Reconnaissant, le chanoine lui donne de l'argent (vers 85–9), Sachs (après le vers 92):

> *Er greifft in sein Taschen, gibt ihr Geldt und spricht ...*

Elle aborde ensuite la jeune femme (vers 104–108), Sachs (après le vers 163):

> *Die alt Kupplerin tritt hinzu und spricht ...*

Celle-ci lui donne quelque argent (vers 172), Sachs (après le vers 206):

> *Die Jung Frau geyt ihr ein Thaler und spricht ...*

Toutes deux se séparent (vers 173), Sachs (après le vers 1213):

> *Sie gehn alle drey ab ...*

La vieille aborde alors le mari (vers 389–90), Sachs (après le vers 264):

> *Die alt Kuplerin tritt hinzu und spricht ...*

Tous deux vont au rendez-vous (vers 399–400), Sachs (après le vers 286):

> *Sie gehn mit einander ab ...*

La belle les voit arriver, postée à la fenêtre (vers 401), Sachs (après le vers 300):

> *Die Meyd geht und schawet zum Fenster auß, kombt gach wider und spricht ...*

La belle gifle son mari (vers 440), ce que Sachs transpose après le vers 334: elle le prend par les cheveux et le jette à terre. Toute la trame gestuelle et narrative du fabliau se retrouve ainsi chez Sachs sous forme d'indications scéniques.

JEAN-MARC PASTRÉ

On voit combien il pourrait être facile de mettre en scène un fabliau pour en faire un Jeu de Carnaval. A thème identique, il arrive même que le *maere* soit plus dramatique que le *Fastnachtspiel*, à preuve *Der Bawer mit dem Plerr* de Sachs et le fabliau *Weiberlist*.[10] Le *maere* est en effet beaucoup plus proche de la scène que le Jeu. Presque tout en dialogues, il introduit chaque réplique par 'il dit / elle dit', '*si sprach / er sprach*', mots constants dans les deux pièces, intégrée dans le vers pour le fabliau et indications scéniques chez Sachs, si bien que si l'on mettait les amorces de réplique en indications scéniques, on aurait un *Fastnachtspiel*, de même qu'on aurait un fabliau si l'on intégrait ces dernières dans le texte rimé. Les notations de style narratif y ont en outre le style d'indications scéniques: il prend une bûche et frappe sa femme dans le dos, la prend par les cheveux et la jette au sol (vers 44–7); les voisins font tout pour les séparer (vers 55–8); elle pleure et se tord les mains lorsqu'elle s'explique avec son époux (vers 177–9); l'époux éclate de rire lorsque la vieille prétend lui voir deux nez (vers 192); enfin la vieille rit de sa bêtise et s'en va (vers 243). Les quelques rares passages de style indirect s'y mettraient sans peine en style direct: les voisins demandent à la jeune femme ce qui se passe (vers 59–61), demandent ensuite une trêve (vers 79), et la décision prise (vers 86); la jeune femme essaie de calmer son époux par toutes sortes de paroles (vers 157–61); il lui demande ce qu'elle lui a donné à manger ce jour-là (vers 246–9). Quelques pensées d'un personnage en style indirect feraient sans peine un petit monologue, comme aux vers 87–90 où la belle se demande par quelle ruse elle pourra éviter les coups. Le petit monologue intérieur du mari qui pense qu'il a mangé du cerfeuil (vers 228–38) deviendrait même sans modification un monologue parlé.

Hans Sachs eut pour source une autre version du conte, sans quoi il aurait eu peu de mal à le mettre en scène et aurait créé un Jeu plus dramatique. Et c'est bien ce qu'il fait dans *Der schwanger Bawer*, jeu repris du *Malade imaginaire* de Boccace (9: 3); la nouvelle était déjà presque entièrement en style direct, et Sachs reprend tout simplement en indications scéniques les notations de style narratif de Boccace, telles que: le docteur se prononce au vu de l'urine, Sachs (après le vers 184):

Der Artzt begreift den Pulß und spricht ...

Calandrin remet à Bruno cinq livres, Sachs (après le vers 148):

Der Artzt gibt Merten das Geldt ...

Le malade boit sa clairette, Sachs (après le vers 268):

Der Kranck trinckt und spricht ...

Le docteur enfin lui tâte le pouls à nouveau, Sachs (après le vers 273):

Der Artzt kombt, greifft jin den Pulß und spricht ...

Cette manière dut tant plaire à Sachs qu'il ajouta même à sa source deux indications scéniques de ce genre: le malade se prend la tête entre les mains et se plaint de son sort (après le vers 195) et serre plus tard la main du médecin par reconnaissance pour la si rapide guérison (après le vers 280).

Ce qui par contre éloigne ces Jeux des récits brefs relève de l'éloignement dans l'espace et le temps, le déplacement spatial et l'intervalle temporel. Sachs évite en général l'un et l'autre. Dans *Von Joseph und Melisso, auch König Salomon*, jeu tiré d'une des nouvelles de Boccace,[11] Sachs supprime ainsi le voyage au cours duquel les deux jeunes gens se rencontrent en route pour Jérusalem et se racontent pourquoi ils vont consulter Salomon. Sachs se contente d'annoncer leur voyage, sur quoi les jeunes gens quittent la scène qui reste alors vide, ce qui permet, ailleurs que sur scène, et en un temps raccourci le voyage. Sachs de même supprime le voyage qu'ils font au Pont de l'Oie où Salomon les a envoyés; le voyage est transformé en récit dans le rapport qu'ils font à Salomon de leur expérience. Dans *Der jung Kauffman Nicola mit seiner Sophia*, tiré d'une autre nouvelle de Boccace,[12] Sachs supprime de même les deux voyages à Naples du jeune marchand Nicolas, le premier pour aller, dans son désarroi d'avoir été dupé par une belle, demander conseil à un vieil ami de son père, le second pour lui rapporter l'argent avancé et lui raconter comment il réussit, grâce à ses conseils, à duper à son tour Sophia. Sachs fait en effet opportunément apparaître le vieillard au moment où Nicolas pleure son infortune et souhaite aller lui demander conseil (vers 147–52), puis il supprime le second voyage et fait annoncer par Nicolas sa décision de retourner à Nice, le Jeu se terminant non sur le voyage chez le vieillard, mais par une scène de déconvenue pour Sophia et sa soubrette.

Lorsqu'il ne peut supprimer la diversité des espaces et des décors, Sachs recourt alors à une structure dramatique en actes ou en scènes, ce qui l'éloigne à la fois de la forme narrative et du *Fastnachtspiel* primitif. Raison pour laquelle Sachs sans doute appelle certains de ces Jeux 'comedi', pièces dans lesquelles les parties démarquées par une scène vide sont appelées 'actes' – par exemple *Die jung Witfrau Francisca* – ce qui toutefois ne distingue en rien ces Jeux de la plupart de ceux qu'il appelle *Fastnachtspiel*. Le jeu *Die Kupplerin mit dem Thumherrn* présente ainsi quatre petits actes démarqués par des scènes vides et par quatre décors différents, et introduits par les annonces de déplacements contenus dans de petits monologues à fonction dramaturgique: la scène se passe d'abord devant chez le chanoine (un monologue de la vieille annonce qu'elle s'y rend, vers 29 et 32), puis au marché (auquel vient la vieille, à ce qu'elle annonce, pour chercher une jolie femme, vers 129–35), ensuite devant chez le mari (la vieille vient y chercher un autre homme, vers 259–64), enfin chez la vieille, qui amène le mari au rendez-vous (après le vers 286). Cette forme déjà très théâtrale du Jeu est chez Sachs la plus fréquente.

Hans Sachs connaît toutefois encore une forme plus primitive du Jeu, moins attachée aux conventions dramaturgiques du théâtre renaissant, déjà très moderne dans sa conception. Dans *Das Weib im Brunnen*, tiré de *La noyée* de Boccace,[13] un monologue de transition sert ainsi à rendre la durée d'une action qui se passe en dehors de la scène: en l'espace de vingt vers, la jeune Gitta explique qu'elle trompe son mari, lequel vient de partir boire chez son frère et reviendra, comme d'habitude, fin saoul; elle le couchera alors et rejoindra son amant. La fiction du Jeu veut qu'il revienne dès après ce monologue, fin saoul comme elle l'avait annoncé, vingt vers suffisant à rendre la durée du départ, des beuveries et du retour du mari (vers 31–50). Dans *Von Joseph und Melisso*, Joseph interrompt un dialogue entre Salomon et Marcolfus, figure qu'il emprunte à un autre Jeu, et présente en sage son cas – sa femme est acariâtre; après la reprise du dialogue entre Salomon et Marcolfus, Melisso vient à son tour exposer son cas – il ne sait se faire aimer malgré sa fortune – et part, comme Joseph, au Pont de l'Oie. Pour meubler la scène pendant ce déplacement et cet épisode, longuement narré chez Boccace, Sachs invente un court débat entre Salomon et Marcolfus sur la vertu des femmes, raillées par Marcolfus et défendues par le sage. Ces quelque vingt vers de considérations générales et philosophiques (vers 252–72) servent d'intermède et font passer par l'interruption de l'action l'interruption du cours du temps, ce qui permet à Joseph, puis à Melisso de réapparaître déjà sur la scène.

Cette manière était en fait celle des *Fastnachtspiele* plus anciens, à preuve *Der Bauer und der Bock* de Hans Rosenplüt:[14] un seigneur confie à son fermier en qui il a pleine confiance, son bouc; une femme apparaît alors et parie avec le seigneur qu'elle fera mentir le paysan avant deux jours. Rosenplüt introduit alors trois messieurs sur la scène, auxquels le seigneur demande de dire leur avis. Après pas même 40 vers de conversation sentencieuse (vers 73–110), la femme réapparaît déjà, laquelle a séduit le paysan en plein champ et a gagné le bouc. Un jour s'est donc écoulé en peu de vers et sans que la scène se vide des personnages, ce qui rappelle le rôle du choeur antique dans la tragédie grecque. Cette notion de durée, éliminée la plupart du temps par Sachs, n'est donc pas un obstacle insurmontable à la dramaturgie du *Fastnachtspiel*.

Le Jeu de Carnaval 'primitif' semble par contre attaché à l'absence de changement de lieu et à l'absence de scènes vides qui, pour rendre ces déplacements, interrompent l'action à la manière du théâtre moderne. *Der schwanger Bawer* en est un bon exemple. La structure par élargissement de ce Jeu permet la présence croissante de personnages sur la scène et la mise à l'arrière-scène de ces mêmes personnages, sans que la scène soit jamais vide et sans que les personnages quittent vraiment le lieu qui sert de scène. Arrive d'abord Merten, paysan auquel viennent s'ajouter deux autres, Hans et Urban (vers 1–116); puis arrive Kargas (vers 127), celui que l'on veut malade: Urban dit alors aux deux autres de s'écarter afin qu'il aborde seul Kargas:

Thut ji zwen hindr den Stadel stan! vers 116

Kargas et Urban restent donc seuls à l'avant-scène, Urban essaie de convaincre Kargas qu'il est malade. Urban se met ensuite probablement à l'arrière-scène pour permettre à Kargas de se demander en monologue quel mal il peut avoir. S'avance alors Merten (*Merten, der ander Pawer, kompt und spricht*, après le vers 129), qui joue la même comédie vis-à-vis de Kargas. Restant à l'avant-scène, il est bientôt rejoint par Hans (indication scénique avant le vers 142) qui poursuit le même jeu: tous deux l'assoient sur une chaise. Urban s'avance à son tour (indication scénique avant le vers 157) et conseille au malade de donner un peu d'urine, tandis qu'Urban court chercher le médecin (avant le vers 162). Kargas se désespère alors dans un monologue (vers 162-72) au cours duquel il écarte expressément Hans et Merten:

O weicht! last mich ein weng verschnauffen! vers 161

Simon, le médecin, arrive alors (vers 173), analyse l'urine, envoie Merten acheter un bon repas (vers 250) et va préparer une potion. La dernière scène, peut-être séparée du reste par une scène vide, fait revenir Merten qui donne à Kargas la potion (vers 272), suivi du médecin (vers 273); enfin guéri, Kargas serre la main à Hans et à Urban manifestement revenus de l'arrière-scène pour participer au finale. On retrouve dans cette forme ramassée d'action ininterrompue la forme plus primitive du *Fastnachtspiel*, et l'on ne s'étonnera pas de voir ce Jeu introduit par 10 vers où le paysan Merten définit dans un court monologue expressément la pièce comme un Jeu de Carnaval, seule pièce à le faire parmi celles que nous comparons à des récits brefs (*idem* au vers 54).

Der farend Schuler mit dem Teuffel pannen est à cet égard plus exemplaire encore. Il y a là un acte unique qui se déroule dans un même lieu et dans un temps limité, tout à l'instar des *Handlungsspiele* décrits par E. Catholy.[15] Comme dans le *maere* de Rosenplüt, un étudiant demande l'hospitalité à une paysanne que le prêtre, son amant, a rejointe; tous deux l'ayant mis dehors, l'étudiant décide de leur forcer la main en leur jouant un bon tour: il revient à la charge lorsque le paysan, revenu inopinément, fait que le prêtre doit se cacher dans un galetas. Il propose au paysan pour divertissement de faire apparaître le diable, le prêtre couvert de suie que l'étudiant fera quitter sain et sauf la pièce en gagnant par là bon gîte et bonne chère. Hans Sachs y fait apparaître puis disparaître de la scène les personnages, successivement en deux grandes branches dans lesquelles la paysanne d'abord prend l'initiative, puis l'étudiant dans la seconde (vers 1-135 et 157-325), les entrées et les sorties étant réglées selon le principe d'élargissements successifs du nombre des personnages, de un à trois dans la première branche, de un à quatre dans la seconde.

Le fabliau de Rosenplüt est par contre manifestement fait pour être lu, avec ou sans mimique, et n'a pas le style scénique. Il n'en va pas toujours de même. Certaines pièces appelées dans les recueils *maere* sont en fait de vraies petites pièces dramatiques, à preuve *Die Beichte der zwölf Frauen*.[16] En deux lignes d'introduction, l'auteur s'adresse, tel un acteur, au public et l'invite à écouter comme à voir cette histoire, tant il est vrai qu'il y avait là effectivement, mimé ou joué à plusieurs, un spectacle. Douze femmes y viennent se plaindre, en guise de confession, de la mauvaise besogne amoureuse de leur mari. Chacune d'entre elles a sa confession introduite par un vers qui pourrait servir d'indication scénique: l'une arrive à pas rapides (vers 76), l'autre accourt (vers 93). Chacune commence par dire au prêtre qu'elle a sujet à se plaindre puis décrit par périphrases ambiguës l'insuffisance du mari et le meilleur usage qu'il devrait faire de sa force virile. A chaque fois le prêtre propose ses services, se disant bon artisan en la matière, et chacune conclut l'invitation en acceptant la pénitence, 'ich halt die pueß'. Chacune ayant la même introduction, le même type de récit et la même conclusion, chaque rôle forme un tout autonome, sans transition de l'un à l'autre, constituant à chaque fois un paragraphe clairement délimité d'une vingtaine de vers: il s'agit là en fait d'un véritable *Reihenspiel*, d'un jeu de rôles successifs qui viennent sur la scène comme en revue. De ce type de Jeu, tout à fait bien répertorié, Rosenplüt donna deux très bons exemples avec le *Arztspiel*,[17] où un médecin analyse successivement l'urine de cinq personnages qui tous posent les mêmes questions, et encore avec *Das Eggenziehen*,[18] où sept femmes, attelées à une herse, viennent expliquer à tour de rôle pourquoi elles sont restées vieilles filles; ou c'est encore les *Liebesnarren* de Hans Folz,[19] revue de treize fous qui racontent leur aventure amoureuse devant Vénus.

Pour rester dans le domaine de la confession comique, on pourrait citer un autre *maere*, *Die zwei Beichten*,[20] très proche encore à sa manière du Jeu scénique. Il s'agit d'un fabliau du 15e siècle à deux personnages, fait d'un dialogue constant, serré et manifestement destiné à être mimé ou dit par deux personnes. Dans ce *maere*, où deux époux décident de se confesser mutuellement, chaque réplique est introduite par l'indication très scénique: 'il dit / elle dit'. La femme y avoue avoir eu huit amants, et ce toujours selon le même schéma; elle nomme l'amant, explique pourquoi elle a cédé, et le mari conclut en lui donnant raison: le berger du village pour ne pas avoir à payer la quote-part de garde des troupeaux, le messager du seigneur pour qu'il dise à son maître du bien d'eux, le prêtre pour qu'il prie pour eux, le juge pour qu'il les laisse en paix, le sommelier et le cuisinier pour qu'ils leur donnent à boire et à manger, le vieux pâtre par pitié, le fils du voisin assisté de trois gaillards pour avoir leur appui en cas de détresse, enfin le sacristain pour qu'il lui ouvre à son gré l'église. Il n'y a là de véritable action que lorsque le mari avoue une seule infidélité, châtiée par la colère de l'épouse qui menace de le battre et l'absout. Tout autant que pour être lu ou mimé, ce genre de *maere* est bien fait pour être joué sur la scène. On est là tout proche d'ailleurs du genre français du 'dialogue dramatique' de la fin du 15e siècle que Jean-Claude Aubailly a bien décrit, où un monologue est interrompu par les questions ou les commentaires d'un second personnage présent pour rendre plus vivant la scène.[21] Même le *maere* du Stricker de même thème et composé dès le milieu du 13e siècle se révèle très dramatique au-delà de la courte exposition (vers 1–10) où l'auteur explique que les deux époux vivent en lisière de forêt et que la neige les empêche d'aller à confesse.[22] La femme y avoue encore d'une traite quatre amants (vers 11–44); tout le reste du *maere* est dialogué, suivi de la narration du châtiment du mari, très proche d'indications scéniques: elle le prend par les cheveux, le jette dehors et le frappe à coups de balai (vers 69–73).

On voit que la proximité des deux genres, le fabliau et le Jeu, est grande. Les *maere*, y compris les plus anciens, ont parfois une forme tout à fait dramatique et

FASTNACHTSPIEL ET RECIT BREF: L'INTERFÉRENCE DE DEUX GENRES

furent probablement mimés par les jongleurs. Le *Fastnachtspiel*, en tant que genre, apparut de toute façon plus tard, vers le milieu du 15e siècle, et s'inspire souvent, directement ou indirectement, d'un récit bref, nouvelle ou fabliau. La vraie différence tient à ce que la plupart des *maere* furent faits pour être dits et pouvaient pour beaucoup d'entre eux être mimés et joués, tandis que les *Fastnachtspiele* furent d'abord, en tant que Jeux, faits pour être joués. La vraie différence relève donc de la distinction des genres littéraires, le genre narratif étant lui-même souvent à la limite du genre dramatique auquel il donna progressivement jour. Tout à fait comme en France, où les monologues dramatiques donnèrent naissance aux dialogues dramatiques, lesquels donnèrent le jour aux farces, il s'est dégagé en Allemagne peu à peu de l'art narratif la conscience d'une technique de présentation dramatique. Par affinement de l'art dramatique, de Jeu qu'il était, le théâtre devint peu à peu, et très vite avec Hans Sachs, un art, et le Jeu de Carnaval une vraie comédie.

Paris

NOTES

1. Pour les sources du théâtre de Hans Sachs, voir A.L. Stiefel 'Über die Quellen des Hans Sachsischen Dramen' *Germania 24* (1891) 1–60, et 25 (1892) 203–230; A. MacMechan *The Relation of Hans Sachs to the 'Decameron'* (Dissertation, Baltimore: Halifax, 1889); Carl Drescher *Arigo, der Übersetzer des 'Decamerone' und des 'Fiore di Virtu'* (Quellen und Forschungen zur Sprach- und Kulturgeschichte der germanischen Völker 86: Strasbourg, 1900); Julius Hartmann *Das Verhältnis von Hans Sachs zur sogenannten Steinhöwelschen Decameronüberzetzung* (Acta Germanica, Neue Reihe, Heft 2: Berlin, 1912).
2. Hans Sachs *Sämmtliche Fastnachtspiele* édition E. Goetze, Bd 1–20 (Neudrucke deutscher Litteraturwerke, Halle, 1880–1887) 16; Boccace 'Le malade imaginaire' *Décaméron* traduction J. Bourciez (Paris, 1952); Giovanni Boccaccio *Decamerone* ... édition Enrico Bianchi (La litteratura italiana Studi e Testi 8: Ricciardi, Napoli, 1952) 628-33.
3. 'Et tous les trois d'envisager le moyen de se graisser les babines aux frais de Calandrin. Ils ne furent pas long à ourdir un plan.'
4. *Der groß Eyferer, der sein Weib Beicht hoeret*, Goetze 45; *Decameron* 7, 5: 'La précaution inutile'.
5. *Der farend Schuler mit dem Teuffel pannen*, Goetze 3 124–35.
6. Goetze 57; 'Alten Weibes List' in *Gesammtabenteuer* édition Friedrich Heinrich von der Hagen, 3 vols (J.G. Cotta'scher Verlag, Stuttgart et Tübingen, 1850: nachdruck Wissenschaftliche Buchgesellschaft, Darmstadt, 1961) *1* no. 9, 189–207.
7. Goetze 23; *Decameron* 8, 10: 'Liaison dangereuse'.
8. Goetze 46;. *Decameron*, 7, 4.
9. Goetze 84; *Decameron* 9, 1.
10. Goetze 54; *Gesammtabenteuer* no. 38.
11. Goetze 26; *Decameron* 9, 9: 'Le Pont de l'Oie'.
12. Cf. note 7.
13. Cf. note 8.

14. *Fastnachtspiele aus dem 15. Jahrhundert* édition [Heinrich] Adelbert von Keller (Bibliothek des litterarischen Vereins in Stuttgart 28–30, 46: Stuttgart, 1853–1858; Wissenschaftliche Buchgesellschaft, Darmstadt 1965–1966) 46, Bd. 1, 351–8; Dieter Wuttke *Fastnachtspiele des 15. und 16. Jahrhunderts* (Reclam, Universal Bibliothek 9415[6], Stuttgart, 1973) 13–20.
15. *Fastnachtspiel* édition Eckehard Catholy (Sammlung Metzler 56: Metzler, Stuttgart, 1966).
16. Hanns Fischer *Die deutsche Märendichtung des 15. Jahrhunderts* (Münchener Texte und Untersuchungen deutschen litteratur Mittelalters 12: München, 1966) A 13, 520–25.
17. H.A. von Keller *Fastnachtspiele 2* 85, 696–9; Wuttke *Fastnachtspiele* 8–12.
18. H.A. von Keller *Fastnachtspiele 1* 30, 247–51; Wuttke *Fastnachtspiele* 27–33.
19. H.A. von Keller *Fastnachtspiele 1* 32, 258–63; Wuttke *Fastnachtspiele* 82–90.
20. Hanns Fischer *Die deutsche Märendichtung* 268–73.
21. J.-C. Aubailly *Le monologue, le dialogue et la sottie, essai sur quelques genres dramatiques de la fin du moyen âge et du début du 16e siècle* (Champion, Paris, 1976).
22. 'Die bîchte', *Gesammtabenteuer* no. 44.

HOCKTIDE:
A Reassessment of a Popular Pre-Reformation Festival
Sally-Beth MacLean

One of the least noticed but more widespread annual folk festivals in pre-Reformation England was held on the second Monday and Tuesday after Easter, a period known as 'Hocktide'. Reference to this event is most often found in guides to calendar customs such as Hazlitt's *Faiths and Folklore*, where a summary account of the festival will include scattered references from medieval and Renaissance parish accounts, sometimes mingled with much later descriptions of the custom as it was revived in the eighteenth and nineteenth centuries.[1]

One of the more recent standard works in this field is A.R. Wright's *British Calendar Customs: England*, which can serve as a starting-point for reassessing the evidence for Hocktide.[2] While noting a 1450 document that suggests that Hocktide was 'a time for unbridled sport and merriment', Wright focuses on the more sober side of the festival, which he defines as 'the season for tripping up and binding in order to enforce payment of dues'.[3] These dues were collected for local parish church repairs or other charitable purposes, and for this reason Hock gatherings are commonly featured in parish churchwardens' accounts. As Wright remarks, the accounts show clearly that the women were more effective fund-raisers, sometimes extracting from their victims three or four times the amount gained by the men. Before the Reformation the women bound the men who passed by on one day and the men reversed the process on the other, but after the Reformation there was an attempt to confine the sport of taking captives by the substitution of ropes or chains set across roadways for the physical binding of passers-by. Despite evidence to the contrary from his earlier sources, Wright assigns Tuesday to the women, probably influenced by some later antiquarians also quoted.

Other local observances mentioned by Wright in the context of Hocktide are wrestling matches in Cornwall (cited by the eighteenth-century poet Chatterton), and plays at Dursley, Gloucestershire, before 1760. Hock Tuesday also had legal significance as a Quarter Day when rents and other payments were due. A suggestion of this tradition blended with the festive game element can still be found at Hungerford in Berkshire, where colourfully appointed 'tutti-men' chosen by the Hocktide Court of Feoffees patrol the town collecting penny tolls from the men and kisses from the women.[4]

While Wright refers to plays at Dursley, he does not mention the Hock Tuesday Play performed at Coventry in the later Middle Ages and Renaissance. This play, which will be discussed in more detail below, had as its subject matter the defeat of

233

the Danes by Saxon women, a shadowy historical event that has given rise to inconclusive speculation about the origins and etymological derivations of Hocktide.

Wright prudently omits speculation about the origins of the festival, but antiquarians such as Brand and Ellis set forth puzzling alternatives that have so far failed to satisfy anyone.[5] One proposal is that Hocktide is a commemorative – even mimetic – festival celebrating the massacre of the Danes in the reign of Ethelred on St Brice's Day 1002. The fact that St Brice's Day fell on 13 November somewhat confounds the plausibility of this theory, but the other proposal is no more convincing. Not until the death of Hardicanute in 1041 were the English released in any real sense from Danish dominance – his sudden expiry at a wedding feast has allowed the conjectural link between the term 'Hocktide' and the Middle Dutch word for 'high time, festival, wedding', a derivation that the *OED* dismisses as 'out of the question'.[6] In addition, Hardicanute died on 8 June, well beyond the traditional Easter season.

Whatever the origins of the term, there is no doubt that Hock Day or Hock Tuesday occurs as early as c.1175 in its status as an important term-day on which rents were paid.[7] Evidence for a folk festival over a two-day period is cited from the fifteenth century onwards and, apart from a lapse in the seventeenth century, variations of the custom have continued into the modern era. At the heart of the festivities was the ransom taken by various means from members of the opposite sex with women and men taking the lead on alternate days. There has also been some notice made of plays performed at Hocktide, most remarkably the Coventry Hock Tuesday Play which was performed in 1575 for Elizabeth I at Kenilworth.

In reassessing the evidence for this or any other popular festival at a distance of five centuries or so, it is vital to bear in mind the limitations on the attempt. The older the custom, the more obscure its origins will be. Sixteenth-century antiquarians were no more inhibited about speculative derivations than their Victorian counterparts, yet they do have the advantage, for our purposes, of being contemporary observers. The chances of the folk keeping written records of their own popular culture in the medieval period are slight, although iconography in local parish churches can sometimes give us a glimpse of their activities. Where a folk custom brought expense or profit to the local church, there may be accounts surviving to prove it. Here the odds favour equally the deterioration or destruction of centuries and the taciturnity of medieval churchwardens who sometimes preferred – for obvious reasons – the hastily-written summary account. Otherwise, written records were more likely kept when conflict with authorities developed and episcopal statutes or court cases ensued. Folk plays that may have been performed at popular medieval festivals were the least likely candidates for written transmission, although reference to their performances may turn up in the form of expenses for costumes or profits taken, if a parish or guild sponsored the event.

What more, then, can we learn about the Hocktide festival in medieval and Tudor England? Research in local records organised by the Records of Early English

Drama project does offer a fresh opportunity to survey the contemporary evidence and set aside more detailed descriptions of the post-Restoration festivity that may distract us from what pre-1642 records can tell us. I am not questioning here the validity of Peter Burke's approach to the study of early modern European popular culture; as he says, there is 'a strong case for writing the history of popular culture backwards and for using the late eighteenth century as a base from which to consider the more fragmentary evidence from the seventeenth and sixteenth centuries'.[8] Some of the more recent material can be used in a responsible critical way to suggest 'connections between elements which can themselves be documented for the period being studied, or for making sense of descriptions which are so allusive or elliptical that they do not make sense by themselves'.[9] Nonetheless, my purpose is to focus here on the records from the earlier period, as contemporary witnesses to Hocktide in its original context, one of several significant folk festivals set within the supportive framework of the pre-Reformation church calendar.

The earliest references remain the 1406 and 1409 proclamations in *London Letterbook I*: *Qe null persone di ceste Citee ... teygne, ou constreyne ascun persone ... deinz meason ou de'hors pur hokkyng lundy ne marsdy proscheins appelles Hokkedayes* ('that no person of this city ... should hold or constrain any person ... in their house or outside for hocking on Monday or Tuesday next, called hockdays': fol. 49ᵛ).[10] If it is not immediately clear why the London authorities would move against this activity, the next relevant document is more revealing. John Carpenter, the Bishop of Worcester in 1450, was more specific about the 'noxious corruptions' of Hocktide:

> vno certo die heu vsitato. hoc Solempni festo paschatis transacto ? mulieres homines. Alioque die homines mulieres ligare ac cetera media vtinam non inhonesta vel deteriorare facere m[enti]untur. et excretere lucrum ecclesie fingentes. Sed dampnum anime Sub fucato colore lucrantes. quorum occasione plura oriuntur Scandala. Adulteriaque. & Alia crimina committuntur enormia in dei manifestam offensam ...[11]

> 'on one particular accustomed day, alas, when that solemn Feast of Easter has passed, women make a show of tying up men and on another day men [make a show of tying up] women, and of doing other means (provocative things?), would that they were not immoral or worse, and pretending to collect money for the church, but gaining the loss of the soul under this cosmetic colour, by the occasion of which things many scandals arise, and adulteries and other gross misdemeanours are committed, in a manifest transgression against God ...'

The familiar elements are present – the binding of the opposite sex over a two-day period, with ransoms extracted for the profits of the church – but the festive excesses, whether of sex or violence, are reminiscent of those associated with the better-known English May Games or even the continental pre-Lenten Carnival.[12]

SALLY-BETH MACLEAN

By 1455, local parish accounts from Hock gatherings begin to survive, the first from St Margaret's, Southwark. At this point in REED's march across the counties of England Hocktide's evidence comes from the south and centre of the country, not because hocking was unknown in the north, but because Northumberland and Yorkshire have not been surveyed yet. In the North-West, itemised parish records for Cumberland/Westmorland do not exist. From a variety of parishes with known hocking accounts, it is possible to choose one as representative, in this case, St Mary's, Lambeth.

The church of St Mary lies beside the palace of the Archbishop of Canterbury, facing the Thames and Westminster beyond. The parish account book starts in 1504 and from the first year until 1557 there are regular receipts from the Hocktide gatherings of men and women.[13] At Lambeth the women apparently took their captives on Monday, but local practice did vary: at Southwark just a few miles downstream, the St Margaret's women hocked on Tuesday.[14] Here as elsewhere, the women were the more formidable captors: their profits are typically two or three times the amount raised by the men. The organisers of the women, or 'wives' as they are often designated, may have been women of considerable status in the parish: in the 1518/19 accounts, the two churchwardens' wives are specified as responsible for delivering the profits.[15] In another instance, when the otherwise dry accounts hint at domestic crisis, a churchwarden's wife, Mistress Bever, has control of the gathering money and refuses to relinquish it. For a couple of years, gloomy note is made under 'Debts Owing' of the 13s 4d hock money for 1517, not paid until 1521/2 when Bever was no longer churchwarden.[16] The status of the men who participated in Hock gatherings is not revealed by these accounts, although specific reference is made at St Laurence, Reading, to 'bachelors' or young men and it is possible that Hocktide provided an opportunity, like the Robin Hood or Summer Lord Games, for the young men of the parish to release energy in a positive festive context.[17]

The ransom taken was not just from parishioners or regular visitors to the village. At Greenwich, the women hocked the King one year, collecting 6s 8d from Henry VII in 1505/6.[18]

Not mentioned in the Lambeth accounts, but cited in a number of others, are expenses for feasting associated with Hocktide. At Allhallows, Staining, for example, the parish laid out 3s 4d for bread, meat, cheese, and a harper at the 'drinking' when the wives had gathered money.[19] It is worth noticing that it is the women who have the feast. In some places and in some years only their hock receipts are listed, but even in years when both men and women participate, it is typically the women who gain the greater profit and drink the ale.[20] This does call to mind one much later description, of the women's day at Birmingham:

> Many a time have I passed along the streets inhabited by the lower orders of people, and seen parties of jolly matrons assembled round tables on which stood a foaming tankard of ale. There they sat in all the pride of absolute sovereignty, and woe the luckless man that dared to invade their prerogatives!

As sure as he was seen he was pursued – as sure as he was pursued he was taken – and as sure as he was taken he was heaved and kissed, and compelled to pay sixpence for 'leave and license' to depart.[21]

Corroborative evidence from our period for the women's zeal in pursuit comes from a Shrewsbury notice of a 1549 accident when two men hiding from hocking women were 'Smootherd vnder the castell hill' when part of the hill fell on them.[22]

Parish accounts, with their predictable focus on finances over description, have little else to tell us about Hocktide. So far, at least, revealing court cases have not been discovered, although there are a couple of documents that have more to say about local practices. One of these is the Town Minute Book of Wallingford in Berkshire, where an apparently lavish dance was held on Hock Tuesday until 1538. In the following year the town burgesses agreed to abolish the dance because of the 'sumptyous Costes' involved in borrowing raiment for the dancers.[23] This may be the only instance of dancing associated with this festival.

Another traditional element of festival may be peculiar to one location as well. Despite the Hocktide plays noted by Wright at Dursley in Gloucestershire, there is no evidence for such drama surviving from the period before 1642.[24] Regretfully, we must admit that the REED survey indicates, at its midway point, that the play at Coventry may have been unique. The Coventry evidence is the closest we are likely to come to a 'play text'; while very few of the Coventry parish records survive – and none of relevance to this study – there is a remarkable document from 1575, written by an eyewitness to the performance of the Coventry Hock Tuesday play before the Queen at Kenilworth. Robert Laneham's letter describes this play as an 'olld storiall sheaw' presented by local amateurs led by a town mason, Captain Cox.[25] The 'historical' subject of the play was the massacre of the Danes on St Brice's Day 1002: Danish mercenaries on horseback held mock combat with English forces on foot carrying alder poles, until English women arrived to carry the day, taking the Danes captive. This action is reminiscent of other rough-and-tumble English folk combat plays: the 'rymez' alluded to by Laneham were probably orally transmitted and formed a fluid text that was less important to the entertainment than the action itself.[26] The play is described by Laneham as 'woont too bee plaid in oour Citee yeerely: without ill exampl of mannerz, papistry, or ony superstition ...'[27] A unique annal, transcribed by the antiquarian Thomas Sharp but now lost, dates the origin of this play at Coventry as 1416, but between that date and 1561 when the play was first put down there is no further mention of it in the admittedly incomplete civic records.[28]

Clearly, the Coventry play falls into the category of medieval folk drama performed within a festive seasonal context. The decisive rôle played by the women in capturing the Danes parallels the aggressive binding game played by women in parishes across the country at Hocktide. In no other location, however, is the historical theme of the action recorded and we may reasonably ask whether the binding game with its rôle reversals on adjacent days was consciously imitating the rout of the Danes. As we have seen earlier, St Brice's Day in November does not sit easily with a commemoration in the post-Easter season of Hocktide.

E.K. Chambers discusses Hocktide in his chapter on 'Festival Play' and cites it along with other spring folk customs or *ludi* linked with primitive rituals of sacrifice.[29] While noting the historical associations of the play at Coventry, Chambers comments: '... I think it may be taken for granted that, as in the Lady Godiva procession, the historical element is comparatively a late one, which has been grafted upon already existing festival customs'.[30] Is Hocktide, then, another example of myth invented to explain pre-existing ritual, such as St John the Baptist's association with Midsummer?[31]

In discussing Renaissance French youth groups and charivaris, Natalie Davis makes an observation relevant to this topic: 'Nor were these activities, as E.K. Chambers and others have claimed, a mere playing with primitive and magical customs of forgotten meaning. Rather they were a carnival treatment of reality, with an important function in the village'.[32] The economic purpose of Hocktide has already been illustrated from parish accounts. That it had a practical function to perform in this area is well summed up by the alternative measures taken by the church of St Laurence, Reading, in 1572/3 when Hock, May, Whitsun, and other gatherings were suspended by the authorities: an annual levy for seat rentals was established to replace the income lost.[33]

Like other popular customs such as Whitsun Ales, however, Hocktide had a social purpose as well as an economic one. In England, at least, it offered occasion for release after a long Lent, in the first of the spring folk festivals, dated with reference to the ecclesiastical calendar and justified to the authorities as a fund-raising event for the parish. Its ritual links lie outside the church, with customs associated with the carnival spirit. The functions outlined by Burke for Carnival apply to Hocktide as well: outdoor entertainment in warmer weather; a communal celebration organised by the people rather than by church or civic authorities; an opportunity for different groups (in this case different sexes) to compete with one another in a variation on the mock battle or siege also popular in the mumming tradition; and finally and perhaps most importantly, a cathartic release of social tension channelled through ritualised inversion of the hierarchical social order that is characteristic of the Middle Ages.[34] Hocktide performed all these functions and, if we are to believe the 1450 Worcester document ordering its suppression, incorporated the key elements of continental Carnival – food, sex, and violence.

The identification of Hocktide as an inversion-of-order ritual deserves more attention. Rather than continuing to explain the hocking custom as a mimetic game re-enacting a somewhat obscure historical event, we should follow the clues in surviving contemporary records that lead to a conclusion that this was predominately a woman's festival, with the sexual rôles reversed and the women in command: organising, pursuing, and feasting. Natalie Davis again has something relevant to say in this context, from her study of 'Women on Top': 'Play with the unruly woman is partly a chance for temporary release from the traditional and stable hierarchy; but it is also part of the conflict over efforts to change the basic distribution of power within society'.³⁵ Hocktide may provide some evidence of this conflict, but in the medieval context at least, it does not seem to have been an agent of social change. Rather it was another example of status-reversal rituals that reaffirm 'the hierarchical principle' as described by Victor Turner, who argues that such rituals 'lead to "an ecstatic experience", an enhanced sense of community, followed by a "sober return" to the normal social structure'.³⁶ It is also worth noting that the Hocktide season falls immediately before or during the month of May, Flora's month, thought to be 'a period in which women were powerful, their desires at their most immoderate'.³⁷ Just as the May and Whitsun games served a useful function in channelling the energies of the young unmarried men of the parish who played a dominant festive rôle, so Hocktide may have given a similar opportunity to women.

In light of these associations with license, disorder, and even paganism, it should not be surprising that Hocktide fell victim to social and religious changes at the Reformation. The distaste felt by the fifteenth-century Bishop of Worcester for the physical excesses and moral corruption of Hocktide would have found sympathy with the Puritans of the seventeenth century. Although Philip Stubbes does not mention the hocking festival among the abuses in his *Anatomie*, a general comment on festivals from this source can act as its opponents' epilogue:

> ... wherfore shuld the whole towne, parish, village and cuntrey, keepe one and the same day, and make such gluttonous feasts as they doo; And therfore, to conclude, they are to no end, except it be to draw a great frequencie of whores, drabbes, theiues, and verlets together, to maintaiue [sic] whordome, bawdrie, gluttony, drunkennesse, thiefte, murther, swearing and all kind of mischief and abhomination. For, these be the ends wherto these feastes, and wakesses doo tende.³⁸

Records of Early English Drama, Toronto

NOTES

1. See W. Carew Hazlitt *Faiths and Folklore of the British Isles* 2 vols (Reeves and Turner, London, 1905; reprinted New York, 1965) *1* 316–18; and Joseph Strutt *The Sports and Pastimes of the People of England* edited J. Charles Cox (Methuen, London, 1903) 274–5.
2. A.R. Wright *British Calendar Customs, England* (Publications of the Folk-Lore Society 97: London, 1936) 124–9.
3. Wright 124.
4. See, for example, a more recent account of the Hungerford custom by Christina Hole in *A Dictionary of British Folk Customs* (Hutchinson, London, 1976) 146–8.
5. See John Brand and Sir Henry Ellis *Observations on the Popular Antiquities of Great Britain* (Bohn, London, 1849) 185, 189.
6. *OED* s.v. *Hock-day*, with reference to Middle Dutch *hogetide, hoochtide*.

7. The *OED* and other standard sources cite the Caen Cartulary (Paris, Bibliothèque Nationale: MS Lat. 5650) fol.54^v, as the earliest occurrence for this usage of *Hock-day*.
8. Peter Burke *Popular Culture in Early Modern Europe* (Temple Smith, London, 1978) 82.
9. Burke 83.
10. As quoted by the *OED* s.v. *Hock* 2; the full text of both proclamations is translated by Henry Thomas Riley in *Memorials of London and London Life in the XIIIth, XIVth, and XVth Centuries* (Longmans, London, 1868) 561 and 571.
11. From the notebook of John Lawarn (Bodleian Library, MS Bodley 692, fol 163^v): see *REED: Herefordshire/Worcestershire* edited David N. Klausner (University of Toronto Press, 1990) 349–50. The conventions of transliteration and the translation are not precisely those provided by this volume.
12. For an analysis of the 'world of Carnival', see Burke 178–204.
13. St Mary's Churchwardens' Accounts at the Minet Library, Lambeth: P/1/1, fols 2–54. The accounts begin in 1504 and then jump to 1514; between 1523 and 1554, the entries are summary and hocking receipts are not recorded. All the Hocktide references will be published in my edition of Surrey records for REED (now in progress). A full edition of the parish accounts was published by Charles Drew *Lambeth Churchwardens' Accounts, 1504–1645, and Vestry Book, 1610* 2 vols (Surrey Record Society, London, 1941–1950).
14. See St Margaret's, Southwark, Churchwardens' Accounts: Greater London Record Office, P92/SAV/1, pages 8, 12 (also to be published in the Surrey collection).
15. Minet Library P/1/1, fol 19: '*Receyved* of the Gaderyng of the wardens weyffis on hoke mondaye viij s iij d'.
16. There is no hocking receipt from the women in 1517/1518. 13s 4d is noted as owing under 1518/1519 (fol 22^v) and 1519/20 (fol 26), with the debt finally paid by Bever's wife in 1521/1522 (fol 30^v).
17. See, for example, St Laurence, Reading, Churchwardens' Accounts: Berkshire Record Office D/P 97 5/2, page 16 (1503/1504 expenses, to be published in Alexandra F. Johnston's Berkshire collection for REED, in progress):
    Item for mete & drynk at hoktyde to the Wyvis soper   xviij d
    Item for mete & drynk þe same tyme to þe bachelers soper   xij d
    The rôle of male youth groups in Renaissance festive customs has been analysed by Natalie Zemon Davis in 'The Reasons of Misrule: Youth Groups and Charivaris in Sixteenth-Century France' *Past and Present* 50 (1971) 41–75.
18. The Greenwich hocking entry comes from the Privy Purse Expenses of Henry VII, quoted by Hazlitt 1, 317. There is a payment by Henry VIII to the wives at Lambeth in 1521/1522 that may be related, although the exact day of their gathering is not indicated in the accounts (see Minet Library: P/1/1, fol 32^v).
19. All Hallows, Staining, Churchwardens' Accounts: London Guildhall MS 4956/1, fol 6^v, 1491/1492 expenses (to be published in Mary Erler's collection of London parishes for REED, in progress).
20. See, for example, St Mary at Hill, London, Churchwardens' Accounts: Guildhall MS 1239/1 part 1, fols 163^v, 165 where the wives collect 14s 6d. and are feasted with beef, bread and ale at a cost of 1s. 2d. The men gathered 6s. in this year (1499).
21. Roy Palmer *The Folklore of Warwickshire* (Batsford, London, 1976) 158.
22. Shrewsbury School Library: Dr Taylor's MS History, fol. 68^v, published in *REED: Shropshire* edited J. Alan B. Somerset (University of Toronto Press, 1994) 202.

23. Wallingford Town Minute Book: Berkshire Record Office W/ACa 1, fol. 55^v (to be published in Johnston's Berkshire collection for REED).
24. The surviving dramatic records for Gloucestershire before 1642 have been published by Peter Greenfield in *REED: Cumberland/Westmorland/ Gloucestershire* edited Audrey Douglas and Peter Greenfield (University of Toronto Press, 1986). The Dursley plays must post-date this period.
25. Robert Laneham *A Letter: Whearin, part of the entertainment vntoo the Queenz Maiesty, at Killingworth Castl in Warwik Sheer in this Soomerz Progress 1575. iz signified ...* (STC: 15191: facsimile reprint, Scolar Press, Menston, 1968) 32.
26. Thomas Pettitt, in a personal letter, has suggested to me that 'The action of the Coventry show parallels not so much the mummers' plays, which usually involve duels between two swordsmen, as other customs involving a *melée* of numerous warriors, like the Irish wake-games "Sir Sopin" and "The Defense of the Fort".' I am also grateful to Mr Pettitt for pointing out a continental analogue to the English hocking custom. This competitive sexual game was not seasonal, but rather was played at weddings in several variations. These are described by Tyndal Roper '"Going to Church and Street": Weddings in Reformation Augsburg' *Past and Present* 106 (1985) 92, drawing from the sixteenth-century *Weltbüch, Spiegel vnd bildtnisz des gantzen erdtbodens* by Sebastian Franck. The closest variant involved the bride and other young women holding the young men to ransom in what Roper terms 'a fascinating reversal of the carnival custom at Nuremburg where nubile women who had not married that year were forced to "pull the plough" (*Eggenziehen*) through the streets'.
27. Laneham *A Letter* 33.
28. See *REED: Coventry* edited R.W. Ingram (University of Toronto Press, 1981) xx, 7, and 542.
29. E.K. Chambers *The Mediaeval Stage* 2 vols (Oxford University Press, London, 1903) *1* 154–9.
30. Chambers 155.
31. See Burke 180–1 for a discussion of ritual influencing myth in festivals associated with St John the Baptist at Midsummer and Robin Hood in May.
32. Davis 'Reasons of Misrule' 53.
33. St Laurence, Reading, Churchwardens' Accounts: Berkshire Record Office D/P 97 5/2 page 349.
34. Burke 199–204.
35. Davis 'Women on Top' in *Society and Culture in Early Modern France* (Stanford University Press, 1975) 131.
36. Victor Turner, as quoted by Burke 201.
37. Davis 'Women on Top' 141.
38. Philip Stubbes *The Anatomie of Abuses* with preface by Arthur Freeman (Garland, London and New York, 1993 reprint of London edition by R. Jones, 1583) sig M7. *STC* no. 23376.

'SLAWPASE FRO THE MYLN-WHELE':
Seeing between the Lines
Malcolm Jones

The relatively neglected *First Shepherds' Play* of the Wakefield Pageants in the Towneley Plays[1] seems to divide into two halves: the knockabout comedy of the argument over the imaginary sheep and of the grotesque feast of the 'secular half' of the play, followed by the more serious playing-out of the Gospel account of the Annunciation to the Shepherds and their Adoration of the Infant.

The folly of the argument between the First and Second Shepherds over the sheep which the First Shepherd imagines he has already bought is forcefully demonstrated to them by the Third Shepherd (nicknamed 'Slowpace')[2] who empties a sack of meal he has just brought from the mill onto the ground before them,[3] and then compares the empty sack to their heads, similarly empty of wits.[4] At this point, a fourth character named Iak Garcio speaks, whose epithet and tone seem to characterise him as the traditional impudent servant, like Garcio (nicknamed 'Pikeharnes'), Abel's servant in the Towneley *Killing of Abel*. Iak's comment on the folly of all three is:

> Sagh I neuer none so fare bot the foles of Gotham.   180

After the 'lawe' of the meal-sack, the Third Shepherd, probably punning on the still current idiom of 'gathering one's wits',[5] orders them to

> Geder vp
> And seke it agane!   173–4

At this point I believe that they do, indeed, begin to gather up the meal and put it back in the sack. There is a – probably deliberate – confusion over the concord of *wyttys* in the previous line, so that *it* can still punningly refer to their wits as well as to the spilt meal, though the *up* of *geder up* does seem to relate to the actual physical process of gathering the meal up from the ground, and *seke* probably has the primary sense, 'sack', i.e. 'put into a sack', though doubtless also puns on *seek*, implying that the two must 'seek' to rediscover their wits. An important difference between this episode and its later appearance in the jestbooks (including the *Merie tales of the mad men of Gotam*),[6] is that in our play the meal is at least able to be gathered up, and not lost irretrievably by being poured into a stream, as in the printed versions.[7]

We know that Slowpace, the Third Shepherd, has a horse with him, for at line 164 he says, 'Hold ye my mare', and then asks one of the two to throw the meal-sack onto his back. Assuming he enters on horseback, it seems unlikely that he has not dismounted by this point – though there are no stage directions in the unique manuscript – as it would be very difficult to throw a sack of meal onto a rider's shoulders from the ground. Iak Garcio's entrance is placed by the most recent editor of our text at the *end* of the scene with the meal-sack, but I suggest that he enters precisely at the point where he is in time to see the sack over the Third Shepherd's shoulder as he stands by his mare, offering her halter to one of the two shepherds, so that it appears to Iak that Slowpace has walked all the way from the mill with the sack over his shoulder, rather than across his horse's back! Although Iak has witnessed him emptying the meal onto the ground – which, at first sight, might seem reason enough for Iak to think him a fool – I suggest that he then sees the other shepherds gathering it up again, so that, while quite prepared to take the Third Shepherd's word for it that they are fools as well, Iak believes *him* to be manifestly the biggest fool of the three, having apparently himself carried the heavy sack from the mill while leading his mare. As further support for this reading, we might adduce the implications of his name, Slowpace.

It may be that the Third Shepherd does indeed enter on foot, leading his mare, with the sack across its back, as seems to have been Cawley's understanding, to judge from his stage direction, *Enter the Third Shepherd, with a horse carrying a sack of meal*,[8] a perfectly rational procedure if one is worried about the burden to one's beast,[9] but whatever the precise stage mechanics of the scene with the meal-sack, it is my opinion that the Wakefield Master intended here to allude to the well-known folly motif of the 'humane' rider who carries the heavy sack on his shoulders, thinking thereby to save his mount some of the burden.[10] If performance predated the surviving manuscript, which is likely, the play was probably already being acted in the second half of the fifteenth century. By this time, this was already a venerable 'Gothamite' motif, and had been long available in England – as on the Continent – as both literary and, above all, pictorial sources show.

In what must be one of the earliest post-classical lists of the follies of the inhabitants of a particular village or country, an anonymous monk of Peterborough Abbey, at the end of the twelfth century, compiled an unflattering account of the stupidity of the people of Norfolk.[11] Most of the follies he retails were, or were to become, proverbial folklore motifs: e.g. thinking that a dung-beetle is a bird, and a toad a partridge, calling out that one is not there, telling travellers who ask for directions simply to go past the crossroads and then on 'as the crow flies', no matter which town they are asking for, and

> On the days when they go to market, carry(ing) their sacks of grain on their shoulders to save their horses. lines 122–5

This is an ancient and international jest,[12] and has its own motif-number in Stith-Thompson's encyclopaedic *Motif Index of Folk Literature*,[13] where it is J 1874.1, 'Rider takes meal-sack on his shoulders to relieve the ass of his burden', and it is a constituent of Folk-Tale Type 1242A.[14]

MALCOLM JONES

A surprising number of contemporary authors seem quite happy to accept as illustrations of everyday life in the Middle Ages, villagers riding to or from their local mill with their only burden a sack of grain or meal, on their *heads* rather than across their animals' backs! Common sense needs to be invoked at this point – there is no reason to believe that our medieval forebears were any stupider than we are – and a greater familiarity with the medieval sense of humour; furthermore, we should know a motif by the company it keeps. On a mid-fourteenth-century monumental brass of Flemish manufacture in the church of King's Lynn in Norfolk,[15] for example, we find our motif with birds of a similar feather: the mounted knight who flees before the threatening horns of a snail,[16] and the man who carries his horse,[17] rather than it him.

The example of the motif on a Bristol misericord of 1520[18] (see Fig. 1) is next to another depicting a man riding his horse back to front,[19] while a third nearby depicts two men trying to drive a slug forward, one tugging at its lead, the other beating it with a flail: as that most proverbial of poets, John Skelton, put it:

> What can it avayle
> To drive forth a snayle ... ? [20]

Obviously, nothing – it is sheer folly. Curiously, there is another fourteenth-century Norfolk instance, found on one of the cloister bosses of Norwich Cathedral (1318–1330).[21] The King's Lynn brass of c.1349 (see Fig. 2) is of Tournai manufacture, exactly contemporary with another instance of our motif represented in a manuscript of the *Saint Graal*, written and illuminated by Piérart dou Tielt in Tournai in 1351.[22] Other Northern French or Flemish examples known to me are Meermanno-Westreenianum Museum (The Hague) MS 78.D.40, a Missal produced in Amiens in 1323, and British Library MS Stowe 17, a Book of Hours produced probably at Maastricht c.1300.[23] The chronology of these examples might tempt one to suggest a Flemish origin for the pictorialisation of this motif and especially for its introduction into England, were it not for an example carved in stone on the Portail des Libraires of Rouen Cathedral in the thirteenth century,[24] the earliest representation of all those known to me.

Three later Flemish examples (one without the mill), of the second half of the fifteenth century, belong to a fascinating and little-understood class of artefact, the non-religious lead badge.[25] One of these foolish riders (see Fig. 3) is depicted with his head on one side and holding the sack on his head with his left hand, while he makes a gesture with three fingers of his right hand: the gesture is one of derision (presumably self-derision here), as may be seen in an *Ecce Homo* woodcut by Cranach (1509).[26]

The motif continues to be portrayed in the sixteenth century, on a bench end in a Somerset church,[27] for example – in which context it is perhaps to be interpreted as symbolising the folly of unregenerate humankind – and, again in significant company, on the titlepage of a German parodic sermon published in 1524, and

'SLAWPASE FRO THE MYLN-WHELE'

Fig.1: Bristol misericord of 1520. Photo: Malcolm Jones

Fig. 2: King's Lynn brass c.1349: Tournai manufacture.
Illustration after Waller *Monumental Brasses* (1842–64).

Fig. 3: Flemish lead badge
from the collection of J.B. van Beuningen, reproduced with his kind permission.

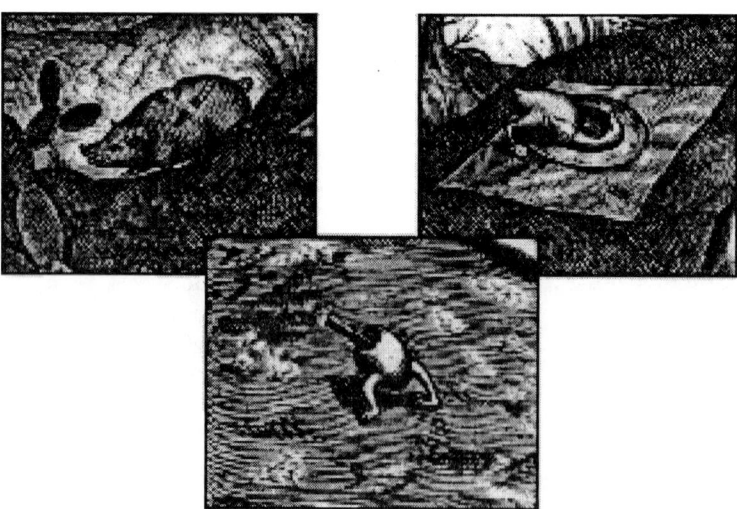

Fig. 4: Roast Pig, Roast Goose, and Perambulating Boiled Egg from
Pieter Brueghel *Luilekkerland*, engraved van der Heyden (1567).
From H. Arthur Klein *Graphic Worlds of Pieter Bruegel the Elder* (London, Dover, 1963) 83.

entitled 'The Sermon of the Wolf to the Geese'.[28] Along the bottom margin plods an obviously weary horse, stumbling under the weight of its rider, who holds a heavy sack in his arms. Horse and rider are surrounded by large flies – a well-attested motif of criticism.[29] The ridiculous horse and rider are further ridiculed by a fool who points at them (or possibly makes the derisive 'horns' gesture)[30] while in the upper corners are two more fools, identified by the familiar ass-eared hoods, and the fact that one, barefoot, carries his club, while the other has only one shoe on, another well-known motif of criticism.[31]

Another late, literary reference to our motif – albeit in slightly variant form – is to be found in Noel du Fail's *Propos Rustiques* (1547). He refers to the

> charretier qui, pour ayder à ses cheuaux attellez à la charette trop chargee, met son chapeau entre son espaule & la roue, pour aucunement (= certainement) les soulager, aucunefois (= quelquefois) beuuant a son baril, attaché au collier du cheual de deuant. [32]

> 'carter who, in order to help his horses which are harnessed to an over-heavy cart, puts his hat between his shoulder and the wheel, in order to lighten their load, from time to time drinking from the barrel which is attached to the collar of the horse in front.'

I believe a familiarity with the images of medieval art is also able to illuminate another reference in the play, namely the Third Shepherd's sententious remark that

> It is far to byd 'hyte'
> To an eg or it go.[33]   150–1

Cawley compares the proverb counselling against 'counting one's chickens before they are hatched', though this is only attested from c.1570 in English. *Far* here is glossed by him as 'absurd', and the whole sentence as 'it is absurd to tell an egg to move before it is even hatched'. It may be absurd, and yet it is twice depicted by Brueghel, both in his 'Netherlandish Proverbs' (more of which below), and in his 'Land of Cockaygne' (1567: see Fig. 4), though I have not so far noted it in any literary description of this very earthly paradise, nor is it in Brueghel's immediate source for his painting, Pieter Baltens' engraving.[34] The notion of urging an egg to walk before it is hatched is, indeed, absurd, and yet it is one of the ultimate 'convenience meals' available on the menu of Schlaraffen-land, as we see in 'Cockaygne', where a soft-boiled egg, already broached and with spoon inserted, waddles about on two legs in the foreground, no doubt advertising its readiness to be eaten by this perambulation, in much the same way as the roast pig in the background, thoughtfully carrying round its own carving knife, or like the 'gees irostid on þe spitte' in the Middle English poem describing the sensual pleasures of the 'lond ihote cokaygne',[35] who squawk out 'gees, al hote! al hot!'

Apart from this poem of c.1300, the theme of the Land of Cockaygne[36] and its constituent motifs is poorly represented in English medieval literature, and even more so in English medieval art, but onomastics comes to the rescue here: the surname *Cocaine* is found in Warwickshire as early as the end of the twelfth century,[37] and seems to imply a familiarity with the topos in England even earlier than the famous allusion to the *abbas Cucaniensis* in the *Carmina Burana*. Already by the thirteenth century, there are two different places called *Cockaynes* in Essex alone,[38] presumably referring to land of such fertility that it hardly needed to be tilled to bring forth abundance, while for the North of England, one Hawisa *de Cokaingne* is named on a Yorkshire assize roll for 1219, and *Cocken* in Lancashire is attested from 1336.[39] Although surnames and placenames preserve the memory of the Land of Cockaygne in England throughout the late Middle Ages in however attenuated a form, it is in the drama that we next make out the outline of its distant shore, from another fleeting allusion. If we allow that the *First Shepherds' Play* does, indeed, refer to one of the constituent motifs of Cockaygne, the mid-sixteenth-century Biblical play *Jacob and Esau* refers to another, closely related:

> I shall with a trice make such meate certain,
> As shall say 'come eat me' [40] 4.1.1031–2

Given that at that date *meat* could refer more generally to 'food', rather than just 'flesh', it is even possible that this could also refer to the egg motif, though when it is next met with, in Jonson's *Tale of a Tub*, it again relates to the self-advertising goose:

> And then, a goose will bid you call
> 'Come cut me'. [41] 3.1.151

It is curious, but doubtless suggestive of the comparative rarity of our motif, that Shakespeare seems to make no mention of it even in passing,[42] unlike many other major Continental writers, e.g. Rabelais's reference to the well-known motif of being paid for sleeping in *Pantagruel*;[43] Sach's poem *Das Schlaweraffenlandt* (c.1530),[44] which has the distinction of giving rise to the first extant illustration of this fabulous land, a woodcut by Erhard Schoen (see Fig. 5); and Brandt's reference to the ready-roasted dove that flies into one's mouth, in chapter 57 of his hugely influential *Narrenschiff* (1494), also included in the woodcut illustration. Perhaps the most significant parallel, however, is to be found in the Melk *Salbenkrämerspiel*, a contemporary and very similar genre of work to our own, in which ready-roasted and seasoned geese waddle up, bread in beak, spit in rump, and carving knife in back.[45]

By 1600, the Middle English 'Cockaygne' was known as 'Lubberland', and the Christmas Revels at St John's College, Oxford in 1607 included an 'Embassage from Lubberland',[46] probably inspired by the appearance earlier that year of Bishop Joseph Hall's satirical *Mundus Alter et Idem*. This must have enjoyed a certain popularity, because it was translated from the Latin two years after publication by John Healey as *Discovery of a New World, or Description of the South Indies, hitherto unknowne*.[47] In 1627, William Hawkins, Master of Hadleigh School, Suffolk, wrote *Apollo Shroving*

'SLAWPASE FRO THE MYLN-WHELE'

Fig. 5: *Das Schlauraffenlandt*: woodcut by Erhard Schoen.
Reprinted by kind permission of the Graphische Sammlung Albertina, Vienna.

for his boys to act on Shrove Tuesday, in which a young sluggard rejoices that he is to be banished to Lubberland:

> I shall earn my fourteen pence a day there by snorting ... It is a fine country. There are rivers of Muscadine, bridges of Brawn, parks of Venison Pasties, paled about with puddings and Sausages ... [48]

For those who have pointed out the debt the modern Mummers' Plays owe to the medieval stage, it is interesting to note such survivals of the motifs we have been discussing as are to be found, for example, in Jack Finney's speech in the Western-sub-Edge play:

> Now my lads we come to the land of plenty, roast stones, plum puddings, houses thatched with pancakes, and little pigs running about with knives and forks stuck in their backs crying, 'Who'll eat me?' [49]

The *Prima Pastorum* is particularly rich in material of popular origin; we have examined the Cockaygne and Gothamite folktale motifs, and the relevance of secular art in their elucidation, but not yet looked in detail at any of the many proverbs that encapsulate folk wisdom[50] and are liberally distributed throughout the play. Slowpace, the would-be wise Shepherd, is a dispenser of proverbial wisdom, a trait which is perhaps hinted at in his very nickname, for, according to a contemporary piece of physiognomic lore,

> Whoso hath the Paas large and slow, he is wyse and wel spedynge in al his dedys ... [51]

In addition to attempting to point up the absurdity of the other two Shepherds' actions, by his demonstration with the meal-sack, and by comparing their behaviour to yet another folk-tale, that of the 'Mowll that went by the way',[52] he further reproaches them with a brace of proverbs, the first of which is:

> Ye fysh before the nett [53]   139

In 1559, a century or so after the date of our play, Pieter Brueghel, that great observer of the folk and folk-ways, painted this remarkable 'anthology picture', usually known as 'The Netherlandish Proverbs', which might well be seen as a bird's eye view of well over one hundred proverbial follies acted out by the villagers of a Flemish Gotham, and indeed, the sign on the building which dominates the left-hand side of the painting is an obviously symbolic inverted globe, for this is the World Turned Upside Down. In the top right-hand corner of his 'Allegory of Temperance' drawn the following year, of especial interest to the student of medieval theatre, he depicted a *rederijker* Morality play: on a trestle stage before a curtain two actors labelled 'Faith' and 'Hope' are speaking, while above them, hanging from a pole, the sign of the inverted globe appears again, and round the curtain peers a fool in ass-eared hood with marotte in hand. Our own Thomas Nashe, the Elizabethan writer, remarked on a similar and evidently popular inn sign of his day (c.1590):

> It is no maruaile if euery Ale house vaunt the table of the world upside downe, since the child beateth his father, and the Asse whippeth his Master.[54]

But to return to the 'Netherlandish Proverbs': in the middle of the picture we see a river across which a net is stretched, forming a barrier behind which a man is attempting to fish from a small boat with a hand-held net. From the direction in which the barrier-net is bellying out, we can tell that the stream is flowing from right to left, which therefore means that the would-be fisherman compounds his folly by not only 'fishing before the net' but also 'striving against the stream'.[55] This familiar proverb, I submit, explains the hitherto inadequately understood line which immediately follows on from the Third Shepherd's first proverb. The manuscript reads:

> And stryfe on this bett   140

which Cawley emends (rightly in my opinion, but for the wrong reason) to

> And stryfe on this flett

suggesting that the manuscript reading is 'possibly a corruption of *flett*, "floor"'.[56] Clearly this line must present another folly as proverbially foolish as 'fishing before the net' – this, I suggest, is the 'striving against the stream', where *on* has the sense it may sometimes have of 'against',[57] and *flett* is a spelling of *fleet*, 'stream'.[58] It has not before been suggested the Brueghel painting also depicts the folly of 'striving against the stream',[59] but Brueghel is a master of the significant detail, and this particular detail has simply not been remarked before (in common with several others); if my interpretation of the conjunction of the two proverbs in both sources can be accepted, it is interesting testimony to the way in which a fifteenth-century play and a sixteenth-century painting may be mutually illuminating.

It has long been appreciated that the Wakefield Master included several local allusions in his plays: in our play, for example, he has the Second Shepherd refer favourably to the 'good ayll of hely', i.e. the village of Healey, some four miles south-west of Wakefield,[60] between Ossett and Horbury, itself mentioned in the *Second Shepherds' Play*[61] – and it is not difficult to imagine the natives of Healey sending up a cheer at this point, out of pride at their local brew. If my interpretation of the word *flett* as *fleet*, i.e. 'stream', is accepted, then we need to remind ourselves of the word which immediately precedes it, *this*. '*This* fleet' suggests that there is a stream envisaged as close at hand, and one which the Third Shepherd may well indicate at this point: it is even possible that, as in the Gotham tales, he empties the meal from the sack directly into 'this fleet', though I still believe that the *up* of the instruction 'geder up' implies that the meal is shaken out onto the ground, from where the two shepherds begin to collect it up again. It would not be possible to identify the 'fleet' in question definitively, though perhaps we are intended to think it is the same stream that powers the 'mylnwhele' from which, we are told, Slowpace has just come. (There was a *mylne of Wakfeld* mentioned in a document of 1538, and a *moldendini de Wakefeld* as early as c.1225.)[62] A further possible local allusion might be preserved in the name of a field in Wakefield, called in a Survey of 1608, *Sheprote land*,[63] which reminds us of the opening of our play in which the First Shepherd tells us of his plight, which is, after all, the mainspring of the action in that it leads directly to the argument over the imaginary sheep:

>   All my shepe ar gone,
>   I am not left oone,
>   The rott has theym slone ...   24–6

CECTAL, University of Sheffield

NOTES

1. All line numbers etc. are cited from *The Wakefield Pageants in the Towneley Cycle* edited A.C. Cawley (Manchester University Press, 1958). Since this paper was originally written, there has been a new edition of *The Towneley Cycle* by M. Stevens and A.C. Cawley *EETS SS 13* and *14* (1994).
2. *Slawpase* sounds like an ideal name for a slug or snail: compare 'Limax ... crepeþ, þough it be wiþ slowe paas', cited s.v. *pas(e)* 2 *(e)* in *Middle English Dictionary* edited H. Kurath and others (University of Michigan Press, Ann Arbor, 1954–). At sense 6 *(a)*, M.E.D. lists some parallels: *Petipas* (1191, 1299, 1342) and *Smalpas* (1377–80). I add from J. Jönsjö *Studies on Middle English Nicknames 1: Compounds* (Lund Studies in English 55: Gleerup, Lund, 1979) *Slafot* (1379) i.e. 'Slowfoot'.
3. I attempt to justify this assertion below by close examination of the text.
4. An interesting parallel to the parable of the meal-sack may be found in the report of the *ommegang* which took place in Antwerp on 15 August 1563, in which there walked *iemand met de meulen in de hand, bestoven zijnde met de meelbuidel, omdat zulke haar wijsheid verloren hebben* ('someone with a mill in his hand, dusty with the meal-pouch, because such (people) have lost all their wisdom'). See *Ordinantie van de nieu Punten van onser Vrouwen Ommeghanck half Oogst 1563* (Hans de Laet, Antwerp, 1563).
5. The first attestation of this idiom I have found, however, dates from 1533: see R.W. Dent *Proverbial Language in English Drama Exclusive of Shakespeare, 1495–1616: An Index* (California University Press, Berkeley and Los Angeles, 1984) W 583.11. See also *Middle English Dictionary* s.v. *gaderen* 2 *(e)* *(b)*, from a text of c.1440: 'If þou ... had ... þi mynd gedirde to-gedire & not distracte'. (Note, however, that neither citation uses the word *up*.) For the sense of *lawe* here (162) see *Middle English Dictionary* s.v. *lawe* 10 *(c)*: 'authoritative instruction, magistral teaching'. The quotation is from lines 174–5.
6. The earliest extant version of the book is the unique copy at Harvard, dated to c.1565 (STC 1020.5), and edited by S.J. Kahrl as *A.B. of Phisike Doctour: Merie Tales of the Mad Men of Gotam* (Northwestern University Press, Evanston, 1965). The title-page states that the tales were 'Gathered together by A.B. of Phisike Doctour', conventionally taken to be Andrew Boorde (died 1549). However, the first appearance in print of the argument over the imaginary sheep and the lesson of the meal-sack is as Tale xxiv, entitled 'Of the .iii. wyse men of gotam', in *A Hundred Mery Talys* published by John

Rastell in 1526, conveniently available in *A Hundred Merry Tales and other Jestbooks of the Fifteenth and Sixteenth Centuries* edited P.M. Zall (University of Nebraska Press, Lincoln, 1963) 87-8.

7. *Pace* M.M. Morgan '"High Fraud" in Shepherds' Plays' *Speculum* 39 (1964) 680, see below for my contention that there is, indeed, 'indication in the dialogue of water near at hand', though I would agree with her that there is 'no obvious reason why the others should not collect most of it and put it back in the sack at the words ... "Geder up / And seke it agane!"'. Cawley also seems to imply a belief in the reality of the gathering up of the spilt meal: see 'Iak Garcio of the *Prima Pastorum*' in *Modern Language Notes* 68 (1953) 171, though his main thesis in this paper, that Iak Garcio and the Third Shepherd are one and the same character has, rightly in my opinion, been rejected. See further Rosemary Woolf *The English Mystery Plays* (Routledge and Kegan Paul, London, 1972) 388, note 26: '[it is not clear] that lines 74-5 are an order to the shepherds to recover the meal rather than their wits (the second shepherd certainly understands these lines in the latter sense)'. I argue below that both senses are to be understood by the Shepherds. S. Speyser 'Dramatic Illusion and Sacred Reality in "The Towneley *Prima Pastorum*"' in *Studies in Philology* 78:1 (1981) 10, implies that she does not believe the Shepherds (attempt to) recover the spilt meal.
8. Placed between lines 45 and 46.
9. See Morgan 'High Fraud' 679.
10. It is significant for my hypothesis that the motif of 'the emptying of the meal-sack' was conflated with that of the 'humane rider'; and that the latter is the very short second tale, following on immediately from the first tale of the quarrel over the imaginary sheep and the meal-sack demonstration in the first extant (c.1565) edition of the Gotham tales.
11. Lines 122-125. Printed by Thomas Wright in *Early Mysteries and Other Latin Poems of the 12th and 13th Centuries* (Nichols and Son, London, 1838) 93-8. See the same author's *A Collection of Latin Stories* (Percy Society, London, 1842) 80, for the tale of the fools who, late with their rent, decide to send it in a purse round the neck of a hare ('*De simplicitate hominum de Wilibege*' – probably Wilby, also in Norfolk). I discuss this and related 'Gothamite' tales alluded to in late medieval art in my paper 'Folklore Motifs in Late Medieval Art 1: Proverbial Follies and Impossibilities' *Folklore* 100:2 (1989) 201-17, especially 207.
12. For example, it is one of the many stories told about the Middle Eastern trickster/fool Nasreddin Hodja: see *202 Jokes of Nasreddin Hodja* (Minyatür Yayinlari, Istanbul, no date), no. 137 and facing illustration.
13. Stith Thompson *Motif Index of Folk Literature* (Rosenkilde and Bagger, revised and enlarged edition, Copenhagen, 1955). Another act of foolish kindness to a horse is referred to by the Fool in King Lear: "Twas (the cockney's) brother that, in pure kindness to his horse, buttered his hay' (2.4.125). No convincing parallels to this anecdote have yet been found.
14. A. Aarne *The Types of the Folk Tale* translated and enlarged Stith Thompson (FF Communications 184: 2nd edition, Helsinki, 1961).
15. See H.K. Cameron 'The Fourteenth-century Flemish Brasses at King's Lynn' in *Archaeological Journal* 136 (1979) 151-72 and plates XXXV, XXXIX (A), and XL (B). Cameron's illustrations of this brass are from John G. and Lionel A.B. Waller *A Series of Monumental Brasses* (London, 1842-1864).

16. The classic discussion of this motif is L. Randall 'The Snail in Gothic Marginal Warfare' *Speculum* 37 (1962) 358–67, now supplemented by R. Pinon 'From Illumination to Folksong: The Armed Snail, a Motif of Topsy-Turvy Land' in *Folklore Studies in the Twentieth Century: Proceedings of the Centenary Conference of the Folklore Society* edited V. Newall (D.S. Brewer, Cambridge, 1980) 76–113.
17. For the illustration of a man carrying an ass in the margin of a mid-fourteenth-century Franco-Flemish manuscript (New York, William S. Glazier Collection MS 24, fol. 32), see fig. 328 of Lillian Randall's seminal *Images in the Margins of Gothic Manuscripts* (University of California Press, Berkeley and Los Angeles, 1966); for another miniature of a man carrying his horse through water, from a Flemish Psalter of the first quarter of the fourteenth century (Oxford, Bodleian Library MS Douce 5, fol. 147), see Randall *Images* fig. 373.
18. See G.L. Remnant *A Catalogue of Misericords in Great Britain* (Clarendon Press, Oxford, 1969) 46:1.
19. On occasion this may be purely a folly motif, but see R. Mellinkoff 'Riding Backwards: Theme of Humiliation and Symbol of Evil' *Viator* 4 (1973) 153–76 and illustrations.
20. See B.J. and M.W. Whiting *Proverbs, Sentences, and Proverbial Phrases* (Harvard University Press, Cambridge, Mass., 1968) S 420. All references to proverbs are taken from this indispensible reference work, unless otherwise stated.
21. Reproduced on page 32 of Arthur Whittingham *Norwich Cathedral Bosses and Misericords* (Jarrold and Sons, Norwich, 1981).
22. Reproduced as fig. 20 in H. Martin 'Un caricaturiste du roi Jean (Piérart dou Tielt)' *Gazette des beaux-arts* 103 (1909) 89–102.
23. The Stowe manuscript image is reproduced in Randall *Images* as fig. 696.
24. I have not been able to see J. Adeline *Les Sculptures grotesques et symboliques – Rouen et environs* (Auge, Rouen, 1879), but the figure is discussed in L. Pillion *Les Portails latéraux de la cathédrale de Rouen* (A. Picard et fils, Paris, 1907).
25. See the catalogue of the exhibition entitled *Schatten uit de Schelde* with introduction and text by L. Hopstaken (Markiezenhof, Bergen-op-Zoom, 1987), exhibit no. 275, since acquired by J.B. van Beuningen, and identical to another already in his collection. The badge which includes the gesture but omits the mill is item no. 283. I am most grateful to Mr van Beuningen for providing me with a slide of this badge, and indeed for keeping me informed of the latest discoveries in this fascinating field.
26. Reproduced in M. Geisberg *The German Single-Leaf Woodcut: 1500–1550* revised by G.L. Strauss (Hacker Art Books, New York, 1974) as G 550. The study of historical gesture is still in its infancy, and although there is an increasing amount of scholarly attention being given to this branch of iconography, I know of no discussion of this particular gesture. (For a bibliography of the subject, which does not pretend to completeness, see note 74 of my paper in *Folklore*, cited in note 11 above. Such Passion scenes of the Mocking of Christ are a rich source of similar gestures of derision, see for example J.H. Marrow '*Circumdederunt me canes multi*: Christ's Tormentors in Northern European Art of the Late Middle Ages and Early Renaissance' *Art Bulletin* 59 (1977) 167–81, and Marrow *Passion Iconography in Northern European Art of the Late Middle Ages and Early Renaissance* (Ghemmert, Kortrijk, 1979), and especially L. Röhrich 'Gebärdensprache und Sprachegebärde' in *Humaniora, Honoring Archer Taylor* edited W.D. Hand and G.O. Arlt (J.J. Augustin, Locust Valley, New York, 1960) 121–49, in

particular figs 23 and 24 for the 'Rübchenschaben' gesture, and fig. 25 for the 'Gähnmaul', all three in scenes of the Mocking of Christ. The gesture described by Paul Vandenbroeck 'Verbeeck's Peasant Weddings: a study of iconography and social function' *Simiolus* 14 (1984) 79–124, especially 98–99 and notes 113–115, though similar, is not the same.

27. Reproduced in P.P. Wright *The Rural Bench-Ends of Somerset* (Avebury, Amersham, 1983).
28. Reproduced in S.L. Gilman *The Parodic Sermon in European Perspective* (Franz Steiner Verlag, Wiesbaden, 1974): this particular 'humane rider' is a reversed copy of that in the lower margin of a print of St Ursula or St Dorothy by Hans Springinklee issued in 1519/20 (Geisberg G 1341).
29. For this motif, see Paul Vandenbroeck 'Zur Herkunft und Verwurzelung der "Grillen"' *De zeventiende Eeuw* 3 (1987). I am most grateful to this author for sending me a copy of this typically informative paper.
30. For the most recent discussion of the origin and meaning of this often enigmatic and apparently polysemous gesture, see J. Engemann 'Der "cornu" Gestus – ein antiker und frühchristlicher Abwehr- und Spottgestus?' in *Jahrbuch für Antike und Christentum* Ergänzungs-Band 8 (1980) 483–98.
31. I hope to discuss this motif in due course elsewhere.
32. *Propos rustiques et Baliverneries* edited by L.-R. Lefèvre (Garnier Frères, Paris, 1928) 15.
33. See Dent *Proverbial Language* (see note 5) C292. See further, note 52 below.
34. Reproduced in W.S. Gibson *Bruegel* (Thames and Hudson, London, 1977) 179. A full-length discussion is to be found in L. Lebeer 'Le Pays de Cocagne: Het Luilekkerland' in *Bulletin des Musées royaux des Beaux Arts* 4 (1955) 199–214.
35. There is an edition and discussion in P.L. Henry 'The Land of Cokaygne: Cultures in Contact in Medieval Ireland' in *English Studies Today* (Istanbul) 5 (1973) 175–203. See also a two-part paper by J. de Caluwé-Dor 'L'Anti-Paradis de Cocagne: Cocagne I' in *Marche Romane: Mélanges de philologie et de littératures romanes offerts a Jeanne Wathelot-Willem* (A.R.U. Liège, Liège, 1978) 103–23, and 'Cocagne II' in *Linguistique et philologie* (Centre d'Études Mediévales, Université d'Amiens, Colloque 1977: Champion, Paris, 1977) 95–104, as well as the same author's 'L'élément irlandais dans la version moyen-anglais de "The Land of Cocaygne"' in *Mélanges de langue et littérature françaises du moyen âge et de la renaissance offerts à C. Foulon* (Institut de Français, Université de Haute Bretagne, Rennes, 1980) 1 89–97.

Mr Peter Millington of Nottingham has kindly drawn my attention to the use of this motif-complex in a parodic recruiting speech, recorded in a local Nottingham newspaper, satirising the extravagant claims made during efforts to recruit for the Loyal Nottinghamshire Foresters in 1796:

– I will lead you into a country where the rivers consist of fine nut-brown ale – where the houses are built of hot roast beef, and the wainscots papered with pancakes. There, my boys, it rains plum-pudding every Sunday morning, the streets are paved with quartern loaves, and nice roasted pigs run about with knives and forks stuck in them, and crying out, 'Who will eat me? Who will eat me?'

The source is J. Granger *Old Nottingham: Its Streets, People &c.* 2nd Series (Nottingham Daily Express: Nottingham, 1904) 60.

36. For a selected bibliography of the literature on Cockaygne, see note 63 of my paper cited in note 11 above.
37. See *Cockayne* in P. H. Reaney *A Dictionary of British Surnames* (Routledge and Kegan Paul, 2nd revised edition, London, 1976).
38. See P. H. Reaney *The Place-names of Essex* (English Place-Name Society, Cambridge, 1935) 325, and J. Field *English Field Names: a Dictionary* (David and Charles, London, 1972) s.v. *Cockaigne*.
39. Reaney *British Surnames* and E. Ekwall *The Placenames of Lancashire* (Publications of the University of Manchester, Manchester, 1922).
40. Dent *Proverbial Language* (see note 5) P315.
41. Dent *Proverbial Language* P315.
42. I cannot accept A.L. Morton's contention in *The English Utopia* (Lawrence and Wishart, London, 1952) 24, that Shakespeare 'puts into the mouth of Gonzalo (*Tempest* 2:1) what appears to be a sympathetic if rather classicised account of Cokaygne ...'.
43. Rabelais *Pantagruel* (1532) edited Verdun L. Saulnier (Textes littéraires français: Droz, Geneva, 1959) 172–3.
44. See the exhibition catalogue *Die Welt des Hans Sachs* edited by den Stadtgeschichtlichen Museen Bearbeiter, R. Freitag-Stadler and others (Verlag Hans Carl, Nüremberg, 1976) no. 59.
45. Lines 550–8 edited by C. Bühler and C. Selmer 'The Melk "Salbenkrämerspiel": an Unpublished Middle High German "Mercator" Play' *Publications of the Modern Language Association of America* 63 (1948) 60. (There is a similar passage in the Erlau text.) In line 550 of the Melk text, the land is said to be called 'Leckant'; the analogy with Flemish 'Luilekkerland' would seem to suggest that we should restore an original *Leckerlant.
46. See E.K. Chambers *The Mediaeval Stage* 2 vols (Oxford University Press, London, 1903) 1 408–10. The *OED*'s first citation of *Lubberland* from Florio (1598) is slightly antedated by its occurrence in Sir John Harington's *Metamorphosis of Ajax* (1596).
47. See Morton *English Utopia* 25–6 and G. Bullough 'The Later History of Cockaigne' in *Festschrift Prof. dr. Herbert Koziol* (Wiener Beiträge zur Englischen Philologie 75: Wilhelm Braumuller Universitäts-Verlagsbuchhandlung, Vienna and Stuttgart, 1973) 22–35, especially 25–6.
48. Bullough 'Later History of Cockaigne' 28: for full text see William Hawkins *Apollo Shroving* edited Howard Garrett Rhoads (Philadelphia, 1936).
49. Morton *English Utopia* 21. See now F.B. Jonassen 'Lucian's *Saturnalia*, the Land of Cockaigne, and the Mummers' Plays' *Folklore* 101:1 (1990) 58–68.
50. However 'learned' their ultimate origin may be: see the Second Shepherd's reference to 'Caton' (line 392), i.e. to the *Distichs of Cato*, a very popular medieval schoolbook, of which there are several Middle English versions extant.
51. See *Three Prose Versions of the Secreta Secretorum* edited R. Steele EETS ES 74 (1898) 235: the quotation is from the 1422 translation by John Yonge, the section entitled 'Of the Feete'.
52. For this tale, see G.H. Gerould 'Moll of the *Prima Pastorum*' *Modern Language Notes* 19 (1904) 225–30. Rabelais has Echephron in chapter 31 of *Gargantua* (1534) allude to Picrochole's dreams of world-conquest in which he gets as far as giving away kingdoms to his advisers as if they were already conquered, as

'SLAWPASE FRO THE MYLN-WHELE'

semblable à la farce du pot au laict, duquel un cordouannier se faisoit riche par resverie; puis, le pot cassé, n'eut de quoy disner.

(Rabelais *Gargantua* edited Ruth Calder and M.A. Screech (Textes littéraires français: Droz, Geneva/Minard, Paris, 1970) 199.) Whether or not this ever appeared as a farce in the dramatic sense is not known. The story is found in the later English jestbooks, at least: e.g. the 1613 edition of *Scogin's Jests* via R.D./T.D.'s *The Mirrour of Mirth, and Pleasant Conceits* (1583), a translation of Bonaventure des Periers' *Nouvelles recreations et joyeux devis* (1558) in which the present tale is nouvelle no. 12. Before entering such 'facetious' literature – it occurs at much the same time in one of Domenichi's Italian collections, and slightly earlier in Pauli's *Schimpf und Ernst* (1522) – the tale of the imagined wealth which would eventually accrue from the sale of the pitcher of milk was part of the *exempla* collections which preachers were advised to dip into to enliven their sermons, as early as the thirteenth-century *Sermones vulgares* of Jacques de Vitry and the *Tractatus de diversis materiis praedicabilibus* of his contemporary Etienne de Bourbon. From Etienne's collection the tale entered the influential fourteenth-century *Dialogus creaturarum moralizatus* which exists in many Latin manuscripts from all over Europe, and was translated into English and printed c.1530 as *The Dialoges of Creatures Moralysed* (in which edition it forms a part of dialogue 100). In some versions of the tale, rather than a bowl of milk, it is a basket of eggs which is to be sold and which thus motivates the daydream, but the earliest such variant known dates from 1524 – it is this form, however, which is illustrated in a German popular print of c.1700 (see W. Fraenger 'Deutsche Vorlagen zu russischen Volksbilderbogen des 18en Jahrhunderts' *Jahrbuch für historische Volkskunde 2* (1926) 136). Rabelais would also seem to allude to 'not counting one's chickens' in the mock-learned guise of one of Judge Bridoye's Latin maxims: *Ad praesens ova cras pullis sunt meliora* ('Today's eggs are better than tomorrow's hens'): *Le Tiers Livre* (1546) edited M.A. Screech (Textes littéraires français: Droz, Geneva, 1964) 287.

53. B.J. and M.W. Whiting *Proverbs, Sentences, and Proverbial Phrases* (Harvard UP, Cambridge, Mass., 1968) N91.
54. From his Preface to Greene's *Menaphon* (1590); see *The Works of Thomas Nashe* edited R.B. McKerrow, revised F.P. Wilson (Blackwell, Oxford, 1958) 3 315. The latest thorough enumeration and discussion of the proverbs depicted in this painting (listing 115) is A. Dundes and C.A. Stubbe *The Art of Mixing Metaphors: a Folkloristic Interpretation of the 'Netherlandish Proverbs' by Pieter Bruegel the Elder* (FF Communications 230: Suomalainen Tiedeakatemia, Helsinki, 1981). For a useful discussion of the picture as a whole, see D. Kunzle 'Bruegel's Proverbs Painting and the World Upside Down' *Art Bulletin 59* (1977) 197–202. For a discussion of the inverted globe as a house-sign, see M. Deruelle 'Een Gentse Gavelteken' *Oostvlaamsche Zanten 33* (1958) 8–12.
55. Whiting *Proverbs* S830. For an earlier depiction of 'fishing before the net', see the woodcut illustration to chapter 90 of Thomas Murner's *Narrenbeschwörung* (1512), entitled 'vor dem berren vischen': *Thomas Murners Narrenbeschwörung: Text und Bilder der ersten Ausgabe ...* edited M. Spanier (Neudrucke deutscher Litteraturwerke des 16. und 17. Jahrhunderts 119–24: Halle, 1894).
56. Cawley *Wakefield Pageants* 100.
57. *Middle English Dictionary* s.v. *on* 8 (c).
58. *Middle English Dictionary* s.v. *flete*. *OED* s.v. *fleet^2* lists *flett* as a sixteenth-century spelling, but does not illustrate this form. However, see the following West Riding place-name

MALCOLM JONES

spellings which include this element, from A.H. Smith *The Place-names of the West Riding of Yorkshire* (English Place-Name Society, Cambridge, 1961) Part 2: *Swinflett* (1557) 10; *Addlenfflett* (1574) 2; *Usflett* (1592) 7. For *fleet* in the sense 'stream', see *West Riding* Part 7, 128: '... *fleot*, here in the sense "stream", as in other (West Riding) stream-names'.
59. See note 54.
60. This identification was first proposed by A.C. Cawley in 'The Grotesque Feast in the *Prima Pastorum*' *Speculum* 30 (1955) 215.
61. Cawley *Wakefield Pageants* line 455.
62. Smith *West Riding* Part 2, 172.
63. Smith *West Riding* 173. I am tempted to interpret the Lancashire nickname of William *Rotenflock* (1325) as the epithet of a similarly unfortunate shepherd, and not, as does Jönsjö (see note 2 above), by analogy with his contemporary, John *Rotenhering*, as 'one who sells rotten flukes (i.e. flounders)'.

THE MEDIEVAL ENGLISH AND FRENCH SHEPHERDS PLAYS

Christine Richardson

The comparative method seems to be particularly appropriate to the study of medieval drama for it allows us to distinguish what may be seen as variants on a universal given theme as the result of certain local conditions of place, associations, or tradition. By comparing the different national traditions we can learn much about the creative force of medieval drama, to discover where it drew its constitutive material from and how the absorption or continuation of specific literary, social or entertainment themes was brought about.

A comparison between the English and French traditions of medieval drama is especially rewarding, for the relationship between these two countries in the fifteenth and sixteenth centuries was close enough to reveal common assumptions, yet consciously distant enough, as England developed its own individual language and literature, to create notable differences which may be seen in the drama. The cultures were close, but not identical, and the variants which are revealed in the drama may thus be more easily related to both the background and the individual intentions of the playwrights and the play-makers, that is, the actors and audiences.

The Shepherds Plays in both traditions offer perhaps the richest field for a comparative study because of the nature of the rôle of the Nativity Shepherds in the organised religious drama. The Shepherds within the scriptural narrative represent Common Man to whom the news of the promise of salvation is brought. Patristic writings had emphasised this rôle of the Shepherds and from Origen onwards had explicitly stated that the news of the Saviour's birth was announced first to poor and humble shepherds, for the offer of salvation which Christ brought was to all humankind, not merely the rich and powerful. Ambrose had pointed out that the Shepherds knew of the birth of the Christ-Child and came to recognise and worship Him before the Magi: *Unde non mirum est quod redemptionem saeculi ante pastores saeculi potuerunt scire, quam principes; non enim angeli nuntiaverunt regibus, non judicibus, sed hominibus rusticanis* ('Whence it is no wonder that shepherds of that time were able to know of the redemption of the world before princes; for the angels did not announce [it] to kings, or to judges, but to countrymen').[1] The Shepherds therefore stand for the audience of the medieval drama to whom the plays' message of wonder and repentance is directed. No other characters within the plays have quite such a strict relationship with the audience. The torturers in the Crucifixion plays also have a close relationship with the audience but the identity suggested is expressed in negative terms, awakening feelings of guilt and responsibility for all

CHRISTINE RICHARDSON

Mankind in the murder of Christ, whereas the Nativity Shepherds offer a positive invitation for identification.

It is perhaps from the point of view of the authors of the plays that the Nativity Shepherds offered the most interesting possibility, for they offered the potential for individual dramatic creativity, an occasion to exploit and develop the dramatic form. Unique among the characters of the organised religious drama (except for the torturers mentioned above), the Shepherds are unnamed, historically undefined participants in the biblical action. Luke, the only one of the Evangelists to include a reference to the Shepherds, does not even state their number, still less provide details of names, personalities, or later activities which would have limited the dramatists to adhere to a pre-defined pattern for their part in the plays. The Shepherds offer no risk of contradicting the biblical narrative in their dramatic development and instead, because of their Everyman rôle, invite creative elaboration and experimentation to establish firmly the identification with the audience. Even though characters such as Herod or Noah were indeed richly developed by the medieval dramatists, they remained fixed in their set patterns in the biblical history and symbolic meaning; no matter how lengthily developed, Herod had to massacre the children and Noah eventually to build the Ark.

In the creation of the Shepherds Plays, dramatists and their actors as co-authors were free to turn to material from areas outside the religious or even apocryphal traditions in order to exploit the audience's associations of shepherds and thereby render effective audience identification with the Nativity Shepherds. The Shepherds Plays therefore became a vehicle for moving the organised religious drama out into other areas of social, literary and, most importantly, dramatic activity.

A comparison of the Shepherds Plays of the English Corpus Christi Cycles with the Shepherds sequences in the French *Passions* reveals that a basic sequence of events remains constant. This is the structure which was set first by the Luke 2:8–20 narrative. The Shepherds are addressed unexpectedly by an angel who tells them that the Saviour of the world has been born and that they should go to worship Him. The Shepherds are surprised and frightened, but agree to hurry to Bethlehem. They worship the Christ-Child, usually presenting gifts, are thanked by the Virgin, and told to spread the news to others. It is often assumed that the basic sequence for the medieval Shepherds Plays was established by the liturgical *Pastores* plays. Although these might have had a rôle of reinforcement on the Luke pattern, the characteristic feature of the Latin *Pastores* plays, the questioning of the Shepherds by the Midwives, providing the Easter-parallel trope of *Quem quaeritis in praesepe, pastores, dicite?* ('Whom do you seek in the manger, shepherds, say?'), is never used by the vernacular plays. When the apocryphal Midwives are used in the Cycles or *Passions* they are separated from the Shepherds and the two sets of characters never meet. The Shepherds' fear and their haste to reach Bethlehem had been underlined by patristic writings and were also comprehensible reactions which were natural enough to allow them to be included in the vernacular plays on the realistic as well as the symbolic level.² The gifts, of course, have no part in the Luke narrative and are an apocryphal addition, found also in narrative sources, which was probably inspired by analogy with the Magi.

However, the basic Luke sequence is expanded in all the vernacular plays by an additional sequence before the appearance of the angel. Only in the least developed of the English Shepherds Plays, that of the N.Town Plays, does the annunciation by the angel open the play. All the other Shepherds Plays devote a notable portion of the entire play to pre-annunciation activities of the Shepherds which serve to establish their rôle as recognisable types of Common Man.³ The notorious Mak sequence of the Towneley *Secunda Pastorum* is simply the best-known and most highly-elaborated of these sequences. It is for this reason that an examination rather of the Chester *Shepherds Play* and the Towneley *Prima Pastorum* and a comparison of them with the Shepherds sequences in Eustache Marcadé's *Passion d'Arras* and Jean Greban's *Passion* may be more revealing.⁴

On the most immediate level, what is most obvious when comparing these plays is that in the English plays the Shepherds make numerous references to their sheep while in the French plays sheep are remarkable for their absence. The sheep do not actually appear in any of the plays, of course, except possibly a live wether for Mak to steal in *Secunda Pastorum* as a piece of stage business in keeping with the Wakefield Master's sense of theatre and apparent fondness for props, but their welfare and the difficulties of the practical tasks of sheep-keeping provide much of the material for dialogue and action both in *Prima Pastorum* and the Chester play. Both plays open with a Shepherd lamenting his lot and listing the misfortunes which have befallen his flock:

> On wouldes have I walked wylde ...
> my seemely wedders to save ...
> My taytfull tuppes are in my thought,
> them to save and heale ...
> Lord, what thay ar weyll that hens ar past! ...
> All my shepe ar gone,
> I am not left oone,
> The rott has theym slone;
> Now beg I and borow.⁵

The Chester Shepherd's list of herbs which he uses to treat the sheep is no poetic invention, but an accurate reflection of medieval methods used to treat sheep diseases. *Gerard's Herbal* corroborates the curative properties of the Chester Shepherd's herb pouch, and the remedy the Third Shepherd has been mixing in his 'wiffes ... ould panne' (lines 74–6) matches very closely a remedy prescribed by the *Liber di diversis medicinis*.⁶ The *Prima Pastorum* Shepherd recounts the devastating effect of 'the rott' on his flock, referring to a frequently-occurring circumstance in fifteenth-century England, and Europe in general, when thousands of sheep were affected by liver-fluke disease and scab. Both Chester Third Shepherd and Trowle have their tar-boxes containing the tar used to treat scab, the iconographical identifier *par excellence* of the medieval shepherd.[7] The knowledge we can draw from medieval treatises on animal husbandry, such as Walter of Henley's *Hosbondrie*, the anonymous *Seneschaucie*, a portion of *Fleta* and Robert Grosseteste's *Rules*,[8] and especially Jehan de Brie's *Le Bon Berger*, support all the details mentioned by the Chester and Towneley Shepherds, including the ever-present threat of theft of sheep. Not only do the Towneley *Secunda Pastorum* Shepherds suffer from this frequent feature of a shepherd's life, but so do their Chester colleagues. When the angel appears in the Chester play, the Third Shepherd's instinctive reaction is to suppose that it is someone planning to steal their sheep.[9]

The existence of *Le Bon Berger* shows that details of sheep-keeping were known, or at least available, in fifteenth-century France, so why then did the French *Passion* authors choose not to use them in their portrayals of the Nativity Shepherds? We can trace the reasons primarily in the different socio-economic conditions of shepherds and shepherding in the two countries, and then in the more local factors of place of provenance of the individual plays. The wool trade in fourteenth- and fifteenth-century England was extremely vigorous and provided the country's principal source of wealth. Originally the wool had been bought and exported by Italian wool traders, then taken to be woven in Italy and elsewhere on the European continent. By the fifteenth century, however, the English cloth-weaving industry had developed sufficiently to utilise most of the home-grown wool and to produce cloth at significantly lower prices, with no transport costs, than those possible in France and Italy. An English shepherd, at the time of the Towneley and Chester plays, was thus a participant in a flourishing and nationally-important economic activity. This explains first of all why the details of sheep-keeping would have been familiar enough to author and audience in the English plays. However, the economic status of the shepherd in the two countries is also important. Following the Black Death and consequent lack of manpower to tend arable land in England, much of the land previously used for crops was rented as pasture for sheep. The tenant would keep his own sheep on the land, sell their wool direct to the 'wool broggers' and thus keep for himself the money made in this transaction, paying out money merely for rent of the pasture.[10]

In France the situation was very different. Here the wool trade was a very minor economic activity and the value of sheep was more in terms of the milk, cheese and meat which they provided. Shepherds were usually employed by a land-owner or even a bourgeois in the cities, to tend flocks of sheep, or by a village to look after the one or two animals each villager owned. The welfare of the sheep therefore was of much less direct interest to the French shepherd; if one of his sheep died from the 'rott' or the *rongne* ('sheep scab') he would not necessarily lose his livelihood, for he would nonetheless be paid his wages and had no direct interest in the profits to be made from the products of the sheep. The practical details of sheep-keeping were thus much less an important element of life and survival for the French shepherd and by reflection for the general population. It should be remembered too that Wakefield was a town which grew up around the wool and cloth trade, and Chester also was a centre for the import and weaving of wool. The audience of the Towneley and Chester plays would therefore have had a very lively interest in the details of sheep-keeping, as would the actors who performed in the play, and they would have responded to the practical Shepherds in the plays both as convincing shepherds and as people like themselves, the kind of people to whom the message of Salvation was first announced. It is not, it would seem, by chance that the *Shepherds Plays* of the York Cycle and N.Town Plays are much less developed.

There is limited reference to sheep in Greban's Shepherds sequence, but the terms are revealing with respect to the motivation and range of connotation for this practical detail. At the beginning of the Shepherds sequence in Greban's *Passion* the three Shepherds are exchanging news, and Rifflart, the foolish clown-type Shepherd in this sequence, recounts how he had saved one of his sheep from the jaws of 'maistre Ysangrin', the wolf. The constant interruptions and rude comments of his fellow Shepherds suggest that this is a tall story not to be taken seriously and the use of the animal-fable term 'maistre Ysangrin' for the wolf adds to the impression of fantasy rather than reality. At the end of the conversation, the Shepherds go off to check their flock for the night and they agree that if any of them sees a wolf he must warn his companions:

> car anuyt nous convient veiller
> sur le trouppeau, chascun pour soy ...
> qui verra le lou, maine bruit![11]

> 'Because at night we must watch
> Over the flock, each one for himself ...
> If anyone sees the wolf, shout loudly!'

Like the *Passion d'Arras*, Greban's *Passion* separates the pre-annunciation development of the Shepherds from the scriptural narrative sequence. As the action of the *Passion* switches to the scene of Joseph leaving the Virgin to find things for the baby and then to God speaking to the angels in Heaven, telling them to go down to worship the Christ-Child at His birth, there is interposed a very brief episode of the Shepherds beating the bushes, checking that there is no wolf lurking in them:

> Gardez bien, pour le lou garder;
> pastoureaulx, faictes bonne garde.[12]

> 'Keep a good look out, look out for the wolf;
> Shepherds, keep a good look out.'

This reference to the wolf would appear to be a detail taken from the real-life activities of shepherds and indeed Helen Cooper suggests that the lack of actual wolves in the English countryside with respect to the later survival of wolves – and thus the real threat they posed to shepherds – in Europe is the reason for the inclusion of this detail of practical sheep-keeping in the French Shepherds sequences.¹³ However, an examination of the appearance of this episode in *pastourelle* and *bergerie* reveals that it was a frequent motif used, and the only one which had anything to do with sheep. It appears in a *pastourelle* by Jean Bodel (c.1200) where the Poet-figure comes upon a shepherdess who is distraught because the wolf has carried off one of her sheep. In order to calm her distress, the Poet-figure offers to retrieve the sheep in return for her virginity. The shepherdess consequently refuses her part of the bargain once the sheep is returned, calls on 'Robin' for help, but he arrives too late.¹⁴ It is clear that the interest in the motif here lies in the love-game and not in the welfare of the flock. The incident also appears in Adam de la Halle's *Jeu de Robin et Marion*, but here the seducer figure is removed and Robin rescues the sheep and receives the reward, this time in the form of a kiss, and the episode also found its way into later popularised fifteenth-century versions of *pastourelle* songs.¹⁵ It is therefore an element from the literary view of shepherds, not the real-life conditions of sheep-keeping. The fact that threats from wolves do not feature in the concerns of the Towneley and Chester Shepherds is not so much due to the existence or not of real wolves in fifteenth-century England but rather to the lack of a *pastourelle-bergerie* tradition in this country.

The Shepherds in the *Passion d'Arras* make no mention of their sheep whatsoever, they too suggest references rather to the strongest connotational range for shepherds within the French social and cultural tradition, the idealised literary world of *bergerie*. Throughout the fourteenth and fifteenth centuries in France the shepherd world originally brought into literary expansion through *pastourelle* developed into *bergerie* which used it consciously to contrast an ideal, innocent, rural world with decadent life at court or in the towns. Narrative pieces such as *Les Dicts de Franc Gontier, Le livre de la deablerie, Le Banquet du bois,* and even the more overtly political *Pastoralet*¹⁶ use the shepherd world as a means of social criticism whereby the simplicity and tranquillity of the shepherds' rustic life is shown to be superior to the luxury, sophistication, and corruption of power and position. The *Bergeries moralisées* of the sixteenth century translated the idea into dramatic form, but retained the trappings of the shepherd world, the merry-making and feasting, the clothing and equipment, and the music, not the harsh details of caring for sheep. Gontier in the *Passion d'Arras* opens the first Shepherds sequence with an appreciation of the shepherd's lot which comes directly from this tradition:

> Car pastouriaux grans et petis
> Ont mieulx le temps que n'ont les rois
> Qui maintennent les grans arrois.¹⁷
>
> 'For shepherds, large and small,
> Have a better time than kings
> Who keep great entourages.'

Robechon continues the theme and agrees with his companion:

> Mais vrayement je ne vorroie mie
> Avoir toute la seignourie
> De tout le monde, est il bien grant,
> Et on me deist maintenant
> Que je laissasse pastourrie.
> Car c'est la plus joyeuse vie
> Que homs puist jamais demener.[18]

> 'But truly, I would not wish in the least
> To have all the lordship
> Of all the world, big as it is,
> If I were to be told now
> That I should give up shepherding;
> For it is the most joyful life
> That man can ever lead.'

The authors, actors, and audience of the French medieval organised religious drama were already familiar with a literary tradition of shepherds which presented them as inherently good and naturally more worthy than the rich and powerful. This is the rôle the Nativity Shepherds play in the Luke narrative and in later exegetical developments of it, of course, and the *Passion* Shepherds could assume this rôle by reference to the pre-existing literary conventions. The Corpus Christi Cycle Shepherds have no such ready-made associations and the English playwrights must therefore adopt other methods to demonstrate the worthiness of the Shepherds to hear the news of the Saviour's birth. This doctrinal point is generally conveyed in the English plays by demonstrating how hard the Shepherd's life is. All the English Shepherds complain. The length and content of the complaints varies, but, except for the undeveloped N.Town play, it remains a constant. The *Prima Pastorum* Shepherds make a series of complaints which have been seen as political protest.[19] The *Secunda Pastorum* Shepherds make similar complaints, but they also incorporate conventional forms of complaint, such as that of the hen-pecked husband, which have little to do with political protest and far more to do with standard complaint topics and use of possibly stock popular-entertainment turns on the level of present day mother-in-law jokes. Like the Coventry Shepherds, they also complain about the cold, an acknowledgement of the supposed play world and situation which is entirely lacking in the French sequences.

By complaining, the Towneley and Chester Shepherds also establish their identity with the audience, for the problems caused by inclement weather, by rents, taxes, purveyancing, by masters who do not pay wages promptly,[20] and women are problems shared by or at least recognisable to members of the audience. Their complaints strengthen their representation as Common Men as did their listing of the practical details of sheep-keeping. How then do the French playwrights establish the recognisable universal humanity of the Nativity Shepherds? They do it by reaching out into the world of popular entertainment and introducing the episode of a trick on an unknowing friend which is so frequent a component of even the very small repertory of popular entertainment turns and secular drama which have come down to us. Immediately after the idealised shepherd-world speeches mentioned above, the *Passion d'Arras* Shepherds Gontier and Robechon plot a trick on the third Shepherd, Gombaut, whom they discover sleeping under a bush. Overheard by the audience, but not apparently by the sleeping Gombaut, they decide to put mud into Gombaut's hands so that when he awakes, when they tickle him, he will rub the mud over his face (lines 1648–67). It is a double trick, for not only does Gombaut not know what has been plotted but neither will he know that he has smeared his face with mud for this will appear only to his friends – and of course the audience. This is the kind of trick which can be found in one of Hrotswitha's plays, *Dulcitius*, where it also takes the form of face-smearing, and in Adam de la Halle's *Le Jeu de la Feuillée* where the monk is tricked into paying the bill for debts he supposedly incurred while sleeping through a dice game and letting others play his hand.[21] It is the theme of *Le Garçon et l'Aveugle*, though here the friend is not sleeping but unknowing because blind, and it features also in *Courtois d'Arras* when the two prostitutes plan to steal Courtois' purse while he is 'off-stage' relieving himself.[22] In all these instances actors set up complicity with the audience against another actor who remains supposedly innocent and the humour is created explicitly through this imbalance of awareness. It is obviously an extremely effective means of involving the audience in the events of the drama for they become participants. Used in the *Passion d'Arras* Shepherds sequence, the trick on an unknowing friend establishes the identity of the audience with the Shepherds both through the dramatic technique used, the complicity, and the range of reference it conveys, that of the secular entertainment familiar to the audience.

The trick is not entirely unknown in the English Shepherds Plays either: it features most famously in the Mak episode of *Secunda Pastorum* where Mak tricks his sleeping friends with the double complicity of the audience, who are aware of both the theft and the subsequent disguise of the sheep.[23] The invisible flock of sheep in *Prima Pastorum* which confounds Slawpace is another trick on an unknowing friend set up with the complicity of the audience. However, in the English tradition it is not the sole means of establishing the identification and is used only in addition to the complaints in the most extensively developed plays. This reveals yet again that the area of popular entertainment provided an obvious source of material for the medieval dramatist when faced with the possibility of extension of a play.

The *Passion d'Arras* trick is contained in the first, pre-annunciation section of the Shepherds sequence. When dramatic attention returns to the Shepherds 428 lines later, it is to the strict scriptural sequence with the annunciation of the angel. In this first sequence, then, the three Shepherds are identified as shepherds by placing them within the established literary convention of the idealised shepherd world of *bergerie* and also by their very names which conform to the conventional shepherd names of both *pastourelle* and *bergerie*. Their first sequence starts in fact by one Shepherd greeting the other simply by name which immediately establishes them as shepherds in the expectations of the audience. Within the time-sequence of the *Passions* there is no clear division between separate episodes of the biblical history as there is with the waggon-play staging of the Corpus Christi Cycle. Episodes follow one another along the set of the multiple-locational playing area and the audience's attention must be captured and information provided at the beginning of each new episode so that they might recognise what is about to be shown. In contrast, it is not until line 24 of *Prima Pastorum* that the key identifying word *shepe* is given, for the new play, the new waggon, the new cast, and the previous play matter had already set up the audience's expectations for a new play and a Shepherds play.

Once the shepherd identification has been established, the *Passion d'Arras* sequence moves on to establish the common humanity of the Shepherds through the exploitation of the trick motif. When the Shepherds sequence resumes at line 2130, the actors have already been identified and their representative rôle been assured so that the scriptural sequence can continue and achieve its doctrinal aim.

In the other Shepherds Plays, the same techniques of shepherd identification and demonstration of the Nativity Shepherds' universal humanity can be seen. The initial shepherd recognition is achieved by reference to the strongest connotational range for shepherds in both traditions, in England to real-life economically important shepherds, in France to the literary conventions which had developed in the extensive shepherd-world literature. The humanity of the Shepherds is then established by moving into other spheres of shared dramatic expectations. Lack of space precludes the possibility of looking at these in detail and it must suffice simply in passing to indicate the references out to the world of farce in the opening section of the *Passion de Semur* Shepherds sequence and of the trick once again in the *Rouen Nativité*.[24] In the English plays the references to material from folk play and popular entertainment are striking in the absorption not only of the Mak tale in *Secunda Pastorum* and the Fools of Gotham sequence in *Prima Pastorum*[25] but also in the use of an episode from the Hero-Combat play in the Chester *Shepherds Play* wrestling match.

In order to develop and identify his Shepherds, a medieval playwright in both England and France was drawn particularly to the realm of popular entertainment and folk material. Within the freedom of the didactic intent of the Shepherds Plays and the lack of rigid pre-established patterns a playwright and his actors could extend the form of the organised religious drama and adopt elements currently used in secular entertainment. In this way the Shepherds Plays represent an active force in the development of the drama in the medieval period.

Florence

NOTES

1. Ambrose *Sermo V: De natali Domini III, PL 17* cols 612–14, at col. 613. Ambrose appears to be making use of the two meanings of *saeculum* 'a particular generation', and 'the world'.

2. See Ambrose *Sermo III: In die natalis Domini (i)*, PL 17 cols 608–10, at col. 609; Origen *Homilia XIII*, PL 26 cols 244–6, at col. 246; Bede *Homilia VI*, PL 94 cols 34–8, at col. 36.
3. The York Shepherds Play seems to be a special case, for the version of the play which has survived is incomplete and shows signs of having undergone major revisions. See Richard Beadle *The York Plays* (Edward Arnold, London, 1982) 130 and 427–8; and 'An unnoticed lacuna in the York Chandlers' Pageant' in *So Meny People Longages and Tonges: Philological Essays in Scots and Mediaeval English presented to Angus McIntosh* edited Michael Benskin and M.L. Samuels (Benskin and Samuels, Middle English Dialect Project, Edinburgh, 1981) 229–35.
4. See *Le Mystère de la Passion: Texte du manuscrit 617 de la Bibliothèque d'Arras* edited Jules-Marie Richard (Imprimerie de la Société du Pas-de-Calais, Arras, 1891; reprinted Slatkine, Geneva, 1976); *Le Mystère de la Passion d'Arnoul Greban* edited Omer Jodogne (Mémoires de l'Académie Royale de Belgique, classe de lettres, 2me série, tome 12, fasc. 3: Bruxelles, 1965).
5. *The Chester Plays* edited R.M. Lumiansky and David Mills EETS SS 3 (1974) 7 (The Painters' Play) lines 1–12; *The Wakefield Pageants in the Towneley Cycle* edited A.C. Cawley (Manchester University Press, 1958/1971) *Prima Pastorum* lines 1–27.
6. *Liber di diversis medicinis* edited Margaret Sinclair Ogden EETS OS 207 (1938, reprinted 1969) 2 line 21.
7. ... *le bon bergier ne doit non plus estre trouve sans la boiste a l'ongnement, que le notaire doit estre sans escriptoire, Car ce est le plus notable et necessaire de ses instruments et outilz* ('the good shepherd must no more be found without his box of ointment than the notary should be without his writing materials, because it is the most noteworthy and necessary of his instruments and tools': Jehan de Brie *Le Bon Berger*). See Marie-Thérèse Kaiser-Guyot *Le berger en France aux XIVe et XVe siècles* (Editions Klincksieck, Paris, 1974) 41.
8. See Dorothea Oschinsky *Walter of Henley and Other Treatises on Estate Management and Accounting* (Clarendon Press, Oxford, 1971).
9. Chester lines 394–5. It may be that this is an acknowledgement of the *Secunda Pastorum* episode, become famous even in Chester.
10. The First Shepherd of *Prima Pastorum* is worried about not being able to pay his rents now that his sheep are dead and cannot provide wool to sell:

> Fermes thyk ar comyng, my purs is bot wake,
> I haue nerehand nothyng to pay nor to take.
> I may syng
> With purs penneles,
> That makys this heuynes,
> 'Wo is me this dystres!'
> And has no helpyng.   30–6

11. Greban *Passion* lines 4822–33.
12. Greban *Passion* lines 4944–5.
13. See Helen Cooper *Pastoral: Mediaeval into Renaissance* (D.S. Brewer, Ipswich, 1977) 48. The use of the wolf occurs also in the *Passion de Semur* (see below, note 24) and in Marguerite de Navarre's *Comédie de la Nativité*: see *Comédie de la Nativité de Jesus Christ* in *Les Marguerites de la Marguerite des Princesses* edited Ruth Thomas, 2 vols (French Renaissance Classics: SR Publishers, East Ardsley, 1970, facsimile reprint of John de Tourné's edition of Lyons, 1547; B.M.G. 18190).

14. See *Romances et Pastourelles Françaises des XIIe et XIIIe siècles* edited Karl Bartsch, 3 vols (Altfranzösische Romanzen und Pastourellen, Leipzig, 1870; reprinted Slatkine, Geneva, 1973) 2, no.14, line 64.
15. See *Chansons du XVe siècle* edited Gaston Paris (Société des Anciens Textes Français: Didot, Paris, 1875; reprinted Johnson Reprint Corporation, New York, 1965) no. 29. See also William Powell Jones 'The Pastourelle and French Folk Drama' *Harvard Studies 13* (1931) 129–63 at 137 for another example of this motif in later folksong.
16. See Eloy d'Amerval *Le liure de la deablerie* edited Charles Frederick Ward (University of Iowa Humanistic Studies 2:2: Iowa, 1923); 'Les Dicts de Franc Gontier' in *Recueil de poésies françoises des XVe et XVIe siècles* edited A. de Montaiglon and James de Rothschild, 13 vols (Bibliothèque elzévirienne, Paris, 1855-1878) 10 (1875); 'Le Banquet du boys' in *Recueil de poésies françoises* 10 206–22; 'Le Pastoralet' in *Chroniques relatives à l'histoire de la Belgique* edited Baron J.M.B.C. Kervyn de Lettenhove, 3 vols (Commission Royale d'Histoire, Brussels, 1873).
17. *Passion d'Arras* lines 1628–30.
18. *Passion d'Arras* lines 1641–7. The use of the shepherd world for social criticism does appear in *pastourelle* but it is usually used only for direct reference to political events as in *pastourelles* by Jean Bodel or, later, Froissart. See Bartsch *Altfranzösische Romanzen und Pastourellen* 3 nos 40; 54; 59.
19. See V.J. Scattergood *Politics and Poetry in the Fifteenth Century* (Blandford Press, London, 1971) 360.
20. Chester's Trowle and *Secunda Pastorum*'s Third Shepherd both make complaints about abuse by their masters: see Chester lines 218–25 and *Secunda Pastorum* lines 154–71. Like all the complaint topics, this too fits in with the structural importance of the world-out-of-joint in the pre-Nativity situation.
21 See Richard Axton *European Drama in the Early Middle Ages* (Hutchinson, London, 1974) 27; Adam de la Halle *Le Jeu de la Feuillée* in *Adam Le Bossu, Le Jeu de la Feuillée* edited Ernest Langlois (Classiques français du moyen âge: Champion, Paris, 1951; second edition 1978) lines 963–1016.
22. See *Le Garçon et l'aveugle, Jeu du XIIIe siècle* edited Mario Roques (Classiques français du moyen âge: Champion, Paris, 1921; second edition 1969); *Courtois d'Arras, Jeu de XIIIe siècle* edited Edmond Faral (Classiques français du moyen âge: Champion, Paris, 1911; reprinted 1967) lines 236–78.
23. Mak seems to draw attention to the dramatic irony of his trick when he leaves the Shepherds to return home to Gyl's 'child-bed':
    I pray you looke my slefe, that I steyll noght   396
24. See the *Passion de Semur* edited Lynette Muir (Leeds Medieval Studies 3: Leeds, 1981); *Mystère de l'Incarnation et Nativité de Notre Sauveur et Rédempteur Jésus-Christ représenté à Rouen en 1474, publié d'après un imprimé du XVe siècle* edited Pierre le Verrdier 2 vols (Société des Bibliophiles Normands: Rouen, 1884–1886).
25. See the article by Malcolm Jones in this collection.

THE OLD CZECH APOTHECARY AS CLOWN AND SYMBOL
Jarmila F. Veltruský

Among the more perplexing features of medieval religious drama is its use of a type of ribald and seemingly blasphemous comedy difficult to reconcile with the plays' religious orientation. Some of the most scurrilous examples are associated with the Apothecary, the character representing the supplier of the spices with which the holy women meant to embalm the body of Christ on Easter morning. Several of the Easter and Passion plays of Central Europe portray him as the protagonist of a grossly burlesque episode, which seems to have only a tenuous connection with the other episodes as regards the plot and to express an essentially godless spirit of irreverence and absurdity. A text which poses the problem in a particularly acute form but at the same time offers pointers to a more general solution is a fourteenth-century Bohemian fragment of an Apothecary episode known as Mastičkář.[1] It is the only known version that contains a parody of the Resurrection.

Master Severin, the Old Czech Apothecary, is a semiotically complex figure. Like several of his German-speaking counterparts, he appears on one hand as a descendant of the stylised Spice Merchant of the liturgical drama, a part of whose sung Latin dialogue with the three Maries appears in the midst of the episode, and on the other hand as a burlesque charlatan with a shrewish wife and two disreputable servants. At the same time his rôle contains two additional features which seemingly complicate but in fact clarify his function as a character in a play designed to celebrate Easter: he is a clown who expressly sets out to provoke laughter; and at the same time, as a parodic image of Christ the Healer, he bears a load of symbolic meaning pertinent to the Resurrection.

At the beginning of Mastičkář, when the scapegrace Rubin comes running to offer his services, Severin welcomes him with the words Dávě liudem dosti smiechu ('We two will give the people lots of laughter': line 4). This establishes him as a comedian, whose first object is to amuse the audience rather than to convince it of his qualifications as an apothecary or persuade it to buy his wares. The two aims are not necessarily incompatible. A huckster may clown or tell jokes in order to draw a crowd in preparation for a hard sell, and much of Rubin's comic patter, for instance, can be interpreted in this way. But Severin's case is different, because he does not present himself as an apothecary who amuses in order to sell his wares, but as an entertainer who enacts a caricature of an apothecary in order to amuse. This apothecary appears ridiculously angry or pompous, but quite serious from his own point of view. He is funny in spite of himself, so to speak, chiefly as the butt of

Rubin's mockery. The spectators laugh *with* Rubin, but *at* his master. But this is only one aspect of Severin's rôle.

His initial remark to Rubin serves to frame their subsequent wrangling, so as to establish that the ostensible conflict between master and servant is in fact the product of collaboration between entertainers working in harmony. (This state of affairs in its turn is only a meaning conveyed through the play; it is the play that supplies the framing remark as well as all that it frames.) Severin's words indicate that the Apothecary's supposedly involuntary comic features are to be perceived as gags, produced by the character in his rôle as market-place entertainer. This image of the entertainer then interposes itself between the actor implied by the dramatic text as such (which by its nature tends to evoke a performance) and the image of the apothecary who supplied the Maries' ointments. The actor's rôle includes the comic entertainer as well as the ridiculous Apothecary. In fact, it comprises several other images as well.

The most remarkable part of *Mastičkář* is the mock-resurrection scene. A character named Abraham appeals to master Severin to bring back to life his dead son Isaac, for whom he pronounces an absurd lament. Severin states his price, and when Abraham accepts, he proceeds to resuscitate the son in a grotesque rite which combines a parody of sacramental prayer with obscene stage action. He starts with a prayer for divine help and protection; then, turning to the dead boy himself, he announces that he is anointing him in God's name, and commands him to rise and praise the Lord. The rubric that describes this 'anointing' says *fundunt ei feces super culum* ('they pour faeces over his backside': sd at 308) and the text makes it quite clear that whatever substance is actually used, it is meant to represent excrement. While outrageously scatological action of this kind is not unparalleled in medieval religious drama, it is particularly startling here because it is associated with apparently serious prayer and because it takes place in the presence of the Three Maries.

Isaac returns to life with wails of woe, which form a ludicrous counterpart to Abraham's show of grief at his death, itself a travesty of the Maries' laments for Christ. Isaac goes on to declare that he has slept long but risen as from the dead (*avšak jako z mirtvych vstach*: line 311), giving a striking twist to the represented reality by means of the simple word 'as' (*jako*). He ends his first sentence with a characteristically bathetic shift into scatological triviality: 'Also, I nearly beshat myself' (*k tomu se bezmál neosrach*: line 312); here it is the word 'nearly' (*bezmál*) that produces a curiously oblique reference to the situation he is shown in. Finally, he thanks the master for having done him so much honour as to pour the 'ointment' not on his head, as other masters would, but all over his backside. The scene ends with a *silete*, a sort of musical punctuation that recurs all through the episode, during which Abraham and Isaac perhaps leave the playing area. They are not mentioned again.

The scene does little to advance the action. Although Severin supposedly revives Isaac in order to show the Maries what he and his wares can accomplish, when he learns that they are mourning a man they loved he does not speak of resuscitating him or healing his wounds, as the Apothecary is known to do in certain other versions, but only offers to lower the price of the ointment for his embalming. Yet, as Roman Jakobson[2] has shown, the scene is the key to the whole Apothecary episode, and to the rôle of its protagonist.

In the context of a religious Easter play, the return of the dead son to life would most likely be perceived as a grotesque echo of Christ's Resurrection even if the son were nameless. In fact several elements other than the name serve to bring out the parallel, such as the parodic correspondence that links the lament for the son with the Maries' laments for Christ a short time before, or that which links Severin's words to Isaac and Isaac's reply with liturgical chants associated with the Resurrection: yet more noticeably, Severin's formula of resuscitation couples a reference to Isaac's father with a double reference to Christ's Sonhood, calling him both 'God's son' (line 301) and 'holy Mary's son' (line 308).

But the fact that the son bears the name of Isaac, who was perhaps the most famous typological figure of Christ, gives the parody a much richer symbolic content. This is not because it reinforces the central point of the character's likeness to Christ, the fact that he rises from the dead, since the biblical Isaac never did anything of the sort. It is because the name brings to mind the typological interpretation of the Old Testament story about Abraham's intended sacrifice of his son. According to this, Isaac was a figure of Christ, the innocent victim offered up in atonement for sin. So by giving his name to the character, the playwright supplements the theme of physical death and resurrection, actually, though parodically, represented through the character's dramatic rôle, with the themes of Christ's redemptive sacrifice and its efficacy in saving humanity from sin and death, which are crucial to the theological significance of Easter.

The grossly comic fashion in which the play treats the character may recall that the name *Isaac* signifies 'laughter'. The sense is explained in the Bible (Genesis 21:3–6) and was often discussed by later commentators. So the better-informed members of the audience would have been familiar with it, and hence in a position to appreciate the playwright's wit in choosing this particular *figura* of Christ for the purpose of his laughter-provoking parody.

Together with his burlesque return to life, Isaac's name makes the point that he is to be seen as a parodic reflection of Christ, the innocent victim raised from the dead. Though he has only ten lines to say, his rôle is of the utmost importance, both on its own account, because of the particular contribution it makes to the subject the whole Easter drama celebrates, and because of the light it throws on the relationship between the religious play and its seemingly incongruous element, the burlesque Apothecary episode: it furnishes the clearest indication that even an extremely bawdy and apparently blasphemous scene is apt to bear a symbolic sense which makes it an integral part of a play in honour of the Resurrection.

Like Severin the Apothecary, Isaac is a figure of fun; like Isaac, Severin is a parodic figure of Christ. This parallel, too, comes to the fore most clearly in the scene of Isaac's resuscitation, although hints of it can be found much earlier in the episode.

The scene sets up a whole network of echoes, parallels, and correspondences with several different passages in the Gospels, with the result that it can be seen as a burlesque analogue of Christ healing the sick, like the epileptic boy brought to Him by his father as Isaac is brought by Abraham (Matthew 17:14–18; Mark 9:16–29; Luke 9:37–42); and restoring dead children to their parents, like Jairus's daughter (Matthew 9:18–25; Mark 5:22–43; Luke 8:41–56) or the son of the widow of Nain (Luke 7:14). The scene does not match any one of the Gospel accounts exactly, so that rather than a particular instance, it recalls the entire set of stories about Christ restoring people to life and health, which were seen as prefiguring His salvation of humanity as a whole.

The image of Christ as healer of both bodies and souls is a commonplace, solidly rooted in the Scriptures and in the liturgy, and reflected in many medieval plays as well as theological and devotional writings. In *Mastičkář* it is called to mind in the Third Mary's lament for

> Jesu Krista nebeského,
> ješto nás často utěšoval
> a mnoho nemocných usdravoval
>
> 'Heavenly Jesus Christ
> who often comforted us
> and healed many sick people.' 260–2

Once the character of the Spice Merchant in the Easter drama acquires the traits of a healer or physician, he is very likely to evoke this image of Christ, whether directly or by parodic contrast. That may be the reason why the Apothecary episode figures so prominently in the different sorts of Easter plays. For the seemingly negative relationship between a parody and the model it parodies also has a positive aspect. The parody necessarily brings to mind what it mocks, and may serve to draw attention to aspects of the model which would otherwise pass unnoticed. Such is the case of *Mastičkář* in general, and the mock-resurrection scene in particular, in relation to the content of Easter. This celebrates not just an event but a mystery involving a whole cluster of biblical and doctrinal themes. The play breaks up this cluster into separate and separately burlesqued elements, and reorganises them in an entirely different pattern. The reorganisation prevents the spectators from taking the parody simply as a transposition of the well-known event into the comic mode. It brings to the fore themes and meanings which would be less likely to spring to the spectators' minds if the parody followed the model more faithfully, and so in fact highlights what it mocks.

Hints that Master Severin is not just a comically boastful apothecary begin to emerge early on in the fragment: they may, of course, have done so even earlier when the episode was complete. Rubin and Pusterpalk, the two servants, first introduce him to the public in a macaronic patter-song set to a melody which is taken from the liturgical *Visitatio Sepulchri*, more precisely from the scene representing Christ's appearance to Mary Magdalene. In this song they declare, first, that the master (i.e. the Apothecary) has come 'by divine grace' (*de gracia divina*: line 28), and then, that he will make those whom he treats lose their souls (*musí duše zbýti*: line 34), implying at least death and possibly also damnation. This sets the pattern of the relationship, made up of similarities and contrasts, that the episode goes on to develop between the quack Master Severin and the truly unequalled Physician who came 'by divine grace' to heal the sick in body and soul. The burlesque scenes that follow contain many such allusions, discreet in themselves, but mutually reinforcing.

The sense of all the episode's components is strongly marked by its context, that of a Resurrection play. This holds good irrespective of whether it was preceded by scenes from the Resurrection story, as in the Easter play from Innsbruck[3] and Vienna,[4] or whether it opened the play, as seems to have been the case in Melk.[5] In any event, the spectators knew that what they were watching was part of a play about the Resurrection.

Easter was a vitally significant occasion in the Middle Ages, when the liturgical calendar ruled the life of the whole community, not only through the numerous and elaborate church services which most people attended as a matter of course, but also through the multifarious popular customs which were tied in with it. Of all the many feasts that punctuated the medieval year, none was celebrated more intensely than Easter, coming as it did after the grim mortification of Lent and the deep mourning of Good Friday. The cluster of ideas associated with the feast would have been very much alive in the minds of the spectators watching *Mastičkář*, for whom attendance at the play was part of the celebration. This would naturally have influenced their perception of the episode, helping to give a special resonance to words and phrases apt to evoke ideas belonging to this cluster and at the same time to bring out the unity that underlies the seemingly disparate elements.

As is the case in other forms of art, the unity is not of a static but of a dynamic nature; it relies on oppositions, conflicts, and tensions between the parts, as much as on their complementarity, congruence, and harmony. The heterogeneous elements are integrated, and unity of meaning is created, by a process based on temporal succession. The meaning of each element and the unity of sense of all the disparate or even incongruous elements depend not only on the general context, but also on its unfolding in time. The burlesque macaronic song the two servants sing near the beginning of the episode is particularly important from this point of view. Besides raising a laugh, it serves as a multi-faceted signal, placed at the start in order, on the one hand, to alert the spectators to the contradictions and complexities it is about to face them with and, on the other, to indicate where they are to seek the underlying unity of meaning. It would have prepared at least the better-schooled members of the audience, such as the students who are mentioned more than once in the dialogue, to grasp the more or less covert allusions to the play's religious context, which are scattered through all the burlesque scenes.

It is the resuscitation scene which most clearly establishes the Apothecary's parodic likeness to Christ, the healer and restorer of life. At the same time it adds yet another important dimension to Severin's rôle as a character in an Easter play. The revival of a dead person is a typical feature of folk rites celebrating the renewal of life and fertility of nature in Spring, and the uproariously scatological procedure by which Severin resurrects Isaac gives him a distinct resemblance to the folk Doctor or reviver. A broad range of folk-plays and customs in which a 'dead' person is brought back to life have been discovered all over Europe, including Bohemia. None of them was actually recorded until long after *Mastičkář*, and many contain elements which are obviously far more recent; but it is generally agreed that at least the mimetic ritual of death and resurrection which forms their essential core is of great antiquity.[6] It is worth noting that several of the recorded examples, especially from the Balkans, Russia, and Bohemia, display what Jakobson called 'puzzling coincidences' with the *Mastičkář* scene, in spite of the distance in time, and sometimes also of space, that separates them. It would be vain to try to reconstruct the folk customs of fourteenth-century Bohemia; but it appears justifiable to suppose that they included at least one form of the common death-and-revival type, that the audience of *Mastičkář* was familiar with it, and that this familiarity with the folk performance coloured their perception of the Easter play.

Master Severin the Apothecary combines in his own person the image of the folk Doctor with that of Christ the healer, and life-giver, so that he becomes a symbolic embodiment of the health-and-life-restoring power which these two figures represent in their different ways and spheres. This being a Christian play about the Resurrection, the parallel with Christ is brought out more strongly, but the fact that the same character conveys, at the same time, the image of the folk Doctor serves to affirm a certain harmony between the world of ritual customs on the one hand and organised religion on the other. The implied reconciliation between these two usually opposed spheres is a not unimportant part of the play's message of joy and celebration.

The double image of the supernatural dispenser of life and death connects up with the secular and down-to-earth image of the Apothecary as a quack healer. What is more, both of its facets have a comic aspect, the folk Doctor because laughter seems inherent in the personage, the Christ-like healer because he is parodically rendered; and this comedy links up with Severin's parody of Christ the conqueror of death, thanks to the tradition of the *risus paschalis* ('Easter laughter').

JARMILA F. VELTRUSKY

The solemn Easter liturgy, commemorating the greatest mystery of the Christian faith, would suddenly switch into the comic mode as the celebrant, instead of preaching a seriously edifying sermon, set out to make the congregation laugh, by whatever means seemed aptest to achieve that end: as a rule it was by telling bawdy jokes. The tradition may have derived from the pagan ritual laughter, which was supposed to signify 'the return to life and the beginning of a new life'.[7] But whatever its origin, the medieval *risus paschalis* owed its existence to the clergy, who regarded it as an appropriate component of the Easter services. It was interpreted in Christian terms, as a way of fulfilling the injunction of the paschal psalm, 'This is the day that the Lord has made: let us rejoice and be glad in it' (*haec est dies quam fecit Dominus: exultemus et laetemur in ea*: Psalm 117:24, Vulgate).

The underlying idea is evidently that Easter is an occasion when the whole Church should rejoice, and laughter is a means not only of expressing one's own joy, but also of imparting it to others. The practice, with its horseplay and obscenity, was deplored by some stricter and more austere spirits even in the Middle Ages, and especially from the sixteenth century onwards. But for hundreds of years it was widely regarded as a customary element of the Easter ritual, and although the post-Reformation Church authorities made strenuous efforts to extirpate it, it displayed an extraordinary persistence, above all in the more rural parts of Central Europe. Its widespread and lasting popularity proves that the most irreverent laughter might actually be conducive to religious worship and spiritual edification.

The medieval conception of the feast as a celebration of the life of the whole community assigned a prominent, and indeed indispensible, rôle to ribaldry and irreverence of every kind. The traditional popular celebration of the religious festivals was characterised by the 'carnivalesque' spirit, subversive of rationality, hierarchy, and all rules imposed from above.[8] The Easter plays were very much part of the festivities in honour of the Resurrection, and that helps to account for the wide scope some of them give to outrageous comedy like that associated with the Apothecary episode.

Mastičkář would have earned its place in an Easter play if it had simply made the people laugh, as did the bawdy sermons of the *risus paschalis* tradition. Indeed, that was probably its sole point for some of the spectators. But this is clearly an impoverishment, since it discounts many signs of a deeper significance. As is often the case with dramatic texts designed to be performed, the question arises how far such signs, though apparent to a reader who can go over the text any number of times, could have been grasped by spectators watching a single performance. But in the Middle Ages, when books were relatively rare and most communication, even in the field of scholarship and learned speculation, was by word of mouth, people were accustomed to absorb long and complicated sermons and speeches of various kinds: those who had studied were trained to grasp all the subtleties of what they had heard. They were also trained to look for several layers of meaning not only in the divinely-inspired Scriptures, but also in secular literature, all the arts, and just about any phenomenon apt to be invested with the power of signification. So it is safe to assume that when faced with a play about the most solemn mystery of the faith, and in the course of it with a burlesque episode that yet signals its intention to convey all sorts of meanings over and above the simply comic – especially if it does so as plainly as does *Mastičkář* – they would have been ready to notice and interpret every possible allusion.

Many medieval plays incorporate a wide range of materials which are apt to be understood in different ways and degrees by spectators possessed of different amounts of erudition, perspicacity, or sophistication. But being destined for an audience drawn from all sectors of society, they do so in such a manner that all can enjoy and profit from them without feeling left out. Each additional kind of meaning a spectator is able to understand enriches his total perception of the play, but the inability to understand a given kind does not produce a noticeable gap in that perception, so that those capable of grasping only the most superficial and obvious sense can still experience the play as satisfactorily complete.

But while everybody could have enjoyed *Mastičkář*, there are indications which suggest that it was destined in the first place for the better-educated members of the public, particularly the students, who were growing in numbers in fourteenth-century Bohemia, even before the foundation of Charles University in 1347–1348. Such spectators could be expected to apply their customary pursuit of multiple interpretation to the Apothecary farce, too. This in turn was well fitted to offer them, in reward, the pleasure of tracing out intricate patterns of meaning, as well as the edification resulting from the process of detecting the multifarious allusions to the religious content of the feast of Easter.

Paris

NOTES

1. The title is commonly given to two fragmentary texts, each belonging to a different variant and both lacking the beginning and end of the episode itself as well as the whole context of the Easter plays they manifestly belonged to. It is the older and considerably longer fragment (431 lines), dating from the middle of the fourteenth century and kept in the National Museum in Prague, that is especially significant and that I concentrate on in the present paper. Both that and the later fragment (195 lines), dating from around 1365–1385 and kept in the monastery of Schlagel (Austria), were published in a diplomatic edition by Jan Máchal *Staročeské skladby dramatické původu liturgického* (Rozpravy České akademie, class 3, no. 23, Prague, 1908). A more accessible edition can be found in Heinrich Kunstmann *Denkmäler der alttschechischen Literatur* (Deutscher Verlag der Wissenschaften, Berlin, 1955). Both texts are also reproduced, with an English translation, in Jarmila F. Veltrusky *A Sacred Farce from Medieval Bohemia: Mastičkář* (Michigan Studies in the Humanities 6: University of Michigan, Ann Arbor, 1985).

2. Roman Jakobson 'Medieval Mock Mystery: The Old Czech *Unguentarius*' in *Selected Writings 7: Contributions to Comparative Mythology, Studies in Literature and Philology* edited Stephen Rudy (Mouton, Berlin, 1985) 666–90.

3. *Das Innsbrucker Osterspiel: Das Osterspiel von Muri* edited Rudolf Meier (Reclam, Stuttgart, 1962).
4. *Das Wiener Osterspiel* edited Hans Blosen (Erich Schmidt Verlag, Berlin, 1979).
5. Curt F. Bühler and Carl Selmer 'The Melk *Salbenkrämerspiel*: An Unpublished Middle High German *Mercator* Play' *Publications of the Modern Language Association of America* 63 (1948) 21–63.
6. E.K. Chambers *The Mediaeval Stage* 2 vols (Oxford University Press, London, 1903) *1* 182–204, and *The English Folk Play* (Clarendon Press, Oxford, 1933) 197–235; R.J.E Tiddy *The Mummers' Play* (Clarendon Press, Oxford, 1923) 70–80; Alan Brody *The English Mummers and Their Plays: Traces of Ancient Mystery* (Routledge and Kegan Paul, London, 1970) 117–27; Richard Axton *European Drama of the Early Middle Ages* (Hutchinson, London, 1974) 1–21; Glynne Wickham *The Medieval Theatre* (Cambridge University Press, 3rd edition 1987) 125–49.
7. Salomon Reinach *Cultes, Mythes et Religions* 5 vols (Ernest Leroux, Paris, 1908–23) 4 121 'Le rire rituel'.
8. See Mikhail Bakhtin *Rabelais and His World* translated Helene Iswolsky (MIT Press, Cambridge, Mass. and London, 1968) 1–144.

CARNIVAL'S END:
Puritan Ideology and the Decline of English Provincial Theatre
John Coldewey

> The verse that pleasde a *Romaine* rashe intent,
> Myght well offend the godly Preachers vayne.
> Deformed shewes were then esteemed muche,
> Reformed speeche doth now become us best.
>
> George Gascoigne, Prologue to *The Glasse of Governement* (1575)

By the mid-sixteenth century, when the cycle plays had virtually ceased as a widespread form of popular dramatic entertainment in England, there still remained two other essentially medieval forms of drama: first, the religious non-cycle plays, those miracle and saints' plays that arose during the late fifteenth and early sixteenth centuries under the sponsorship of small towns and parishes, mainly in the Southeast; second, the morality plays and polemical interludes performed by travelling troupes all over the country. Both these forms were also destined to disappear, and their disappearances would be linked, like that of the cycle plays, to the rising tide of reformed ideology. If for the larger corporations that undertook the cycle plays, the self-reflexive nature of the cycle plays and the social meaning inherent in their performances projected a doctrinally unacceptable and perhaps politically dangerous subtext for an increasingly reform-minded oligarchy, what happened in the smaller communities that periodically sponsored single, non-cycle plays had more to do with the growing opposition towards outward display and clerical privilege. I have dealt elsewhere[1] with the ways in which the demise of town drama was intimately connected with the Vestiarian Controversy, a bitterly fought battle that rocked the English Church during the 1560s and 1570s. Let me rehearse it briefly here, for it acts as the swelling prologue to the swan song of the travelling companies.

Put simply, in parish after parish in town after town during the first two decades of Elizabeth's reign, ecclesiastical vestments – 'popish rags' – were zealously de-sanctified and, in many instances, transformed into stage costumes. These theatrical wardrobes were maintained by the parish, which used them in ordinarily quite profitable theatrical performances, sometimes hiring them out to other towns and parishes. Eventually the presence of these 'remnants of popery' in any form seems to have become intolerable, and the towns and parishes willingly sold off their wardrobes. The plays disappeared along with the costumes. There were no further vestments to transform, and even if some *had* survived there was no further will to use them in the towns.

JOHN COLDEWEY

This much, then, is clear: the cycle play tradition and the non-cycle plays came to their ends in quite different ways. While the cycles fell under the censorious eye of powerful prelates whose admonitions about their contents were taken to heart by the governing body of sponsoring towns, the non-cycle plays suffered as casualties in a process largely unconnected to their own ideological and doctrinal roots. The spoliation and transformation of vestments, and their sale as costumes – indeed, the entire Vestiarian Controversy – were all manifestations of the reformist impulse to oppose clerical privilege, one of the worms at the heart of Roman church practices. It had little to do with the non-cycle *texts*, but a great deal to do with their contexts – the historical frames, that is, within which they resonated. The demise of these plays, most notably, is linked to a movement that was *ideological in its opposition to privilege, but political only with regard to ecclesiastical rank*.

With this in mind, we might now push beyond the deaths of the corporate cycle play form and locally-sponsored non-cycle plays to consider how it happened that plays put on by travelling troupes, that last vestige of medieval theatrical practices, came to end *their* days of plenty. Like the cycle and non-cycle plays, the travelling players were dependent on the continued co-operation of ordinary townsfolk and the approval of the town officials. Beginning in late Elizabethan times, and continuing for the next 30 or 40 years into the reigns of James, and then Charles, the increasingly reformed circumstances of towns and villages all over the country brought about a generally recognisable sequence of actions regarding travelling troupes. First, their performances were identified with moral decadence and were eschewed in favour of more godly performative arts like preaching and prophesyings. Next, in a logical extension of humanist opposition to privilege, whether clerical or aristocratic, plays put on by noblemen's men were discouraged, with only royally-connected companies – which could not be dismissed lightly – left to perform. Finally, even *those* companies were no longer tolerated, and they were, in fact, paid *not* to play.[2]

The town of Maldon in Essex offers a unique opportunity to trace this pattern, for the records of its drama and the records of godly preachers there have both survived relatively intact. There are plenty of other towns in Essex whose civic or ecclesiastical accounts are extant; for most of them, however, documents pertaining to their social history have perished; and very often for towns with fuller documentation of social history the opposite is true. But Maldon can offer a compelling example of larger cultural patterns at work, both here and elsewhere in the country. The dramatic traditions in Maldon were old, rich, diverse, and documented by a greater variety of records than in any other town in the county of Essex[3] – one measure of how thoroughly performances had become part of everyday life there. Among the Maldon records we can find fifteenth-century references both to town players and to noblemen's companies – the earliest in the county. Starting in the second quarter of the sixteenth century we find detailed accounts of locally-sponsored productions on a very large scale, and, at the same time, the beginning of a steady stream of references to performances by travelling troupes. Between 1563 and 1573, following the pattern outlined above for the non-cycle plays, local productions dwindled and finally ceased altogether after the sale of the town's costumes, which had been made from church vestments. In the proceedings of the Borough Court is found the agreement by town officials to sell their wardrobe; in the Chamberlain's Accounts the payments for it are recorded.[4]

But travelling players continued to visit. An overview shows that in the 1560s travelling companies performed 25 times in Maldon, including the players of at least twelve different noblemen, plus the Queen's Players and the Queen's Majesty's Players. In the 1570s the number of visiting players dropped to nine, including six different noblemen's men and the Queen's Majesty's Players. The 1580s brought only three named noblemen's companies, all in 1581, and no royal companies; but there may have been others travelling players, for in 1585 appears for the first time in the accounts a generalised entry of payment 'for diverse gyftes & rewards as well to noblemens players & pursyvants as other wyse bestowed in benevolence boith upon personags of woorship & others at Mr Baylieffs Appoyntmt ...'[5] In the 1590s only the Earl of Derby's Players, 'other players', and the Queen's Majesty's Players appear, but as we shall see this was a very tumultuous decade in Maldon.[6] In the first decade of the seventeenth century only the King's Players came, in 1602/3.[7] Between 1610 and 1620, fifteen companies performed, including multiple performances by six royally-connected players plus an appearance of those of the Earl of Sussex. Eight playing companies appeared in the 1620s, all royally connected. Only two companies came to Maldon in the 1630s: the Children of His Majesty's Revels appeared in 1633; and in 1635, in the very last entry concerning travelling troupes, an unnamed company of players came but was paid 15s. by the town *not* to play.[8]

What is important to note here is that over the course of seven decades the patronage of the companies that were allowed to play in Maldon shifted radically from being predominantly noblemen to being exclusively royal or royally connected. One of the reasons for the decreasing frequency of travelling players' appearances during the closing decades of the sixteenth century was surely the growth of new professional theatres in London and the opportunities these afforded the companies. But another main reason that fewer playing companies came to Maldon was an extraordinary growth of reformed sensibility in the town, and that is a matter towards which we should now turn.

Starting in the late 1560s and early 1570s, payments to godly preachers begin to show up in the Maldon Chamberlain's Accounts. In 1573 an entire section of expenditure was devoted to them, much like the part of the accounts quoted above which kept track of gifts and rewards split between playing companies and 'personags of woorship'. Times were changing, and sermons could now be publicly underwritten as legitimate instructive public entertainment. The preachers mentioned in the section devoted to them in the 1573 accounts included the 'Deane of Powles' and the Archdeacon of Colchester. Also among the 1573 items occurs a telling entry that records 2s. paid 'at the blewe [boar] for the dinner of Mr Archdeacon Walker & for wine, at that tyme when he preached agenst o^r playe this year'. 'Archdeacon Walker' was John Walker, Archdeacon of Essex from 1571 until 1585,[9] and whatever 'playe' he may have been preaching against, his sermon did not bode well for the future of drama in the town.

Beginning in August of 1582 an outspoken adherent of the puritan cause, George Gifford, became incumbent as vicar at the Church of All Saints in Maldon, and his presence apparently shook the town like a whirlwind.[10] Gifford was a zealous preacher, a prolific pamphleteer, and a radical nonconformist. He published collection after collection of sermons; he attacked powerful prelates to his right and puritan intellectuals to his left. In January and February of 1584 he joined a synod of nonconformist Essex ministers in London, publicly refusing to subscribe to the articles of the established church. Within two months he was suspended and charged with preaching limited obedience to civil magistrates, using conventicles and secret teachings. This disproved, he was arrested again, this time for nonconformity, and tried before the high commissioners. Some of his parishioners sent in a petition asking that Gifford be restored. Despite this, and despite the intercession of Lord Burghley and Sir Francis Knowles, Gifford was deprived of his living in June 1584 by John Whitgift, Archbishop of Canterbury, and John Aylmer, Bishop of London, who considered him 'a ringleader of the nonconformists'. But he was allowed to continue preaching in Maldon as a lecturer. Within two years, by 1586, his replacement, Marcus Wiersdale, attempted to resign his living in favour of Gifford, but now Aylmer suspended Gifford from his lectureship (1587) and replaced Wiersdale with Robert Palmer. As will become clear, Palmer did not share Gifford's enthusiasms.

Not to be discouraged, Gifford continued preaching in Maldon, attending radical synods, and taking part in theological controversies. He fought furiously against the Brownists (followers of Robert Browne, the Separatist clergyman and precursor of the Congregationalists) in several tracts, the most notable of which was dedicated to Sir William Cecil. Its full title may give something of Gifford's rhetorical style: *A Plain Declaration that our Brownists be full Donatists, by comparing them together from point to point out of the writings of Augustine. Also a replie to Master Greenwood touching read prayer, wherein his grosse ignorance is detected, which labouring to purge himselfe from former absurdities, doth plunge himselfe deeper in the mire. by George Gyffard, Minister of Gods word in Maldon. 1590* (STC 11862).[11] His activities extended for another thirty years until he died at Maldon, according to the *D.N.B.* 'at a good old age' in 1620.

Gifford's style, like that of many puritans, was confrontational, and it was inevitable that he would raise hackles wherever he lived. Some inkling of the mood he seems to have inspired in Maldon can be found in a Borough Court case of 1592 that involved Robert Palmer, still the Vicar of All Saints, and certain supporters of Gifford:

> Thomas Pearce, Thomas Purcas and John Holdinge say that one Sturgion coming into the church of All Saints asked Mr. Palmer, minister there, being

there present whether he would preach that day. The said Mr. Palmer made answer that he would not make him account. Presently after there came into the church one Richard Williams and John Pratt, who rang the bell there to a sermon and the said Mr. Palmer did forbid them, charging them in God's name, the Queen's Majesty's and his own to leave ringing. Then the said Richard Williams said though he forbade them to ring yet they might toll and (the said Mr. Palmer holding the bellrope in his hand) took the same and tolled certain times, and said that Mr. Giffard had showed forth an order from the Lord Bishop of London that he might preach then. The said Mr. Palmer made answer that Mr. Giffard should not preach there, nor none such as he was, except he did wear the surplice, administer the sacraments, make the cross in baptism and subscribe as he had done. They say further that the said Mr. Palmer forbidding the said Richard Williams and John Pratt to ring, plucked the bellrope out of the said Richard Williams' hand and with that thrust him on the breast.[12]

Clearly, bitterness and animosity in the town were coming to a head. While the issue might seem, at this remove, mainly personal, or perhaps a matter of ecclesiastical conformity, the real problems went much deeper, and a better idea of the stakes in this game can be found in another court case involving Gifford's supporters and detractors, a case that occurred shortly after the 1592 fracas above. It involved some 'acusors & trobblers' of the governors and government of Maldon, who were hauled into court for a hearing, ostensibly so the town might defend itself against their charges. But there was another agenda. One of the 'acusors', John Spigurwell,

affirmeiths that there is a great faccon in the Towne of Maldon that the like is not in anye Towne in Englande, And saith that the faccon in his opinion lyeth on the pts of Mr Gyffards favorars, wherbye it appeareith he directlie chargeith the Baylieffs & governors to make the faccons, being mr Gyffards favorers.[13]

Spigurwell's claim that the group in power – the 'faction' – in the local government had a strong Puritan cast to it was doubtless true, though it is unlikely that Maldon's situation was unique in England. In any case the charge was ignored. The real purpose of the session emerged when the court brought forth its *own* charges *against the plaintiffs*, and among these appears the main charge to concern us here. It was made against a 'Mr Morrys', who had at one point 'thretned the constable to runn him through wth a pitchforck in doing his office'. The 'article' or complaint is worth quoting in full:

Article 12.   Also the said mr marrys hath often sett himself against the Baylieffs & governors in mistifyinge & defendinge the misdemeanors of disordred Unrulie & contemptious persons in their evell behavior, as when certain players playd on the Lords daye in the nyght, contrarie both the Earle of Essex letter & Mr Baylieffs comaundement, and m^r Baylieffs rebuking them for the same, Mr Morrys spake openlie in the hall, that before tyme noble mens menn hadd such entertaynment when they came to the Towne, that the Towne hadd the favor of noble men, but now noble mens men had such entertaynement, that the Towne was brought into contempt with noble men, And when the said m^r morris was gonne out of the hall into the street, he spake these woords alowde 'A sort of precisions and Brownists'.[14]

This last remark was probably meant as a rebuke to Gifford, whom we recall had fulminated in print against the Brownists. Beyond that, however, there are two important points to note about this article. First, although the players were supposed to have offended because they performed on the Lord's Day, it is clear that *the play itself* was considered by the court as 'evell behavior' of 'disordred unrulie & contemptious persons'. Second, the political wisdom of the reform-minded town council is called into question for discouraging the visits of playing companies.

It was true, as we have seen, that visits by travelling players had diminished since Gifford and his group had come into power in Maldon. The last named nobleman's company paid to perform had been in 1581, perhaps a dozen years before. But the Town Council's position would not change. Within the next year or so of Spigurwell's and Morrys's testimonies, in April of 1594, the townsman William Gillman was fined *ijs vjd* because 'he in the open market cryed a playe at the appoyntmt of certen players, w^tout m^r Bayliffs Appoyntmt to the great reproche of the towne'.[15]

The truth of the matter was that the Maldon Town Council represented the reformed ideology, now politically empowered. It was no longer *concerned* that the noblemen's men – or, I would suggest, the noblemen themselves – were not well-received or that the town was 'brought into contempt' with them. Maldon's treatment of travelling players over the next forty years bears this assertion out. Of the thirty-one travelling players who were allowed to perform in the town between this moment in the mid 1590s and 1635, only *four* were not royally connected-sponsored, that is, by a member of the royal household, and therefore irresistible. But even well-connected players were watched carefully. In April of 1619 members of the company of Princess Elizabeth's Players were prosecuted

> because when they prolonged ther plays vntill xi of the clocke in the Blue-Boore in Maldon, Mr Baylyff coming and requesting them to breake off ther play so that the companye might departe, they called Baylyff Frauncis 'foole', to the great disparagement of the government of the borough.[16]

So noblemen's players were banished from the town of Maldon and, as time went on, from other towns across the land as well. A similar trajectory of events might be traced where other godly preachers were empowered and the temper of the town altered: Richard Rogers at Wethersfield for example, or William Negus of Leighs, or William Dyke at Coggeshall, or further afield in towns like Ipswich and Bungay in

Suffolk, or even Tewkesbury in Gloucestershire.[17] In the end, by 1635, the payment for playing company, royal or not, *not* to perform, would be common. Maldon was simply one of the first to the mark.

From a larger vantage point such a development should come as no surprise. Margo Todd has pointed out that inherent in the puritan position, developing as it did out of Christian humanism, was a social ideology that rejected privilege and external show.[18] The fate of the non-cycle plays, we recall, had been sealed by puritan opposition to the trappings that signalled clerical privilege. In Maldon such opposition had turned, within a generation, into an opposition to *social* privilege, especially when it encouraged 'Unrulie & contemptious persons in their evell behavior'. What we are witnessing in Maldon, then, is a process that rejects stage plays as part of a larger *social* ideology, rather than a psychological or material impulse. This process presages both the rationale and the treatment of other playing companies, later and elsewhere, and in fact foreshadows the closing of the popular theatres in London in 1642, all at the hands of politically empowered Puritans. In 1642 the opposition to privilege was taken to its radical but logical implication: the attempted extirpation of hereditary aristocracy and, ultimately, the monarchy itself. In 1642 not only the King's Players but the King himself would be banished for life. Both Kings and plays would return to England, but never again in the forms familiar to the medieval experience.

At the start of this essay I quoted George Gascoigne, who in 1575 in his *Glasse of Governement* already was reflecting the vision of reformed sensibilities that would come to dominate provincial towns like Maldon. The end result of this signal shift in ideological terms was clear for every form of the dramatic legacy of the middle ages: whether cycle or non-cycle, or the visits of travelling troupes, the plays together were finished, theologically obsolete, ideologically bankrupt, their social rituals a net loss. With the passing of the generation of the English revolution, they were lost from view for the next three hundred years.

University of Washington, Seattle

NOTES

1. 'The Last Rise and Final Demise of Essex Town Drama' *Modern Language Quarterly* 56:3 (September 1975) 239–60.
2. In his useful and wide-ranging survey of REED material, Andrew Gurr has recently suggested that the declining numbers of travelling troupes appearing in civic records is linked to changes of recording procedures practised in towns, and to changes in possible venues for the players ('The loss of records for the travelling companies in Stuart times' *REED Newsletter* 19:2 (1994) 2–19). Clearly, both of these are important factors that bear on our knowledge of travelling companies' visits; they do not, however, account for or provide a register for the recorded animosity often lurking behind the unrecorded or unrewarded visits.
3. These records form part of my forthcoming *REED: Essex* volume.

4. For the relevant Chamberlain's Accounts for the 1560s, see Essex Record Office (hereafter E.R.O.) MSS D/B 3/3/248 to 3/3/255; for the 1570s, see E.R.O. MSS D/B 3/3/256 to D/B 3/3/262. The Borough Court record of the town's wardrobe sale is found in E.R.O. MSS D/B 3/1/5, fols 86, 92, 104.
5. The relevant Chamberlain's Accounts for the 1580s are E.R.O. MSS D/B 3/3/263 to D/B 3/3/266. The generalised entry occurs first in D/B 3/3/265.
6. The relevant Chamberlain's Accounts for the 1590s are E.R.O. MSS D/B 3/3/268 to D/B 3/3/273 and D/B 3/3/162.
7. E.R.O. MSS D/B 3/3/274.
8. For the relevant Chamberlain's Accounts from 1610–1620, see Essex Record Office (E.R.O.) MSS D/B 3/3/280 to D/B 3/3/289; for 1620–1630, see E.R.O. MSS D/B 3/3290 to D/B 3/3/297 and D/B 3/3/217 no. 25; there are no relevant payments for 1630–33; for the 1635 reference see E.R.O. MSS D/B 3/3/80 no. 2. The payment for companies not to play, as Gurr indicates (see note 2), is not uncommon.
9. For terms of the early archdeacons in Essex, see John Le Neve *Fasti Ecclesiae Anglicanae* (Institute of Historical Research, London1969), I, 9.
10. For more detailed treatments of Gifford in Maldon, see Patrick Collinson *The Elizabethan Puritan Movement* (University of California Press, Berkeley, 1967) 263–72, and William Hunt *The Puritan Moment: The Coming of Revolution in an English County* (Harvard University Press, Cambridge, Mass., 1983) 150–5.
11. Peter Milward *Religious Controversies of the Elizabethan Age: a Survey of Printed Sources* (Scolar Press, London, 1977) 99.
12. Maldon Borough Records: E.R.O. MS D/B 3/1/8.
13. Maldon Court Records: E.R.O. MS D/B 3/3/423/1, Article 19.
14. Maldon Court Records: E.R.O. MS D/B 3/3/423/1, Article 12.
15. Maldon Sessions Book: E.R.O. MS D/B 3/1/8, fol. 132v.
16. Maldon Sessions and Leet Papers: E.R.O. MS D/B 3/3/476.
17. See Collinson *passim*; Hunt 99–103.
18. This increasing animosity towards clerical (and ultimately social) privilege from its original impulse in humanism through its development during the later Tudor and Stuart societies, culminating in its bloody manifestation in the 1642 revolution, is a much more complicated matter than can be indicated here. Todd states the main issue well from the vantage point of Caroline society: 'it was only when Laud and Charles, in their drive for control and conformity, attempted to divert the mainstream into an apparently absolutist channel, that Puritans found themselves in opposition. They were alienated not by the religion of Protestants, but by Laudian innovation and Caroline enforcement. When this happened, when those in authority rejected humanist reform, puritans and parliamentarians had a radical social ideology at hand with which to legitimate their revolutionary actions: the logical implications of humanist anticlericalism and opposition to hereditary aristocracy and monarch were released': *Christian Humanism and the Puritan Social Order* (Cambridge University Press, 1987) 21.